THE BLAMELESS VICTIM

Our Ten-Year Legal Battle against Zurich American Insurance and American International Group

HAROLD S. RHODES

Copyright © 2014 Harold S. Rhodes
All Rights Reserved.

ISBN: 149954328X
ISBN 13: 9781499543285
Library of Congress Control Number: 2014908917
CreateSpace Independent Publishing Platform
North Charleston, South Carolina

www.TheBlamelessVictim.com

CONTENTS

Dedication v
Selected Quotations vii
Acknowledgments ix
Prologue xiii
Timeline One: 1
  The Crash and the Catastrophic Injuries
Timeline Two: 145
  The Criminal Trial of Carlo Zalewski
Timeline Three: 161
  The Personal Injury Trial
Timeline Four: 227
  Did Zurich, AIG, or Both Commit an *"Unfair or Deceptive Act"*?
Timeline Five: 289
  Did Zurich, AIG, or Both Commit an *"Unfair or Deceptive Act"*?
Timeline Six: 312
  Did Zurich, AIG, or Both Commit an *"Unfair or Deceptive Act"*?
Afterword 355
About the Author 357
The Blameless Victim Website 359

DEDICATION

The Blameless Victim is dedicated to the many catastrophically injured persons who must battle not only large insurance companies but also the purportedly protective civil courts just to get their due and timely compensation for their injuries. They are brave. They change the world for future blameless victims.

Insurance companies know from the start that they have the advantage over blameless victims. They know blameless victims must strain to cope with their immediate catastrophic injuries, tirelessly work to recover from the resulting medical difficulties, and suffer enormous emotional devastation and painful family deterioration.

Worse yet, blameless victims need money without delay. Blameless victims must immediately have their homes renovated; acquire medical equipment; purchase medical supplies and medicines; pay hospitals, doctors, and therapists; and buy accessible transportation.

Civil courts are supposed to guard against the injustices committed by insurance companies. Blameless victims presume that civil courts will protect their insurance rights. When an insurance company first systematically denies and then methodically delays compensation, a blameless victim believes the legal system will promptly require an insurance company to fulfill its financial obligation.

This belief is far from true. Civil courts are slow. Civil courts are expensive. Civil courts will make public every embarrassing aspect of a blameless victim's life. Worse, earlier personal injury decisions by civil courts are legally confusing and often side with the insurance company. As painful as the catastrophic injury might be, civil courts, time and again, cause so much more pain for a blameless victim.

SELECTED QUOTATIONS

"We (Zurich) know plaintiffs would never have accepted Zurich's $2 million if it was offered the day after the accident, six months after the accident, a year after the accident, or even beyond that."

—Opening statement by Mr. Greg Varga (attorney for the Defendant Zurich American Insurance) in *Rhodes et al. v. Zurich American Insurance and AIG Domestic Claims, Inc.*

Massachusetts Superior Court, Civil Action No. 05-1360BLS
February 5, 2007

"She was a blameless victim, you know, whose entire life was changed."

—Trial testimony by Ms. Tracey Kelly (complex claims director, American International Group) in *Rhodes et al. v. Zurich American Insurance and AIG Domestic Claims, Inc.*

Massachusetts Superior Court, Civil Action No. 05-1360BLS
March 13, 2007

"The record also supports the judge's determination that Zurich, the primary insurer, satisfied its duty to effectuate settlement by tendering the policy limits to AIGDC, where it was clear that the case would not settle for an amount within the primary policy limits, necessitating the involvement of the excess insurer."

—Decision by the Massachusetts Supreme Judicial Court in
Rhodes et al. v. Zurich American Insurance and AIG Domestic Claims, Inc.

Massachusetts Supreme Judicial Court SJC-10911
February 10, 2012

ACKNOWLEDGMENTS

It is impossible to thank individually all the wonderful people who helped in the writing of *The Blameless Victim*. Over twelve years, many persons—lawyers, paralegals, medical professionals, family members, and friends—provided clarity to my ideas, filled in details, and gave extensive commentary and feedback. Without their assistance, I never would have been able to complete this book. I thank them all for their encouragement over the years.

During the last two years, three professional editors reviewed the tone, direction, and even the smallest details of this book. I owe each one more than a debt of gratitude. More than twenty people read the final manuscript before publication, several of whom described the content as brutally honest and painful to read.

However, any mistakes are mine alone. In particular, I am not an attorney, so my legal conclusions might be inaccurate.

The Blameless Victim website (www.theblamelessvictim.com) includes a searchable database of nearly all the legal documents, as well as a wealth of additional information. (The reader is especially encouraged to review the many letters between the attorneys.) The website was designed by Reflective Innovation Design Studio. My thanks to Jason for his design insights, perseverance, and patience.

A loving thank you to our daughter, Rebecca, who allowed me to include her deepest, most painful young-teenager emotions for all to read.

I especially want to thank my wife, Marcia, for encouraging me to write this book. It lays wide open her unhappy day-to-day life. Never did she say that any topic—even those that have been the most personally uncomfortable—should be excluded. Her bravery in wanting to improve the world for future blameless victims through the telling of this story has been astonishing. She has forever been and will always be my inspiration and my love.

The blameless victim at age thirty.

The blameless victim on our wedding day.

PROLOGUE

The Blameless Victim is sad and, admittedly, emotionally difficult to read.

After my spouse's car was rear-ended by an 80,000 pound tranker-trailer, leaving her catastrophically injured on January 9, 2002, I began keeping a diary as my way to remember everything that I needed to do, all that was happening to Marcia, and the many mistakes that I made. For the the next ten years, I wrote about Marcia's awful physical injuries, her dreadful medical complications, our emotional devastation, and our near financial ruin.

I also wrote about the justice system in Massachusetts from the five courtroom trials which Marcia and I had to endure. During these trials, even though Marcia did absolutely nothing wrong, virtually every aspect of our marriage, our family, our young daughter, and our individual lives was scrutinized by the defendant insurance carriers – Zurich American Insurance and American International Group.

As well, I wrote about the inner workings of these two insurance carriers, based on Zurich's and AIG's insurance claims notes (which are rarely disclosed) and additional legal information (which Zurich and AIG were compelled to provide).

However, these aren't the reasons why *The Blameless Victim* is such a sad narrative. What happened to our family is no worse than what has befallen many other families. Many people suffer horribly from catastrophic injuries from motor vehicle accidents, dreadful medical complications, and awful emotional devastation. All the while, many catastrophically injured people and their families face enormous financial difficulties.

However, even with all the awful medical and legal events, as well as the dreadful emotional and financial consequences, the true calamity—why *The Blameless Victim* is such a sad narrative—would not be known for ten years, until February 10, 2012.

TIMELINE ONE:
THE CRASH AND THE CATASTROPHIC INJURIES

JANUARY 9, 2002 TO OCTOBER 31, 2003
MY DIARY[1]

Wednesday, January 9, 2002

At one o'clock in the afternoon on Wednesday, January 9, 2002, Marcia kissed me goodbye. *"I am going to visit the antiques stores to see how the collectibles are selling,"* she said. She was wearing my favorite blue hat, just like the one Ali MacGraw wore in *Love Story*.

In the garage, she got into her blue Toyota Corolla and clicked her seatbelt. From our home in Milford, Massachusetts, she headed east on Route 109 into the town of Medway. Route 109, a pleasant, well-maintained road, is perfectly straight. The road slightly inclines for a quarter of a mile and then slightly declines.

As she crested the small hill, she saw a tall police officer in her lane, about a quarter-mile ahead. This officer was directing traffic around a work crew, letting the westbound vehicles pass. He raised his hand high, indicating that she should stop and wait her turn. He was in full uniform with a bright-orange work vest and white gloves.

Marcia heeded the officer and came to a complete stop. There were no vehicles in front of or behind her car. Her foot was on the brake pedal and the rear brake lights were illuminated.

Unknown to Marcia, at four o'clock in the morning that same day, Carlo Zalewski began his trip from Edison, New Jersey, to the GAF Materials Corporation roof-shingle

---

1   This daily diary was formally developed many years after the dates of occurrence from my memories, legal documents, medical records, recollections of discussions with family members and friends, personal calendar entries, e-mails, recorded notes, and observations that I wrote down. The entry dates might not be perfectly accurate. I am not an attorney, so my legal observations and conclusions might be inaccurate. I have been told that the circumstances regarding Marcia's crash might be rare and, as such, might not be typical of personal injury accidents. A nearly complete record of the litigation documentation can be found at www.theblamelessvictim.com.

production facility in Millis, Massachusetts. The facility was directly east of Medway on Route 109. Zalewski had made this drive for his employer, Driver Logistics Services, on behalf of GAF, many times before.

After filling out paperwork and doing a brief inspection, Zalewski drove the tanker-trailer from a Penske truck-leasing facility to another facility where it was filled with liquid asphalt. After the tanker was loaded, the truck, the tank, and the liquid asphalt weighed approximately 80,000 pounds.

Making only one stop along the way, Zalewski traveled north through Connecticut to reach the Massachusetts Turnpike. He headed east on the turnpike and then turned south onto Route 495. At the Route 109 intersection, he headed east through Milford.

A moment after crossing from Milford into Medway, the tanker-trailer crested the slight hill, heading directly toward the clearly visible police officer and the work site area on Route 109.

At the top of the slight crest, Zalewski had a quarter of a mile of clear view on a straight road with no vehicles between his 80,000-pound tanker-trailer and Marcia's car.

Traveling at thirty miles per hour, he had more than twelve seconds to stop before reaching the work site.

He did not slow down.

He did not stop.

Carlo Zalewski crashed his forty-ton tanker-trailer, filled with liquid asphalt, into Marcia's Toyota.

The impact threw Marcia's car 100 feet down an embankment and straight into a large tree.

At 1:20 p.m., the phone rang.

When I answered, an unfamiliar male voice said, *"Mr. Rhodes? This is the Medway Police Department calling. I am sorry to tell you that your wife has been in a serious automobile crash and that she is asking for you. We are at the corner of Trotter Drive and Route 109. Do you know where that is?"*

"Yes. Trotter Drive is close. I will be there quickly."

I ran to my car in the garage. As I drove, I felt frozen. What did the police officer mean by *serious*?

As I drove east on Route 109, I passed a large tanker-trailer stopped on the south side of the road. I didn't think much about what it was doing there because I was intent on getting to Marcia.

I reached the crash site within five minutes. I parked on Trotter Drive and hurried to the site. I saw Marcia's Toyota with its front in the embankment, almost vertical, against a large tree. The car had been smashed so forcefully that the entire rear end was now in the front seat. I was stupefied. *My wife is inside that folded-up accordion?*

Medway emergency medical technicians (EMTs) surrounded the car. I got closer and saw Marcia. Her body was bent forward in a way that human beings can't bend. Many thoughts rushed my mind, but the first was of Rebecca, our thirteen-year-old daughter.

A police officer approached and said, *"Are you Mr. Rhodes? Your wife is calling for you."*

Somehow, Marcia was alive and conscious but screaming in pain. I ran to her. When I reached out to her, she grabbed my hand and said, *"Harold, please take care of me."*

"Of course I will. I'll take care of you forever. I love you."

The officer returned. *"Mr. Rhodes, could you please step over there?"* He pointed to one of the fire trucks. *"We are going to try to get your wife out of the vehicle now."*

The Jaws of Life tore off the roof of the Toyota. I watched as EMTs, firefighters, and police officers slowly removed Marcia from the Toyota and placed her on a stretcher.

I was transfixed while an EMT removed her shoes and scratched the bottoms of her feet. I knew that she was testing whether Marcia could feel her legs. Marcia did not react. The EMT scratched a second time and then a third. No reaction. The EMT looked over at me and shook her head.

I rushed to the ambulance while the EMTs strapped Marcia to the gurney. An EMT said, *"We are going to take her to the Milford hospital right now."*

The ambulance sped away, and I followed as quickly as I could to the Milford Regional Medical Center, about three miles away.

By the time I arrived, Marcia was on a medical bed in the largest room in the emergency department, with many doctors and nurses surrounding her. She was conscious but in shock, and broken glass was all over her face and body. In a hurry to remove the glass, the nurses began to cut away her clothing and jewelry.

The doctors and nurses began asking me questions. *"What medicines is she taking? What medicines is she allergic to?"* I was unprepared to answer these questions, even after nineteen years of marriage.

Marcia's voice reached me above the din. *"Harold, I am really hurt, aren't I? I can't feel my legs."* I tried to reassure her.

One of the doctors came over to me and said, *"Mr. Rhodes, your wife appears to have sustained serious damage to her back, and she apparently has several other serious medical issues. With your approval, we are going to inject a substantial amount of steroids to hold the* swelling down around her spinal cord. We are going to medicate her to relieve the pain as well as administer several other medications. As soon as she is stabilized, she will be transported to the trauma unit at UMass Memorial Hospital in Worcester. We know that this has been a shock to you. We have already called the emergency department. When you arrive, go to the front desk, where you will be met by a trauma nurse."

It took me nearly an hour to drive to UMass Memorial Hospital. Concerned for Rebecca, I called Diane, Rebecca's school counselor. I explained to Diane what had happened. Diane said she would talk to Rebecca and let her know I wanted to talk to her.

I telephoned Elaine, the mother of Rachel, a good friend of Rebecca's.

"Please don't worry, Harold," Elaine told me. "I will pick them both up at school, and Rebecca will sleep over tonight."

At approximately four o'clock, I arrived at the front desk of the emergency department. "My name is Harold Rhodes. My wife was in an auto crash and was brought here by ambulance."

A woman with dark hair approached me. "I am the on-duty social worker. Let's go to the family room and talk." I followed her.

She said, "Mr. Rhodes, as you know, your wife has been in a serious auto crash. For the next several hours, she will be evaluated to determine the extent of her injuries by an orthopedic surgeon and a neurologist. I can assure you that both doctors are the best at UMass. As soon as they have completed their initial evaluation, they will come here and talk to you. This is going to take several hours, so please be patient, but please do not hesitate to ask for me if you have any questions while you're waiting. We know that this is a difficult time for you. Do you have a health care proxy for her?"[2]

It was five o'clock. I had been waiting for more than an hour, and I had to make several difficult phone calls. I called my brothers, Steve and Mike; my sister, Lisa; Marcia's sister, Susan; her parents, Moe and Elayne; and her best friends, Cyndi and Pam. The conversation was always the same: "Marcia was in a serious accident, and I am waiting to hear the extent of her injuries."

---

2 Colossal Mistake #1: I did not have any advanced medical directives for Marcia (living will, power of attorney, or health care proxy). Because she was conscious, she was able to direct that I make her medical care decisions. Under different circumstances, not having these documents could have been dire. For more information, see http://www.medicinenet.com/advance_medical_directives/article.htm.

Then I called our daughter. "Rebecca, this is Dad. I know that Elaine told you Mom was in a car crash, and that is why she picked you up at school. I am at the hospital in Worcester with Mom, and the doctors are caring for her now."

"Is Mom going to be all right?"

"We will know more later tonight or tomorrow after the doctors are done looking at her. For tonight, you will sleep over at Rachel's, and when I know more, I will call you. I am going to stay with Mom at the hospital tonight. She is being taken care of very well."

"How long is she going to be in the hospital?"

"We don't know yet."

I heard Rebecca softly crying, but she didn't push me for more information.

At around nine o'clock, I met Dr. James Bayley,[3] the orthopedic surgeon, and Dr. Bennett Blumenkopf,[4] the neurosurgeon.

Dr. Bayley began by explaining anatomy. "*The spinal column, commonly called the spine or backbone, consists of thirty-three vertebrae and the intervertebral discs between each two vertebrae. The spinal column extends from the skull to the pelvis and houses and protects the spinal cord. The spinal canal is the natural passage through the center of the spinal column that contains the spinal cord.*[5] *The spinal cord is a long, thin, tubular bundle of nervous tissue and support cells within the spinal canal. It has three major functions: as a conduit for motor information, which travels down the spinal cord; as a conduit for sensory information in the reverse direction; and as a center for coordinating certain reflexes.*"

Dr. Bayley continued. "As you know, Marcia has been seriously injured. Her spinal column has suffered an acute burst fracture[6] at the thoracic T-12 vertebra along the spinal column, which is the lowest thoracic vertebra. In addition, she has at least seven broken ribs, internal organ damage not yet determined, and potential head trauma and edema. A more complete picture of her injuries will be known when the swelling around her spinal cord has subsided."

I had never been the type of person to have outbursts of emotions, but I felt myself screaming inside.

---

3   Dr. Bayley is a leading board-certified orthopedic surgeon whose special expertise includes degenerative spine, lumbar spinal stenosis, spinal fractures, and spinal stenosis.

4   Dr. Blumenkopf is a leading board-certified neurological surgeon whose special expertise includes epilepsy, neurosurgery, pain, and the spine and peripheral nerves.

5   "Spinal Canal," *Collins English Dictionary*, last modified July 11, 2014, http://www.collinsdictionary.com/dictionary/english/spinal-canal.

6   "*A burst fracture is a type of traumatic spinal injury in which a vertebra breaks from a high-energy axial load (e.g., car accidents), with shards of vertebra penetrating surrounding tissues and sometimes the spinal canal. In the long-term, varying degrees of pain, function, and appearance may affect the traumatized region during the subject's lifetime. Over the subject's lifetime, the subject experiences ancillary pain and discomfort in the spine and limbs caused by increasing neurological dysfunction.*" "Burst Fracture," *Wikipedia*, last modified March 9, 2014, http://en.wikipedia.org/wiki/Burst_fracture.

A while later, Dr. Bayley visited again. He told me that Marcia would be stabilized and heavily sedated. To prevent further damage, she would be kept immobile. *"When the swelling does subside, a spinal cord fusion surgery[7] will be performed. The basic idea is to fuse together the damaged vertebra with other vertebrae so they heal into a single, solid bone. Two eight-inch titanium rods—one on each side of her spinal column—will be attached, using as many as eight titanium screws, in order to support her spinal column to prevent further damage. During the surgery, Dr. Blumenkopf will attempt to repair the nerve damage to the spinal cord, if at all possible."* He went on. *"After surgery, she will be transferred to a recovery floor. Upon recovery from the surgery, she will be transferred to a spinal cord rehabilitation hospital of your choosing. She will be here for ten to thirty days."*

That night was the first of twenty-three that I slept at UMass Memorial Hospital.

Thursday, January 10, 2002

Marcia's arms flailed. Restrained in a special medical bed, she was desperately trying to remove the tubes inserted into her body.

The intensive care nurse approached me. *"May I have your permission to strap her arms down?"* This was the second of the many questions for which I was unprepared to answer but had to, as her patient advocate.

"Yes." That was the logical answer. She needed those tubes and would pull them out otherwise, but another part of me demanded, *What are you doing to your wife?*

The memory of meeting Marcia for the first time flooded my mind. The day was Sunday, July 11, 1982, and I was standing on the balcony of my apartment at Natick Village in Natick, Massachusetts.

After growing up in Indianapolis, I entered Harvard Business School in 1978 and graduated in 1980. A year later, a three-year relationship ended, and I moved to Natick, where I worked for Prime Computer.

The most beautiful girl I'd ever seen was sunning on a deck chair at the pool, and she was alone. I wasted no time getting to the pool area. *"Is someone sitting here?"* I asked.

"Sit where you want. It's a free country," she said, so sarcastically.

---

7   "Spinal fusion is a surgical technique used to join two or more vertebrae. Supplementary bone tissue, either from the patient or a donor, is used in conjunction with the body's natural bone growth processes to fuse the vertebrae. In most cases, the fusion is augmented by a process called fixation, involving the placement of metallic screws (pedicle screws often made from titanium), rods, plates, or cages to stabilize the vertebrae and facilitate bone fusion. The fusion process typically takes 6 to 12 months after surgery. During this time, external bracing (orthotics) may be required. Fusing of the spine is used primarily to eliminate the pain caused by abnormal motion of the vertebrae by immobilizing the faulty vertebrae themselves, which is usually caused by degenerative conditions." "Spinal Fusion," *Wikipedia*, last modified June 4, 2014, http://en.wikipedia.org/wiki/Spinal_fusion.

I was not one to shy away from a flip response like this. I chuckled and sat down next to Marcia Goldy from New Jersey. We talked, and we had our first date the following night.

Marcia wore red high heels on our first date. I'd never dated a woman who wore red high heels. I was a country boy from Indiana. Girls wore black shoes, maybe navy or blue, but never red. I was hooked.

Marcia was so New Jersey: funny, fabulously East Coast stylish, and gorgeous. We had similar backgrounds. Her father was an engineer like mine. She worked as an accountant at Zayre, but she went to work mostly to socialize and to have fun. The point of work and everything else, she said, was to have fun.

After immersing myself in business school, where the focus was earning money, Marcia was a breath of fresh air. I was in love before dinner ended.

The physicians, specialists, and trauma nurses closely monitored Marcia. No procedures would be performed until the swelling in her back subsided, which could take ten to fourteen days.

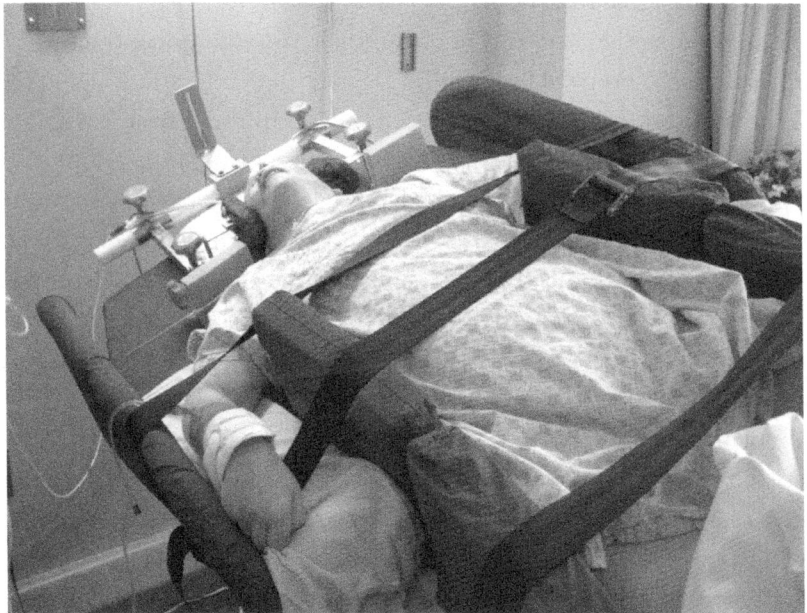

Figure 1. Marcia was immobilized until the internal swelling stabilized.

During the night, one of the treating physicians gave me a more detailed accounting of her complications:

1. Spinal cord burst fracture at the thoracic-12 vertebra, including fractures in the lamina, facets, and spinous process with bone fragments in the spinal canal
2. Attenuated lesion on liver
3. Likely loss of bowel control
4. Likely loss of bladder control
5. Multiple rib fractures
6. Left pneumothorax (a collection of air or gas in the space around the left lung)
7. Psoas hematoma (an unusual blood clot on the muscle that flexes the thigh)
8. Pancreatitis (inflammation of the pancreas)
9. Subarachnoid hemorrhage (bleeding in the area between the brain and the thin tissues that cover the brain)
10. Deep venous thrombosis (a blood clot that forms in a vein deep inside the body)
11. Paraplegia, complete

In the following days, I learned of additional complications:

1. Flail chest (a life-threatening condition that occurs when a segment of the chest wall breaks under extreme stress and becomes detached from the rest of the chest wall)
2. Pneumonia due to contracting methicillin-resistant *Staphylococcus aureus* (MRSA), a bacterial infection
3. Colon inflammation and severe abdominal pain due to contracting *clostridium difficile* (*c. diff*), a type of bacteria
4. Pleural effusion (excess fluid that accumulates in the pleural cavity and impairs breathing by limiting the expansion of the lungs during inhalation)
5. Hypernatremia (an electrolyte disturbance, defined by an elevated sodium level in the blood, that can cause lethargy, weakness, irritability, and edema)
6. Diabetes insipidus (indicating the inability of the kidney to concentrate urine)

An article about the crash appeared on the front page of the *Milford Daily News*, and Marcia was identified as the crash victim. As expected, the telephone messages started to pile up.

At midmorning, while at the hospital, I called Rebecca's school, Milford Middle School East, and spoke again to the school counselor, Diane. She had seen the article. I could tell that she knew Rebecca would need all the support the school could provide. Diane was kind on the phone, and she made me understand that she, as well as the teachers and school administrators, would do their best to take care of Rebecca while at school.

I called several of Marcia's friends: three Cindys, Marion, Elaine, Jessica, and Pam. All were supportive. Marion told me she would speak to Lisa (her daughter and Rebecca's close friend) and make sure that she took care of Rebecca.

I called the Medway Police Department to speak with William Boultenhouse, the officer who had been on duty during the crash. He reiterated the details of the crash that were in the newspaper. He also made me understand that he was extremely thankful that Marcia had avoided hitting him with her car. *"I would have been killed, you know. I am sure that steered clear of crashing into me."*

I called Marcia's parents in Florida. They said they would fly up as soon as possible. I called Julie, a close friend, and she told me to call if she could do anything at all for Marcia or me.

I called Metropolitan Insurance, our auto insurance carrier, to establish a claim number. The service representative told me that Marcia's crumpled car had been taken to a local storage facility. *"When can you remove the valuables and the license plate?"*

Removing the license plate was low on my priority list.

Later in the day, Dr. Bayley told me that Marcia would undergo spinal cord fusion surgery the following Wednesday. Until then, she would be sedated, restrained, fed intravenously, and kept on a respiratory ventilator in the intensive care unit (ICU). The sight of her with all those tubes, being slowly rotated on the medical bed to maintain air passage in her lungs to prevent pneumonia, was a horrifying image. Rebecca wanted to visit her, but I put that off until Marcia was more stable.

After surgery and recovery, she would be transported to a spinal cord injury rehabilitation facility where she would receive intensive medical, physical,[8] and occupational[9] therapies for six weeks. If the therapies were successful and if the necessary modifications to our house were complete, she would be able to return home. She would be angry and grief-stricken for a long time.

Friday, January 11, 2002

Earlier in the morning, a nasogastric (NG) tube was inserted into Marcia's stomach via her nose and throat. Among other functions, an NG tube is used to remove the contents of the stomach in case emergency surgery was required. The tube was uncomfortable, and it irritated the inside of her nose and throat. Although sedated, she tried to pull it out.

---

[8] *"A physical therapist is a health care professional who is primarily concerned about the remediation of impairments and disabilities through physical activity."* "Physical Therapy," *Wikipedia*, last modified July 3, 2014, http://en.wikipedia.org/wiki/Physical_therapy.

[9] *"An occupational therapist is a health care professional who is primarily concerned about the treatments to develop, recover, or maintain the daily living and work skills of people with a physical, mental, or developmental condition."* "Occupational Therapy," *Wikipedia*, last modified July 2, 2014, http://en.wikipedia.org/wiki/Occupational_therapy.

I watched while the nurse restrained and affixed her arms to the rails of the medical bed and confirmed that her neck and head brace were well placed. This image of Marcia flailing in her medical bed, trying for freedom still haunts me.

In the ICU on the fifth floor of UMass, the medical bed slowly rotated her body from left to right and back again. She was agitated and sleeping lightly despite sedation.

Many health care providers began to educate me about my responsibilities and the actions that I had to take before she would be allowed to return home.

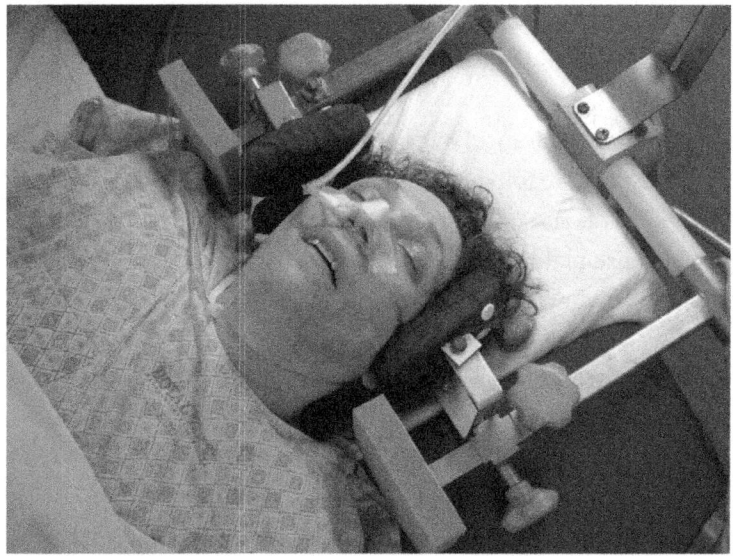

Figure 2. Marcia was sedated while the swelling decreased around her spinal cord.

In order for her to be discharged from the rehabilitation hospital, our home had to be substantially renovated to accommodate her. In my notebook, I began my list of what I had to accomplish:
1. Acquire an appropriate manual wheelchair
2. Acquire a wheelchair-accessible minivan
3. Complete the following home renovations:
    - A wheelchair-accessible bathroom to accommodate her special needs
    - A wheelchair ramp to enable entering and exiting our home
    - Rehab-grade carpet to enable a manual wheelchair to easily maneuver
    - Inside and outside doors widened to accommodate a manual wheelchair
    - Corner edge guards to prevent inside damage
    - Additional closet space to safely store the many medical supplies
4. Acquire a fully functioning medical bed with lateral rotation

5. Acquire an air mattress featuring lateral rotation, alternating pressure, and true low air loss to prevent pressure ulcers
6. Acquire a large array of medical supplies

The cost would exceed $125,000, but fortunately, we had enough savings for now.

How would other victims, with little or no money, be able to manage this? Where would they get $100,000? Because we knew that the crash couldn't be Marcia's fault, shouldn't Carlo Zalewski's insurance carrier advance the money for her care and recovery?[10]

My brother Steve, an attorney, encouraged me to get legal representation as soon as possible. Three days had already passed, and Zalewski's insurance carrier had yet to contact me.

I called Julie (my close friend) again and asked if her sister, Abby Hechtman, could recommend an attorney. Abby[11] was a senior partner at Brown Rudnick Berlack Israels, one of Boston's most prestigious law firms. She put me in touch with M. Frederick Pritzker,[12] who chaired the Brown Rudnick litigation department. According to Brown Rudnick's website, Pritzker *"successfully generated the second highest settlement for a single claimant personal injury client recorded in Massachusetts."*

Saturday, January 12, 2002

I continued to receive many calls and e-mails from friends and family, but I had no desire to talk. I had to be with Marcia day and night inside the ICU. Having been hospitalized myself for surgery, I knew that Marcia had to have a full-time patient advocate. Someone knowledgeable and caring had to be with her at all times to answer any medical questions, make sure that no mistakes were inadvertently made, and provide for her care when the nurses' aides were unavailable. I did this, and over time, I asked Marcia's friends to take shifts.

---

10 Years later, I realized that this thought was the moment when our battle, on behalf of all blameless victims, began against Zalewski's insurers, Zurich American Insurance and AIG.

11 Over the years to follow, my friendship with Abby grew. Besides being an outstanding attorney, her continued compassion allowed me to pour my heart out to her many times. I will never be able to thank Abby enough for introducing me to Fred Pritzker as well as what she did for Marcia and me.

12 The selection of Fred Pritzker, with the substantial resources of Brown Rudnick, was one of the two best decisions that I made. Along with the members of his team, Fred is a gifted attorney and litigator. His legal skills are remarkable. He has an amazing ability to predict the actions of the defendant attorneys well in advance and to simplify complex situations. He became a compassionate member of our family. Marcia and I are grateful for his commitment to us.

At around ten o'clock that night, Marcia pulled out the nasogastric tube. At two o'clock in the morning, a doctor reinserted it. She was again in pain and stressed, and she relentlessly tried to break free from the arm restraints. I felt so helpless.

The only relief Marcia got was when the nurse gave her a dose of Ativan (a high-potency, intermediate-duration sedative). The relief never lasted long. Whenever she was awake and somewhat lucid, she was in tremendous distress. I was allowed to give her some ice chips, and that was all I could do to comfort my wife.

At four o'clock in the morning, the ICU nurses demanded that I get some sleep. They showed me a room that visitors rarely used and gave me sheets, a pillow, and a blanket.

During these nights when I was alone in the hospital, shock, worry, and fear tore at me. I could cope only by analytically figuring out what to do and doing it.

I advocated for Marcia, dealt with the insurance companies, called the lawyers, and arranged for the home renovations. I moved forward, asking myself, *What do I need to do next?* At night I thought, *What if I can't handle this? What if I'm not capable?* That was when the tears flowed.

Sunday, January 13, 2002

I woke at six thirty and went to Marcia's room in the ICU. She was already agitated and in considerable pain.

I managed to catch the resident doctor doing her rounds. I asked for additional Ativan to calm Marcia, and the doctor said she would look into it. Clearly, I had to advocate on Marcia's behalf all the time. By seven, the pain medication and Ativan made Marcia more comfortable. She was still agitated but appeared to be more stable.

I was grateful for Judy, the supervising registered nurse on duty. She was competent, and she followed up on Marcia extremely well. I could tell she took a great interest in Marcia during her two-day shifts. *"Marcia had a bowel movement,"* Judy told me. *"This is important because it is a positive indication that her digestive system appears not to have been completely damaged."*

With a complete T-12 burst spinal fracture, Marcia would never again have normal bowel and bladder control. Most people took these bodily functions for granted. For a person with a spinal cord injury, learning to regulate the bowel and bladder could be extraordinarily challenging.

For bowel control, I was told, Marcia would have to transfer herself from her bed to her wheelchair and then from her wheelchair onto the commode. If unable to transfer herself, she would need assistance by a caregiver. If she could not be transferred at all, a caregiver would have to attend to her bowel movements in bed.

For bladder control, an injured female had to initially use a full-time Foley catheter,[13] a flexible tube that passed through the urethra and into the bladder, allowing urine to flow into a urine collection bag that was periodically emptied.

However, a full-time in-dwelling Foley catheter risked serious repeated urinary tract infections (UTI),[14] bladder infections, kidney infections, or even sepsis, an illness resulting from an infection that often led to organ failure and even death. Due to the likelihood of infections, over time, an injured female had to try to learn to dispose of urine via intermittent self-catheterization through her urethra, typically every four to six hours. If intermittent self-catheterization was not possible, she would have to use an in-dwelling Foley catheter for the rest of her life.

For persons whose mobility was limited due to a spinal cord injury, sepsis is especially life threatening. According to the Mayo Clinic, *"Sepsis is a potentially life-threatening complication of an infection. Sepsis occurs when chemicals released into the bloodstream to fight the infection trigger inflammation throughout the body. This inflammation can trigger a cascade of changes that can damage multiple organ systems, causing them to fail. If sepsis progresses to septic shock, blood pressure drops dramatically, which may lead to death."*[15]

According to *Wikipedia*, "Approximately 20–35 percent of people with severe sepsis and 30–70 percent of people with septic shock die."[16]

In the afternoon, while Marcia was not heavily sedated, Dr. Bayley talked with her for the first time. *"Marcia, four days ago you were in a very serious auto accident. You are now*

---

[13] "A Foley catheter is a flexible tube that is passed through the urethra and into the bladder. The tube has two separated channels, or lumens, running down its length. One lumen is open at both ends, and allows urine to drain out into a collection bag. The other lumen has a valve on the outside end and connects to a balloon at the tip; the balloon is inflated with sterile water when it lies inside the bladder, in order to stop it from slipping out. A major problem with Foley catheters is that they have a tendency to contribute to urinary tract infections (UTI). This occurs because bacteria can travel up the catheters to the bladder where the urine can become infected. To combat this, the industry is moving to antiseptic-coated catheters. This has been helpful, but it has not completely solved this major problem. An additional problem is that Foley catheters tend to become coated over time with a biofilm that can obstruct the drainage. This increases the amount of stagnant urine left in the bladder, which further contributes to the problem of urinary tract infections. When a Foley catheter becomes clogged, it must be flushed or replaced." "Foley Catheter," *Wikipedia*, last modified March 11, 2014, http://en.wikipedia.org/wiki/Foley_catheter.

[14] "The urinary tract is comprised of the kidneys, ureters, bladder, and urethra. A urinary tract infection (UTI) is an infection caused by pathogenic organisms (for example, bacteria, fungi, or parasites) in any of the structures that comprise the urinary tract." "Urine Infection," RxList, last modified March 11, 2014, http://www.rxlist.com/urine_infection/page2.htm.

[15] "Sepsis," Mayo Clinic, last modified March 11, 2014, http://www.mayoclinic.org/diseases-conditions/sepsis/basics/definition/con-20031900.

[16] "Sepsis," *Wikipedia*, last modified March 11, 2014, http://en.wikipedia.org/wiki/Sepsis.

in the intensive care unit at UMass Memorial Hospital. You have sustained many injuries. Most significantly, your spinal column has been seriously damaged, and your spinal cord has been severed. The damage to your spinal cord has caused other medical complications. Our plan is that after the swelling around your spinal column goes down in a few days, we are going to fuse your spine back together. We will see what can be done neurologically."

Given her state of mind, I was not sure how much of this information she was able to understand and process.

With the increase in medication for pain and sleep, she seemed calmer. Her breathing sounded okay, and she was only occasionally aggravated. Again, I spent the night at the hospital. I slept in one of the two waiting rooms but woke every two hours to look in on her.

Monday, January 14, 2002

At five fifteen in the morning, Marcia was constantly moaning in pain. She repeatedly jerked her arms, trying to get loose from the restraints.

I stared at my broken, suffering wife. Twelve seconds of recklessness on the part of Carlo Zalewski, and Marcia's life was changed forever. Zalewski had walked away from the crash.

Marcia's case manager, Melissa, continued to educate me about caring for a spouse who had a spinal cord injury. Most importantly, she provided me with the contact information for the Spinal Cord Injury Hotline.[17]

The knowledgeable individual who answered the hotline phone told me about several high-quality rehabilitation hospitals in the area: Whittier Rehabilitation Hospital (Westborough), Fairlawn Rehabilitation Hospital (Worcester), Spaulding Rehabilitation Hospital (Boston), and New England Rehabilitation Hospital (Woburn).[18] Although seemingly premature, the hotline personnel said that I should begin my research as soon as possible, because we did not know how long Marcia would be at UMass.

Melissa set up referral visits for the first three rehabilitation hospitals for the end of the week.

Marcia's spinal cord fusion surgery was scheduled for Wednesday, January 16. After that, the nurses would try to get her to sit up. I continued to pray that she would have normal bladder and bowel control. Without that, life for her would be extremely challenging.

---

17   "Our mission is to assist spinal-cord-injured individuals and their families to reach the best possible care. We strive to educate medical professionals and others about caring for spinal cord injuries. Through a grant from the Paralyzed Veterans of America, we have established a large media library on educational topics relating to spinal cord injury and disability. We aim for spinal-cord-injured individuals to live life fully and productively." "About Us," Spinal Cord Injury Network, last modified March 11, 2014, http://spinalcordinjury.org/joomla1/index.php?option=com_content&view=article&id=46&Itemid=54.

18   Colossal Mistake #2: I did not ask if there were hospital facilities that specialized in acute spinal cord injury. Later, I learned about the Craig Hospital in Englewood, Colorado, a world-renowned rehabilitation hospital that specialized in neurorehabilitation and research of patients with spinal cord injury (SCI).

Managing the relationship with our medical insurance provider, UnitedHealthcare, has become nearly a full-time job. Like many other people, I had never read our medical insurance policy in detail. I didn't understand all the limitations, exclusions, and types of coverage. Nonetheless, the good people at UnitedHealthcare were, without fail, compassionate.[19]

I was struck with the thought that without money from Zalewski's insurance carrier and without excellent health care insurance, how could Marcia, or any blameless victim, receive the best medical care after a catastrophic injury?

I wondered whether Zalewski's insurance carrier understood that lacking health care insurance, a blameless victim would likely suffer even greater harm. Moreover, how could a spouse be a full-time patient advocate while working full-time? Did Zalewski's insurance carrier understand that a spouse would likely have to stop working to provide care for the spouse? Did Zalewski's insurance carrier know that the spouse who had to quit a job to provide care wouldn't be compensated for lost wages?

For a blameless victim without the financial resources for home modifications and transportation, without health care insurance, and without compensation for the lost wages of a patient advocate who was a spouse, Zalewski's insurance carrier would be able to exert enormous, unrelenting financial pressure on us.

Marcia's parents, Moe and Elayne, arrived that night at the hospital, and I prepared them before seeing their daughter in the ICU. As their youngest daughter, Marcia had always had a special, loving relationship with her parents. Their grief must have been enormous.

We entered the ICU and saw the ventilator forcing Marcia to breathe. When her parents saw her, I felt their anguish. They stayed with her that night.

---

19 UnitedHealthcare has consistently lived up to its policy requirements and, in most every case, supported Marcia's special needs, all of which significantly enhanced her medical outcome. We will always be thankful to her case managers, especially Jackie West, and the medical directors at UnitedHealthcare. Marcia and I have been quite fortunate to have UnitedHealthcare as our health insurance provider.

At four o'clock in the afternoon, I went home to take Rebecca to her first psychologist appointment since the crash. Earlier in the day, I had spoken to Harriet Melrose, a licensed independent clinical social worker (LICSW), about the crash, as well as about how I thought Rebecca was doing.

On the surface, Rebecca seemed to be accepting her mother's condition. However, I knew that she generally held her troubles inside and then showed her anger and depression in large bursts. I felt sure that when she understood the full gravity of her mom's injuries, she would feel devastated.

For years to come, while Marcia recovered, I would be both mother and father to Rebecca. Like most fathers, I had no idea how to be a mother to a thirteen-year-old girl. I was scared about how Rebecca would be scarred by this crash for the rest of her life.

Harriet gave us two goals: whenever we were home together, we must eat dinner together, and, when things were not working well between us, we must tell each other.

That night, Rebecca waited for me to talk about her mom. I emphasized that Marcia had great doctors and was getting excellent care. I said that her mom would be in a wheelchair, but I didn't discuss paralysis. I knew that, at some point, Rebecca would need to see her mother in the hospital. Having Rebecca see her mom with all the tubes and wires was a dreadful thought.

A phone call interrupted us. Marcia's mother had terrible news. She said that Marcia had developed a pneumothorax: a pocket of air in her body but outside her lungs. A pneumothorax was painful and could lead to pneumonia. Additionally, Marcia's most recent blood test results were outside of normal ranges in several areas, particularly her electrolytes. The endocrinologist said that this probably accounted for her continued agitation.

Over the next six months, I learned much about endocrinology. Each day, a pleasant medical resident explained Marcia's blood test results to me. If an anomaly was found, the medical resident told me how it would be managed.

Tuesday, January 15, 2002

Before school, I asked Rebecca how she was feeling. Because of the way she usually held her emotions inside, her feelings were sometimes difficult to read.

I spoke to Diane at Rebecca's school. Diane said she talked to all of Rebecca's teachers, and they were watching out for her. We agreed to talk each morning. As I looked back, Diane's compassion was remarkable. While I was at the hospital, I felt much better knowing that Diane and all of Rebecca's teachers were caring for our daughter.

Almost a week had passed, and I had not begun planning for the home renovations or the acquisition of a wheelchair-accessible minivan, a full-functioning medical bed with lateral rotation, an air mattress to prevent pressure ulcers, or the many other required medical supplies.

By chance, we had a family friend who was an architectural designer. He had extensive experience with the residential building requirements described in the American Disabilities Act (ADA). Before going to the hospital, I spoke with him about the renovations. He told me that he could come over the next day to begin. In the best-case scenario, Marcia would be at UMass for three weeks and in the rehabilitation hospital for five weeks. Therefore, our home had to be renovated within eight weeks. The designer assured me that he would take care of everything so that the house would be ready for her.

The initial home renovations would cost at least $50,000. The other items (including the wheelchair-accessible van) would cost at least $60,000. I was thankful that we had the money on hand.

While the architectural designer was discussing the costs, I wondered again how the families of other blameless victims managed financially. Was Zalewski's insurance carrier betting that Marcia didn't have the money on hand or the time to manage these and other large expenses? Did the insurance carrier believe that Marcia would be forced to settle quickly for an amount of money that was much less than she needed?

Our living room would become Marcia's new bedroom. To fit her medical bed, her piano had to be put in storage, which would make her unhappy. The openness of the living room-turned-bedroom would also make her unhappy. Every time that she went to her new bathroom, she would have to traverse the entire home, likely in front of anyone who was in the house, including Rebecca's friends. I was certain that Marcia would detest this arrangement.

After having spoken with the architectural designer, I arrived at the hospital at eleven o'clock in the morning.

Marcia's parents and I had the initial meetings with the intake representatives from the Spaulding, Whittier, and Fairlawn rehabilitation hospitals while at UMass.

Afterward, I made calls to friends and others for their input. I was leaning toward Spaulding, which appeared to offer everything: state-of-the-art rehabilitation facilities, excellent medical personnel, and closeness to the Harvard medical community.

Later, our lawyer, Fred Pritzker visited Marcia in the hospital. I could tell that he felt the pain that she was feeling. I looked into his eyes and knew that he would forever have an emotional commitment to her.

After reading information and having discussions with other attorneys, I understood that Zalewski's insurance carrier would likely try to delay settlement for as long as possible. Zalewski's insurance carrier would likely presume that we had very little savings and would therefore require us to accept a lowball settlement offer. I understood that an insurance carrier would never want to settle for any more than necessary and that Marcia and I would want as much as possible. However, I never thought that an insurance carrier would wait to settle until we were in dire financial hardship. How very stupid was I?

I called Rebecca's school to check in. Diane told me that Rebecca was having a good day. Her science teacher had taken the time to explain to her what the spine did and why the spine was important.

Diane called back to tell me that Rebecca had had a crying spell that afternoon. Diane invited Rebecca to talk with her in her office. After a little while, Rebecca had started smiling again. I was relieved that Rebecca had a safe place to go when her emotions overwhelmed her.

I do not know if schools in other communities were as accommodating, but I will never forget how wonderfully caring Milford's tightly knit community is.[20]

Wednesday, January 16, 2002

I spent last night at the hospital and checked on Marcia three times during the night.

Today is surgery day—a critical day for Marcia. The spinal cord fusion surgery was scheduled to begin at noon. I was filled with nervousness, fear, and hope. I thought, *Maybe there will be a miracle. Maybe she will be able to walk again.*

I met Dr. Bayley and Dr. Blumenkopf before the surgery began. They told me the surgery might take as long as seven hours depending on the extent of the orthopedic and nerve damage.

---

20 Milford, known around the world for its pink granite, is a wonderful community. Most everyone knows everyone else; caring for one another is just a normal part of life in Milford. Our teachers, the medical professionals and staff at the Milford Regional Medical Center, our town employees, our police and fire professionals, our religious congregations, and the many town volunteers make sure that any Milfordian in need is well cared-for. I am certain that the care Marcia, Rebecca, and I received in Milford was the best that any community could provide.

At eight thirty, Marcia, was on the gurney and headed to surgery. I held her hand, and I managed to hold back my tears. I waited in a private family room near the surgery center.

Two hours into the surgery, Dr. Blumenkopf visited me in the family room. His news extinguished all hope for a miracle. Given the extreme extent of the burst fracture to the spine, Dr. Blumenkopf said he couldn't do anything neurologically for her. The spinal cord had been completely severed, and the nerve damage couldn't be repaired. Dr. Bayley would manage the surgery alone.

Marcia would never walk again.

The official medical report of the operation read as follows:
Spinal Fusion Surgery—Report of Operation. *"Midline incision from T-6–L-3; midline fascia was totally ripped in half by trauma. In fact, a finger can be placed down between the spinous process of what appeared to be T-12 and T-11 and perhaps L-1 right through the subcutaneous tissue. In any case, the remaining spinal processes from L-2 up to T-9 were stripped of surrounding soft tissue and muscle. Drill used to locate screws on vertebra and attach two titanium rods."*

When Marcia awoke from surgery, Dr. Bayley broke the awful news to her. He explained the details of the surgery in his straightforward but kind way. He told her that this burst spinal fracture was the worst he had ever seen. Her spinal column had been severed into two parts, separated by more than one inch, and Dr. Blumenkopf could stick his finger all the way into the now-lower portion of her spinal column.

Dr. Bayley said he believed the spinal cord fusion surgery was successful. The two portions of the spinal cord were fused, and her spinal column was now being held together by two eight-inch titanium rods and eight titanium screws.

As warmly as he could, Dr. Bayley explained that Dr. Blumenkopf couldn't do anything neurologically. The burst fracture had sheared the spinal cord into two portions, and the ends of the severed nerves had already died. Dr. Bayley said that medical science didn't have a method to reattach traumatically separated dead nerves in the spinal cord.

I could see that she was horrified. Her expressions ranged from shock to repulsion as though she were thinking, *"Why is this happening? Why did this happen to me? Harold, you need to take care of me. Will you take care of me? Take care of me, Harold."*

I would do everything to take care of her for the rest of her life.

Thursday, January 17, 2002

I spoke to Officer Boultenhouse of the Medway Police Department. He told me that in addition to the Medway police report, the Massachusetts State Police had been developing a comprehensive accident reconstruction report, because a semitrailer truck was involved.

Zalewski had been given a criminal citation for *"Operating a Vehicle Negligently so as to Endanger,"* as governed by Massachusetts General Laws Chapter 90 Section 24(2)(a).[21] The punishment was *"a fine of not less than twenty dollars nor more than two hundred dollars or by imprisonment for not less than two weeks nor more than two years, or both."* Officer William Kingsbury of the Medway Police Department was leading the investigation.

Officer Boultenhouse expressed his deep concern for Marcia's recovery. He said he thought Marcia had recognized that she was going to be struck by the oncoming tractor-trailer and that *"somehow she had the presence of mind to turn the wheels of her car to the right in order to avoid colliding into and perhaps killing me."* That was why she had gone down the embankment. Officer Boultenhouse offered to provide any assistance he could.

Marcia's parents and I visited Spaulding Rehabilitation Hospital in Boston. It was a modern facility and part of the esteemed Brigham Hospital community. It had earned national recognition for its spinal cord injury rehabilitation unit.

The hospital was in a modern high-rise building, and the spinal cord unit occupied two of the floors. We were met by the director of admissions and his assistant, and the tour was conducted by one of the physical therapists.

Friday, January 18, 2002

MetLife Auto's claims representative continued to call me to request that I clean out Marcia's car so that it could be moved to Met's facility. I had been putting this off. I knew that I would be emotionally overwhelmed when I saw her crumpled car.

I spoke to a fellow named Charlie who was quadriplegic and lived in the Milford area. He offered remarkable compassion and wonderful support. I was confident that he would be a great source of strength for us in the years to come. He introduced me to Tami at the Greater Boston Chapter of the National Spinal Cord Injury Association. Tami offered to send me details about spinal cord injury care and services.

Marcia's parents and I visited Fairlawn Rehabilitation Hospital in Worcester. Fairlawn had a close alliance with UMass; many health providers at UMass knew it well. While not having a specific spinal cord injury unit, it was a well-regarded rehabilitation hospital. It was in an older, three-story building with forty or so beds on each floor. The rooms were small, and most of the patients were much older than Marcia.

---

21 "Reckless and Unauthorized Driving," Massachusetts General Laws, last modified March 11, 2014, https://malegislature.gov/Laws/GeneralLaws/PartI/TitleXIV/Chapter90/Section24.

Marcia's parents liked Fairlawn, because its location was more convenient than Spaulding. I thought that Spaulding was well worth the extra distance.

Saturday, January 19, 2002

Ten days have passed since the crash. The time had come for Rebecca to see her mother. I cringed at the idea but I asked her, *"How do you feel about visiting Mom today?"*

I waited. I could tell she was doing her best to decide.

"Okay," she said. *"Am I going to be able to talk to her?"*

I explained that Mom was often sedated and in pain, but I did not think Rebecca heard me. I called ahead to let the nursing staff know that Rebecca was coming for her first visit.

At about one o'clock, Rebecca and I entered the ICU. The door to Marcia's room was mostly open.

"Let's go in together, okay?"

After taking two steps into Marcia's room, Rebecca saw her mother connected to many tubes, agitated, and moaning. Rebecca fainted and fell hard onto the floor. Two nurses, whom I hadn't noticed standing close to Rebecca, rushed to her aid, saying, *"Wake up, Rebecca! Are you okay? Does anything hurt?"*

They took her into an examination room to make sure she was okay. I guessed they were well prepared for this kind of reaction.

Sunday, January 20, 2002

I awoke to the sound of the phone ringing. The nurse from UMass said Marcia had been pulling on her IV and the physician wanted to have the wrist restraints put on again. *"Would that be okay with you?"*

In the afternoon, I went to Fairlawn by myself. After I met with Dr. Elizabeth Roaf, I agreed to have Marcia's rehabilitation conducted at Fairlawn. I could tell Dr. Roaf was a wonderfully caring person and a gifted physiatrist.[22] I knew Marcia would like her a lot.[23]

Monday, January 21, 2002

Rebecca and I had an appointment this day with Harriet Melrose. While I was certain therapists saw many complicated cases, I suspected ours was one of her most challenging.

---

[22] A physiatrist is a medical doctor who leads the rehabilitative and medical care to treat injuries or illnesses that affect bodily movement. Physiatrists are expert in damage to nerves, muscles, and bones as well as other secondary medical complications. The physiatrist is the quarterback of the rehabilitation and medical team. In particular, the physiatrist designs the physical and occupational therapies. According to the Association of Academic Physiatrists, there are only 10,000 board-certified physiatrists in the United States.

[23] The selection of Dr. Roaf was the second of the two best decisions that I made on Marcia's behalf. Over the next seven years, a special bond developed between them. Dr. Roaf consistently guided every aspect of Marcia's emotional, physical, and occupational therapies. Later, she played an important role in our civil litigations. Marcia and I will never be able to express the considerable gratitude we have for everything Dr. Roaf did for us.

I was now responsible for managing Rebecca's life, a substantial change from when Marcia had been in charge. Rebecca and I needed to work out a way to get along, even with all her sadness and my anxiety. Through each session, I learned much about Rebecca and even more about myself.

Wednesday, January 23, 2002

I slept at UMass last night. I thought at length about what Marcia would need upon her discharge from Fairlawn: a home with a wheelchair-accessible bathroom, a wheelchair ramp, enlarged doorways to accommodate the wheelchair, a wheelchair-accessible van, an appropriate manual wheelchair, and items to continue her antiques business.

The construction for what would be the first phase of the home renovations was moving along. A new wheelchair-accessible bathroom and a wheelchair ramp in the garage were being built. All of the door openings were being enlarged, and some changes were being made to the kitchen. Nonetheless, Marcia's bedroom would still be in the living room.

In the afternoon, Rebecca and I had another appointment with Harriet Melrose. Harriet recommended that psych medicine might be able to help Rebecca cope with her anxiety and fear. She said she would call Dr. Virginia Merritt, a child psychiatrist, and that I should call Dr. Merritt later to schedule an appointment.

In the late afternoon, Rebecca and I had our first appointment with Dr. Merritt. After learning from Rebecca how she felt about her mom, dad, and life in general, Dr. Merritt prescribed a low dose of an antidepressant. Rebecca and I met with Dr. Merritt at least once a month from then on.

Tuesday, January 29, 2002

A few days earlier, the physicians recognized that Marcia's right leg had swollen. She was diagnosed as having an obstruction in the femoral vein of her right leg, referred to as a blood clot or a deep vein thrombosis (DVT).

If untreated, a pulmonary embolism could develop. This was *"a blockage of the pulmonary artery or one of its branches, usually occurring when a blood clot from a vein becomes dislodged from its site of formation and embolizes to the arterial blood supply of one of the lungs."*[24]

Marcia had surgery. A Greenfield filter, also referred to as an inferior vena cava filter, was surgically inserted below her heart. It prevented a blood clot from traveling from her leg through her veins and into her heart.

---

[24] "Pulmonary Embolism," *Wikipedia*, last modified March 11, 2014, https://en.wikipedia.org/wiki/Pulmonary_embolism.

Tuesday, February 5, 2002

Marcia was discharged today from UMass Memorial Hospital with the following complications:

1. Paraplegia, complete
2. T-12 spinal fracture, fused by surgery, and supported by two titanium rods
3. Anemia
4. Attention deficit hyperactivity disorder (ADHD)
5. Autonomic dysreflexia[25]
6. Body bruises
7. Broken ribs
8. Cerebral hematoma[26]
9. Abdominal pain and fatigue
10. Clostridium difficile colitis (c. diff)[27]
11. Contusion of abdominal wall
12. Deep vein thromboses (chest, leg) with Greenfield filter inserted
13. Depression and anxiety, severe
14. Diabetes insipidus (results in excessive thirst and urination, which can lead to dehydration)
15. Elevated blood function tests (particularly lithium level)
16. Flail chest
17. Hyperosmolality (increase in concentration of body fluids)
18. Hypernatremia (excessive sodium in blood)
19. MRSA[28]
20. Loss of bladder control
21. Loss of bowel control
22. Multiple fractured ribs
23. Pain

---

[25] *"AD is an abnormal response which occurs when your body is experiencing pain or discomfort below the level of your spinal cord injury [SCI]. Because the pain or discomfort message does not get to the brain because of the spinal cord injury, the body's blood pressure increases to dangerous levels. If the cause of pain or discomfort is not found and treated immediately, serious complications such as stroke, seizure, organ damage, permanent brain injury, or even death may occur."* Publication #765, "Autonomic Dysreflexia," Craig Hospital, last modified March 11, 2014, https://www.craighospital.org/repository/documents/HeathInfo/PDFs/765.AutonomicDysreflexia.pdf.

[26] *"CH involves bleeding into the cerebrum, the largest section of the brain, resulting in an expanding mass of blood that damages surrounding neural tissue."* "Gale Encyclopedia of Neurological Disorders: Cerebral Hematoma," Encyclopedia.com, last modified March 11, 2014, http://www.encyclopedia.com/doc/1G2-3435200089.html.

[27] Colossal Mistake #3A: C. diff is most often a hospital-acquired infection, mostly due to poor infection control within the hospital. I should have investigated the incidence rate of C. diff at UMass and made sure that the best infection control had been arranged for Marcia. C. diff is preventable, with effective infectious disease control.

[28] Colossal Mistake #3B: Like C. diff, MRSA is most often a hospital-acquired infection, mostly due to poor infection control within the hospital. I should have investigated the incidence rate of MRSA at UMass and made sure that the best infection control had been arranged for Marcia. MRSA is preventable, with effective infectious disease control.

24. Pancreatitis
25. Pneumonia due to MRSA
26. Pneumothorax without open wound into thorax
27. Spasticity[29]
28. Subarachnoid hemorrhage after injury
29. Unspecified pleural effusion[30]
30. Urinary tract infection

Marcia was transported via ambulance to Fairlawn Rehabilitation Hospital. Upon her arrival, Dr. David DeGrande, an internist, conducted her intake medical examination and made the following notes:

Seroquel was discontinued as patient showed no evidence of psychotic problems; patient was generally stable from psychiatric viewpoint during hospital stay. Patient did have extreme stress during her hospitalization. Her husband and her parents got into an argument. Patient had to schedule their visits at separate times.

Patient is frustrated with being restricted to her room because of staph infection.

Functional Independence Measure (FIM) Score [31] –13.

Functional Assessment Measure (FAM) Score [32] –27.

Pain when Marcia tries to roll from side to side.

Describes self as irritable as result of pain—goal of patient to decrease pain.

Saturday, February 9, 2002

Because of the MRSA infection, Marcia was given a private room at Fairlawn. Unfortunately, having MRSA meant that anyone—family members, visitors, and health care providers—who had contact with Marcia had to wear a complete gown, gloves, and mask to prevent acquiring MRSA. MRSA would tremendously limit the effectiveness of her physical, occupational, and emotional therapies while at Fairlawn.

---

29 "*Spasticity is a velocity-dependent resistance to stretch, where a lack of inhibition results in excessive contraction of the muscles, ultimately leading to overly flexed joints.*" "Spasticity," Wikipedia, last modified March 11, 2014, http://en.wikipedia.org/wiki/Spasticity.

30 "*PE is a buildup of fluid between the layers of tissue that line the lungs and chest cavity.*" "Pleural Effusion," MedlinePlus, last modified March 11, 2014, http://www.nlm.nih.gov/medlineplus/ency/article/000086.htm.

31 "*The Functional Independence Measure (FIM) Score is a uniform method to evaluate the degree of disability. The score measures the assistance required in eighteen categories (such as "upper body dressing"); each category is rated on a scale of 0 to 7, depending on the assistance required. A fully independent individual would score 126. A score of 13 indicates nearly complete disability.*" "Functional Independence Measure," Rehabilitation Measures Database, last modified March 11, 2014, http://www.rehabmeasures.org/lists/rehabmeasures/dispform.aspx?id=889.

32 "*The Functional Assessment Measure (FAM) was developed by clinicians representing each of the disciplines in an inpatient rehabilitation program as an adjunct to the FIM to specifically address the major functional areas, including cognitive, behavioral, communication, and community functioning measures. The FAM consists of twelve items (such as "employability"); each item is rated on a score of 0 to 7. A fully cognitive individual would score 98. A score of 27 indicates substantially limited cognitive abilities.*" "Functional Assessment Measure," Rehabilitation Measures Database, last modified March 11, 2014, http://www.rehabmeasures.org/Lists/RehabMeasures/DispForm.aspx?ID=1090.

In addition, Marcia had to wear a thoracolumbosacral orthosis (TLSO) body jacket to protect her spinal cord and broken ribs. According to the information provided, *"The TLSO is to function as an immobilization device to restrict excessive motion in your thoracolumbar spine."* Worse, the TLSO aggravated her existing rib fractures and caused substantial additional pain. The TLSO would also substantially limit the effectiveness of her physical, occupational, and emotional therapies.

Monday, February 18, 2002

While Marcia was at Fairlawn, the manager from the Worcester office of Griswold Special Care visited me. She explained that Griswold provided home health aides (HHAs)[33] for home health care.

With Griswold, I would pay the HHA directly, and I would also pay Griswold a fee each week for its service. She told me that the advantages of using Griswold were that it did background checks on the aides and had replacement aides available.

Wednesday, February 27, 2002

Today was exceptionally grueling for Marcia and me. I argued with her parents, which completely upset her. I was devastated when I left.

Years later, I had the opportunity to review the hospital's patient care notes for this day:

"Patient reports her husband threatened divorce today; split in family between her parents and husband causing increased stress. She says abdominal pain was better until he came for visit. Add daytime dose of Valium—patient can use it. Pastoral care—experiencing exceptional family stress."

Thursday, February 28, 2002

In the evening, I had another horrible argument with Marcia. Arguing with Marcia was so stupid. I was devastated when I left. We are in a demanding situation, but I expect much more out of myself. It was another rotten day all around.

Years later, I had the opportunity to review the hospital's patient care notes for this day:

"Neuropsychology—there is ongoing marital/family stress in addition to stress of coping with disability. Argument with husband tonight—patient quite upset."

The issues that I was having with Marcia's parents have made me extremely protective of Marcia.

❖ ❖ ❖

---

33 "A home-health aide is a trained and certified health-care worker who provides assistance to a patient in the home with personal care (as hygiene and exercise) and light household duties (as meal preparation) and who monitors the patient's condition." Merriam-Webster Dictionary, last modified March 11, 2014, http://www.merriam-webster.com/medical/home%20health%20aide.

For the next several weeks, the hospital patient care notes detailed how Marcia was doing.

Sunday, March 3, 2002

"Family brought dog for visit. Patient in good spirits. In wheelchair for 1.5 hrs—later was weepy off and on."

Tuesday, March 5, 2002

"Pastoral Care. Frustrated by slow progress and inability to leave room. Feels unproductive being stationary with lack of activity. Very difficult for Attention Deficit Disorder sufferer like herself."

Friday, March 8, 2002

"Has c. Difficile colitis (inflammation of colon)/clostridium."

Monday, March 11, 2002

"Good spirits. Improvement in abdominal pain. Still gets pain in back when out of bed."

Wednesday, March 13, 2002

"Hope c. Difficile colitis explains abdominal pain. Complaint of new pain whenever takes deep breath. Chest x-ray shows broken rib at location of pain—ends not in contact. New fracture?"

Sunday, March 17, 2002

"Patient says she wished she can go home. Everything happens here—ribs...infection...cough—has cough/cold symptoms."

Friday, March 22, 2002

Roaf Progress Note. *"Brace interfering with arm movement; swollen leg; Husband concern re: mood; should be OUT OF BED more. Dr. Meyers consult concerning Wellbutrin/Prozac—notes frustration with being isolated. At Fairlawn 6 weeks and confined to room."*

Monday, March 25, 2002

"Allowed out of room for therapy per Sue Nelson; remain on contact precaution."

Roaf Progress Note. *"Husband thinks she is more depressed. She says she feels that she is at her baseline and husband keeps asking for a divorce,*[34] *and so she feels anxious about*

---

[34] Before the crash, I would have been described as cool, calculating, and analytical—almost emotionally stoic. Nonetheless, these last three months were brutal for me. I showed my irritation at Marcia's family members. On occasion, I

that. Leg still swollen—on Coumadin[35] (delayed because of concerns with sub-cranial hemorrhage). Patient allowed out of room—showed progress in physical therapy as a result."

Marcia's depression, anxiety, and anger at me are heartbreaking. I later learned that people who are paraplegic have a high divorce rate given the intense grief, stress, and caretaking involved.

Tuesday, March 26, 2002
"Left leg swollen from foot to thigh."

Sunday, March 31, 2002
"Left leg swollen from foot to thigh."

---

expressed my anger directly at Marcia. As expected, Marcia reacted by becoming angry with me. Although only mentioned twice in this diary, we discussed divorce more than a few times during these months, although neither of us did anything more than talking. To this day, I remain horrified at myself for losing emotional control, no matter the circumstances.

[35] *"Coumadin is a prescription medicine used to treat blood clots and to lower the chance of blood clots forming in your body. Blood clots can cause a stroke, heart attack, or other serious conditions if they form in the legs or lungs."* Unfortunately, people who take Coumadin must have their blood level endocrinology checked several times per week. "Coumadin," Bristol-Myers Squibb, last modified March 11, 2014, http://www.coumadin.com/html/index.htm.

April 2002 to June 2002

Monday, April 1, 2002

This morning, I spoke with an attorney from Brown Rudnick. He told me about the insurance coverage for the crash. There are four defendants: Carlo Zalewski (the truck driver); GAF Materials Corporation (the company that leased both the truck driver and the tanker-trailer); Driver Logistics Services (the company that employed Zalewski); and Penske Trucking (the company that owned the tanker-trailer).

There are two insurance carriers representing the four defendants. The *primary insurance carrier* is Zurich American Insurance. The insurance policy limit with Zurich is $2 million, meaning that any claim below $2 million would be paid by Zurich.

The *excess insurance carrier* is American International Group (AIG).[36] The insurance policy limit with AIG was $50 million, meaning that the amount of any claim above $2 million but less than $50 million would be paid by AIG.

Monday, April 8, 2002

Rebecca turned fourteen years old today. To celebrate, Dr. Roaf allowed Marcia to come home by ambulance for the day. We had a great time together. At five thirty, she returned to Fairlawn by ambulance.

Tuesday, April 16, 2002

Today was our nineteenth wedding anniversary. After thirty-two days at UMass Memorial Hospital and another sixty-six days in rehabilitation at Fairlawn, Marcia made up her mind to come home today.

I would have preferred that she stay another week or two at Fairlawn, but she was sick and tired of being in a hospital and wanted to get back to some normalcy. Who could blame her?

The good news was that both the wheelchair-accessible ramp and the wheelchair-accessible bathroom had been completed and approved by Fairlawn's occupational therapists. They would have liked a second wheelchair-accessible exit to be available, but they said this could wait until later.

In addition, a medical bed—albeit working quite poorly—was ready for her. This bed was at least twenty years old and creaky. I should have made certain Marcia had been given

---

36 The actual insurance policy was written through one of AIG's subsidiaries, National Union Fire Insurance Company of Pittsburgh, Pennsylvania. The people who did the claims investigation and processing are employed by another AIG subsidiary, AIG Domestic Claims, Inc.

only new durable medical equipment (DME), including this medical bed. Too often, old equipment breaks down and usually at the most inopportune time.

As the ambulance turned into our driveway, I remembered what the health care professionals at Fairlawn had taught me:
1. I am not a health care professional.
2. I must never set medical goals for Marcia's rehabilitation.
3. I must not nag Marcia about doing her rehabilitation.[37]
4. Only health care professionals could set Marcia's rehabilitative goals. If I have a concern, I should speak to them, not to Marcia.
5. Marcia needs me to always be her husband, the one person who would love her exactly as she was. She needs to know that she could never fail in my eyes.

Almost immediately, however, I realized how utterly unprepared I was to take care of her, now that she was home.[38]

I thought that I had done everything required. I had even arranged for a morning HHA (7:00 a.m. to 9:00 a.m.) and an evening HHA (5:00 p.m. to 9:00 p.m.) to begin the next day.

However, I had completely forgotten to arrange for an evening HHA to care for Marcia when she got home. How stupid could I be?

First, I was scared to transfer Marcia from her wheelchair to her medical bed.[39]

Second, just after I transferred her into bed, she defecated. I had absolutely no idea what to do. With great fear, I had to leave Marcia by herself in bed. I hurried to CVS, where a wonderfully helpful pharmacy technician, Evelyn, took pity on me.

Evelyn found refastenable briefs, wipes, and other items. She explained how to use them to clean an unexpected bowel movement. Then, Evelyn said to call her if I had any questions. I did, several times.

Third, I didn't know how to get Marcia ready for bed. This included cleaning her body, knowing what to feed her, knowing what medicines to give her, knowing how to manage her Foley catheter, and everything else a well-trained HHA would know.

---

[37] Later, a defense attorney would challenge me on this in open court in front of Marcia and Rebecca. This attorney tried to prove that I was an uncaring husband who did not show her (as the attorney said) *"tough love."*

[38] Colossal Mistake #4: I am sure that Fairlawn's physical and occupational therapists did their best to prepare me for this day. However, I failed to connect what I was taught at Fairlawn's rehab facilities to the realities of our home. Given Marcia's MRSA, the required use of a TLSO, and her desire to come home early, Marcia's physical and occupational therapies had only limited success.

[39] Colossal Mistake #5: While I am sure that the Fairlawn therapists did their best to teach me how to perform each type of transfer, I failed to make sure that I learned to do transfers in our home. At Fairlawn, I practiced wheelchair transfers in a large, open room onto a large, low therapy bed, equal in height to the wheelchair. Transfers in our home were onto a medical bed that was higher than the wheelchair and in a much smaller area.

Fourth, I was not told about additional durable medical equipment that would have been especially useful to have from day one.[40]

Fifth, I didn't learn about backup medical support from.[41]

Sixth, I didn't learn how to provide immediate care for a new pressure ulcer.[42][43]

Seventh, and most important, we didn't learn how to live together as a family with a family member who had a spinal cord injury.[44]

Wednesday, April 18, 2002

Because of the crash, Marcia lacked bowel control. To avoid defecating during the day, the goal of her morning bowel program is to completely empty her colon after being transferred onto the commode. Without bowel control, there are many concerns, two of which were starting the bowel movement via *digital stimulation* as well as knowing when the colon is empty.

Unfortunately, Marcia hadn't been taught digital stimulation during rehabilitation. While just a clinical activity for bowel management, it could be a difficult emotional hurdle to overcome for a person who lacks bowel control. Each day, in order to begin to defecate, the injured person had to insert a lubricated, gloved finger into the rectum, via the anus, and then move the finger gently in a circular motion for several minutes, causing the anal sphincter to relax. Occasionally, a suppository is used at the same time.

The first time Marcia had to do this, I showed her how. Having me stick my gloved finger inside her rectum to help her begin defecating must have been an incredibly degrading experience for her.

Digital stimulation and using suppositories can have their own secondary medical complications. For Marcia, repeated digital stimulation later caused horrible internal and external hemorrhoids as well as extensive bruising on her wrists. The bleeding hemorrhoids could become infected. Suppositories could cause persistent stomach pain, bloody stools, rectal bleeding, a persistent urge to have a bowel movement, and persistent diarrhea.

---

40 Colossal Mistake #6: I was not told about other beneficial durable medical equipment that we should have purchased, including an alternating lateral rotation air mattress (to prevent pressure ulcers), a fully automatic alternating pressure relief wheelchair cushion (also to prevent pressure ulcers), and a Hoyer lift (to ease transfers).

41 Colossal Mistake #7: I was not told about Life Care Planners. With extensive expertise in nursing, case management, and spinal cord injury, a Life Care Planner would have likely mitigated both my initial and ongoing mistakes. This would have helped Marcia to achieve a better medical outcome and relieved me of much of my own stress. For more information, see http://www.aanlcp.org.

42 Colossal Mistake #8: I was not told that the best place to receive medical care for a pressure ulcer was at a wound care center. Worse, I was not told that there was an excellent wound care center at Sturdy Memorial Hospital (Attleboro, Massachusetts), thirty minutes away.

43 In 2007, an excellent method to treat pressure ulcers became available. For more information, see http://www.kci1.com/KCI1/activactherapyunit.

44 Colossal Mistake #9: I was not told about the Craig Hospital (Englewood, Colorado). The Craig Institute is perhaps the finest inpatient facility for families and their caregivers to learn about coping with spinal cord injury.

Starting that day, Marcia was intensely fearful that her colon wouldn't completely empty and that during the day, there might be an unexpected bowel movement. To compensate, her daily bowel program on the commode typically lasted three hours or more.

What a horrible life.

Friday, April 19, 2002

After one hundred days, Zurich American Insurance had not communicated with us, let alone provided any financial assistance. We had already spent or planned to spend more than $150,000.

❖ ❖ ❖

Zurich, how can a blameless victim without financial resources return to good health? Zurich, why hasn't a claims adjuster from Zurich contacted us?

❖ ❖ ❖

This morning, several nurses from the Milford Visiting Nurse Association (VNA) met with Marcia to begin her home care medical program. Typically, the home care medical program includes nursing, physical therapy, occupational therapy, and psychological therapy. From the beginning, I developed a special fondness for the wonderful medical professionals from the Milford VNA. They are angels.[45]

Later, I had the opportunity to review the Milford VNA's medical notes from their first visit: *"Identifies support system as a problem. Lives with husband and 14-year-old daughter. Strained relationship with husband."*

Monday, April 22, 2002

Today, a social worker and an occupational therapist from the Milford VNA met with Marcia. The notes from this visit stated the following:

Social Worker Visit Report. *"Patient is in private therapy as is the rest of her family. Family is financially well off and pays for additional care for patient. Patient reports having ADHD. Patient has difficult time focusing, complains of marital problems with controlling husband. Patient reports husband has been very supportive—family is involved with private therapists. Patient is continuing with own business. Patient didn't speak of medical condition, just her life."*

---

[45] I cannot say enough about the Milford VNA home care for nursing, physical therapy, occupational therapy, and home aid. Milford is fortunate to have such a terrific organization. Each of the therapists approached Marcia with care and love. The consistent, dedicated caring for Marcia made our lives much better.

Occupational Therapy Visit Report. *"Apparently, there are multiple family issues. Husband does much to ready the house for her return."*[46]

Wednesday, April 24, 2002

Marcia had her first medical appointment with Dr. Donna Krauth, who had been her primary care provider for many years.[47]

Thursday, April 25, 2002

An occupational therapist from the Milford VNA met with Marcia. The medical notes for this day stated, *"Patient seen for kitchen activities and suggestions to help modify kitchen so patient can be more independent. Patient needs redirection back to task. Discuss need to stay focused on objective. Patient tends to get off track."*

Monday, May 6, 2002

We have so much tension between us. We are not adjusting well. *"I want to go stay with my sister,"* Marcia told me.

Trapped in her own body, Marcia needed to get out—go somewhere, anywhere. She depends on me to meet even her most basic needs—needs that people take for granted, like eating or going to the bathroom. The paralysis, constant discomfort, and complete reliance for personal care cannot be anything less than torture.

Tuesday, May 7, 2002

The Milford VNA notes stated, *"Telephone communication with Nursing Supervisor, Diana Haynes, informed Medical Social Worker that patient called and informed VNA that she will be relocating to the Cape indefinitely. VNA services will be transferred to Cape."*

Wednesday, May 8, 2002

The Milford VNA notes stated, *"Patient not available last two days, being at sister's for two days. It was even questionable her returning."*

---

46 Colossal Mistake #10: It has taken me much too long to understand my new role as Marcia's patient advocate. As a husband, I expected Marcia to express how grateful she was for everything that I did. Because she did not do this, I was angry and difficult to be around. It took me much time to realize that besides being her husband, I was, much more importantly, her patient advocate—a person to whom she did not have to say *please* and *thank you*, because the awful predicament in which she lived was not her fault. After realizing this, I was much less angry with her.

47 Dr. Krauth is both an outstanding physician and a wonderful person. Not only is she an expert medical doctor, but she has the best "bedside" manner imaginable. With Marcia, she is especially gentle. She vigilantly examines Marcia for any possible medical complication. She compassionately encourages Marcia to achieve her rehabilitative goals. Dr. Krauth never rushes with Marcia, always asks the best questions, and provides the very best advice. Marcia and I will be forever thankful to Dr. Krauth.

Thursday, May 9, 2002

Marcia returned home today. The Milford VNA notes stated, *"Patient and husband are working on their relationship. Patient has support from family members when things get too difficult. Patient now realizes to go to her sister's at Cape is not appropriate without preparation due to her medical needs. Patient and husband now know how to access resources they need."*

Friday, May 24, 2002, to Tuesday, May 28, 2002

Marcia woke me in the middle of the night to tell me that her stomach pain was growing worse.[48] She has had awful diarrhea for a few days, and her temperature was 101. I gave her a Percocet and a Valium and stayed with her for two hours. Finally, she went back to sleep.

We went to Dr. Krauth in the morning. She told us that Marcia had several infections, including one that was causing the diarrhea. Her pain continued, so Dr. Krauth said to take her to the emergency room (ER) at Milford Regional Medical Center. She looked unusually pale, and her temperature had risen to 101.5.

About forty people were waiting in the ER, and we had to wait more than an hour just to see the triage nurse.[49] I was asked, *"What medications is Marcia taking, and what medications is she allergic to?"* I was unprepared for these questions.[50]

Generally, ERs are not well equipped to care for people with paraplegia. Several male nurses and I had to lift Marcia onto a stretcher. Because no examination room was available, she had to wait on a stretcher in the hallway for almost two hours before being transferred to an exam room. By three thirty in the afternoon, she was a mess. The medical personnel gave her strong painkillers to comfort her, but something was seriously wrong.

A third-year medical student, an intern, a resident, and an attending resident examined her. Given her severe pain and growing fever, the resident doctor had her admitted to the hospital. Many tests were run to determine the cause of her stomach pain.

A little while later, Dr. Albert Crimaldi,[51] a leading gastroenterologist in Massachusetts and the chairman of the board of trustees of the Milford Regional Medical Center, exam-

---

48 Colossal Mistake #11: I had not been taught that whenever any secondary medical complication became apparent I had to take Marcia to the ER by ambulance so that she could receive immediate medical attention. Until now, I did not realize how fragile she was. I did not understand that her immune system would always be compromised. I did not realize that because she could not feel pain below her waist, any pain that she felt always required going to the ER.

49 Colossal Mistake #12: When she did go to the ER, she had to immediately be seen by an ER doctor. I should have been much more insistent.

50 Colossal Mistake #13: Not having the appropriate documents for the hospital was inexcusable.

51 When Dr. Crimaldi met Marcia for the first time, I could see that he had a special fondness for her, and she developed a special fondness for him. Over the years, she saw him many times. Even with all of his many responsibilities, he always had time for her, which I deeply appreciated. He never rushed with Marcia, and he always asked about other aspects of her life. Marcia and I will always be thankful for the care that he has given her. Someday, Marcia and I will figure out an appropriate way to thank him.

ined Marcia. With a touch of her abdomen, he diagnosed Marcia with a gall bladder infection that needed surgery without delay. The complicating factor was her high international normalized ratio (INR) level, which indicated a decreased ability for her blood to clot. Because of the DVT in her right leg, she was taking Coumadin to prevent future blood clots.[52]

During surgery, blood had to be able to clot quickly. To prepare for the gall bladder surgery, the medical professionals hurriedly injected massive doses of vitamin K and blood platelets to lower her INR level.

After surgery, Dr. Crimaldi told us that Marcia's gall bladder was not only infected but also gangrenous.[53] He said that he had never seen a gall bladder so gravely infected.

Although ordinarily serious, a gangrenous gall bladder is life threatening for a person who is paraplegic. Normally, the onset of bodily pain is an excellent indication of a medical complication such as a gall bladder infection. With no feeling below her waist, Marcia could only feel pain that had reached an enormous proportion, putting her at even more risk for not recognizing a dangerous medical condition in time. Not feeling pain when sick or injured is one of the cruel realities of spinal cord injury.

After the surgery, Marcia was admitted to the ICU, where Rebecca, once again, had to see her mother. Rebecca was suffering more grief than any fourteen-year-old should.

After three weeks in the hospital, Marcia was admitted to Whittier Rehabilitation Hospital in Westborough to continue her recovery from surgery, including additional physical therapy. After sixty-six days at Fairlawn, I thought she would like a new environment.

Friday, June 14, 2002
Marcia was discharged from Whittier.

Saturday, June 22, 2002
Happy birthday, Marcia. This was not the type of birthday I ever thought she would ever have.

Friday, June 28, 2002
In a follow-up appointment with Dr. Krauth, Marcia was diagnosed with bursitis and tendonitis in her shoulders from the physical therapy, another urinary tract infection, and blood in her stool (likely from an intestinal infection).

---

[52] A blood clot from a DVT in the heart, lungs, or brain could cause a lethal heart attack, pulmonary embolism, or brain stroke.

[53] *"Gangrene is a serious and potentially life-threatening condition that arises when a considerable mass of body tissue dies (necrosis)."* "Gangrene," *Wikipedia*, last modified March 11, 2014, http://en.wikipedia.org/wiki/Gangrene.

In the afternoon, a VNA nurse examined her. The nurse noted that her bursitis and tendonitis made it *"more difficult to become self-sufficient, and it intermittently interrupts her progress in physical therapy."*

Years later, I reviewed notes from a social worker visit for this day: *"Relationship with husband has improved."*

Saturday, June 29, 2002

Louise, our new HHA from Griswold Special Care, called to say that she was sick and wouldn't be coming in this morning. Griswold was unable to locate a fill-in aide.

Even so, Marcia wanted to take a shower. Showers require two people to safely manage the transfers. I knew that transferring her onto the shower bench by myself would be a grueling maneuver. I also knew that a one-person-assisted transfer into and out of the shower increased the likelihood of an accidental fall, in which Marcia, the floor, and I would all be wet. Idiotically, I attempted to transfer her onto the shower bench by myself. During the transfer, she unexpectedly defecated. When I tried to transfer her back to the wheelchair, she fell to the floor.[54] Did I hurt her? I was scared to death. Why was I so stupid?

Sunday, June 30, 2002

With everything going on in Marcia's life, I had not paid much attention to what Fred Pritzker and his fellow lawyers were doing. Fred sent me a copy of the legal complaint that would soon be filed. After reading it, I was livid.

More than 170 days had passed since the crash. Zurich American Insurance still had not begun to talk about settlement. We were in for a grueling fight—not just for us but also for all blameless victims.

❖ ❖ ❖

Zurich, is this your settlement strategy? Will you later claim that everything was lost in the mail or some other silly excuse?

❖ ❖ ❖

---

54   Colossal Mistake #14: Even more foolishly, I did not take Marcia to the ER for an X-ray to see if any bones had been broken in the fall. I knew that every time she fell, she had to be taken to the ER. I was too lazy or just too stupid.

July 2002 to September 2002

Tuesday, July 2, 2002

An occupational therapist from the Milford VNA came this morning to continue to work with Marcia on her transfers. Regrettably, she cannot do any transfers by herself; she remains completely dependent on others. Developing the necessary upper body strength for an independent transfer is an impossible challenge for her.

Friday, July 5, 2002

Almost six months have passed since the crash and I still cannot work. While Marcia receives assistance in the morning and in the evening, I have to take care of her day and night. I have so much to do each day—doctor's appointments, laundry, cleaning, prescriptions, insurance, legal issues, caring for Marcia, making plans for her future needs, and more.

We have now begun to dip into our savings.

❖ ❖ ❖

Zurich, is your goal to put the family of a blameless victim in financially unbearable circumstances?

❖ ❖ ❖

Massachusetts laws and judicial decisions substantially favor insurance carriers. They make no provision for the lost wages of the spouse who has been required to become a full-time caregiver. If a spouse caregiver could recover lost wages, then insurance carriers would have much more incentive to settle as soon as possible.

Saturday, July 6, 2002

Marcia, Sue (Marcia's sister), Rebecca, and I tried to take Marcia to one of her favorite flea markets. Marcia's manual wheelchair couldn't traverse the sand and pebbles on the ground. She broke down in tears.[55]

Sunday, July 7, 2002

Marcia went to see Dr. Jill McAnulty, her psychologist. She was in tears when I picked her up. We had a lengthy talk in the car. *"My life is miserable,"* she cried. *"I can't take it."*

---

55 Colossal Mistake #15: I did not check to see if the location was wheelchair-accessible. From now on, before going to a new place, I must make sure that the location really is wheelchair-accessible.

Monday, July 8, 2002

At Marcia's request, I woke her early this morning. Unfortunately, she defecated during the transfer to the commode. Her stress level sharply increased.

At midmorning, the VNA occupational therapist worked with Marcia. The therapist told me that she saw blood in her urine. She called Dr. Krauth, and by two thirty, we were at the ER.

Rebecca had an appointment with Harriet Melrose at four o'clock. I had to leave Marcia alone at the hospital in order to pick up Rebecca at home and take her to see Harriet. During Rebecca's appointment, I went back to the hospital to see how Marcia was doing.

Then, I left her again to bring Rebecca home. Not surprisingly, Rebecca was utterly depressed and angry. I left Rebecca at home, all alone. I felt miserable.

I returned to the hospital. Marcia was diagnosed with another urinary tract infection. After being given a prescription for an antibiotic, we left the hospital at eight thirty and stopped at CVS to get the medicine.

When we returned home, Marcia was exhausted and overwrought. Her back pain was enormous. I rubbed her back until eleven, when she finally fell asleep. I was able to get to bed at eleven thirty.

Before going to sleep, I realized that I was not being much of a father to Rebecca. We had not done anything fun together this summer, as we had done every summer before. I didn't even know if she had been doing her summer reading assignment and I didn't know anything about how she was feeling. It was another awful day.

Tuesday, July 9, 2002

Today was exactly six months from the crash.[56]

Thursday, July 11, 2002

At midmorning, Marcia saw Dr. Roaf at Fairlawn. Dr. Roaf was distressed to see Marcia so unwell—medically, physically, psychologically, and emotionally. She diagnosed Marcia with bursitis and tendonitis and told her that she had to avoid using her manual wheelchair and stop physical therapy. She gave me a prescription for a powered wheelchair.

Powered wheelchairs are expensive and more than the durable medical equipment limit that we had with UnitedHealthcare. We would have to pay several thousand dollars above the DME limit for the powered wheelchair.

---

56 At the trial five years later, a Zurich attorney said, *"We (Zurich) know plaintiffs would never have accepted Zurich's $2 million if it was offered the day after the accident, six months after the accident, a year after the accident, or even beyond that."* This was not true. We would have been ecstatic to accept Zurich's $2 million today.

Friday, July 12, 2002

Brown Rudnick filed our personal injury lawsuit in the Massachusetts Superior Court in Norfolk County against Carlo Zalewski, Driver Logistics Services, GAF Materials Corporation, and Penske Truck Leasing Group.

I went to Dr. Krauth, because my diarrhea won't go away. She asked me how I was doing, but I was sure that she already knew the answer. Physically and emotionally, I felt more than awful.

Saturday, July 13, 2002

Early in the morning, I transferred Marcia to the commode. I brought her breakfast, brought her medicines, and attended to her other needs, including cleaning the Foley catheter and emptying the urine collection bag.[57]

At eleven thirty, I transferred her back to bed. While cleaning her, I noticed a stage III pressure ulcer and two stage II pressure ulcers on her backside.

Pressure ulcers are a constant worry. Once discovered, the best solution is bed rest until the pressure ulcer has healed. In Marcia's case, this bed rest could take many months.[58] [59] [60] [61]

---

[57] Each time the urine collection bag is emptied, the urine has to be examined for bacterial colonization that might lead to a UTI. The urine examination includes checking the color of the urine (it should be bright yellow), determining if there is any foreign matter (there should not be any), and smelling the urine for any odor.

[58] "Pressure ulcers, also known as decubitus ulcers or bedsores, are localized injuries to the skin and/or underlying tissue that usually occur over a bony prominence as a result of pressure, or pressure in combination with shear and/or friction. The most common sites are the sacrum, coccyx, heels, or the hips. Pressure ulcers occur due to pressure applied to soft tissue resulting in completely or partially obstructed blood flow to the soft tissue. Shear is also a cause, as it can pull on blood vessels that feed the skin. Pressure ulcers most commonly develop in persons who are not moving about or are confined to wheelchairs." "Pressure Ulcer," Wikipedia, last modified March 11, 2014, https://en.wikipedia.org/wiki/Pressure_ulcers.

[59] "A pressure sore (ulcer) may start simply with a change in skin color or temperature (stage 1), then progress to an abrasion, blister, or skin crater (stage 2). By the time it reaches stage 3, there is a deep crater with loss of skin and damaged or dead subcutaneous tissue, possibly extending down to the underlying fascia. In stage 4, the damage extends to muscle, bone, or supporting structures such as tendons, possibly accompanied by sinus tracts. (1) With no skin to present a barrier comes the threat of infection, which can lead to the death of the patient. It's amazing—and alarming—to think that what started out as just a little red spot on the derriere can result in the need to plan a funeral. But it happens." "Performing Under Pressure: Preventing Pressure Ulcers," last modified March 11, 2014, HighBeam Research, http://www.highbeam.com/doc/1G1-182662183.html.

[60] "The cost of treatment is $2,000-$40,000 per pressure ulcer, depending on the stage of development." "Pressure Ulcers and Wound Care: Scope of the Problem," Medscape, last modified March 11, 2014, http://emedicine.medscape.com/article/319284-overview.

[61] Colossal Mistake #16: I should have known about the wound care center at Sturdy Memorial Hospital (Attleboro, Massachusetts), just twenty minutes from our home. As soon as a Stage II pressure ulcer appears, I should have taken Marcia immediately to the wound care center for the best medical treatment. I did not learn about the Sturdy Wound Care Center until May 12, 2003. She could have received much better medical attention if I'd known better.

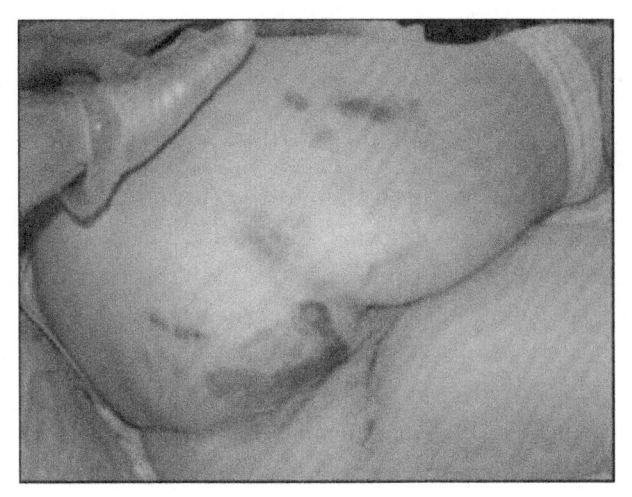

Figure 3. Several stage I, stage II, and stage III pressure ulcers.

According to the National Pressure Ulcer Advisory Panel, pressures ulcers are staged as follows:
1. (Suspected) deep tissue injury: a purple or maroon localized area of discolored intact skin or blood-filled blister due to damage of underlying soft tissue from pressure or shear
2. Stage I: intact skin with signs of impending ulceration, initially presenting blanchable erythema indicating reactive hyperemia
3. Stage II: a partial-thickness loss of skin involving epidermis and dermis
4. Stage III: a full-thickness loss of skin with extension into subcutaneous tissue but not through the underlying fascia
5. Stage IV: a full-thickness tissue loss with extension into muscle, bone, tendon, or joint capsule
6. Unstageable: a full-thickness tissue loss in which the base of the ulcer is covered by slough or eschar to such an extent that the full depth of the wound cannot be appreciated[62]

Monday, July 15, 2002

The VNA occupational therapist and an HHA arrived at eight o'clock. We worked with Marcia on the seemingly impossible transfers from the commode to the wheelchair, to the shower, to the wheelchair, to the bed, and back to the wheelchair.

Later, I took Marcia to Bio-Lab to have her blood drawn to determine her INR level. The nurse was unable, even after three attempts, to stick a needle into a vein to draw blood,

---

[62] "Pressure Ulcers and Wound Care: Practice Essentials," Medscape, last modified March 11, 2014, http://emedicine.medscape.com/article/190115-overview.

meaning that we would have to go back again. Marcia was depressed about having to do this again tomorrow. I had to figure out how to make blood draws less painful for her.

Tuesday, July 16, 2002

UnitedHealthcare notified me that we had reached the reimbursement limit for HHAs. Going forward, we had to pay out-of-pocket. Marcia and I decided that she would receive four hours of caregiving in the morning and four hours in the evening from an HHA, seven days per week. At eighteen dollars per hour, the expense would be $55,000 per year or $1.3 million over twenty-five years.

Louise arrived at six forty-five to learn Marcia's morning care routine. I explained to her that before waking Marcia, to avoid any bowel movement accidents, the urine collection bag had to be emptied and examined for any symptom of a UTI.

We had four minutes to wake her, transfer her onto the wheelchair and transfer her onto the commode. During the transfer, she was not allowed to use her arms, to prevent exacerbating her tendonitis and bursitis.

Louise examined the urine. It was bright yellow with no sediment and no odor (therefore, no symptoms of a UTI).

Between the two of us (called a max transfer), we transferred her, within four minutes, onto the commode. She was unhappy that I had to assist in the transfer—she knew that my shoulder was hurting.

Later in the morning, a Milford VNA occupational therapist visited. She told us that UnitedHealthcare would pay for only one more occupational therapy visit.

Marcia had to have as much outpatient occupational therapy as possible, particularly because of the lack of occupational therapy at Fairlawn and Whittier. Are we supposed to pay for these therapies at $135 per hour?

I knew I had to appeal this decision. Making an appeal would take a lot of my time, and I was unsure whether additional occupational therapy visits would be approved. In that case, Marcia and I would have to pay for the two visits per week out-of-pocket, costing $14,000 per year.

❖ ❖ ❖

Zurich, do you know that we must pay for the care provided by Marcia's HHAs as well as occupational therapists from our savings, further dwindling our financial resources? Zurich, shouldn't you, as the primary insurance carrier, be paying for these critical medical needs? Zurich, are you being fair to us?

❖ ❖ ❖

Saturday, July 20, 2002

After her morning bowel program, Marcia stayed in bed all day, letting the pressure ulcers heal. She was beyond bored—she was miserable.

She could not use a manual wheelchair on the current carpeting because pushing the wheels hurt her arms too much. For $4,000, we were having industrial-grade, no-nap carpeting put down throughout our home.

Monday, July 22, 2002

After waiting more than six months, we received the initial draft of the Massachusetts State Police Collision Reconstruction Report.[63] It provided a detailed, analytical review of the crash. Nothing in it changed the fact that Zalewski crashed his forty-ton tractor-trailer, going at least thirty miles per hour, into the rear of Marcia's car.

Tuesday, July 23, 2002

Unexpectedly, one of the Milford VNA nurses came by. The nurse redressed an open pressure ulcer on Marcia's foot. This pressure ulcer would take several months to heal, and Marcia wouldn't be able to wear shoes for a while. In addition, the nurse told us that the urine sample taken on Sunday showed, yet again, another bladder infection. Marcia had to take an antibiotic for ten days and then have a new urine sample done.

She was so depressed in the evening. Due to all her maladies, she had not left our home for a while. She was bored and cranky, especially because she could not use her arms for anything.

Wednesday, July 24, 2002

Marcia began taking Macrobid (an antibiotic) for the bladder infection. She was taking the following prescription medicines:
1. Ambien (sleep)
2. Amoxicillin (infection)
3. Cipro (urinary tract infection)
4. Coumadin (blood)
5. Cylert (ADHD)
6. Diflucan (fungal infection)
7. Dulcolax (bowel program)
8. Levaquin (bacterial infection)
9. Macrobid (bacterial bladder infection)
10. Metronidazole (trichomoniasis infection)
11. Percocet (pain)

---

63 To review the State Police Collision Reconstruction Report, see www.theblamelessvictim.com.

12. Prilosec (stomach)
13. Prozac (anxiety and depression)
14. Reglin (stomach)
15. Ritalin (ADHD)
16. Valium (stress)
17. Wellbutrin SR (depression)
18. Zyprexa (bipolar disorder)

Marcia has slid downhill psychologically and has become tearful about life. She went to bed at five thirty—mostly, I think, to escape.

Thursday, July 25, 2002

For the fourth day, Marcia decided not to leave the house.

At the urging of the Milford VNA, UnitedHealthcare agreed to provide in-home physical therapy treatments for Marcia's tendonitis and bursitis.

I located a website (www.dmv-driving-record.com) that provided driving records, and I requested Zalewski's record.

Marcia was increasingly miserable. She talked to me about the crash—and about suicide. She went to sleep—in her dress—at five o'clock. This was so sad.

Friday, July 26, 2002

Marcia began the day worried about having a Coumadin blood test. She was so afraid of the multiple needle insertions for the blood draw. *"I just can't go, Harold. It's so painful,"* she said. She became so anxious that we decided not to have the blood test today.

After calling around with the help of Dr. Krauth's office, we found that the cardiology department at the MetroWest Medical Center in Framingham, Massachusetts, had a calibrated machine to do a blood stick INR test, which was much easier than a blood draw. We made an appointment for the following Wednesday.

Marcia had an awful evening with painful spasms in her back. The treatments were Valium, Percocet, an electric massager, and patience. I massaged her back for forty-five minutes, and she finally fell asleep.

Saturday, July 27, 2002

I woke at six thirty with the attitude that one way or another, we were going to have fun today. Rebecca has been so stressed out that she was literally pulling out her hair, a condition called trichotillomania.[64] Being home with her mom and me has noticeably increased her anxiety.

---

64 *"Trichotillomania is the compulsive urge to pull out one's own hair, leading to noticeable hair loss, distress, and social or functional impairment. It is classified as an impulse control disorder by DSM-IV and is often chronic and difficult to treat.*

Louise had to leave early, at nine o'clock, so I helped Marcia with her morning routine. In the course of helping her to dress, the leg urine collection bag sprang a leak, and urine went all over the place. Just as the leak occurred, Rebecca came downstairs. I hadn't closed the door, and Rebecca peered in. I became angry and yelled at her for staring. More realistically, I was angry at myself for not closing the door—a horrible mistake on my part. For a long time, I relived these moments and cried.[65]

At eleven fifteen, I had awful diarrhea again. I was exhausted and cranky for the rest of the day.

Sunday, July 28, 2002

Today is Day 200 since the crash.

Zurich American Insurance has not communicated with us, let alone provided any financial assistance to Marcia. We had already spent or had planned to spend more than $225,000.

❖ ❖ ❖

Zurich, how will a blameless victim without financial resources return to good health? Zurich, are you trying to send me a message that you expect us to run out of money before settlement discussions even begin? I have to believe that your own claims processing manual wouldn't allow for this delay.

❖ ❖ ❖

Louise called at six o'clock in the morning. She said that she was not well and wouldn't be coming in. I dreaded not having any assistance. I had to have help with Marcia in order to prepare for the carpet installers.

While helping Marcia dress, I noticed a large black-and-blue mark on her buttocks. The odd issue was how rigid the bruise was. The VNA nurse needed to look at her skin early this week.

She slept most of the afternoon but woke at nine o'clock in the evening. She washed up in bed because I was too drained to transfer her to the bathroom.

Trichotillomania may be present in infants, but the peak age of onset is 9 to 13. It may be triggered by depression or stress." "Trichotillomania," *Wikipedia*, last modified March 11, 2014, https://en.wikipedia.org/wiki/Trichotillomania.

65 Colossal Mistake #17: How stupid could I be? I had to be in full control of my emotions when Rebecca was nearby. The loss of her mother-daughter relationship must have been terrible for her, and my getting angry made everything worse.

Monday, July 29, 2002

I woke at five thirty to hear a voice message that, again, Louise was not coming today. I tended to Marcia's morning routine and prepared for the carpet installers by myself. Her sister took her out for the day while the carpet installers worked.

She returned at five o'clock in the evening. I could tell she was not feeling well and was exhausted. While getting her into bed, she had another back spasm attack. I gave her Valium, Percocet, and Tylenol. I massaged her back for an hour until the meds kicked in and she fell asleep.

Tuesday, July 30, 2002

For the third day, Louise was unable to come in, but Marianne, another Griswold HHA, came instead. She was a considerable help.

We had the whole crew from the Milford VNA here today. The nurse checked Marcia's bruise on her buttocks and the skin lesion on her toe. The occupational therapists coached her on managing transfers, especially in the shower. The physical therapist used ultrasound therapy on her arms and shoulders to relieve the tendonitis and bursitis.

Given the large size of the bruise, the nurse asked Marcia to stay in bed with her buttocks raised to relieve the pressure. She was miserable about having to stay in bed.

I woke her at six thirty. If she didn't have dinner, she wouldn't sleep through the night.

Today, I received Zalewski's driving record in the mail.

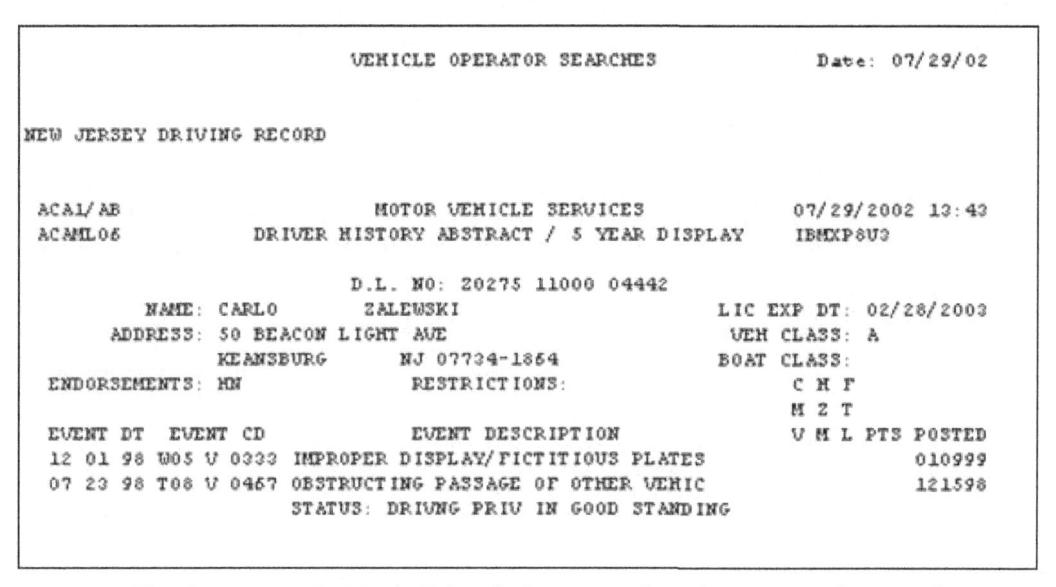

```
                    VEHICLE OPERATOR SEARCHES              Date: 07/29/02

NEW JERSEY DRIVING RECORD

  ACA1/AB                    MOTOR VEHICLE SERVICES        07/29/2002 13:43
  ACAML06          DRIVER HISTORY ABSTRACT / 5 YEAR DISPLAY    IBMXP8U3

                    D.L. NO: 20275 11000 04442
            NAME:  CARLO         ZALEWSKI             LIC EXP DT: 02/28/2003
         ADDRESS:  50 BEACON LIGHT AVE                VEH CLASS: A
                   KEANSBURG       NJ 07734-1854      BOAT CLASS:
    ENDORSEMENTS:  HM            RESTRICTIONS:        C H F
                                                      M Z T
       EVENT DT  EVENT CD          EVENT DESCRIPTION       V H L PTS POSTED
       12 01 98  W05 V 0333  IMPROPER DISPLAY/FICTITIOUS PLATES    010999
       07 23 98  T08 V 0467  OBSTRUCTING PASSAGE OF OTHER VEHIC    121598
                             STATUS: DRIVNG PRIV IN GOOD STANDING
```

Figure 4. The driving record of Carlo Zalewski from www.dmv-driving-record.com. Why was a driver of a forty-ton tanker-trailer allowed to continue to drive when he already had two citations?

Wednesday, July 31, 2002

It was another difficult morning. We had to leave the house by eight thirty to get to Marcia's INR testing at MetroWest Medical Center. Instead of drawing blood by syringe, a Fingerstick Device pricked her fingertip, and we got the INR results immediately. The Fingerstick Device was definitely less painful and scary than drawing with a syringe.[66] [67]

Our attorneys sent me the final version of the Massachusetts State Police Collision Reconstruction Report.[68] After I read it, all I could do was cry. When Rebecca asked me what was wrong, I didn't know what to say. Zurich American Insurance must have known that Carlo Zalewski was 100 percent at *fault*.

❖ ❖ ❖

Zurich, do you know that we have already spent a huge amount of money? Zurich, why won't you give us some money to help alleviate our financial stress?

❖ ❖ ❖

I didn't know why, but Marcia went to sleep at five o'clock today. She doesn't have much of a life. I am so sad.

Thursday, August 2, 2002

A nurse from the Milford VNA saw Marcia. Years later, I had the opportunity to review the nurse's patient care notes:

Treatment for shoulder bursitis. *"Patient had been followed by physical therapy three times a week initially for transfer training. Prescription change to focus on building upper extremity strength until patient developed bilateral shoulder bursitis and is applying hydrocortisone cream to shoulders against application of phonophoresis (using ultrasound to enhance the delivery of topically applied drugs) to both shoulders."*

---

[66] It was difficult to understand why it took seven months to learn that there was a much less stressful method to check her INR level.

[67] *"Over the past 10 to 15 years, the CDC and the FDA have noted a progressive increase in reports of blood-borne infection transmission (primarily hepatitis B virus) resulting from the shared use of finger stick and POC [point-of-care] blood testing devices."* "Medical Devices," US Food and Drug Administration, last modified March 11, 2014, http://www.fda.gov/medicaldevices/safety/alertsandnotices/ucm224025.htm. On August 26, 2010, the FDA issued a safety alert on the use of Fingerstick Devices.

[68] To review the final version of the Massachusetts State Police Collision Reconstruction Report, see www.theblamelessvictim.com.

Friday, August 3, 2002

I finalized the purchase for the new powered wheelchair EZ-Lock[69] system, which would take three weeks for delivery. UnitedHealthcare would pay the first $3,000, and we had to pay the remaining $4,500.

I made a list of what needed to be done to improve our lives.
1. Obtain additional home health care. We must have someone who is in charge of her personal care, household chores, prescriptions, medical supplies, daily sterilization of her work and sleep areas, and ordinary transportation needs. This will be expensive, but it must be done.
2. Improve Rebecca's psychological health. She has started to pull out her hair again. The causes are likely complicated: seeing Mom each day incapable of taking care of herself, being fearful of a new school next year, being unprepared for independence, not having many friends or knowing how to have fun, and, many times, having an overbearing father.
3. Plan a substantial addition to the house. With the first renovation, Marcia has a place to sleep (the old living room), an office (the old dining room), and a wheelchair-accessible bathroom. Nevertheless, she has no privacy and no place to be alone with Rebecca.
4. Marcia must have a private bedroom that can accommodate a medical bed, an enormous amount of medical supplies, and two exits as well as a state-of-the-art wheelchair-accessible bathroom.
5. We must have a larger dining room, so that we can be together as a family, as well as a larger living room so she can exercise, have friends over, play piano, and not feel cramped.
6. Improve my understanding of the pending legal activities. I must be able to explain to Marcia the forthcoming criminal case and the civil cases.
7. Have fun with Marcia and Rebecca each week.

Sunday, July 28, 2002

Marcia's sister visited today. Marianne, the HHA, also came, so I went out.

When I returned, Marcia informed me that she fell during a transfer from the wheelchair onto the commode. Her sister and Marianne couldn't pick her up and had to call the fire department for assistance.

Years later, I had the opportunity to review the nurse's patient care notes: *"Patient and sister both relayed that there was a slip/fall or 'controlled slide' onto the toilet, but position*

---

[69] *"The EZ Lock Wheelchair Docking System easily secures a wheelchair to the vehicle floor, saving you both time and effort. Even better, the automatic docking base allows the user to lock the wheelchair into place without the assistance of others. No more struggling to cinch the straps down; no more hassle."* "Welcome to EZ Lock," EZ Lock, last modified March 11, 2014, http://www.ezlock.net.

of patient and inability to assist due to bursitis and sister's bad back required call to 911 for assistance back to the toilet. Patient denies any injury or hitting anything."

I was beside myself that I hadn't been there.

Sunday, July 28, 2002

I ordered additional Foley catheter replacement trays, Foley catheters, urine collection bags, and saline. The cost was $632.40, none of which was covered by UnitedHealthcare.

The architectural designer came by to discuss the home addition. In the end, the addition would cost at least $150,000. This would be a significant renovation, but Marcia required additional space to give her considerably more freedom in our home.[70]

Thursday, August 8, 2002

I took Marcia to see Dr. Roaf for her monthly appointment. To have UnitedHealthcare reimburse the $3,000 for the powered wheelchair, Dr. Roaf had to provide a prescription. She indicated that the eighteen-inch-seat wheelchair to be ordered wouldn't be appropriate for Marcia. She had to have a twenty-inch seat to prevent skin breakdown. I was mad at the wheelchair specialist for not catching this. Moreover, the wheelchair specialist could not return for two weeks. Not unexpectedly, Marcia was dejected after the appointment.

Rebecca continued to have awful difficulties coping with the stress. We went to see Dr. Merritt in the afternoon, and Rebecca was given a different prescription.

Sunday, August 11, 2002

Yesterday, Cindy R. took Marcia shopping and to flea markets, which was kind of her. Today, Marion and Lisa made an unplanned visit and then took Rebecca and Marcia shopping. It was a beautiful day.

When Marcia got into bed, I measured the circumference of her legs and abdomen, both of which appeared to be swollen. Was this a new medical condition? I had to do something, but what?

Monday, August 12, 2002

Marcia saw her psychologist today. While I waited, I thought that in terms of rehabilitation, her psychological rehabilitation would be the most troublesome. I couldn't imagine all the concerns and fears that must have been in her head. She got through each day but without any joy. She would need many years of therapy to be content, if contentment was even possible.

---

[70] Even as large as this addition would be, years later I realized that it should have been much larger. Further, instead of installing a wheelchair stair lift to move Marcia to and from the basement, I should have installed an elevator, which I did several years later, because of her fear of using the stair lift. However, the cost of the elevator would exceed $65,000.

One unspoken problem was that Marcia struggled with her parents. I think that she had been afraid to disappoint them and constantly sought their approval. Sometimes she was honest with her parents about how she was doing. She wouldn't be able to accept herself until she knew that others, especially her parents, accepted her as she was now.

Tuesday, August 13, 2002

I took Marcia to see Dr. Kelly Clark, her psychiatrist. Marcia said, *"I haven't menstruated since the crash, and my short-term memory is getting worse."*

She talked to Dr. Clark about her increasing depression and anxiety. Dr. Clark gave her a prescription for a more powerful time-release version of Cylert. I hoped it would make her feel better.

The Brown Rudnick attorneys called. They wanted to know about Marcia's pain and suffering, so I sent this list to them:

Medical

1. Painful medical recovery. T-12 spinal fusion, titanium rods, infected gall bladder, MRSA, blood function, multiple urinary tract infections, multiple bladder infections, skin ulcers, second leg clot, head edema.
2. Current medical condition: cannot walk, cannot stand, loss of bowel control, loss of bladder control, pain, second leg clot with extended leg swelling, depression and sadness, short-term memory loss, teeth pain, bursitis, tendonitis, multiple skin ulcers.
3. Unrelenting abdominal pain.
4. Many doctor visits, therapy sessions, and blood tests.
5. 120 hospital nights as an inpatient.

Psychological

1. Loss of spousal intimacy.[71]
2. Loss of parental intimacy.
3. Unrelenting depression, anxiety, and stress.
4. Loss of personal independence.
5. Embarrassment.

Physical

1. Restricted living conditions.
2. Requires assisted transfer to bed, commode, and wheelchair.

---

71 This was an extraordinarily difficult topic to openly present. While many individuals who have suffered a spinal cord injury find ways to continue to have sexual intercourse, Marcia and I were not able to, and we would likely never be able to do so. The emotional impact on our lives was devastating.

3. Demanding physical therapy.
4. Cannot play piano and cannot drive.

Friday, August 16, 2002

Michelle, our VNA nurse, visited today. The timing was fortunate. Marcia's brief was soaked with urine, because the catheter balloon had become dislodged. Michelle was able to adjust the balloon into position. If the problem continued, the catheter would be replaced.

In addition, Susan, the physical therapist from the Milford VNA, came to treat Marcia's bursitis and tendonitis. She told me Marcia's arms were getting better, but it seemed to me she was still hurting.

Marcia went to bed at five fifteen. When I woke her at seven thirty, she needed to defecate. After emptying the urine collection bag, I transferred her to her wheelchair and then the commode, where she remained for about two hours. I transferred her back to the wheelchair and back to bed. I cleaned the bathroom before going to bed.

Saturday, August 17, 2002

Marcia tried to organize her antiques in the garage, but she kept calling for Rebecca or me to help her reach the boxes. We didn't hear her. She was sad and frustrated about being so dependent. *"I can't do anything myself!"* she said. We had a long talk.

Sunday, August 18, 2002

After last night's lengthy talk, I thought about what I had done poorly.
1. Not understanding the alternative standards of care for the immediate treatment of her spinal fracture.
2. Not knowing about Life Care Planners, the Craig Institute, or nearby wound care centers.
3. Not maintaining Rebecca's psychological health.
4. Not understanding our health insurance policy's DME limit and how to get around it.
5. Not requiring the proper care at UMass Memorial Hospital to prevent MRSA and C. difficile infections.
6. Not understanding infection control and not demanding prophylactic antibiotics after hospitalization.
7. Not having the appropriate training to care for her.
8. Not understanding the potential medical problems (UTI, pressure ulcers, bone fractures, tendonitis, and bursitis), how to prevent potential medical problems, how to detect a medical problem, and how to best care for a medical problem.

9. Not having or knowing how to acquire the needed medical supplies when she came home (briefs, wipes, Foley catheters, urine collection bags, saline, equipment, creams, rinses).
10. Not having or knowing how to acquire the needed medical equipment including an air mattress ($12,000), a standard Hoyer Lift ($5,000),[72] and a portable Hoyer Lift ($3,000).
11. Not knowing about the Fingerstick Device at MetroWest Medical Center.
12. Not understanding the care she would require.
13. Not having an HHA when she returned home.
14. Not understanding she always needed at least one HHA for transfers.
15. Not recognizing that Whittier was an out-of network medical provider and would result in substantial copayments.

Tuesday, August 20, 2002

Determined to try to do something enjoyable as a family, I planned a two-night trip to Cape Cod. We need to have new fun family experiences. We could not be stuck in the house, fearful of going to a new place.

I did extensive research to find a wheelchair-accessible hotel on Cape Cod. I made reservations at a resort hotel in West Yarmouth for two nights, based on the hotel's website and its AAA approval. I called the hotel to be certain. The hotel clerk assured me the hotel room was suitable for wheelchairs and that our room would have a wheelchair-accessible bathroom with a roll-in shower. I planned for Marcia, Rebecca, and me to have plenty of fun at the hotel, eat out at our favorite seafood restaurants, go to flea markets, and goof off.

The trip didn't work at all. We arrived at the hotel at six o'clock in the evening. The hotel was not as advertised; it didn't easily support wheelchairs. While it did have a roll-in shower, the bathroom was not wheelchair accessible. In fact, getting Marcia into the bathroom was challenging. Luckily, we had the commode with us, but Marcia felt disheartened. Clearly, we wouldn't be staying two nights.

By seven, she was an emotional wreck. The hotel was terrible, and she was mad at me and at herself. We went out to eat and then went to bed. In the morning, I talked to the hotel manager. She agreed that the room was not as advertised and didn't charge us.

We went to the Wellfleet Flea Market, but Marcia was understandably fatigued. She slept all the way home in the car (about two and a half hours). When I put her to bed at seven o'clock, she felt warm to me.

---

72 "A Hoyer Lift is an assistive device used by caregivers to transfer individuals, whose mobility is limited, between a bed and a wheelchair or other similar resting places, using hydraulic power." "Patient Lift," *Wikipedia*, last modified March 11, 2014, http://en.wikipedia.org/wiki/Patient_lift.

Thursday, August 22, 2002

Marcia had a complete emotional breakdown. She said she had nothing to live for and she wished she were dead.

Saturday, August 24, 2002

In the afternoon, I took Marcia to one of her antiques consignment shops and helped her organize her collectibles for sale.

Before going to sleep, I thought about our gloomy situation. All my life, I had never given in, and I never gave up. I have been taught to keep trying and to never take no for an answer. Maybe this was too much for me.

Sunday, August 25, 2002

Marcia and I went to see my therapist, Linda Eisenberg.[73] Whether we went together or I went alone, the therapy sessions were invaluable to me. We talked about something urgent, something chronic, or nothing at all, but the sessions were my hour each week to stop and talk, or even be quiet, with someone who did not judge me.

We talked about two topics. Did Marcia's parents need to have an accurate understanding of her psychological and emotional condition in order for her to heal? According to Linda, the answer was no. I was surprised and sure that I would overthink this all week.

Did we want Louise to become a live-in caretaker for Marcia? Marcia had come around to this. I found this change in her surprising, given how she valued her privacy. Linda agreed with Marcia. Linda said that my stress and daily anger came, in large part, from having to be her HHA when Louise was absent.

Monday, August 26, 2002

Marcia woke with her catheter out, and the bed was soaked with urine. She was humiliated and sad. I called the Milford VNA, who will send a nurse over to replace the catheter. What a start to the week.

Tuesday, August 27, 2002

Marcia had no medical appointments today. Before she woke, I planned that she, Rebecca, and I would go school shopping at Target and have lunch together.

Marcia said she had a stomachache. Instead of going out, I watched her closely for the possibility of an obstructed bowel or an infection. She took a nap from two to seven. She does not have much of a life. Would she ever?

---

73 I will be forever grateful to Linda Eisenberg for her concern for Marcia, Rebecca, and especially me. On numerous occasions, Linda helped me understand where I had blind spots in my thinking. On other occasions, she let me rant and cry. I am sure that without her, I would have gone off the deep end at some point. I will never know a finer or more caring therapist than her.

I met with the architectural designer today. He showed me three potential renovations ranging from $140,000 to $170,000. We decided that we had to borrow the money. Marcia had to be as comfortable as possible.

Wednesday, August 28, 2002

Louise called at seven o'clock to say that she wouldn't be able to come in. The Griswold manager called to say that a replacement couldn't be found.

I thought again that this lack of predictably by caregivers was a major reason why I couldn't make work commitments. Worse, according to the Massachusetts General Laws, even though Marcia could make a claim for lost wages (if she had been working), I couldn't make such a claim, even though providing care for her meant that I had to stop working.[74]

In the morning, she said that she had not defecated in three days, her stomach ached, and she felt lethargic. Concerned, I called Michelle, who said to give her an overnight laxative. If she developed any additional problems (pain, fever, high blood pressure, or shortness of breath), I should take her to the ER without delay. I worried all day that Marcia might have a UTI or an obstructed bowel.

Thursday, August 29, 2002

Marcia was constipated all day, but she didn't develop any additional symptoms. All day I thought I should take her to the ER, but I didn't. At eleven o'clock in the evening, she defecated.

Friday, August 30, 2002

Marcia woke at seven o'clock, even more depressed than yesterday. I had no idea what to do to make her feel better. Kelly and Debbie, the physical therapists from the Milford VNA, came midmorning. With Dr. Roaf's approval, they planned to begin physical therapy.

At noon, Marcia called her sister. Susan agreed to take her to a hotel for the night, and they left around four o'clock, but she called around nine o'clock and said she was coming home. The hotel didn't have wheelchair-accessible hotel rooms as advertised. Again, she felt dejected.

Saturday, August 31, 2002

I woke Marcia at six o'clock to empty the urine collection bag and transfer her onto the commode. I reminded her that we had a meeting with the attorneys from Brown Rudnick next Tuesday. She told me her parents might be coming to our home that day and staying

---

[74] The legal rationale was that I could hire an aide so I could continue to work, which would be more cost-effective. Given the complexity of Marcia's catastrophic injuries, I had to always be available in addition to an HHA. The advantage went to Zurich American Insurance and AIG.

the night. Normally, I wouldn't care. Getting directly involved with her care, if done appropriately, would be good for her parents, but not on the night when the attorneys were visiting.

Sunday, September 1, 2002

After another month, little had changed. Marcia spent most of the day in bed. She didn't even want to see Linda with me, so I went to therapy alone. She felt miserable about her paraplegia as well as her inability to self-transfer. She was nervous about her parents' visit.

Monday, September 2, 2002

I woke Marcia at seven o'clock, and she stayed on the commode until ten thirty. I examined her stool and noticed blood in it. I decided to check more closely the next day. She asked to go back to bed and to be awoken at twelve thirty. I thought she must have stayed up late last night watching TV. What else was there for her to do?

She spent the whole day in bed.

Tuesday, September 3, 2002

I awoke at five o'clock in the morning and saw that I had forgotten to empty the urine collection last night. Although the urine collection bag was not completely full, I should have remembered to do so.[75] Fortunately, Marcia's brief was dry.

I saw two new open pressure ulcers near the anus.

Our attorneys, Fred Pritzker and Margaret Pinkham, visited. This was their first time seeing Marcia in her home. Margaret was a partner attorney in Brown Rudnick's litigation department.[76]

After Fred and Margaret arrived, I took them to the crash site. I could tell they were amazed to see the length of road Zalewski had traveled and how much time he had to avoid the crash. Their expressions went from amazement to disbelief to shock. I could see the situation seemed incredible to them.

We looked over three spreadsheets that detailed the facts of Marcia's life since the crash. The first spreadsheet showed the hospital days, unplanned nurse visits, unplanned

---

[75] Colossal Mistake #18: Forgetting to empty the urine collection bag was stupid. The consequences would be horrendous if urine filled her body instead of voiding.

[76] Over the years to follow, Marcia and I came to know Margaret as an amazing person. She would spend hours on the phone with Marcia talking about family, parenting, therapy, medical issues, and Margaret's new twins. The friendship between them would last a lifetime. Margaret's legal skills, like Fred's, were extraordinary, both in strategic preparation and inside the courtroom. In particular, in a future trial, Margaret's cross-examination of a defense witness was considered masterful. Marcia and I could not have had two finer attorneys than Fred and Margaret. I was often asked what my best and worst decisions were. I could easily recount the poor decisions, but I made two superb decisions—one of which was to have Brown Rudnick represent us.

ER visits, doctor appointments, blood tests, physical therapy sessions, occupational therapy sessions, and HHA hours.

The second spreadsheet showed projected overall expenses for the next thirty years. The third spreadsheet showed a summary of Marcia's surgeries, her previous and current medical complications, and her daily life.

Reading the expression of an attorney was challenging; good lawyers were practiced at not revealing their emotions, but I saw that Fred and Margaret left our home deeply troubled by what they had learned.

In the evening, Rebecca was tired and irritable, but Marcia cheered her up before bed. I had to figure out why Marcia was able to be so caring with Rebecca tonight. By ten thirty, she was ready to go to sleep, but again she complained about back spasms. I knew the drill: Valium, Percocet, and a good massage.

Wednesday, September 4, 2002

Ninth grade started today for Rebecca. After Rebecca got on the bus but before Marcia woke, I thought about Rebecca. She had gotten through her first summer with her mom in her new condition. All summer, people asked me how Rebecca was doing, but from one day to the next, I never knew for sure.

What effect did Marcia's medical, emotional, and physical conditions have on Rebecca? Rebecca was more withdrawn from her friends over the summer. All she wanted to do was be in her room. I was sure she was scared of high school, but that was normal. Nonetheless, I suspected we would have a challenging adjustment for the first month.

Marcia was gloomy after Louise left. I knew she was apprehensive about her parents' visit. Worse, she had gotten into an inappropriate sleep pattern—from twelve thirty at night to seven in the morning and then from one to three in the afternoon. I kept her awake all day so she would sleep through the night normally.

In the afternoon, I took Marcia to see Dr. Clark, who prescribed Prozac and Zyprexa for her increasing depression.

Marcia's parents arrived around five thirty. I kept a low profile. They went out to dinner and returned at nine o'clock, just in time for her to go to bed. Her parents left for Falmouth, where Marcia's sister lived.

Saturday, September 7, 2002

We went out to lunch today and had a pleasant time. Marcia said she thought I should take a more active role in Rebecca's daily care, because she could not. As the words came out of her mouth, she became terribly distraught.

Thursday, September 12, 2002

Marcia and I had a busy day seeing her gynecologist, Dr. Leonard DiGiovanni, and her therapist, Jill McAnulty. Dr. DiGiovanni gave us some dreadful news. Marcia had an enlarged uterus, which might be the cause of her chronic stomach pain or the spasms, as well as not having menstruated. *Please, no more surgeries*, I thought.

Sunday, September 15, 2002

Marcia and I had a productive session with Linda today. We both agreed that Rebecca had continued to grow more disaffected and withdrawn. Sometimes she looked like she was doing okay, but most of the time she stayed in her room.

Because of Marcia's medical appointments the following Monday, I had to cancel Rebecca's session with Harriet. I was not happy about that.

Monday, September 16, 2002

I stayed in bed with Marcia this morning, contemplating our lives. She was depressed about being in a wheelchair, Rebecca hated her life, and I was mostly sad.

Marcia decided to have Louise at the house for eight hours each day. Although it was expensive, if doing so made her happier, I would do it. Regrettably, we had to begin using our line of credit on the equity in our home to pay these expenses.

❖ ❖ ❖

Zurich, do you know that not one dollar had been paid to us?

Zurich, do you know the unbearable emotional and financial pressure that you have put us for the last eight months?[77]

❖ ❖ ❖

When Louise arrived, she discovered that urine had leaked all over the bed during the night. Worse, because I had been especially tired, I had neglected to put a brief on Marcia. Michelle came out and replaced the catheter. A large amount of gunk in the Foley catheter had prevented urine from getting through to the urine collection bag, so the urine escaped around the Foley catheter.

While Michelle was here, she taught me how to avoid pushing the Foley catheter into Marcia's bladder. Doing so loosened the Foley catheter balloon from where it was supposed

---

[77] Sometime later, one of Zurich's attorneys asked me, "*When do you think Zurich should have begun to make payments to Marcia?*" I said, "*On January 10, 2002, since Carlo Zalewski was completely liable for this crash and Marcia had immediate expenses that needed to be paid.*" Obviously, Zurich did not agree.

to rest inside her bladder. She also taught me how to refill the Foley catheter balloon. Maybe next time I would do it myself.

Michelle was concerned about the large black-and-blue bruises all over Marcia's buttocks, most likely caused by rubbing her gloved hand during digital stimulation. Marcia complained to Michelle that her stomach had been hurting even more.

Tuesday, September 17, 2002

When I came home after running errands, I saw the physical therapists. They told me that Marcia was doing better and that outpatient physical therapy should be restarted.

Louise, Marcia, and I went to the MetroWest Medical Center for her Coumadin blood test. Later that day, I taught Louise how to operate the van and transfer Marcia in and out of it. As a result, Marcia won't be as dependent on me to go places.

Wednesday, September 18, 2002

After my dental appointment, I didn't get home until five thirty. I asked Marcia whether Rebecca had taken care of her chores, but Marcia didn't know.

I couldn't let Rebecca backslide on exercising, personal care, walking the dogs, doing her homework, and other responsibilities. I drove her to her theater workshop at six o'clock, and I waited for her until seven thirty. During the ride home, I asked her how she had been doing. She didn't say anything, even after I asked a second time.

Friday, September 20, 2002

Louise took Marcia to see Dr. Roaf this morning. Dr. Roaf told Marcia that she needed to start physical therapy with an EasyStand.[78] An EasyStand is used to put a person who was paraplegic into a standing position so that the body weight could rest on the legs and strengthen the bones. Loss of bone density is common after a spinal cord injury, and fractures could easily occur.

The EasyStand therapy would require regular trips to Fairlawn for outpatient therapy, or we could purchase one for use at home for $3,000. Because of the amount of time required to take Marcia to and from Fairlawn, I decided to purchase it so she could do the therapy at home. Because we had already exceeded our DME limit with UnitedHealthcare, we had to pay for it ourselves.

❖ ❖ ❖

Zurich, are you glad to know this?

---

[78] For more information, see http://www.easystand.com.

❖ ❖ ❖

Dr. Roaf told Marcia that she had to try intermittent self-catheterization. She also told Marcia to spend less time on the commode by using suppositories to speed the bowel movements.

Saturday, September 21, 2002

Louise was not feeling well and didn't come in today. Once more, I was the HHA. I woke Marcia, inspected and emptied the urine collection bag, transferred her to the wheelchair and the commode, attended to her other bathroom activities, transferred her back to the wheelchair and back to the bed, cleaned her female parts, helped her dress, and transferred her back into her wheelchair. I thoroughly cleaned the bedroom and bedding and made her bed.

After she finished in the bathroom, I meticulously sanitized everything. Last, I began the first of five loads of wash.

While cleaning her, I noted a small but open pressure ulcer, which was always a cause for concern. I put medicine on it and covered it with a gauze bandage.

In the afternoon, we all went to the mall. We had an enjoyable time being a family together for a little while.

Sunday, September 22, 2002

For the second day, Louise was not feeling well and didn't come in, so again, I did all the HHA caregiving.

We went to the Abilities Expo in Boston, a convention for people with disabilities and their families. The exhibition hall featured the latest mobility and medical equipment. The expo was valuable. Marcia tried and liked the electric leg exerciser. We learned about intermittent self-catheterization, but she was not looking forward to that.

We met the Adaptive Driving Program team and attended their seminar. We learned about hand controls for driving. They said they could teach Marcia how to drive, and I made an appointment with them. We also saw many other vendors who might help us later on.

We went shopping before our appointment with Linda. Being with Marcia was wonderful.

Monday, September 23, 2002

Even though Zalewski's criminal trial was ten days away,[79] we still hadn't talked to anyone from the district attorney's office. I hoped there would be no complications.

---

[79] The details and transcript of Zalewski's criminal trial are included in Timeline Two.

Louise came in today, though she didn't look well.

I took Marcia to Tri-River Family Health Center in Uxbridge for a mammogram and ultrasound to determine the cause of her enlarged uterus. Although we had been told that Tri-River could do a mammogram with her in a wheelchair, it couldn't. We went ahead with the ultrasound. Because she was unable to hold fluids in her bladder, getting a quality ultrasound was difficult. Being unable to complete these tests was depressing for her.[80]

She would have a computed tomography (CT) scan[81] done on her uterus at Milford Regional Medical Center, which Tri-River would schedule.

Tuesday, September 24, 2002

Marcia woke me at five forty-five in the morning. She told me she had awoken at three thirty in significant pain and took a pain pill to relieve it. I was afraid something was seriously wrong.

She called Dr. Krauth's office. They asked her for a urine sample to see if her pain was related to a bladder infection. She also went to see Dr. Clark, who revised her psych prescriptions.

Wednesday, September 25, 2002

When I woke Marcia at six o'clock, she told me she had been having deep pain in her stomach since three thirty. She had considered waking me to take her to the ER but took some pain medicine and went back to sleep. When she told me this, I was sad and mad at the same time—sad that she had been in such pain and mad that Tri-River Medical hadn't yet scheduled the CT scan.

I made repeated calls to Dr. DiGiovanni's office about scheduling the CT scan. I said that I was unhappy and that they had to schedule the CT scan for today. They called me back to tell me to take Marcia to Milford Regional Medical Center, where they would squeeze her in for a CT scan.

I took Marcia to Dr. Krauth, and we went to the hospital. We were able to get the scan at six o'clock in the evening. We waited only two hours.

I helped Marcia into bed. As a fitting ending to a long day, she unexpectedly defecated. I did the cleanup well and fast.

---

80 Colossal Mistake #19. I was so stupid for not checking out Tri-River in advance. Before going to a new healthcare facility or any public place, I should have checked its accommodations for Marcia.

81 A CT scan, also referred to as computerized axial tomography, or a CAT scan, is *"an X-ray procedure that combines many X-ray images with the aid of a computer to generate cross-sectional views and, if needed, three-dimensional images of the internal organs and structures of the body. A CT scan is used to define normal and abnormal structures in the body and/or assist in procedures by helping to accurately guide the placement of instruments or treatments."* "CT Scan," MedicineNet.com, last modified March 11, 2014, http://www.medicinenet.com/cat_scan/article.htm.

Thursday, September 26, 2002

At three o'clock in the afternoon, I called Tri-River Medical about the results of Marcia's CT scan, but the radiologist still hadn't reviewed it. I called Milford Regional Medical Center CT department and left a message.

At four o'clock, Dr. DiGiovanni called. The CT scan indicated, while not conclusively, that Marcia had a large fibroid at the top of her uterus. To confirm this, she had to have another ultrasound on Monday. If the fibroid was confirmed, she would either have to take an anti-estrogen medication called a gonadotropin-releasing hormone (GnRH) agonist or have a hysterectomy. Each option was terrible to consider: the side effects of GnRH agonists included hot flashes, headaches, and osteoporosis, and the major side effect of a hysterectomy was premature menopause.[82]

Friday, September 27, 2002

I finally had an appointment with Handicap Mobility to have the EZ Lock system installed ($2,000). Along with leg exercisers ($1,900), the consultation with the registered nurse ($500), and Louise ($800), this was an expensive, sad, and stressful week.

❖ ❖ ❖

Zurich, where are you?

❖ ❖ ❖

Sunday, September 29, 2002

Louise called at six fifteen. She wouldn't be coming in.

My blood test results were awful, with my cholesterol at 283. I am back to exercise and a diet.

We had an enjoyable family lunch together. Marcia liked the new EZ Lock system. She was almost able to wheel herself up and then lock herself in the van.

---

[82] "In 2013, the American Congress of Obstetricians and Gynecologists determined that of the more than 500,000 hysterectomies performed in the United States each year, about 11 percent, or more than 50,000, involve morcellation—a surgical method that can be used to perform a hysterectomy. According to the FDA, morcellation can recklessly spread undetected cancers throughout the body and make the disease more lethal in the process. The FDA took the rare step of urging doctors to stop performing morcellation." "Health & Science: FDA Warns Against Procedure to Remove Uterine Fibroids," *Washington Post*, last modified March 11, 2014, http://www.washingtonpost.com/national/health-science/fda-warns-against-procedure-to-remove-uterine-fibroids-says-it-could-spread-hidden-cancer/2014/04/17/f9fe53cc-c64a-11e3-bf7a-be01a9b69cf1_story.html?hpid=z3.

Monday, September 30, 2002

With Marcia's ultrasound at nine o'clock, I woke at five o'clock to transfer her onto the commode by five thirty. At seven thirty, I clamped off her catheter so her bladder would fill. At nine o'clock, the clamp came loose, and her bladder emptied into the urine collection bag. She took in more liquids, and her ultrasound was pushed back to ten thirty.

We had to wait until Wednesday to hear the results from Dr. DiGiovanni.

The trial date for Zalewski was rescheduled to November 26. The criminal justice system in Massachusetts is so slow.

October 2002 to December 2002

Thursday, October 3, 2002

From Dr. Roaf's strong suggestion in September, Marcia went to see her urologist, who said she should be able to perform intermittent self-catheterization. I learned that *"intermittent catheterization is the temporary placement of a catheter (tube) to remove urine from the body. This is usually done by placing the catheter through the urethra (the tube that leads from the bladder to the outside opening) to empty the bladder."*[83]

I thought her urologist did not understand how difficult intermittent self-catheterization would be for her during the day or if she had to wake up at night to do it.

Friday, October 4, 2002

Early this morning, Dr. Krauth told Marcia she had a serious UTI and several large uterine fibroids.

I finally reached Dr. DiGiovanni. He confirmed that she had fibroids in her uterus. He couldn't say with certainty, but he believed the fibroids could be causing her enlarged uterus and the abdominal pain. He suggested radiation treatment to reduce the fibroids before considering a hysterectomy.

Marcia's chronic pain[84] continued to worsen, averaging a seven on a one-to-ten scale. Often, the pain level spiked to more than eight. I couldn't imagine how she lived with such pain each day. I was so heartbroken when I saw her in such terrible pain.

I was unable to find an acceptable prescription treatment method. Ideally, reducing the size of the uterine fibroids would decrease the pain.

Wednesday, October 16, 2002

Today, Marcia had appointments with Diane, her occupational therapist, and Dr. Clark, her psychiatrist.

Her life during the week became routine: wake at seven thirty, be on the commode until ten thirty, take a shower and dress, go to doctor appointments in the afternoon, come home and work on the computer, do needlework and watch television, and go to bed. I guess I should have been satisfied that she could do these activities, but what kind of life was this?

---

83 For more information, see http://www.nytimes.com/health/guides/specialtopic/clean-intermittent-self-catheterization/overview.html.
84 This is the first mention of the term "chronic pain." In the years to follow, Marcia's chronic pain would become the most awful of her secondary medical complications. Finding a medical solution to treat it would be nearly impossible.

Monday, October 21, 2002

Marcia had a dental appointment today to begin to fix the two cracked teeth from the crash. Preparing for the dentist was tricky. She had to stop taking Coumadin several days in advance because it increased the chance of bleeding during dental treatment.

She continued to suffer chronic pain each day. Percocet was unable to decrease the pain level.

Wednesday, October 23, 2002

Rebecca continues to bring me happiness. She is such a wonderful kid. I know she is working harder in school, and I am so proud of her. I am sure her teachers were going to great lengths to make her feel safe. I would never be able to express my deep appreciation for their personal commitments to her.

Sunday, October 27, 2002

Marcia made plans to take Rebecca to Wrentham Mall to buy clothes. At noon, I took Marcia and Rebecca to the mall, where Marcia met her sister, Sue.

I picked up Marcia and Rebecca at two thirty. Marcia told me her parents were coming to visit on Thanksgiving. During the ride home, I told her I had mixed feelings toward her parents. I did not understand why they seldom visited her or why they had shown such little care and concern for her. That comment sparked an intense argument.

Monday, October 28, 2002

Marcia saw Diane and went to see Dr. Krauth. While she was with Dr. Krauth, I picked up Rebecca from her appointment with Harriet. Rebecca overheard the argument Marcia and I had in the car on Sunday.[85]

Tuesday, October 29, 2002

Today was supposed to be an important day for Marcia. With the hope of reducing her awful chronic pain, she had planned to undergo a uterine fibroid embolization (UFE) to reduce the size of her uterine fibroids.[86] Before the UFE, she had an MRI to determine the size of the fibroids. Afterward, we saw the radiologist and his associates. He told us that in his opinion, there were no large uterine fibroids.

---

85   Colossal Mistake #20: This was the second time I failed to be supportive of Marcia in front of Rebecca. I should have made sure Rebecca was not within earshot when we discussed adult issues, especially those about Marcia's medical and psychological health. What an incredibly idiotic thing I did.

86   "In a UFE procedure, physicians use an X-ray camera called a fluoroscope to guide the delivery of small particles to the uterus and fibroids. The small particles are injected through a thin, flexible tube called a catheter. These block the arteries that provide blood flow, causing the fibroids to shrink. Nearly 90 percent of women with fibroids experience relief of their symptoms." "Uterine Fibroid Embolization," The Radiological Society of North America, last modified March 11, 2014, http://www.radiologyinfo.org/en/info.cfm?pg=ufe.

The radiologist didn't recommend the UFE procedure. With regard to the lack of menstruation and the enlarged uterus, he told Marcia not to be overly concerned. With regard to the chronic pain, he agreed with Dr. Bayley that this pain was typical of T-12 spinal injuries. He said she would need to *"learn to live with the pain"* and use painkillers when required. She cried. Living in chronic pain is a miserable life.

Saturday, November 2, 2002

I woke hoping today would be peaceful. Marcia did her personal chores most of the day, but by midafternoon, she was disheartened. She said a word I had not heard her say before—*cripple*. *"Harold, I do not want to be a cripple for the rest of my life."* I was so sad for my wife.

Sunday, November 3, 2002

While life should be full of new phenomena, I had a first-in-a-lifetime experience. After Marcia got into bed, she unexpectedly defecated. The catheter became dislodged, and urine soaked everything. She menstruated, so stool, urine, and blood covered her and the bed.

For the bowel movement and urine, I carefully washed and cleaned her body, changed her brief, and cleansed and rebandaged the pressure ulcers. Even though I hadn't been specifically taught, I opened a new catheter, did the necessary preparation, and placed the catheter into her urethra on the first try. I filled the balloon and connected the catheter to a urine collection bag.

I learned about feminine hygiene from her. With Marcia watching in a mirror, I carefully cleaned her vagina. She instructed me on how to properly insert a tampon. It took a couple of tries.

What was interesting to me was how clinical I had become about taking care of her. I was not bothered about any of this.

Monday, November 4, 2002

Rebecca came home with poor grades on several math quizzes and tests. I realized again that I was not doing a decent job as a parent. I wanted Marcia to be the primary caregiver for Rebecca, as she had been before the crash, but she was not capable of this. Rebecca did not want me to intrude in her life, and she and I had a difficult and complicated relationship.

I put Marcia to bed and again cleaned her menstruation.

Tuesday, November 5, 2002

Today is Day 300 since the crash.

Zurich American Insurance has not provided any financial assistance. We had already spent or planned to spend more than $300,000.

❖   ❖   ❖

Zurich, how will a blameless victim, without financial resources, return to good health? Zurich, am I supposed to get the message that you expect Marcia and me to run out of money before settlement discussions even begin?

❖   ❖   ❖

Wednesday, November 6, 2002

After a day out, I came home at five o'clock. For some reason, I sensed that something was wrong. Marcia was not ready to talk about it. At six thirty, she began. In her session with the school guidance counselor, Rebecca had said that she had been tremendously stressed out. The guidance counselor asked the school psychologist to get involved. The school psychologist called Marcia and Harriet, and Harriet wanted to meet us tomorrow.

When children at school even mentioned that they were thinking about hurting themselves, there is an automatic administrative procedure. While concerned for the child, the school is also concerned for the safety of the other children. The child has to be separated from the other children and go through a comprehensive psychological evaluation to determine the next step, which could range from returning to school the next day to involuntary commitment.

I knew that Rebecca was having a difficult time, but I had no idea that her problems had come to thoughts of hurting herself. Her math grades were down, and I knew she does not feel comfortable with me reviewing her homework each night.

Harriet told Marcia that she wanted me to go to the session, but Marcia asked to go alone. I thought Rebecca needed some space from me.

Thursday, November 7, 2002

I woke Rebecca this morning at six o'clock. She seemed reserved. Maybe she was tired, but more likely she was trying to deal with her stress in her own way. Rebecca would stay home today and tomorrow but would see Harriet today. I am worried about my daughter.

Friday, November 8, 2002

Marcia had an appointment with her gynecologist. While Dr. DiGiovanni agreed that she didn't need a UFE, he disagreed with the radiologist's opinion that the enlarged uterus was not a matter for concern. At Dr. DiGiovanni's request, she made a follow-up appointment in three months for another ultrasound to see how large (or hopefully small) her uterus had become.

Monday, November 11, 2002

Rebecca returned to school.

Tuesday, November 12, 2002

Marcia and I didn't speak to each other the whole day. Yesterday, we had an intense and combative session in Linda's office. I wanted her to consider my perspective and feelings when she made decisions, not just hers. She felt that because she had been rendered paraplegic and she was the one damaged, she should have final authority over her choices, even those that affected me.

After the session, I was upset that Rebecca took over for me and helped Marcia take care of herself and get into bed.[87]

It was fifteen days until Zalewski's criminal trial.

Thursday, November 14, 2002

Rebecca came home with a poor report card. Before the crash, her report cards were consistently excellent. Given what she had to live with each day since January 9, 2002, this report card was not unexpected.

Saturday, November 16, 2002

We had a quiet day. Rebecca and I went shopping, and Marcia had the house to herself. When we returned home, she decided to use the EasyStand. Standing upright was medically beneficial for her but caused intense emotions. After getting into the standing frame, she started to cry. *"Why can't I do this all the time?"* she asked.

Sunday, November 17, 2002

Marcia and I went to see Linda today. After last week's session, I hoped we would have a more productive, more peaceful session. I explained again that Marcia should consider my perspective when making decisions that affected me. She seemed to understand this. We went out to lunch afterward, and things seemed okay.

Sunday, November 24, 2002

I am trying not to be stressed about the upcoming criminal trial. I hoped there would be a guilty verdict and that Zalewski would be severely punished for what he did to Marcia.

---

[87] Colossal Mistake #21: The next day, and for a long time afterward, I could not forgive myself for being so selfish. At fourteen, Rebecca should not be required to take care of her mother.

Tuesday, November 26, 2002

The criminal trial was held today, 321 days after the crash, in a district court in Norfolk County.[88]

Legally, Zalewski *"admitted to facts sufficient for a finding of guilt for negligent operation of a motor vehicle."* This meant that if we had a civil trial, Zurich and AIG couldn't contest the *fault*. Even with *fault* legally established, Zurich continued to take great advantage in delaying any settlement discussion until *damages* were *"reasonably clear."* The Massachusetts Legislature has to fix this law. A blameless victim shouldn't be financially penalized because the injuries are so severe that *damages* could not be easily calculated.

Under the current laws, determining the total financial damage to a seriously injured person, such as a T-12 paraplegic after a catastrophic crash, is a conundrum for the plaintiff but beneficial for the insurance carrier. If the plaintiff began litigation or settlement discussions too early, the financial settlement would likely be too low, because additional injuries might not be known for several years. If the plaintiff waited to begin litigation or settlement discussions until *damages* were completely determined, the plaintiff had to continue to pay all the expenses until then, likely at great financial harm.

Because of this, Zurich could wait a long time to accept *damages* that were *"reasonably clear."* Pretty clever, huh?[89]

Friday, November 29, 2002

Louise took Marcia to the dentist for another root canal. Her teeth are a mess from the crash. Typically, dental patient rooms and dental chairs are small. Transferring Marcia onto the dental chair is next to impossible and dangerous. To accomplish the transfers, we acquired a portable Hoyer lift ($3,000).[90]

Rebecca and I went to the mall to go gift shopping. I purchased a beautiful heart necklace for Marcia for Hanukkah. I knew she would be happy with it.

We exchanged gifts, and Rebecca was happy with her gifts. She is such a blessing.

---

88 See Timeline Two for the complete details of this criminal trial.

89 Later, I learned how clever this legal maneuver is for Zurich. For the most part, the laws and adjudications defining an *"unfair or deceptive act"* in Massachusetts assume that there is just one insurance carrier. In our case, there are two: the primary carrier (Zurich) and the excess carrier (AIG). Zurich's insurance policy limit was $2 million, meaning that the first $2 million of the total *damages* would be paid by Zurich. (Any amount of *damages* over $2 million, up to $50 million, would be paid by AIG.) When Zalewski admitted *"to facts sufficient for a finding of guilt,"* Zurich knew it had to pay some amount of the *damages*. Against all logical thinking and fairness, Zurich was not legally required to pay its $2 million until only after the personal injury trial-three years after the crash. The Massachusetts legislature should require a primary insurance carrier to begin to tender a portion of its policy limits as soon as the blameless victim must begin to pay expenses for damages. Even without the change in the law, Zurich was not prohibited from paying any portion of its $2 million of the total *damages* at any time directly to us. It didn't.

90 The regulations integral to the Americans with Disabilities Act (ADA) specify that medical offices must provide "equal access" to persons with disabilities. As such, the dentist is responsible for providing the method to transfer a patient who is paraplegic. A patient room should include an overhead Hoyer lift that a nurse could safely use to transfer a patient onto the dental chair.

Preparing for bed was the worst. Marcia got her period, so I had to help her clean herself. Although I had become more anatomically and medically prepared, she must have found what I had to do to care for her an enormous invasion of privacy.

Saturday, November 30, 2002

During the afternoon, I heard Marcia crying. She said, *"It's not right that you must take care of me for the next two days while I am having my period."*

At six o'clock, I made dinner for all and finished the laundry. We celebrated Hanukkah again. It was a happy time.

By nine thirty, Marcia was safely in bed. I woke around eleven thirty and heard the TV on downstairs. She had fallen asleep with the bed in an upright position, her glasses on, the lights on, and her needlepoint nearby. I put her to bed.

Sunday, December 1, 2002

Marcia is now taking more than thirty medications each day. Each week, I divided the pills into four bags to be given four times during the day for the next seven days. It took two hours or more to do this. I had to be careful.

After I transferred her onto the commode, I retrieved the first bag of morning medicines, gave her breakfast, and organized in the bathroom. Marcia was on the commode until twelve thirty. After she completed her bowel program, blood was all over the commode and the bathroom floor from her menstruation. I need to be more prepared so that the dripping could be controlled. This meant plenty of cleaning and disinfecting. I transferred her onto her wheelchair, getting the transfer board all bloody, and it, too, had to be cleaned and disinfected.

I transferred her back to her bed. I thoroughly cleaned her female parts. She had a small (half-inch) but growing pressure ulcer on her buttocks. I was concerned about it and put a bandage on it.[91]

While she dressed, I cleaned and disinfected the bathroom and continued the laundry. Because I am paranoid about cleanliness, I cleaned everywhere that I could. Blood had dripped under the commode. Sterilizing was exhausting.

Tuesday, December 3, 2002

Louise's bill for last week was $800. While I am happy she and Marcia get along well, Louise had not been doing the required work. I prepared a written list of the specific tasks she had to do. I shouldn't have had to do this.

---

91 Colossal Mistake #22: I did not realize on December 1, 2002, that this small pressure ulcer would develop into a major medical complication that kept Marcia bedridden for ten months. Additionally, as the skin breakdown grew worse, I continued to believe the ulcer would heal quickly. Nothing could have been further from the truth, and I was an idiot for thinking I knew how to care for a pressure ulcer. I am such a dunce.

Marcia was unhappy when I came home. She told me she fell off the commode while shifting her seating.[92] Because of the cold weather, she was going crazy, being housebound for the fourth day in a row, and Louise (likely in response to my list) had asked her for a raise.

Friday, December 6, 2002

Michelle came over today, replaced Marcia's catheter, and inspected her open pressure ulcers. I wish I knew more about what to do about pressure ulcers.[93]

Sunday, December 8, 2002

We saw Linda today. She was forthright with Marcia, telling her she would be traumatized for a while after having to verbalize her victim impact statement in open court.

Monday, December 9, 2002

I took Rebecca to see Harriet. Rebecca has been in such a foul mood that I did not want to be with her. She should be more pleasant and less sarcastic. However, under the circumstances, what could I expect?

Tuesday, December 10, 2002

Mark Whitehouse from Adaptive Driving Program came to the house today to begin teaching Marcia how to drive the van with hand controls.[94] To show her it wouldn't be difficult, he got her into the driver's seat, which was equipped with hand controls. Using the hand controls, she drove around the block with him twice.

She has plenty to learn. Learning to drive would take ten to twelve two-hour sessions, plus a two-hour road test. Her wheelchair has to be modified, the van seats have to be adjusted, and hand controls have to be mounted in the van. The cost would exceed $4,000, which we would have to pay.

Wednesday, December 11, 2002

Marcia received her new L'Nard boots today.[95] Fortunately, UnitedHealthcare agreed to pay the $400 for them.

---

92 Colossal Mistake #23: Even though Marcia said she did not fall hard and even though I was tired, I should have taken her for an X-ray to see if there were any broken bones.

93 Colossal Mistake #24: As before, I would learn that the wound care center at Sturdy Memorial Hospital was less than thirty minutes from our home. It specializes in providing care for persons with paraplegia and others who have serious pressure ulcers. For more information, see http://www.sturdymemorial.org/serv_woundmanagement.html. This was a serious breakdown in my education about how to care for Marcia.

94 Mark and his associates are superb people who are greatly respected for the excellent work they do teaching people with disabilities to drive and regain the freedom they have lost. For more information, see http://www.adaptivedriving-program.com/index.php.

95 *"L'Nard Multipodus boots are commonly used to decrease pressure or friction on the heel. They are also used to position the foot in a neutral position for the treatment and prevention of foot/ankle contractures. The rotation bar controls hip and*

Marcia was exceptionally unhappy today. I had not seen her this sad in a long time. At five o'clock in the afternoon, all I could do was give her a Valium and transfer her to bed early, which had not happened in a while. I felt such sorrow for her. She did not know why she was sad. While I was putting the boots on, she said: *"I feel like I'm back at the hospital when I have to wear these boots at night."*

Thursday, December 12, 2002

Marcia saw Jill McAnulty today. Jill believes that driving again has been the cause of Marcia's extreme sadness. Driving reminded her of the crash, the hospitalization, the recovery, the trauma, the family pain, her disability, and everything else. I was disappointed in myself that I didn't foresee this sadness. I should have prepared better for this.[96]

Sunday, December 15, 2002

I went to see Linda alone. We talked about how disappointed I was in Marcia's family, particularly her sister. I couldn't understand how her immediate family could be so absent when their loved one was suffering. I know Marcia was upset too, but she wouldn't talk about those feelings with anyone.

Monday, December 16, 2002

This morning, we discovered that even though Marcia was not doing anything differently, she had developed several large pressure ulcers on her buttocks. She called the dermatologist and made an appointment for tomorrow afternoon. In case the dermatologist was not able to provide care for a person with paraplegia, I took several pictures of the pressure ulcers before Marcia got out of bed.

Marcia went to Dr. Clark, who refilled the psych prescriptions she was taking:
1. Cylert (ADHD)
2. Percocet (worsening chronic pain)
3. Prilosec (indigestion)
4. Prozac (anxiety and depression)
5. Ritalin (ADHD)
6. Valium (anxiety)
7. Sonata (sleeping disorders)
8. Wellbutrin SR (depression)
9. Zyprexa (bipolar disorder)

---

leg rotation." "L'Nard Multipodus Boot," The University of Michigan Orthotics & Prosthetics Center, last modified March 11, 2014, http://www.med.umich.edu/op/Patient%20Education%20Forms/5A/L'nard.pdf.

96 Colossal Mistake #25: Again, so stupid. After almost a year, I should have known that caregiving is a process, not a series of events. I need to ask myself, *"How will this new positive event impact Marcia's emotions, potentially in a negative manner?"*

Wednesday, December 18, 2002

Not unexpectedly, the dermatologist's office was not equipped for persons with spinal cord injury. We showed the dermatologist the pictures of the pressure ulcers.[97] The dermatologist diagnosed the pressure ulcers as stage II and stage III, which are serious and could easily result in a grave situation. The only solution is to take all the weight off the pressure ulcers so they could heal.

Thursday, December 19, 2002

Marcia struggled with her bowel program today. After her shower, she unexpectedly defecated. Louise had quite a time cleaning the mess. The pressure ulcers were worse than yesterday, and Marcia had to stay on her side in bed all day so the ulcers wouldn't press against anything.

Being unable to transfer into her wheelchair, she felt dejected. She spoke to Jill by phone. I could do little to improve her mood. To help her, I ordered a different kind of seat cushion ($220) with an opening in the middle area. I hoped she would be able to sit on the cushion without putting stress on the pressure ulcers.[98] I called Michelle (the VNA nurse), who said she would visit tomorrow.

Friday, December 20, 2002

I woke early to prepare for the day and found that the pressure ulcers were worse. They were larger, and there were three blisters that had yet to open. I spoke to the wheelchair specialist and told him that Marcia had been confined to her bed. He said state law dictated that he see her in the powered wheelchair for at least a few minutes, so she sat in the Jazzy 1122[99] when he visited. I was disappointed she wouldn't be able to use the new wheelchair for the next few days.

Michelle came by. She was amazed at the seriousness of the pressure ulcers. She said bed rest was all that could be done. So sad.

I spoke to Dr. Roaf, who was especially concerned. She asked that I have Michelle call her.

Saturday, December 21, 2002

Except for her morning bowel program, Marcia was 100 percent bedridden in order to remove all pressure on the ulcers. She was uncomfortable being in bed all the time. Her

---

97 Later, I learned the appropriate method to care for pressure ulcers. I was bewildered that I did not learn about this much earlier.

98 Colossal Mistake #26: Later, I learned about a new type of cushion for Marcia's wheelchair. Although expensive (more than $2,500), using it would practically stop pressure sores from developing on her buttocks. Again, I was bewildered that I did not learn about this cushion for a long time. For more information, see http://www.aquilacorp.com.

99 For more information about the Jazzy 1122, see http://www.pridemobility.com/pdf/Owners_Manuals/US_Jazzy/US_Jazzy_1122_om.pdf.

powered wheelchair had been sitting in the garage while she waited for the pressure ulcers to heal. She was extraordinarily depressed that she could not use it. The afternoon dragged on slowly. Pam came by for a visit, and I was thankful Marcia had a friend to talk to while being stuck in bed.

I made Marcia one of her favorite dinners to break up the monotony of being restricted to bed. I sat with her until she fell asleep at nine o'clock. I couldn't remember having such a bad day since those first terrible days when she came home in April.

I am so angry at Zalewski for doing this to my family. In twelve seconds of reckless inattention, he changed our lives for the worse.

Sunday, December 22, 2002

In the morning, I saw a puddle of urine in the bed. Fortunately, Michelle would come tomorrow and fix the catheter.

Marcia complained to me last night that Rebecca had not been paying any attention to her. Marcia was heartbroken, but I could see Rebecca's point of view. Rebecca was upset seeing her mom in bed every day, incapable of doing anything. I will try to get Rebecca to spend time with her while I am with Linda today.

I had no doubt Marcia would be in bed all day again. How sad.

Monday, December 23, 2002

Marcia stayed in bed except for her morning bowel program. Michelle came over to check on her. She said Marcia needed to be in bed for several more days.

Marcia was still unable to try her powered wheelchair. It would probably be returned before she got out of bed.

The INR test had to be rescheduled until the following Monday. Marcia could not go to the hospital today, and she remained miserable about being stuck in bed.

Tuesday, December 24, 2002

For another day, Marcia was bedridden. She had been on her side for a week, and I couldn't help but feel dejected for her. She still had many more days in bed ahead of her.

Louise did a first-rate job of cleaning Marcia and helping her dress. We gave Louise a large Christmas present. Although there were times I wished she did more, I knew we couldn't have survived without her.

Marcia was depressed tonight, more so than ever. While the pressure ulcers were healing, the process was so slow. She still had another week or more. In the late evenings, when she was tired of being stuck in bed all day, she was the angriest, the most irritable, and the most depressed.

Marcia's mother called tonight. I never knew whether to answer her calls or not, and Marcia wouldn't answer the phone on her own. On the one hand, she would benefit from staying in touch with people who loved her, but on the other hand, her mother sometimes harped on how she was doing, reminding her of the pitifully awful shape she was in.

Wednesday, December 25, 2002

Could this day have been worse? There was a major snowstorm, so Louise didn't come in.

The pressure ulcers didn't noticeably heal last night, and worse, Marcia got her period last night. Every night for five nights, I had to clean this.

At eleven forty-five in the morning, Marcia was still on the commode. She needed to get back into bed.

In the afternoon, she and Rebecca watched a movie together. She wanted to have Rebecca around more.

We were going to get another major snowstorm. Could life be worse?

Thursday, December 26, 2002

As arranged, the snowplow man came in the middle of the night. What an awful snowstorm. I had to clean off the deck, feed the birds, and snowplow the unreachable portions of the driveway. We had to be able to get out of the driveway in case Marcia required a trip to the ER.

Some of the pressure ulcers looked better, but several were worsening by blistering or bleeding. Marcia needed many more days of bed rest. This situation couldn't have been sadder, especially with my family coming to visit.

Marcia spent a large part of the morning on the commode, which she was not supposed to. I suspected that when she had her period, the bowel program took longer. She did as well as she could to get ready for my family. She didn't have to, but that was Marcia—no matter what the circumstances were, she tried her best.

Louise agreed to stay over tomorrow night. Having additional caregiving time would be expensive, but I wanted to have plenty of time with my brothers and their families.

Friday, December 27, 2002

Today was my brother Steve's birthday. Spending the day with him was terrific. I needed a day off.

Louise arrived at seven thirty, ready to take care of Marcia for the day. The girls went to Solomon Pond Mall. Steve, my other brother, Mike, and I went electronics shopping. I was so happy being with my brothers. We went out to lunch and talked about the renovation. We met up with everyone at the movies, and Rebecca came. The movie was long and boring, but I was proud of her for hanging in there. I dropped her off at home around five thirty, and we all went to Uno's for dinner.

When I returned home at eight thirty, I was shocked, saddened, and disappointed. For whatever reason, Louise had left at eight o'clock, leaving Marcia alone in bed, and Louise had done nothing to prepare Marcia for bed: change her bandages, change her tampon, lay out her pills, or clean the kitchen. I had to do everything that I expected Louise to have done. Forget about having a day off, and I still had to pay Louise for being at the house until eight. I was angry.

Saturday, December 28, 2002

I continued to be happy to have my family with us. While my brothers and I went to the movies, Kathy (Mike's wife) and Lisa (my sister) stayed at home and talked with Marcia. When we returned home, I could tell that Marcia enjoyed talking with Kathy and Lisa. She was more animated and looked more energetic.

While not yet proficient at it, I did my best to change her bandages before she went to sleep. I forgot to have her change her tampon.[100] At nine thirty, my day was finally over.

Sunday, December 29, 2002

Having breakfast with everyone this morning was wonderful. I will miss my family.

I noticed the pressure ulcers were healing, but Marcia still had several more days in bed ahead of her. While I hoped we all would have a pleasantly quiet day, Marcia was stuck in bed—another unhappy day for her.

Tuesday, December 31, 2002

The end of 2002 was here. What am I happy about?
1. Marcia had no head trauma and no quadriplegia due to the crash. She was alive.
2. The Brown Rudnick team has been excellent.
3. The architectural designer did a wonderful job with the design of our new addition and was managing the bidders well. The new addition will be wonderful.
4. Marcia might soon learn to drive (I hope by our anniversary).
5. Most of the time, Louise did a fine job taking care of Marcia.
6. My family provided me with the needed emotional support.
7. Cindy, Bruce, Marion, and Pam S. have been wonderful friends.
8. The Milford VNA, Dr. Roaf, and Dr. Krauth have provided excellent medical care.

---

[100] Colossal Mistake #27: Females know this, but men don't. Not changing a tampon every eight hours can cause a UTI, a yeast infection, or toxic shock syndrome.

What am I depressed about?
1. Marcia's unrelenting chronic pain. I don't know what to do. It is horrible to see her in such pain every day.
2. Marcia's awful pressure ulcers and my lack of knowledge about the best way to care for them. Marcia has been bedridden for two weeks, and she likely has many weeks to go.
3. Marcia is in awful shape in every way—medically, physically, psychologically, and emotionally. She requires an HHA for assistance for almost every activity. Her family has not given her enough in-person, loving support.
4. Rebecca is in her own world—distant from Marcia and me and unhappy all the time. She was doing poorly in school and has been generally asocial. She too had developed substantial psychological problems. I have no idea what to do. Rebecca and I need to start thinking about and preparing for college.
5. I am in poor shape. I worry about Marcia and her future all the time and I am struggling to adjust to her unhappiness. I worry about Rebecca and her future all the time. My body hurts, and I am not taking care of myself. I have so much to do each day.
6. I am worried about the pending litigation.
7. Zurich continues to ignore us. It obviously has a plan to make us run out of money before settlement discussions begin.

We had spent or planned to spend a lot of money. The past and current out-of-pocket medical expenses and costs have been enormous, and we have begun to use our home equity. I hate to be in debt. I am beginning to worry about whether we would receive enough money to care for Marcia for the rest of her life.

January 2003 to March 2003

Wednesday, January 1, 2003

While it was the beginning of a new year for everyone, for Marcia, today was another awful day of being bedridden. Cindy, who continues to be a wonderful friend to Marcia, came over this afternoon, but being with Cindy only reminded Marcia that many other people had deserted her.

Since filing the lawsuit six months ago, Marcia's expenses had increased by more than $175,000.

Thursday, January 2, 2003

When I came home in the afternoon, Louise told me the pressure ulcers had worsened. They looked horrible and were even worse to clean. Marcia was disheartened. She had to be bedridden for at least two weeks, one year after the crash.

Marcia's mother called, and Marcia cried on the phone with her. Her mother wanted to know if she should come up to take care of her.

I did something I had never done before: I called Marcia's mother after she went to sleep. I told her Marcia was in poor shape—medically, emotionally, physically, and psychologically. There didn't seem to be anything that could be done.

Friday, January 3, 2003

Louise and I checked the pressure ulcers this morning. They were not healing and might be getting worse.

For the first time since the crash, I thought I could no longer provide the best care for Marcia. I am worn out. Maybe she should go back to the rehabilitation hospital. The hospital nurses would likely be able to provide her with better care than I could. I told her I would call Michelle, the VNA nurse.

Michelle was kind on the phone. She told me she would rearrange her appointments so she could see Marcia this morning. She said the pressure ulcers were serious but were stabilizing. She called Dr. Roaf, who said she wanted to examine Marcia in person. Michelle arranged for an ambulance to take Marcia to Fairlawn on Monday afternoon. I couldn't take Marcia in the van because she had to be on a stretcher so Dr. Roaf could examine her.

When we came home, I made Marcia dinner and changed her bandages. I had to clean each pressure ulcer, apply zinc oxide, spread Second Skin Scar Gel, and bandage and tape the ulcers with great care. To relieve the weight on the ulcers, I shifted her onto her side. Moving her by myself was scary, even while in bed. I was not well trained in wound care.

I woke around three in the morning to make sure she hadn't turned over.

Saturday, January 4, 2003

The snow came down hard last night, and there was a huge amount everywhere. Our snowplow person was reliable, and he understood the delicate and unpredictable position we were in.

Marcia spent most of the day in bed talking to her girlfriends. That was the best, except she didn't take a nap in the afternoon. At seven thirty, she was predictably cranky and unhappy.

Because of the impending pressure ulcer on her left hip, the side on which she had been sleeping every night and every day, she had to sleep on her right side. I hoped this did not cause a new pressure sore. We would see tomorrow.

I moved another TV, cable box, clock, and intercom to the other side of the bed. I did this quietly around nine thirty while she was asleep. I did something completely out of character. I was so overwhelmed that I took two of her Percocet pills. I had the worst headaches imaginable, but I didn't have the energy or interest to talk with a doctor about it.

Sunday, January 5, 2003

Before I went to sleep last night, I made a significant decision: I had to have more caregiver assistance in the evenings. I could no longer care for Marcia by myself. Having additional assistance would be expensive, so I had been hesitant.

❖ ❖ ❖

Zurich, do you know Marcia requires extensive personal care in both the morning and evening? Zurich, do you know that in order to provide Marcia's patient care, I am unable to work? Zurich, do you know I now must pay an aide to care for Marcia more than eight hours each day? Zurich, do you know the nearly impossible financial burden we carry?

❖ ❖ ❖

Although it was expensive, I arranged for Louise to stay each day until six thirty. I was disappointed in myself that I could no longer provide the care I should be able to.

Monday, January 6, 2003

Today, Marcia was taken by ambulance to Fairlawn. Dr. Roaf made these conclusions: several pressure ulcers were healing, but one large area (about one and a half inches by four inches) was covered with dead skin (slough). This meant it was not healing.

Dr. Roaf prescribed a new prescription enzyme: collagenase Santyl ointment. It destroyed the slough and added collagen to the pressure ulcer, so healing could occur faster. The ointment had to be meticulously applied.

One other ulcer (about one and a half inches by one and a half inches) was severely damaged. Dr. Roaf diagnosed it as being almost a stage III.

Marcia is unhappy, Rebecca is depressed, and I am numb.

Wednesday, January 8, 2003

Marcia had to take three sleeping pills to sleep last night. Michelle visited her and told her the pressure ulcers were improving but slowly. Marcia was depressed.

Years later, I had the opportunity to review the patient care notes from today:

"Overall emotional and behavioral status is deteriorating. Patient affect is flat. Mood is depressed and tearful. Patient ability to cope with illness is inadequate due to patient approaching first year anniversary of accident, very upset that she now has to stay at home due to condition of wounds."

Amazingly, a year had passed: hospitalization at UMass Memorial Hospital; hospitalization at Fairlawn Rehabilitation Hospital; the home renovations, the purchases of the van, manual wheelchair, and other DME; the purchases of a large amount of medical supplies; Marcia's homecoming; gall bladder surgery; a second hospitalization at Milford Regional Medical Center; and the hospitalization at Whittier Rehabilitation Hospital.

There had been occupational therapy, physical therapy, and many medical appointments. There had been depression, anxiety, anger, and fear. Once in a while, we had some happiness.

I had in my mind that this one-year anniversary would be a positive step for Marcia—it would show her all the progress she had made—but it would not be so. Being bedridden with stage II and stage III pressure ulcers was an awful one-year anniversary. By bedtime, she was in tears.

Thursday, January 9, 2003

Zurich American Insurance still has not provided any financial assistance. These are the facts and figures:

1. Medical expenses to date: $400,000
2. Out-of-pocket medical expenses and costs to date: $150,165
3. Forecast medical expenses: $100,000
4. Forecast home renovation cost: $150,000
5. Forecast other out-of-pocket medical expenses and costs for next year: $50,000
6. Forecast HHA expenses for next year: $75,000
7. Number of hospital nights: 120

8. Number of nurse and therapist visits: 113
9. Number of doctor appointments: 69
10. Number of ER trips: 4

I picked up Marcia's mother from the airport. I was so happy for Marcia. Pam, Cindy, and Marcia's mother played mah-jongg with her, and she was in a good mood. I was thankful.

Friday, January 10, 2003

While redressing the bandages, I saw that several pressure ulcers had improved. Thank goodness!

Sunday, January 12, 2003

For the first time in a long time, I was not feeling well today. I had to be careful not to get Marcia sick. I stayed in bed most of the day but got up to help Marcia's mother prepare her for bed. I was in full precaution medical garb with a mask and gown. Fortunately, the pressure ulcers continued to improve.

Monday, January 13, 2003

I was still sick but well enough to get out of bed. When we woke Marcia, she was wet from urine, and she had defecated during the night. Worse, she had a new rash on her legs and bottom—on top of the pressure ulcers.

Tuesday, January 14, 2003

I woke at five thirty to take care of the trash, woke Marcia, and got Rebecca to the bus stop. Marcia was all wet again. I was sure her catheter needed changing.

When I came home from errands, she told me she was wet from urine again. Worse, the rash looked awful.

Wednesday, January 15, 2003

At one o'clock last night, I went downstairs to check on Marcia. She was wet from urine again. Even though she was sleeping, I cleaned the mess as best I could.

Michelle came to see Marcia, and I asked that her catheter be replaced. The pressure ulcers were still healing. We guessed she had two more weeks in bed.

The distressing news was that the urine had caused an awful fungal rash. Marcia had to have new gauze twice per day, including antifungal cream for the rash, zinc oxide for the edges of the pressure ulcers, and silver sulfadiazine for the open pressure ulcers. At least she could sleep on her back now. I thought Marcia's mother was beginning to understand what life had been like for Marcia and me for the last year.

At around six thirty, we got Marcia ready for bed. I noticed she was wet all over. Although I had asked to have her catheter replaced, Michelle had refilled the balloon. I called the Milford VNA on-call nurse, Martha, asking her to come to the house at seven forty-five to replace the catheter.

Thursday, January 16, 2003

Today started off terribly. The company letting Marcia try out the power wheelchair called and said they wanted it back. Not that I blamed them—she had not used it at all. Marcia was sad and thought she had taken a step backward. I felt awful.

Saturday, January 18, 2003

The pressure ulcers continued to heal, but Marcia still had a week or more to go. At least she could sit up in bed now. Her mother has been considerably helpful. For the week I had a cold and didn't feel like doing anything, it was wonderful to have her here.

Sunday, January 19, 2003

Louise called at six thirty. She was not feeling well and would not be coming in. I was beginning to feel better, so I thought I would have the energy to take care of Marcia. I appreciated the comfort her mother had been bringing her.

After six weeks, I was finally able to do something with Rebecca: we went to the mall together. Although it was two short hours, we were alone for the first time, doing something she liked. We had lunch together and talked as a normal father and daughter. I missed being with her so much. She is such a great kid.

❖ ❖ ❖

Zurich knew that Massachusetts law allowed for a claim of *loss of spousal consortium*[101] as well as a claim of *loss of parental consortium*[102] between Marcia and Rebecca. However, the law does not provide for a claim of *loss of parental consortium* between Rebecca and me, even though our relationship greatly suffered because of Zalewski. The Massachusetts legislature has to remedy this inequity.

---

[101] *"Loss of (spousal) consortium is an actionable injury for which money damages may be awarded. The loss of the love, sexual relations, and services of a spouse are being considered tangible injuries to an increasing extent. An action for loss of consortium is based upon the inconvenience of having a spouse who has been injured."* "Consortium," *The Free Dictionary*, last modified March 11, 2014, http://legal-dictionary.thefreedictionary.com/consortium.

[102] *"Damages for loss of consortium cover some of the losses a child suffers when a parent is injured or dies as a result of someone else's negligent or intentional conduct. They include damages for loss of services, loss of financial support, and loss of the relationship between the parent and child, which includes advice, emotional support, and other intangible but highly valued elements."* "Can children claim loss of consortium for a parent's injury, or vice versa?" Rottenstein Law Group, last modified March 11, 2014, http://www.rotlaw.com/legal-library/can-children-claim-loss-of-consortium-for-a-parents-injury-or-vice-versa.

❖ ❖ ❖

Tuesday, January 21, 2003

Marcia had a fun afternoon. Pam and Marion came over, brought lunch, and played mah-jongg. I was happy when her friends came over.

I spent more than $200 in copayments for prescriptions. Enough said.

Wednesday, January 22, 2003

I came home at twelve thirty to learn that Marcia's newest catheter was leaking. Michelle made another trip to our house, and I could tell she was exasperated.

Rebecca was complaining about stomach pains. Understandably, she missed her mother's attention and affection. I was reasonably certain there was nothing seriously wrong with her, but we would wait and see. Tomorrow should be interesting, because she would have her quarterly visit with Dr. Merritt.

Thursday, January 23, 2003

After school, I took Rebecca to see Dr. Merritt. Rebecca was so depressed. She said her life stank. I couldn't blame her for being distressed, for being angry, and for pulling her hair. For the previous six weeks, she had practically no interaction with her mother or me. Dr. Merritt increased her anti-anxiety medicine level. Maybe this would help.

Marcia's mother told me she was beginning to think about going home. I knew I should be thankful for what she had done, but I felt she was abandoning Marcia.

Friday, January 24, 2003

When Marcia woke at seven o'clock, I could tell she wasn't feeling well. She had a slight fever and her dark urine had a pungent odor. After a year, even I could diagnose a UTI. I captured clean urine in a sterile sample cup and brought it to the Milford Regional Medical Center to be analyzed. Around nine thirty, Dr. Krauth's office called to say, *"Marcia has a UTI, and a prescription for antibiotic has been called into CVS. Have Marcia take the full course of the antibiotic, and then have the VNA draw a clean urine sample. If she worsens, immediately go to the emergency room."*

Saturday, January 25, 2003

Marcia had another difficult day. Besides having a UTI, the pressure ulcers had not healed very much, and she got her period. I spent a lot of time caring for her. Nevertheless, I had become so clinical that caring for her (except for the transfers) did not affect me (or so I thought). She was upset at Zurich. She said, *"If Zurich would give us some money, we could have someone on the weekend care for me so you don't have to."* We decided to have a weekend HHA. I wouldn't let Zurich upset her.

Monday, January 27, 2003

In the afternoon, I spoke to the manager at Griswold. She said Louise was pregnant, so a change of home health aides would be necessary. The Griswold manager called Sandy to check her availability, and Sandy said she could come tomorrow and Thursday this week, three days next week, and full-time afterward. I told Marcia that Sandy would be coming in from now on—not Louise. I was struck that she wasn't upset about this.

Later in the day, she told me that while she was on the commode on Friday, she had called loudly for Louise, but Louise had been asleep on the couch. She had used her cell phone to wake Louise. She was devastated and scared to be alone.

A few hours later, I asked her why she hadn't told me about this. *"I didn't want to bother you—you are worrying about so many things already."* On the one hand, this was a caring thought. On the other hand, it meant she felt she could not talk to me when something was upsetting her. I had to change that.

Tuesday, January 28, 2003

Elayne, Marcia's mother, told me she was going home on the coming weekend. Oh, well. Having her here had been helpful, but in the end, I cannot count on anyone else.

Wednesday, January 29, 2003

Elayne told Marcia she was returning home this weekend. Marcia cried. I knew Elayne had her own life, but I still felt she was abandoning her daughter at her time of utmost need. Elayne should have stayed until Marcia asked her to go.

Beginning Monday, Sandy would be Marcia's weekday HHA, and Maggie (another new HHA) would work weekends.

The second semester started at Milford High School. Rebecca was stressed and mad at the world. I know that fourteen-year-old girls could be a challenge, but Rebecca was well beyond this. My heart is broken. She was fourteen years old and without a mother.

With the pressure ulcers still not completely healed, I changed next week's appointment with Dr. DiGiovanni to the end of February. This may have been unwise, but I didn't have any choice.

I called Dr. Krauth for myself. I was getting a colonoscopy done. What fun.

Thursday, January 30, 2003

Today was difficult. Marcia was miserable. She continued to have her period. She was having problems getting used to the new HHAs, and she was not looking forward to the renewed occupational and physical therapies. Elayne's going home was a break in their strong bond. I was dreading how Marcia would feel without her mother.

Rebecca was not being polite to her and was showing her stress. She continued to demonstrate her unhappiness, and I did not know what to do. I decided I would go with her to Harriet on Monday. I had to learn how to be a better father.

Sunday, February 2, 2003

Maggie called to say she wouldn't be coming in. The snow was heavy in Worcester last night. Fortunately, Elayne took care of Marcia this morning while I cleared the driveway. Marcia's sister and brother-in-law came in the afternoon to take Elayne to the airport. Marcia was so dejected.

Marcia and I didn't start off well. With her mother here, Marcia had put on ten to fifteen pounds. I made the dumb mistake of speaking to her about the importance of eating more healthfully and losing the added weight. She was angry at me.[103]

Monday, February 3, 2003

Instead of Sandy, Maggie came in. While Maggie assisted in the transfer from the commode to Marcia's wheelchair, Marcia fell. I hoped there weren't any fractures from the fall, but I knew to inspect her legs for bruising.

Before going to bed, I checked on Marcia. She was weeping. She missed having her mother with her in the evenings.

Thursday, February 6, 2003

I had a blood test today. I hoped my cholesterol would be okay. Next came the colonoscopy.

Marcia was in a pleasant mood today. She even risked taking a shower.

The pressures ulcers were improving. She continued to have one stage III ulcer in the crease of her leg to her buttocks (gluteal crease). The skin in the area was thin, and this ulcer would take several weeks to heal. Even then, the area would be subject to future damage.

Sunday, February 9, 2003

First thing today, I examined the pressure ulcers. The epidermis and dermis of the pressure ulcer in the left gluteal crease had been penetrated. In some places, this pressure ulcer was down to the subcutaneous tissue. Marcia shouldn't get out of bed until this pressure ulcer was healed. I felt so stressed out that I took another of Marcia's Percocets and a Valium.

---

103 Colossal Mistake #28: Nagging Marcia about anything medical violated the therapists' instructions to never pester her or set medical goals. This was really stupid of me to do.

After my appointment with Linda and after Marcia finished playing mah-jongg with her friends, we three had dinner together for the first time in a long time. We were in bed by nine thirty, but, with everything on my mind, I couldn't sleep.

Monday, February 10, 2003

I stayed home most of the day to ensure that Sandy could manage a single-person transfer. In the afternoon, I took Rebecca to see Harriet.

Sandy and I had just transferred Marcia onto the commode when she began to defecate.

I did not think Marcia and Sandy were starting off well. Marcia struggled to understand Sandy's accent (and vice versa), and Sandy struggled to transfer Marcia to the shower, even with my assistance. Marcia was crying when I saw her in the bathroom.

Sandy was not as knowledgeable or as experienced as Louise. I knew we had a long learning curve ahead of us. But, okay.

Wednesday, February 12, 2003

I woke early to transfer Marcia onto the commode at six o'clock. Urine had leaked all over her and the bed, she hadn't put the tampon in the correct location, and the catheter had become squeezed.

Marcia was depressed and felt alone all afternoon. Today was cold, and no one visited except for the physical therapist.

Thursday, February 13, 2003

Today is Day 400 since the crash. Zurich has yet to provide any financial assistance, and we had already spent or planned to spend more than $450,000.

❖ ❖ ❖

Zurich, how will a blameless victim without financial resources return to good health? Zurich, do you want me to get the message that you want us to run out of money before settlement discussions begin? Zurich, please help.

❖ ❖ ❖

Marcia woke soaked in urine again. Sediment in the urine blocked the catheter during the night. She called the Milford VNA nurse to have the catheter replaced.

She was so unhappy this afternoon. I called my sister, Lisa, and asked her to call Marcia. I asked Mike to have his wife, Kathy, call.

Marcia took a laxative at bedtime. She had to stop using a suppository for her bowel program.

Friday, February 14, 2003 (Valentine's Day!)

The laxative worked too well. Marcia defecated during the night. Sandy was able to transfer her from her bed to the wheelchair and onto the commode with me. Training a new HHA took time, but we were getting there.

Rebecca's guidance counselor called from school. She said Rebecca was having a miserable day, so I went to school to pick her up. We bought Valentine's Day cards and gifts, and Rebecca seemed okay. We all had dinner together—swordfish and talk. Being together was enjoyable.

Marcia took half a laxative before going to sleep.

Saturday, February 15, 2003

I woke Marcia at seven thirty and found urine on the bed. I thought there had to be something wrong with the catheter, but I also thought we had become a hassle to the Milford VNA. The catheter continued to leak even while Marcia was on the commode. I did something I had never been taught to do: I flushed the catheter and refilled it with sterile water. With the debris in her urine, which was likely clogging the catheter, I thought she must have a UTI.

Eighteen months earlier, I had had no idea what a catheter was.

To end the evening, Marion canceled dinner with us for Sunday. Marcia took two laxatives before bedtime. Maybe tomorrow would be better.

Sunday, February 16, 2003

Again, the catheter leaked, and it had to be replaced. We made another call to the Milford VNA, even on a cold day like this.

Because Marcia took laxatives last night, I tried to do the transfer quickly. My shoulder and back were hurting, and I didn't feel well. I took two of Marcia's Percocets. At twelve thirty, she was still on the commode. Getting used to the new bowel program—using laxatives—was challenging. She had been sitting there for five hours, and it was still not through. I called Linda and canceled my therapy session.

I called the Milford VNA. Michelle said she would come over. Although Marcia was wet from the urine in the bed, Michelle didn't change the catheter. She showed me how to flush the catheter, empty and refill the Foley catheter balloon, and reset the Foley catheter location. I hoped this would fix the catheter. The pressure ulcers worsened from the urine-soaked dressings.

At five thirty, Marcia defecated in her bed. I spent about forty-five minutes cleaning everything and putting on new bandages.

Even though Cindy came over for a short visit late in the afternoon, Marcia had a truly unhappy day. I did too.

Monday, February 17, 2003

I woke at seven fifteen. While Marcia was able to put out some urine, she was still wet. Sandy arrived at seven forty. I decided she had to take care of Marcia today by herself—after yesterday, I was already tired. I called the Milford VNA to have the catheter replaced, and the nurse said someone would be here later this morning.

At ten o'clock, the snow began, and the forecast was twelve to twenty inches. I sent Sandy home at ten thirty—I didn't want her to have any problems getting home. I doubted she would be back tomorrow.

The Milford VNA called. Unless the problem was urgent, the nurse would come tomorrow due to the snow. I took care of Marcia today. In doing so, I strained my shoulder again. I took two Percocets.

Tuesday, February 18, 2003

Twenty-eight inches of snow—what else could be said? Sandy called at seven o'clock and said she couldn't come in today.

Wednesday, February 19, 2003

I woke Marcia at five thirty. Although she was wet from urine, after I cleaned her and she completed her morning bowel program, she and her friends went to Foxwoods. After many days of bed rest from the awful pressure ulcers, she felt she had to go out without regard for the consequences. What could I say?

Thursday, February 20, 2003

Marcia woke all wet. I called the Milford VNA, and Michelle came at seven forty-five to check her catheter. Michelle didn't change the catheter but adjusted the location and the balloon. She wanted to see if Marcia would be wet again tomorrow.

I saw Dr. Krauth, who recognized my worsening emotional health. She prescribed Lexapro (an antidepressant), and I told her about my painful left shoulder from all the transfers. She entered an order for an X-ray of my shoulder; until then, I should take Motrin. I knew I should tell her about the Percocets I had been taking, but I decided not to.

Friday, February 21, 2003

Michelle was here at four o'clock in the afternoon. She changed the catheter to one that had a slightly larger opening, so any gunk in the urine could pass through without blocking it. The size of the opening of the catheter increased from 12 Fr to 14 Fr, which meant an increase of 0.026 inches, about the width of six hairs.

Saturday, February 22, 2003

After ten days, Marcia didn't wake wet. The first thing she said was that her lower abdomen hurt. The chronic pain had become so substantial that she could feel it, even though there was no nerve connection to the brain.[104]

Without taking a suppository, she was unable to defecate. She was feeling bloated, gaseous, and unhappy that she was off her routine. Nevertheless, the doctors had told her to stop using suppositories and take a nighttime laxative instead. Adjusting took some time.

In bed at ten o'clock in the evening, I noted that she had what I thought was a new bruise that encircled her right leg at midcalf. Was this serious?

Sunday, February 23, 2003

This morning, the bruise appeared the same. It could be from her sock's elastic, or it might be an indication of a blood clot.[105] Not knowing was the worst.

Because I had forgotten to put on her L'Nard boots last night, Marcia developed another pressure ulcer on her big toe from rubbing on the sheet.[106] She was unusually sad tonight. I gave her a Valium, and she fell asleep.

Monday, February 24, 2003

Today was my forty-ninth birthday. I felt eighty-nine.

After her morning bowel program, I took Marcia to see Dr. Krauth. The news was unfortunate all around. The large bruise on her right leg was most likely a DVT, due to the prolonged bed rest to relieve the pressure ulcers. She had to have an ultrasound on her leg as soon as possible.

Dr. Krauth diagnosed her with a UTI, and Marcia began taking Keflex this afternoon. She also told Marcia to go back to the suppositories for her bowel program and not to use laxatives as Dr. Roaf had indicated.

---

104 Later, I learned more about the nature of chronic pain due to an acute injury. For example, what I wrote this day was incorrect. Most people understood chronic pain to be a symptom of an underlying trauma or disease. For Marcia, chronic pain is a disease.

105 Colossal Mistake #29: This decision to not do anything about the leg bruise was particularly stupid. I could make the excuse that I had not been trained to understand the implications of such a bruise. Nonetheless, I failed to follow my own rule to have any medical complication, no matter how slight, immediately reviewed by a doctor.

106 Colossal Mistake #30: I forgot to put on her L'Nard boots at night—how stupid or lazy can I be? I knew better than to do this, but I failed her.

Tuesday, February 25, 2003

At eleven o'clock, I took Marcia to the hospital for the ultrasound on her leg. During the ultrasound, I asked the technician for her opinion, but she said I had to speak to Dr. Krauth. I watched the computer screen during the ultrasound. After seeing many ultrasounds, I could tell Marcia didn't have a blood clot. Therefore, the soreness and swelling on her leg was likely from a skin infection (cellulitis), which the Keflex would heal; a low INR level, which increased Coumadin would heal; or something else altogether.[107]

After dinner, I put her to bed and checked her body. I noted a stage III pressure ulcer on her right leg near her crotch, a stage II pressure ulcer on her left foot, a large swelling on her right leg, and additional open pressure ulcers. I didn't know the medical term, but she was a mess. I changed her dressings and put on new ointments, and the day was complete.

Wednesday, February 26, 2003

Marcia's leg was considerably more swollen. Dr. Krauth called and said Marcia had an infection or the INR level was not correct. However, she didn't have a blood clot.

Marcia continued to take Keflex in case there was an infection. Tomorrow, I would take her to the MetroWest Medical Center for an INR test.

Thursday, February 27, 2003

The swelling of Marcia's leg grew more severe.

Besides being concerned about her worsening medical condition, I was distressed when we went to sign the line of credit papers at Fleet Bank for the home renovation. Very kindly, the loan officers met Marcia outside at the van, in the cold, for her signature. I hated being in debt—it ran contrary to how I was brought up.

❖ ❖ ❖

Zurich, do you know that Marcia and I must go into debt because you have not provided even the first penny to help Marcia return to good health?

❖ ❖ ❖

After the bank, we went to MetroWest Medical Center. Marcia's INR level was unexpectedly high at 3.5. The soreness and swelling on her leg had to be from cellulitis.

---

[107] *"Cellulitis is a bacterial infection of the skin and tissues beneath the skin. Cellulitis usually begins as a small area of tenderness, swelling, and redness that spreads to adjacent skin. As this red area begins to enlarge, the affected person may develop a fever—sometimes with chills and sweats—and swollen lymph nodes ("swollen glands") near the area of infected skin."* "Cellulitis: Cellulitis Facts," MedicineNet.com, last modified March 11, 2014, http://www.medicinenet.com/cellulitis/article.htm.

Friday, February 28, 2003

Mike's Kathy arrived late in the afternoon. We went for a test drive so Kathy could get comfortable taking Marcia in the van. That seemed to work well. Later, I heard Rebecca, Marcia, and Kathy laughing and having fun. I should have done this much sooner!

Steve, Mike, and I went to Phoenix for a weekend of golf.

Sunday, March 2, 2003

While golfing, Steve's Kathy called. She told me the cellulitis was worse. I asked her to call the Milford VNA, and they advised her to take Marcia to the ER. At six o'clock, Marcia received her first dose of intravenous Levaquin.[108]

Steve's Kathy called back to tell me the IV Levaquin had to be given every twelve hours. I planned to return home as soon as possible. However, ever so wonderfully, Steve's Kathy, Mike's Kathy, and Marcia insisted I stay with Mike and Steve in Phoenix and not come home. They said they would take her to the ER every twelve hours. Besides having two great brothers and a sister, I had two wonderful sisters-in-law.

Monday, March 3, 2003

Because Sunday evening's IV Levaquin was given at six, Kathy and Kathy got Marcia up at three o'clock in the morning to start her bowel program. Three hours later, they took her to the ER for her second IV Levaquin. At six o'clock in the evening, they again took her to the ER for her third IV Levaquin.

Tuesday, March 4, 2003

On Tuesday morning at six o'clock—after a three-hour bowel program—Kathy and Kathy took Marcia to the ER for her fourth IV Levaquin.

Steve, Mike, and I returned home Tuesday morning. I have the best brothers and sisters-in-law.

That evening, I took Marcia to the ER for her fifth IV Levaquin.

Wednesday, March 5, 2003

I woke at three o'clock in the morning to transfer Marcia onto the commode. It was the beginning of a long day. We went to the ER just before six for her sixth IV Levaquin. At five o'clock in the evening, I noted the redness on her leg didn't look any better. Twelve hours later, we went back to the hospital for her seventh IV Levaquin.

---

108 "Levaquin is a 'broad spectrum' antibiotic, which means Levaquin is effective against a wide variety of different types of bacterial infections. Levaquin is often used to treat an infection while tests are being done to see which antibiotics are effective for treating a specific infection." "What Is Levaquin Used For?" Clinaero, last modified March 11, 2014, http://antibiotics.emedtv.com/levaquin/what-is-levaquin-used-for.html.

Thursday, March 6, 2003

I took Marcia to the ER in the morning and in the evening for her eighth and ninth IV Levaquin.

She was not in a happy mood, and I didn't help. A letter from UnitedHealthcare, requesting additional justification for the EasyStand, had been hidden on the kitchen counter for more than a week. I missed the return deadline, and we will have to pay $4,500 for the EasyStand.

Friday, March 7, 2003

Instead of having to go to the ER twice a day, Marcia began oral Levaquin today.

When I returned home at three thirty, after my CT scan to check my own medical issues, Marcia was in an okay mood. I hoped the day would be a quiet one.

I spoke to the UnitedHealthcare appeals coordinator. Although I hadn't sent the response to the request for additional information, the coordinator said she would accept any materials for another two weeks, which was kind.

Saturday, March 8, 2003

We didn't do anything today. Marcia spent the afternoon in bed with her leg raised. Kathy (Steve's spouse) called, and that cheered her up.

At nine, although I was ready to put her to bed, she said she needed to get back onto the commode because she felt she was about to defecate. After two hours, she was done. I saw that blood had leaked from her rectum.[109] I cleaned her skin. The skin around the anus was rough and dry from all the rubbing caused by the digital stimulation. I told her to wake me if she felt warm or nauseated.

She told me her chronic pain had worsened even with all the pain medication she was taking. I don't know what to do. I didn't sleep well.

Sunday, March 9, 2003

I woke Marcia at seven thirty. While she was on the commode, I could see her leg was more swollen. Recovering from the cellulitis is going to take a long time. At twelve thirty, after transferring her back to bed, I also saw she had three serious pressure ulcers that needed bandaging. Around seven fifteen in the evening, I heard her speaking to her mother on the phone. After the call, I heard her crying.

I began to reconsider my decision not to have any help on weekends even without any financial assistance from Zurich.

---

[109] Blood leakage is not serious if it is due to skin irritation around the anus or even from external hemorrhoids. However, blood leakage is serious if the leaking is from the intestines or internal hemorrhoids. If either occurs, we must rush to the ER.

Monday, March 10, 2003

First thing this morning, Rebecca's school counselor called saying, *"Rebecca is having an especially difficult day. She asked if you would please come get her."* I went to the school and picked her up. While she seemed fine to me, I was sure there was something she wasn't telling me.

Marcia was so depressed. I sat with her while on the commode. She cried and poured her heart out to me. She was angry at everything. She said she hated the condition she was in and she wanted to die. I did my best not to break down, but I hurt inside from what she was saying. I didn't know what to do, so I sat and listened. I felt so miserable for her.

Michelle came over but didn't have anything to say except that while the cellulitis had improved, we still had a long way to go. The pressure ulcers on Marcia's feet had to be closely monitored.

In the afternoon, we went to see Dr. Krauth, who gave Marcia a prescription for oral Levaquin for another seven days. I hoped this would take care of the cellulitis.

At eight in the evening, with an outside temperature of fifteen degrees, I went to CVS to purchase the Levaquin for the next day. Nancy, the CVS pharmacy technician, told me I was a saint. *No, I'm not*, I thought. *I am just afraid for Marcia.*

Tuesday, March 11, 2003

Finally, a normal day. No medical problem and no home-health-aide problems. We even ate dinner together.

Marcia still had one pressure ulcer on her leg and two on her feet. I hoped they would heal soon. The cellulitis appeared to be improving.

Wednesday, March 12, 2003

Almost another normal day, except dinner with Rebecca was challenging. I don't think Rebecca is going to be able to go to school tomorrow.

Thursday, March 13, 2003

I went to the dentist and had a new crown put on as well as the cavities in my back wisdom teeth refilled. Apparently, I have been grinding my teeth from all the stress and anxiety. I must have had six shots of Novocain.

In the evening, I transferred Marcia into bed, dressed her pressure ulcers, and made sure she was set for the night. I crawled into bed.

Friday, March 14, 2003

I stayed home today to teach Maggie the HHA how to drive the van, but the snow and ice from the previous day's storm put this on hold. Marcia was disappointed. What can I do that is right?

She was despondent. Just as her medical health was improving, her psychological health was declining.

Saturday, March 15, 2003

Before Marcia woke, I checked on her. The pressure ulcer in the gluteal crease wouldn't heal, and it had bled again. The cellulitis—while improving—was still strikingly red. It seemed to grow larger whenever she was in bed.

She stayed in bed until five in the evening. I began to get her out of bed to go out to dinner and saw that her right foot was red and swollen. By six, we were on our way to the ER. We were passed by three ambulances—not a good indication that the ER visit would be quick. When we arrived, the ER was packed. We waited until seven thirty for triage. An hour later, we were in an examination room. The doctor ordered additional IV Levaquin to begin at nine o'clock. Marcia finished the infusion at ten o'clock. The nurse told us to return in twenty-four hours. In case Marcia needed additional Levaquin, the IV was left intact on her wrist and carefully covered.

We were home by eleven, and she was asleep by eleven forty-five. I cleaned the house and was asleep by midnight.

Sunday, March 16, 2003

Before transferring Marcia to the wheelchair, I realized that because her left hand was wrapped for a possible IV Levaquin later today, the transfers were going to be especially difficult, especially without an HHA.

While transferring from her bed to the wheelchair, she fell to the floor—a terrible blunder on my part. I knew I was worn out and had a lot on my mind, but I shouldn't fail her like this.[110] I was angry at myself. It took all my strength to get her back into the wheelchair from the floor.

At eight, we returned to the ER for the second dose of IV Levaquin.

Her psychological health was poor. She was awfully unhappy tonight. I was too, and I hoped she didn't break any bones because of the fall.

---

110 Colossal Mistake #31: I am, after two years, supposed to be able to safely transfer Marcia. While mistakes happen when caring for a person who is paraplegic, blunders such as allowing a fall to the floor just cannot happen. If Zurich had been providing financial assistance, we would have had an HHA that morning.

Monday, March 17, 2003

I woke at five thirty to get an early start on the day. I reminded Rebecca to be out of bed by six o'clock and at the bus by seven.

At one o'clock that afternoon, we went to see Dr. Roaf. Marcia told the doctor about the pressure ulcers on her bottom, legs, and feet; the tendonitis in her shoulders; and the cellulitis on her leg. She had not had the urodynamics testing[111] that Dr. Roaf had requested. As always, Dr. Roaf was supportive, thoughtful, and caring.

While driving home, Marcia started crying. She saw all the places she used to be able to go but now couldn't.

We returned to the ER at eight o'clock for the third dose of IV Levaquin. While Marcia was waiting to be triaged, I went to CVS to purchase Valium. She was going to need it tonight.

The ER doctor told us he was dissatisfied with the medical care Marcia had been getting. He ordered a new set of blood cultures (negative), a new ultrasound (negative), and 500 mg of IV Levaquin.

The IV nurse had an impossible time getting the IV Levaquin to flow through the existing IV. This drove Marcia crazy. After many tries and with additional nursing help, the IV started flowing. At least Marcia didn't have to endure another IV insertion.

Before going home, this doctor told us he was not convinced the bruise was cellulitis. He strongly advised us to see Dr. Krauth as soon as possible.

Tuesday, March 18, 2003

At eleven o'clock in the morning, the physical therapist came over to give Marcia ultrasound treatment on her shoulders for the tendonitis/bursitis.

I called Dr. Krauth's office to get a referral to the infectious disease doctor who ordinarily did not see patients outside of the hospital.

Wednesday, March 19, 2003

Marcia rose early. For the second day in a row, I was able to transfer her onto the commode without letting her fall to the floor.

In the afternoon, I taught Maggie how to drive the van. This will be greatly beneficial for all of us.

Marcia was unhappy tonight. Her leg was even more swollen, so while she wanted to go to an auction where collectibles and antiques were for sale, she could not. The Iraq war had started, and there was nothing on TV that she wanted to watch.

---

111 *"Urodynamic testing or Urodynamics is a study that assesses how the bladder and urethra are performing their job of storing and releasing urine."* "Urodynamic Testing," *Wikipedia*, last modified March 11, 2014, http://en.wikipedia.org/wiki/Urodynamic_testing.

Thursday, March 20, 2003

Michelle came at eight o'clock in the morning to change Marcia's catheter.

At four fifteen, we had an appointment at Dr. Krauth's office. She had arranged for Marcia to see Dr. Michael C. Newstein,[112] a board-certified infectious disease physician, at her office. After examining her leg, he ordered an X-ray of it and her foot. When we left, I thought that an infectious disease doctor ordering an X-ray was odd.

Friday, March 21, 2003

At two thirty in the afternoon, Maggie took Marcia to the hospital for the X-rays.

At five thirty, Dr. Cohan (Dr. Krauth's partner) called me. The X-rays revealed that Marcia had multiple fractures in her right leg, near the location of the cellulitis. According to the radiologist, the fractures looked about a month old (from about the time when the cellulitis had supposedly started). Was there a connection with the cellulitis? We would know more on Monday. Until then, could anything else happen to her?

Saturday, March 22, 2003

Without my knowing, Marcia arranged for a weekend HHA, Glenda. Marcia's kindness in understanding how poorly I was doing made me feel much better.

Glenda was here from ten in the morning until two in the afternoon. During this time, I went out with Rebecca to have some fun. Of course, we had to pay this added cost for the additional HHA.

❖ ❖ ❖

Zurich, do you know what you are doing to us? Please give us some money.

❖ ❖ ❖

Monday, March 24, 2003

Early in the morning, Dr. Krauth called. She told Marcia her right leg had multiple fractures. What looked like cellulitis infection was actually a broken leg. Now I understood why Dr. Newstein had ordered an X-ray. Accurately diagnosing the broken leg took a month.

---

112 Over the next ten years, Marcia and I came to know Dr. Newstein well. Dr. Newstein's expertise in infectious disease in unparalleled. He never hurried with Marcia and always took the time to explain the medical issues to her. While many of the secondary medical conditions resulting from paraplegia can cause a substantial health decline, infections are the worst. Any open orifice can easily become infected, and if not treated quickly and well, septic shock could occur. On multiple occasions, Dr. Newstein treated Marcia for many potential septic infections. In March 2008, along with the other fine doctors at Milford Regional Medical Center, he treated her for sepsis. In December 2013, he treated her for osteomyelitis, an infection of the bone, typically resulting from a stage IV pressure ulcer, which can often result in sepsis.

Even though more than a year had passed since the crash, I learned a vital lesson: if Marcia fell or an odd bruise appeared on her leg, I needed to have X-rays done as quickly as possible.[113]

Dr. Krauth arranged for Marcia to see an orthopedic surgeon on Thursday to determine the course of action. She sent a hospital order for Marcia to have an X-ray on her left leg. She also diagnosed Marcia with osteoporosis.[114] Dr. Krauth increased her daily intake of calcium to 1,500 milligrams, and gave her a new prescription for Fosamax (to combat osteoporosis). She hoped her bones could get stronger or at least not worsen.

When we returned home, I saw that Rebecca continued to show the strain of everything and was unable to cope with life. My heart was broken.[115]

The wheelchair specialist called. He indicated that UnitedHealthcare had declined to pay for the manual wheelchair. I thought this had been taken care of months earlier—Marcia took ownership of the wheelchair in June! This was one more task I had to take care of, or we would have to pay the $2,300 ourselves.

Marcia was not doing well. My fear was that she would require a cast on one or both legs. That would be horrible. Overall, it was an awful day.

Tuesday, March 25, 2003

Before Marcia got out of bed, Michelle came with instructions on how to take care of the worsening pressure ulcer on Marcia's foot. Marcia had to be given Santyl ointment each night.

In the afternoon, I spoke to Margaret Pinkham and Carlotta Patten,[116] other fine attorneys from Brown Rudnick. I brought them up to date on Marcia's worsening medical and psychological condition. I explained our worsening financial condition and asked if Zurich had begun to explore settlement discussions.

It hadn't.

Carlotta was now the third litigation attorney from Brown Rudnick working on our case. Like Fred and Margaret, over the years to follow, she became a close friend, especially to Marcia.

---

113 Hadn't I learned this lesson already? I am such an idiot.

114 *"Osteoporosis is a progressive bone disease that is characterized by a decrease in bone mass and density which can lead to an increased risk of fracture."* "Osteoporosis," Wikipedia, last modified March 11, 2014, http://en.wikipedia.org/wiki/Osteoporosis.

115 Colossal Mistake #32: I failed to take good care of my daughter. I should have taken her to see her doctor. I should have done everything possible to help her feel better. I didn't.

116 Again, I was impressed with Brown Rudnick's litigation attorneys. Carlotta was fully up-to-speed on our case and knew exactly how to befriend Marcia. Later, Carlotta will protect Marcia through a difficult situation, cementing their relationship. I was sure Carlotta had a bright future at Brown Rudnick.

Wednesday, March 26, 2003

In the morning, Maggie took Marcia to get an X-ray on her left leg at the hospital. Fortunately, there did not appear to be any breaks, so she would get one cast on her right leg. Tomorrow, we would go to the orthopedic surgeon and would know for certain then.

Around five in the evening, the manager from Griswold called with unpleasant news. Glenda wouldn't be able to come on weekends. The HHA was not to clean where Marcia didn't go (in this case, upstairs), and Maggie would need additional help for Marcia's transfers.

I decided I had to hire our HHAs.

Dr. Krauth called with more disturbing news. Marcia's left leg was broken. I did not know how to tell Marcia. I had no idea how we would cope with two leg casts. We would find out more tomorrow when we went to the orthopedic surgeon.

When putting Marcia to bed, I saw that her tampon hadn't been replaced recently. I thoroughly cleaned the vaginal area and replaced the tampon. I carefully cleaned the worsening pressure ulcer on her ischium[117] bone and applied a precise amount of Santyl ointment on it.

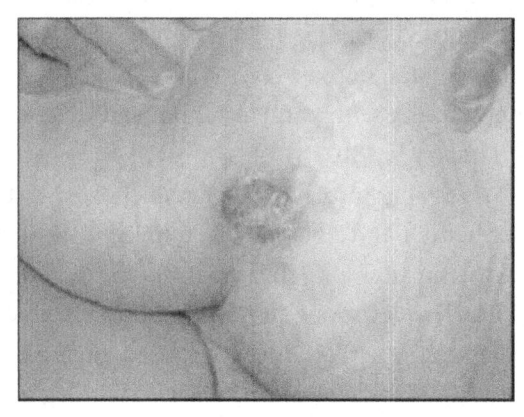

Figure 5. A stage III pressure ulcer on the ischium bone. The ischium bone is directly centered above the buttocks. The skin outside the ischium bone is thin and susceptible to pressure ulcers.

I precisely bandaged her left foot where the pressure ulcers were, and I examined the urine in the urine collection bag—it was clear, without odor. After taking her evening pills, she was asleep by nine fifteen.

---

117 "The Ischium is the curved bone making up the lower part of the pelvis. It is this part of the pelvic bone on which the body rests when sitting." For convenience in describing the whole area where a pressure ulcer could develop, pressure ulcers (such as the one shown) are called an 'ischium pressure ulcer,' instead of the much more specific 'coccyx pressure ulcer.'" "Plastic Surgery: Ischium," About.com, last modified March 11, 2014, http://plasticsurgery.about.com/od/glossary/g/Ischium.htm. For convenience in describing the whole area where a pressure ulcer could develop a pressure ulcer is called an "ischium pressure ulcer" instead of the more specific "coccyx pressure ulcer."

THE CRASH AND THE CATASTROPHIC INJURIES

I was so distressed that I couldn't get to sleep until well past midnight. What was I to do?

Thursday, March 27, 2003

I woke early to transfer Marcia onto the commode at five thirty. Her medical appointment with the orthopedist was scheduled at ten forty, which was too early.

Her current conditions included the following:
1. Left leg fractures (early February fall in shower—diagnosed March 26, 2003)
2. Right leg fractures (early February fall in shower—diagnosed March 23, 2003)
3. Osteoporosis (diagnosed mid-March 2003)
4. Tendonitis/bursitis in her shoulders (diagnosed mid-March 2003)
5. Major pressure ulcer on outer left foot (diagnosed mid-February 2003)
6. Pressure ulcer on left foot heel (diagnosed mid-February 2003)
7. Psychological stress and fatigue (diagnosed January 2003)
8. Multiple pressure ulcers on buttocks (diagnosed December 2002)
9. Stage III pressure ulcer on ischium bone (diagnosed December 2002)
10. Large but now smaller pressure ulcer on right leg (diagnosed December 2002)
11. Chronic pain (diagnosed October 4, 2002)
12. Gall bladder removal (diagnosed May 2002)
13. T-12 burst spinal fracture with paraplegia, no bladder control, and no bowel control (diagnosed January 9, 2002)

At ten forty-five, Marcia's appointment with Dr. Nicholas Mastroianni[118] began. After examining the X-rays for her left and right legs, he told her a full-length cast had to be put on her right leg. He couldn't say how long the cast would be on, but he did say that persons with paraplegia took at least twice as long to heal as persons who could use their legs. He provided a flexible knee brace for her left knee to be used during transfers.

Bottom line, Marcia had a new purple cast on her right leg and had to use a flexible brace on her left leg. She was so unhappy.

Until the leg cast was removed, two people were required for every transfer. On the weekends, transferring her would be especially grueling and risky because now I wouldn't have any assistance. Sadly, Marcia would mostly be on the commode or in bed for the next few months.

Sometime that evening, she told me she remembered that in early February, during a transfer from the commode to the wheelchair, she had fallen to the floor. I realized this fall was the true cause of her broken leg. I developed some new rules:

---

118 Dr. Mastroianni has a long history of treating thousands of patients in the Milford area. Like Dr. Crimaldi, Dr. Newstein, and Dr. Krauth, I could tell that Dr. Mastroianni had a special fondness for Marcia. She saw him many times over the next several years. Marcia and I thank him for the wonderful care he provided.

1. When Marcia fell, even lightly, we had to go straight to the ER for an X-ray.
2. I had to hire another HHA for the weekends.
3. After transferring onto the commode, she had to immediately transfer back to her bed, where she had to stay until the next day unless she had a medical appointment.
4. She should not stay too long on any one side while in bed—we had to be careful that no new pressure ulcers developed.
5. With her right leg stuck out (in the full leg cast), she had to use a hospital-like wheelchair with full leg extensions.

Upon learning all this, Marcia was incredibly miserable. Life sucked.

Friday, March 28, 2003

Because I had to go out early, I transferred Marcia onto the commode by myself. With her broken leg in a cast and the other leg in a flexible knee restraint, this transfer was complicated to the point of danger. Transferring her by myself was plain stupid. Why am I so stupid?

Complicating everything was the fact that she was on the third day of her period. She was bleeding heavily, and everything was a mess. I had an awful headache. I took two of her Percocets.

❖ ❖ ❖

Zurich, do you realize that without any monies, there will be many times that blameless victims and their families will find life unbearable to handle? Is this part of your plan?

❖ ❖ ❖

Saturday, March 29, 2003

Griswold located an additional HHA, Angie, to work weekends. Although she arrived late (she had gotten lost), she appeared capable. I hoped she would come every weekend.

After Angie left at two o'clock, Marcia took a nap. Napping during the day was a double-edged sword. While this passed the time quietly, it tended to cause Marcia to stay up later at night.

Last night was the worst for her. Her mother called at 8:00 p.m., and by 8:05 p.m., Marcia was in tears. I did not think her mother realized the harm being done when Marcia was asked to explain all her medical complications, plans, and prognoses.

I had gently asked her mother not to ask Marcia about her medical complications. I told her that whenever she wanted to know any details of the medical complications, she should talk with me instead. I suggested that when talking with Marcia, she should chat only about topics that made Marcia happy. If Marcia wanted to tell her mother about her medical complications, she would. I also asked her mother to call only before dinner. After dinner, Marcia was typically tired and could easily become upset. I had not been able to get her mother to follow any of these requests.

Linda, my therapist, told me I shouldn't insert myself into this situation. Marcia's relationship with her mother was up to her, but I couldn't help feeling that I was abandoning Marcia if I let it continue.

At seven thirty, I replaced all the bandages. The pressure ulcer on her heel was improving, but the pressure ulcer on the outer left foot was awful. It would require at least another month to heal.

Each evening around eight, Marcia expressed her depression about her life, her family, and everything. I hated to do it, but I gave her a Valium, maybe two, to calm her down. I did not know what else to do.

Sunday, March 30, 2003

This morning, while being transferred to her wheelchair, Marcia defecated. While she was being transferred from the wheelchair onto the commode, she defecated again. I cleaned and sanitized everything as best I could, but I was glad Angie was coming today.

When I returned home at two thirty, Angie had already left, and Marcia was in bed. At five o'clock, Marcia's sister and brother-in-law came over—without calling first. Their remembering Marcia was kind, but they left at six o'clock. *But please call first!* I thought.

When I changed Marcia's foot bandage at eight o'clock (it had to be done daily), she defecated. The worst part was that Angie hadn't put a brief on her. Cleaning was a chore.

I went to bed at nine o'clock but checked on Marcia at eleven fifteen. She was hot and sweaty, so I took her temperature, and it was normal. Even a mild fever was worrisome.

Monday, March 31, 2003

Marcia desperately wanted to take a shower. With the cast and flexible knee brace, she had been unable to wash herself completely in a long time. She had an appointment with Dr. Krauth at eleven thirty. With difficulty and great fear, I transferred her onto the commode at six o'clock by myself. (Again, this was so stupid.)

She was on the commode from 6:15 to 11:15, so she called Dr. Krauth and canceled the appointment. Maggie and I transferred her from the commode to her wheelchair and onto the shower bench. This type of transfer was dangerous.

With her on the shower seat, I carefully wrapped both of her legs in plastic trash bags. The left leg had a bandage from the pressure ulcer, and the right leg had the cast—because neither should get wet. She spent fifteen minutes in the shower.

After carefully drying her off, Maggie and I transferred her back to the wheelchair. This was scary because she was wet and could slip through our arms easily. She was transferred back onto the bed.

In the afternoon, we went to MetroWest Medical Center for her INR test, which came back low at 1.4. The level was not yet concerning, but the INR level had to be checked again in a week.

At eight in the evening, I changed her bandages, taking particular care of the two pressure ulcers on her left foot with Santyl ointment. I was so tired.

By hiring Angie, my plan had been to slow down during the summer while the new addition was being built. I planned to leave Marcia's daily care to Maggie and Angie. That plan had to be put on hold while Marcia recuperated one more time. I prayed that after the pressure ulcers (December, January, February), the misdiagnosed cellulitis (February, March), and the broken leg (March, April), nothing more would happen to her.

I was thankful for Angie and Maggie. They were capable HHAs without whom I couldn't have gotten through the day.

April 2003 to June 2003

Tuesday, April 1, 2003

Marcia had an important appointment with the urologist this morning. During the drive, I opened my heart to her.

"I am running on empty, with just enough energy each day to take care of you, to take care of Rebecca, to take care of me, to manage the home renovation, and to handle only the most critical interruptions during the day. Would you please try to stay as calm as possible, even when I upset you, which I know has been often lately? Could we please speak to each other quietly and politely? Could we please avoid any surprises? I promise I will do all the tasks you want, but please be patient with me. I have so much on my mind that sleeping is difficult even with the medicines, including Ambien. My right knee and my right shoulder hurt considerably from all the transfers, and now I have a constant headache."

I could tell she understood. I loved her so much.

At eleven thirty, we met with the urologist to learn about intermittent self-catheterization. The urologist explained the benefits: the incidence of urinary tract infections would significantly decrease, there was less chance of contracting sepsis, Foley catheters would never be replaced, the upper urinary tract was protected from reflux, and she would likely have a healthy feeling from being more in control of her body.

Additionally, there was the possibility of having sexual intercourse, which promoted well-being and a positive body image.[119]

Unfortunately, our having sexual intercourse was quite difficult to even discuss, let alone resume. Sadly, I just did not think we would ever again have sexual intercourse.

The urologist explained the challenges. Marcia had to self-catheterize at least five times per day and had to wake and self-catheterize during the night, when needed. If intermittent self-catheterization was not successful, she might revert to using a Foley catheter or have urostomy[120] surgery.

The urologist, who was wonderfully sympathetic, scheduled Marcia to return on April 14 for a urodynamics test in preparation for self-catheterization.

I put her to bed at 4:00 p.m. The ischium pressure ulcer hadn't healed even a small amount, and it looked awful. A skin rash had developed on her buttocks, which would

---

[119] *"For individuals with paraplegia, improved sexual function was the number 1 priority for recovery of function."* "Measurement of Sexual Functioning After Spinal Cord Injury: Preferred Instruments," National Center for Biotechnology Information, last modified March 11, 2014, http://www.ncbi.nlm.nih.gov/pmc/articles/PMC2718820.

[120] *"A urostomy is a surgical procedure which diverts the normal flow of urine from the kidneys and ureters into a specially created stoma (an opening on the surface of the abdomen). To create the stoma the surgeon will isolate a short piece of a small intestine from which he will fashion a tube or spout (known as an ileal conduit). The two ureters will be plumbed into this spout which will be brought to the surface of the abdomen. Urine will continue to pass through the stoma, completely bypassing the bladder. The bladder may or may not be removed. A urostomy is permanent."* "Urostomy," Clinimed, last modified March 11, 2014, http://www.clinimed.co.uk/Stoma-Care/Stoma-Types/Urostomy.aspx.

require close attention to avoid blisters. At eight, while she was sleeping, I carefully redressed the bandages on her foot.

Wednesday, April 2, 2003

I woke at five thirty. I liked waking early. The house was quiet, and Marcia and Rebecca were still asleep. I had a few minutes to myself.

At three thirty, Marcia had a short appointment with Dr. Clark to renew her psych prescriptions.

Although contrary to staying in bed, Marcia was happy that she was going out with Cindy tonight to go shopping.

Thursday, April 3, 2003

Rebecca was in a dejected mood this morning. Her depression, anxiety, and stress continued to be dreadful.

All I could think about was how full of life Rebecca had been. Our wonderful Rebecca, before the crash, was so happy. Before the crash, Rebecca possessed Marcia's graceful social skills as well as my analytical abilities; she was funny and smart. We had marvelous times together while she was growing up. Every Saturday, we did something together. One Saturday, when she was twelve, we stood together under the Great Dome in MIT's Barker Engineering Library. Students were scurrying about, laughing, and carrying books. I asked, *"Would you like to go to MIT for college?"* Without missing a beat, she asked, *"Is MIT the best?"* Could a father be happier? I miss that Rebecca so much.

I took Rebecca to see Dr. Merritt, who changed her prescription to something new. I hoped these medicines would be better for her.

Friday, April 4, 2003

Rebecca woke at six fifteen and began complaining of having a stomachache. She wanted to stay home from school. Her stomachache was possibly psychological, but whatever the case, I hated to see her miss classes. Nonetheless, she stayed in her room.

I spent the morning preparing the materials for Brown Rudnick. I developed a spreadsheet that showed that our out-of-pocket past, current, and future medical expenses and costs would be at least $475,000 (legally referred to as *Special Damages*).

While preparing to take a shower, Marcia fell off the commode and onto the floor even with both Maggie and me assisting. Maggie took Marcia to the ER. Fortunately, no new leg fractures were discovered.

Marcia was in bed at four o'clock and asleep by nine.

Rebecca woke at seven o'clock in the evening, and while she didn't feel well, she said she didn't need to go to the ER. She played on the computer, and I went to bed and cried. Could life get worse?

Saturday, April 5, 2003

By ten o'clock, Angie had yet to arrive. I decided to transfer Marcia onto the commode by myself, knowing that I had to be careful.

After the transfer onto the commode, I tied an ACE bandage around Marcia and the commode to prevent it from falling over. I attached her broken leg to the leg of the commode with Velcro to prevent her leg from slipping forward. She looked so pathetic.

Angie arrived at ten forty-five. She was late, but I was glad she was here. We transferred Marcia back to bed at noon. While cleaning and inspecting her, Angie found several potential pressure ulcers on her buttocks.

The pressure ulcers now include: the lower ischium pressure ulcer, which had yet to heal; a new upper ischium pressure ulcer where the epidermis skin layer had torn away; and three new blisters around the anus. These new blisters, filled with pus, would open and become full-blown pressure ulcers or heal without opening. Marcia would have to stay bedridden and remain on her side to relieve any pressure on the blisters.

Sunday, April 6, 2003

I woke Marcia at nine o'clock. She was already unhappy. She felt she did not have anything to look forward to. It was another day home alone in bed.

Again without Angie, I transferred her onto the commode. However, I was sure I did some damage to her buttocks. Angie arrived at ten o'clock and took over caring for Marcia.

I asked Rebecca to spend more time with Mom. Rebecca said that while Mom is so upset she found it difficult to be around her.

Two years ago, Marcia and Rebecca were inseparable.

After errands, I went to CVS to pick up Marcia's meds and supplies. It was $239 for everything.

When I got home, Rebecca told me Lisa and Lisa's mother, Marion, arranged to pick up the girls and take them shopping and to the movies. That was great—I was sure Rebecca and Lisa would have fun together.

Marcia slept from three to six, meaning she wouldn't be able to get back to sleep until late. Cindy called, which made Marcia a lot happier.

Monday, April 7, 2003

This afternoon, Marcia spoke to Dr. Roaf about going back into Fairlawn. I hated the idea, but going back for a few weeks might be for the best. With the pressure ulcers and broken legs (as well as how poorly I was feeling), Marcia needed care from a medical team that was larger and more qualified. Dr. Roaf told Marcia about her concern that the top edge of the cast was chafing against her leg. Dr. Roaf indicated that she would call Dr. Mastroianni.

Tuesday, April 8, 2003

Today was Rebecca's fifteenth birthday. I thought about how Rebecca would be when she turns twenty-one. I really want her to have great teenage years. But it looks like that might not happen.

This morning's transfer went okay. However, even for two people, the transfers were grueling. Effectively, I couldn't do anything until her cast came off. I had to be around the house for every transfer.

We were waiting to hear from UnitedHealthcare about Marcia going back into Fairlawn.

After picking Rebecca up at school, I took her for a medical checkup so she could become a volunteer at Milford Regional Medical Center this summer. She was looking forward to volunteering.

We didn't get home until five. I made Marcia dinner, got her into bed, rebandaged the two ischium pressure ulcers, and cleaned and carefully rebandaged her foot pressure ulcers. We ended the night with a fight. She continues to be angry all the time.

Wednesday, April 9, 2003

I woke at five forty-five with the best of intentions. As usual, I woke with a pounding headache from grinding my teeth and clenching my jaw. Lately, my left foot and left knee had been hurting from the difficult transfers.

Susan and Michelle (the VNA physical therapist and nurse, respectively) dropped by. Neither had anything special to report—Marcia still had two broken legs, tendonitis, bursitis, and multiple pressure ulcers. Maggie took Marcia for the INR blood test at MetroWest Medical Center.

Because Michelle had changed Marcia's bandage while she was here, all I had to do this evening was get her into bed, empty the urine collection bag, make her dinner, and give her meds to her. I was so worn out that Rebecca had to make her own dinner.

Thursday, April 10, 2003

Again, I woke at five forty-five. I had plenty to do this morning, including reviewing the final set of our answers to the first four interrogatories.[121] Marcia slept until seven thirty.

---

121 An interrogatory *"is a set of written questions to a party to a lawsuit asked by the opposing party as part of the pretrial discovery process. These questions must be answered in writing under oath or under penalty of perjury within a specified time."* "Interrogatories," Law.com, last modified March 11, 2014, http://dictionary.law.com/Default.aspx?selected=1005.

Maggie had to leave at eleven o'clock, and I had to go out at two o'clock for my own medical appointment. After finishing cleaning the bathroom at noon, I transferred Marcia back into bed. I gave her lunch and her meds, her pocketbook and needlepoint, her computer, and the TV remote control. She stayed there all afternoon, all evening, and all night. I knew she felt trapped.

Friday, April 11, 2003

Today, Marcia's friend Charlie came over. She was always in a much better mood when friends visited, and I need to make sure more friends visited each week. Having Charlie visit was her best therapy.

Saturday, April 12, 2003

Because Cindy was taking Marcia to get her hair cut at eleven thirty, I woke her at six o'clock and transferred her onto the commode so she would have plenty of time for her bowel program. By eight, I had given her Fosamax, transferred her onto the commode, given her breakfast and her meds, watered the plants, checked the air pressure in the wheelchair tires, checked the brakes, and checked the seat cushion.

I was glad Angie would be here at ten o'clock.

Marcia returned home at six o'clock in the evening. I transferred her into her bed at eight o'clock and gave her dinner and her meds. I changed her wet brief and replaced the bandages. Her big toe on her right foot had a new pressure ulcer that needed to be watched carefully.

Sunday, April 13, 2003

Marcia seems to have recovered from the deep depression she had been in earlier this week. I don't know how she is able to keep going. We went out to lunch and talked. Just being with her cheered me up.

I talked to her about something serious. Most nights, she fell asleep with the lights and TV on, sitting up in bed, with her needlepoint in hand. I got up each night at midnight to put away the needlepoint to prevent any sort of accident. She promised she would stop doing needlepoint after ten o'clock.

We went out for a surprise dinner with Bruce and Marion as well as Cindy and Andrew for our twentieth anniversary. We had fun.

After caring for Marcia for an hour when we came home, I didn't get into bed until eleven thirty.

Monday, April 14, 2003

I woke Marcia and Rebecca up at six o'clock. At six fifteen, I began the transfer to the commode. During the transfer, Marcia slipped, albeit gently, out of her wheelchair and onto the floor. I was so mad at myself. This shouldn't ever happen. Lifting her up onto the commode took all my strength.

She had her urodynamics test at eleven o'clock. When we returned from the urologist, I faxed the urologist's prescription order to the Milford VNA. They called and told me to purchase the intermittent catheter supplies on my own. I had hoped I could get the supplies through the VNA, because UnitedHealthcare, for some odd reason, does not pay for the intermittent self-catheterization supplies.

The rest of the day was quiet. I put Marcia into bed at six o'clock (what a life) and did everything to get her ready for sleep. By the time I was done, it was seven fifteen, and I was wiped out. I barely had the energy to make Rebecca dinner. By eight thirty, I was in bed.

Wednesday, April 16, 2003

Happy twentieth anniversary for Marcia and me. Where had the time gone?

Marcia went to the MetroWest Medical Center for another INR blood test. Sandy, a friend of ours, brought over dinner for us. That was so considerate of her.

After Michelle left a message about the self-catheterization, I realized I had messed up the order, and receiving the supplies would take a few more days.

I put Marcia to bed at eight o'clock. By nine, I was done with my chores with her.

Maybe next year would be better.

Thursday, April 17, 2003

This morning, I updated the attorneys by telephone. Marcia's current medical conditions included the following:
1. Broken right leg (treated with full leg cast)
2. Broken left leg (currently treated with a removable brace)
3. Tendinitis and bursitis in both shoulders (treated with ultrasound three times per week)
4. Pressure ulcers (treated by Milford VNA):
    - One on ischium bone—stage III
    - One on right gluteal crease—stage III
    - Two on left foot—stage III and stage II
    - One on right big toe—stage III
    - Several on buttocks—stage I
5. Mental health—anxiety, depression, bipolar (treated by LICSW)
6. Loss of bowel control (required four-hour daily bowel program)
7. Loss of bladder control (required in-dwelling Foley catheter or intermittent self-catheterization)
8. Low Functional Independence Measure (FIM) score

9. Required two aides for max transfer for all transfers
10. Weekdays—required an HHA from seven thirty in the morning to three thirty in the afternoon and from six to nine in the evenings
11. Weekends—required an HHA from ten in the morning to two in the afternoon and six to nine in the evenings
12. Transportation—required weekly transportation to and from MetroWest Medical Center to check INR ratio
13. Unable to do any physical, aquatic, or occupational therapies

Upcoming medical expenses:
1. Physical, aquatic, and other therapy at $750 per month
2. Supplies and medicines at $2,000 per month
3. HHAs at $4,000 per month
4. Medical and disability insurance at $2,700 per month Upcoming DME expenses and other one-time expenses:
1. New manual wheelchair at $4,000
2. EasyStand standing frame at $5,200
3. Powered wheelchair at $7,400
4. Van renovation for a powered wheelchair at $2,000
5. Home exercise equipment at $4,000
6. Driving lessons at $3,000
7. Home renovation at $250,000

Our net worth had decreased by more than $500,000 since the crash, with large expenses expected in the near future. Unknown expenses included the possible return to an out-of-network rehab facility, additional surgical operations (such as the removal of titanium rods from her spinal cord), new medical conditions as they developed, ongoing medical appointments, and additional doctors (endodontist, periodontist, oral surgeon, dentist, and ophthalmologist).

❖ ❖ ❖

I am so angry at Zurich.

❖ ❖ ❖

Friday, April 18, 2003

I woke at six o'clock. Maggie and I transferred Marcia onto the commode at seven thirty. She remained on the commode until twelve thirty, which was an unusually large amount of time. She didn't feel like taking a shower. Instead, Maggie and she went shopping, at great risk to her medical conditions.

Saturday, April 19, 2003

My brother Steve and his wife, Kathy, arrived late last night for a weekend visit.

I woke at five thirty to get Marcia onto the commode by six fifteen. She wanted to go out with Kathy as early as possible.

We had been unable to get any stability with the HHAs on weekends. Mary, the new weekend HHA, started today. I hoped Marcia would like her. Mary arrived at ten forty-five.

By one, Marcia was finally off the commode, washed, and dressed. Kathy and she went out for the afternoon. This time out of the house is always wonderful for her except for the likely medical problems.

Mary did a fine job, and she seemed better than average in taking care of Marcia and the house.

Steve and I went to lunch and the movies. My being with Steve, as well as Kathy's being with Marcia, was wonderful. I wish we lived closer to them.

We all went out to a pleasant dinner. When we returned home at nine o'clock, I helped Marcia get ready for bed. I was done by ten and in bed and asleep by eleven.

Having Steve and Kathy here was marvelous.

Monday, April 21, 2003

I woke at six thirty and woke Marcia shortly afterward. She wanted to begin intermittent self-catheterization today.

Maggie arrived a little late. We had some unexpected trouble transferring Marcia from her bed to the wheelchair and then onto the commode. At least we didn't drop her. We finally got her settled at eight o'clock.

The Milford VNA nurse came at ten o'clock to teach Marcia how to self-catheterize while on the commode, in bed, or in her wheelchair. The nurse removed the in-dwelling Foley catheter and said she would be back at noon to do the teaching when Marcia's bladder was fuller.

At noon, the nurse showed Marcia how to self-catheterize.

The nurse explained to Marcia that the outer labia are the externally visible portion of the vulva (the external portion of the female genitalia). Marcia had to spread open the outer labia to expose the *"external urethral orifice"* where the catheter is to be inserted.[122]

---

[122] Colossal Mistake #33: While females understand this, male readers likely won't. A female's "external urethral orifice" is tiny and therefore difficult to locate, especially when a female is paraplegic, with pressure ulcers, and two broken legs. I should have realized Marcia would not be able to self-catheterize at that time and her inability would cause distress for her. I am stupefied at how many times I do such idiotic things.

The nurse showed Marcia how to lean forward while holding a mirror between her legs so she could see her outer labia. One hand spread open the outer labia, and she used her other hand to insert the disposable catheter.

This was difficult, but perhaps all she needed was practice. I wanted her to be able to do this, but I did not want her to be upset if she couldn't. The other concern was her ability to wake during the night to self-catheterize. Many of her nighttime medicines made her very sleepy.

Rebecca and I had a helpful session with Harriet in the afternoon, although Rebecca got angry at me several times. Not having a regular mom distressed her very much.

Tuesday, April 22, 2003

I woke at six o'clock to get everything ready for the day. I had done one load of wash by seven thirty when Maggie arrived. Marcia—now without a Foley catheter—woke wet. She wasn't able to self-catheterize last night. I helped her to self-catheterize several times during the day and again before bedtime.

I thought on Thursday, with a bit of luck, she would have her cast removed, and no new cast would be put on her left leg. If that occurred, she could test the new powered wheelchair, start aquatic therapy, have easier transfers, and try to self-catheterize.

Wednesday, April 23, 2003

I woke at one o'clock in the morning to see if Marcia had been able to wake up to self-catheterize. She was already wet. I had to call the Milford VNA to figure out how to handle the evenings. She could not be wet all night every night for the rest of her life.

Maggie arrived at seven forty. With Maggie's assistance, Marcia tried to self-catheterize at nine o'clock.

Returning home at three thirty in the afternoon, it was time for her to catheterize without help. She tried but was unsuccessful at catheterizing in her wheelchair. Transferring her into and out of her bed every three hours to catheterize would be grueling. She couldn't find her urethra opening to insert the catheter.

With no in-dwelling catheter, I had to help her catheterize at seven o'clock and again at ten o'clock. I had to wake up at two o'clock in the morning as well.

Friday, April 25, 2003

Yesterday was so terrible, I couldn't write anything. Not only did Marcia not have her cast removed, but she has to have the leg cast for at least several more weeks.[123]

---

[123] A broken leg for a person who is paraplegic takes at least twice as long to heal because the person could not place any weight on the leg to help speed the healing. A calcium deficiency and osteoporosis are also likely.

In addition, her parents told her they were planning a trip to the Far East. They wouldn't be able to visit or help anytime soon. She was devastated and cried for hours. I felt awful for her.

Today we had no doctor visits. Michelle came over to check Marcia's self-catheterization and to check the ischium and feet pressure ulcers. Susan (the physical therapist) also came over. After examining the pressure ulcers, Michelle said she would bring the wound care nurse from Milford Regional Medical Center on Monday.

When I visited Marcia at ten o'clock this evening, she was crying. She was so depressed. Worse, I was powerless to do anything for her.

I checked on her again at midnight. She was wide awake. Tomorrow, she would be sleepy and cranky.

Saturday, April 26, 2003

I woke at six fifteen so Marcia could self-catheterize at seven o'clock. Because we had a medical appointment at noon, I helped Marcia by inserting the catheter. She had to learn to give herself plenty of time to self-catheterize and safely dispose of the collected urine.

Before transferring her to the commode, I inspected her pressure ulcers. The lower ischium pressure ulcer looked worse to me today—it was larger, open, and still bleeding. I hoped Michelle would know how to improve this pressure ulcer when she visited on Monday.

Mary and I transferred Marcia onto the commode at seven thirty, where she stayed until eleven thirty—a long time. Although a mess, at least she was able to self-catheterize while on the commode.

We went out at one o'clock for the afternoon. While out, I catheterized her in a private area.

We were home by five. I transferred her back to bed right away. I made dinner for her, and she watched TV for the rest of the evening.

At ten o'clock, I helped her to self-catheterize and slathered on the barrier cream, knowing that urine would leak during the night.

Sunday, April 27, 2003

I woke at six thirty to start the laundry and cleaning. At seven o'clock, I woke Marcia and assisted her in the first self-catheterization of the day. She still had trouble locating the urethra opening. Was I helping more than I should?

At seven thirty, I transferred her, by myself, onto the commode. While on the commode, urine leaked onto the floor. She has to do more frequent self-catheterizations. What a mess.

I went to see Linda (my therapist) today. Although it was helpful to talk about what was on my mind, in the end, everything was the same.

Marcia spent the day in bed. With my assistance, she did three additional catheterizations during the day. The last one was at ten o'clock at night.

I am completely worn out.

Monday, April 28, 2003

I woke at six o'clock and woke Rebecca at six ten. I began the laundry and made breakfast for Rebecca. By seven, she was out the door to catch the school bus.

For the next thirty minutes until Maggie arrived, I cried while I thought about our problems.

❖ ❖ ❖

I am so mad at Zurich American Insurance. Money from Zurich at this time would greatly help Marcia and me. Surely, there must be a legal method to prevent insurance companies from being so difficult.

❖ ❖ ❖

At seven thirty, Maggie and I transferred Marcia to the commode, where she stayed until ten thirty.

Michelle and the wound care nurse from Milford Regional Medical Center arrived at eleven o'clock. The nurse examined each pressure ulcer, carefully noting the size depth, stage, color, and other characteristics. She reiterated much of what everyone had previously said.

However, she told me something I did not know: about the Wound Care Center at Sturdy Memorial Hospital. Marcia's pressure ulcers should have been treated there from the beginning.[124] I didn't show it, but I was furious I had not been told about the wound care center.

The nurse said she would call the center to set up an appointment. Sturdy Memorial Hospital was located in Attleboro, only twenty minutes from our home.

At twelve thirty, we left for Marcia's monthly visit with Dr. Roaf. I wish I could say progress had been made since the last visit, but in reality, things were worse. Dr. Roaf was wonderful in her caring for Marcia. She determined that the urine leaking at night

---

[124] Colossal Mistake #34: I am so appalled at myself that I did not know about the wound care center at Sturdy Memorial Hospital until now. Marcia could have been being treated for the pressure ulcers much sooner and better by wound-care experts. I just don't know how I missed this.

was making the lower ischium pressure ulcer worse. She said Marcia could wake up and self-catheterize twice each night, or I could insert a Foley catheter each night before bed. Marcia chose the latter. Dr. Roaf wrote a prescription to the Milford VNA to teach me how to insert a Foley catheter. She warned me that inserting a Foley catheter was not trivial and the risk of infection was significant.

As an experiment, Marcia didn't have anything to drink after seven o'clock. At eleven thirty, before going to sleep, Marcia self-catheterized with my help.

Tuesday, April 29, 2003

I woke at five forty-five and checked on Marcia. No urine had leaked. Without any delay, I woke her to self-catheterize with my assistance. She fell back to sleep.

At eight o'clock, Maggie and I transferred her onto the commode. I noticed the leg cast had been poking into her leg. Due to the paraplegia, she couldn't feel the pain from the poking. I put some soft pads between the cast on her leg to see if this would stop the chafing (and a potential pressure ulcer). If it did not, we would have to go to Dr. Mastroianni to have the cast adjusted.

Marcia took a shower, which entailed much effort on her part. We were able to use the specially made but expensive plastic cast cover on her leg instead of trash bags.

Marcia and Maggie went out and returned home at two thirty.

At three thirty, Marcia and I began a lengthy conference call with Carlotta Patten and Adele Pollard, a registered nurse and a Life Care Planner. Adele assisted the attorneys in documenting a Life Care Plan[125] for Marcia.

After Adele left, I was furious no one had told me to have a Life Care Planner as part of Marcia's medical support system. I am sure that I would have made fewer colossal mistakes.

At seven thirty and at eleven forty-five, Marcia self-catheterized with my help. Selfishly, I didn't want to insert a Foley catheter into her each night for the rest of my life. The procedure ordinarily took an experienced nurse thirty minutes. For me, it took at least at an hour.

Wednesday, April 30, 2003

I woke at five forty-five to catheterize Marcia. Urine had leaked.

I cleaned the house and began to get ready for the day. Rebecca managed to get herself off to school at seven o'clock.

At ten o'clock, Maggie assisted Marcia with catheterization, and she took Marcia to get an INR blood test at MetroWest Medical Center. They rushed home to do the next catheterization at one o'clock.

---

125 Marcia's Life Care Plan is described in detail in Timeline Three.

At four o'clock, I helped Marcia self-catheterize. At seven thirty, I started to help her self-catheterize. She was angry at me for wanting to help, but I knew she couldn't do it without help.[126] I catheterized her again at ten thirty, while she was asleep.

Friday, May 2, 2003

I woke at one o'clock during the night to catheterize Marcia and then went back to bed. I woke again at five forty-five. Without delay, I catheterized her. Fortunately, no urine had leaked. After last night's argument and waking for the nighttime catheterizations, I didn't sleep. Almost every muscle in my body hurt. I took two Percocets.

I began the day by doing the seemingly never-ending laundry. Maggie took care of Marcia in the morning.

I catheterized Marcia at nine o'clock and then went to sleep. Before I knew it, it was three in the morning. I began to catheterize her, but urine had already leaked. I think she drank a large amount of fluid in the evening. I had to clean her and her bedding before going back to bed.

I am tired of waking up in the middle of the night and dejected about what my life had become. I knew Marcia thought the same.

Saturday, May 3, 2003

I woke at seven o'clock and catheterized Marcia while she was asleep. At seven thirty, I woke her and transferred her onto the commode by myself (how stupid!). While on the commode, she did her best to self-catheterize.

At eleven o'clock, I transferred her back to bed. Although we had plans to go out to lunch with Rebecca, after examining the new pressure ulcers, I decided Marcia should stay in bed today and tomorrow if she could stand it.

Besides the two existing pressure ulcers on her left foot (each stage II but healing) and the existing ischium (stage III, large and growing worse), a new stage I pressure ulcer had appeared above the existing ischium pressure ulcer. When urine leaked at night, the ischium pressure ulcers worsened. I thoroughly cleaned and put new bandages and creams on the pressure ulcers.

I was so tired from not sleeping the night before that I napped on and off during the day. At around six o'clock, Marcia called for me, but I didn't answer because I was asleep. When I went to see her, she was in tears. She had defecated. After an hour and a half, I had washed and cleaned her. I replaced all the bandages on the ischium pressure ulcers, replaced the brief she was wearing, and did a catheterization at eight o'clock. She was asleep before I finished.

---

126 Colossal Mistake #35: I was stupid in doing the catheterizations for Marcia. She should determine whether she could self-catheterize and whether she wanted to. All I did was make her less independent.

I napped after the last catheterization but woke again at half past midnight to do the next catheterization. I am determined not to let the ischium pressure ulcers get wet.

Sunday, May 4, 2003

I was able to get back to sleep at one thirty, but I woke at five o'clock. Marcia was dry. I did another catheterization and went back to sleep.

At seven o'clock, I transferred her to the commode. Before going back to sleep, I asked Rebecca to help. If Marcia called for anything, Rebecca had to wake me.[127] Having Rebecca involved in Marcia's care is against our rules, but I rationalized that compromises sometimes had to be made. This was one of those times. I knew I was being selfish.

I woke two hours later; Marcia didn't call for help. After two cups of coffee, I was still drained. I paid the bills, started the laundry, cleaned the house, and did other chores.

Before going to bed, with Dr. Roaf's permission, I inserted a Foley catheter, carefully making sure I took all precautions against infection so I wouldn't have to get up during the night.

Monday, May 5, 2003

Maggie was late this morning, so I emptied the urine collection bag and transferred Marcia onto the commode by myself (again, stupid of me). At least I didn't have to get up to catheterize her last night. I had so much sleep to catch up on.

The pressure ulcers continued to be serious. They could heal only with continued bed rest. Marcia spent a long time on the commode (until noon!). What an awful life for her. We transferred her back into her bed for the rest of the day and evening.

I kissed Marcia goodnight at eight o'clock and went to bed.

I cried and realized I am burned out. Marcia and Rebecca depend on me, but I am doing my job poorly. I am drained, and my body hurts all over. All I wanted to do is go away for a long time. I am shattered and exhausted.

I heard my father talking to me, and I felt so ashamed for having these thoughts.

❖ ❖ ❖

Zurich, will you please give us some money?

❖ ❖ ❖

---

[127] Colossal Mistake #36: I had been taught that Rebecca should not be involved in any part of Marcia's care until she asked to be involved. I was unfair to Rebecca to ask her to help. She had enough just being fifteen.

Tuesday, May 6, 2003

Marcia's chronic pain continued to worsen. Even with Dilaudid (a very powered opioid), her pain was relieved only for a short while. With all my research, all the letters I had written, and all the medical professionals I had spoken to, no one had any idea how to manage it. Somewhere in medical science there had to be a solution. I had to keep looking. I could not give up.

Wednesday, May 7, 2003

I spoke with Fred Pritzker yesterday. He told me that in case there is a jury trial to determine *damages*, it would be useful to have prepared an *"A Day in Marcia's Life"* video.[128]

This video would be shown so the jury members could have a firsthand, visual understanding of how Marcia's life was before the crash, and how she was now as a paraplegic, with her many acute and chronic medical complications. To prepare for filming the video, I organized a list as a guide for the film team:

1. Wake Marcia at seven thirty.
2. Transfer her immediately to her wheelchair and onto the commode.
3. Put the gait belt around her chest.
4. Move the urine collection drainage bag to the floor so the bag can't get caught during the wheelchair transfer.
5. Transfer her to her wheelchair, using the transfer board and plenty of baby powder. Due to the broken legs, she requires max transfer support, meaning she needs two people for all transfers. Have her turn on her left side, and insert the transfer board under her. One person lifts her in the rear by grabbing the gait belt under her arms; the other person lifts her legs. Together, they lift and move her to her wheelchair. One person pushes, and the other person holds her legs up to avoid skin irritation.
6. Push the wheelchair next to the commode. Carefully line up the wheelchair with the commode. Transfer her to the commode.
7. Center her onto the commode such that she has enough area to slide her hand down to the rear (for digital stimulation) but not so far forward that she might fall off.
8. Use the Velcro strap to tie her broken leg to the commode, so the broken leg does not slip forward.
9. Examine the urine for cloudiness, sediment, or odor. Empty the urine collection bag.
10. Have her take the medicines in the first of the four bags of meds that she takes during the day.

---

[128] A viewable copy of this video is available at www.theblamelessvictim.com.

11. Put a med table next to her that has wipes, gloves, and Dulcolax. Using digital stimulation, she does her bowel program, typically for four hours.
12. Give her breakfast while on the commode.

After completing the bowel program:

13. If she is not taking a shower, transfer her to her wheelchair and then to her bed.
14. If she is taking a shower, transfer her to her wheelchair and onto the shower seat. This transfer is the second most dangerous one. Cover her broken leg with the plastic leg wrap. When the shower is completed, transfer her from the shower seat into her wheelchair. This transfer is the most dangerous one. She is wet and can easily slip from your hands. Transfer her to her bed.
15. Wash her carefully.
16. Carefully inspect her body for any new pressure ulcers or skin breakdowns. Reapply any existing dressings with appropriate bandages and medicines. Reapply any ointments or other medicines.
17. Carefully slip on her brief. The brief has to be over the topper bandage and shouldn't rub against the pressure ulcer on her leg.
18. Help her dress while in bed.
19. Assist her with her arm and leg exercises.
20. Depending on the day, transfer her to the wheelchair (for a medical appointment later in the day). In any event, the amount of time she is in the wheelchair should be limited as much as possible. Transfer her back to bed.
21. Examine the urine for cloudiness, sediment, and odor. Empty the urine collection bag.
22. She does needlepoint, reads, watches television, uses the portable computer, talks with Rebecca or me, or talks on the telephone for the remainder of the afternoon.
23. Give her dinner at six o'clock.
24. She does needlepoint, reads, watches television, uses the portable computer, or talks on telephone for the remainder of the evening.
25. At ten o'clock, have her take her evening medications. Empty the urine collection bag. She may be asleep by eleven.

Saturday, May 10, 2003

Because we still hadn't received any money from Zurich, I decided that in spite of how awful I was feeling, we had to stop having HHAs on weekends.

❖ ❖ ❖

Zurich, do you know you are winning? The pressure you are putting on us is becoming unbearable. There must be a law that stops an insurance company from doing this to other blameless victims. If there isn't, there should be.

❖ ❖ ❖

Sunday, May 11, 2003

Marcia spent her second Mother's Day in bed.

Monday, May 12, 2003

After inspecting the pressure ulcers, I realized Marcia had to go to the wound care center soon. I had let this go too long. I took Rebecca to her orthodontist while Maggie took care of Marcia. I could see Maggie taking a leadership role.

I wish Marcia was in better shape to enjoy the spring and summer, do her rehab, and have some fun. Until she could get her bowel program down to three hours, get the pressure ulcers healed, and get into physical and aquatic rehabilitation at MetroWest Medical Center, she wouldn't noticeably improve.

Tuesday, May 13, 2003

I woke at six o'clock and began my chores. When I went to see Marcia, I noticed the urine collection bag was empty. Like a garden hose, the catheter tubing had become kinked. When I unkinked it, the urine flowed, so no damage had occurred. Nonetheless, not checking that urine was flowing in the tubing before I went to bed was stupid. I had to be more careful at night.[129]

Maggie took Marcia to the MetroWest Medical Center for her INR level test. At 1.2, her INR level was low. Upon returning home, she went to bed, and I made her dinner.

She had to go back onto the commode at seven thirty, and she didn't finish until eleven. With her back in bed, I replaced all the bandages and did everything else including cleaning up the bathroom. I was dead tired when I got to bed at midnight. This was a difficult day.

Thursday, May 15, 2003

By seven thirty, Marcia was on the commode, using a Magic Bullet suppository,[130] which I hoped would get her off the commode faster.

---

[129] Colossal Mistake #37: Later, I learned that what I had done was more than stupid. Letting urine back up into her bladder was medically dangerous.

[130] For more information, see http://conceptsinconfidence.com.

At ten thirty (perhaps before completing her bowel program), with Maggie and me assisting, she took a shower. I was scared while she was in the shower. She could easily fall and hurt herself.

At one fifteen, she had an appointment at the wound care center. The team was, as always, helpful. The doctor debrided each pressure ulcer to remove dead tissue (so the healthy tissue could heal), cleaned each pressure ulcer, and put ointment on each one. She was given the same basic message: keep the pressure ulcers clean and moist, keep the weight off the pressure ulcers, eat a lot of protein, and come back in two weeks.

By seven, she was in tears. This time of the evening was always horrendous: stuck in bed, fatigued, and overwhelmed with sorrow and depression. I felt utterly sad for her.

Sunday, May 18, 2003

When she woke, Rebecca complained about something important to her, and I lost my temper.[131] My inability to remain patient and loving toward her is unfair.

I checked on Marcia at midnight. She was still wearing her glasses, and the TV was blaring, but at least she was sleeping. I stayed with her for about a half-hour. She looked so peaceful and so at ease when she was asleep. Only when awake did the nightmare continue for another day.

Monday, May 19, 2003

I woke at six o'clock. Rebecca was in a good mood this morning.

In the afternoon, I received a call from the wound care center. Marcia's ischium pressure ulcers were diagnosed as being infected with MRSA.[132] MRSA was dreadful for many reasons. The wound care center gave the Milford VNA instructions on how to manage a pressure ulcer that was infected with MRSA.[133]

Wednesday, May 21, 2003

Marcia had an appointment at the wound care center at eleven thirty. I transferred her onto the commode at six thirty. Early-morning appointments are especially challenging, but the wound care doctor could see Marcia only at this time. Otherwise, we would have had to wait until next week. I managed to get her onto the commode by myself. My left shoulder, which lifted her right leg in the cast, continued to severely ache.

Appointments at the wound care center are now twice monthly. The nurses and the doctor examined Marcia's five pressure ulcers. The two large pressure ulcers on her

---

131　I should not have lost my temper. Rebecca had enough to cope with, and I should not have added to her burden.

132　"*MRSA, or Methicillin-resistant S. Aureus, is a multidrug-resistant strain that responds to practically no antibiotics developed so far.*" "Outsmarting Deadly Bacteria," WebMD, last modified March 11, 2014, http://www.webmd.com/news/20010419/outsmarting-deadly-bacteria.

133　For more information, see http://www.woundsinternational.com/pdf/content_195.pdf.

buttocks, now diagnosed with MRSA, were being treated with a special silver compound. They were going to take a while to heal.

It is seven in the evening, and I am worn out. I knew I needed to have an X-ray of my left shoulder. I hope there hasn't been any damage.

Thursday, May 22, 2003

At eleven thirty, we went to see Dr. Mastroianni. The news was bad. Marcia had to have a right-leg cast for a long time. This meant everything was put on hold: physical therapy, aquatic, occupational therapy, and the powered wheelchair. She was crestfallen.

In the afternoon, the guidance counselor from Milford High School called. Some boys (as witnessed by a teacher) had sexually harassed Rebecca. The school wanted her to file a formal complaint, but she told the guidance counselor she was afraid of reprisals.[134]

Saturday, May 24, 2003

Today is Day 500 since the crash. We had already spent or planned to spend more than $600,000. Zurich has yet to provide one cent to help Marcia, Rebecca, and me.

❖ ❖ ❖

Zurich, how will a blameless victim without financial resources return to good health? Zurich, are you allowed to do this to a blameless victim?

❖ ❖ ❖

Before going to sleep, I thought about how much I hated weekends now that I did not have HHA assistance. I hated most that I did not have the energy to be with Rebecca in the afternoons.

Thursday, May 29, 2003

Today was the first day of the filming of *"A Day in Marcia's Life."* Our attorneys told us the film would be a significant piece of evidence for the settlement or trial. The jurors had to be able to view Marcia in her new normal home life.

The film would represent a typical day: getting up, transferring to the wheelchair and onto the commode, waiting four hours for Marcia to do her bowel program, transferring back to the wheelchair, and going back to bed.

---

134 The events that transpired after the sexual harassment, although not directly relevant, confirmed again what a wonderful community Milford is. The housemaster of Milford High School, Nancy Angelini, made sure that the boys were punished for their actions and that Rebecca continued to feel safe at school. From that day on, she took a deep interest in Rebecca's psychological health. Marcia and I will be forever thankful to Nancy for the care she provided Rebecca while in school. One day we will do something special for Nancy to let her know how deep our appreciation is.

However, the filming was incredibly intrusive for Marcia.

During the filming, Michelle rebandaged her pressure ulcers and checked her skin and vitals. Maggie assisted her in dressing, helped her to eat, and took her to see Jill McAnulty. Every moment was on tape except the three additional bowel movements that Marcia had in bed. At least Maggie was here to clean up everything.

Friday, May 30, 2003

Today was the second day of filming. Because the film team wouldn't arrive until eleven fifteen, we had a normal morning.

Separately, at our attorney's request, I provided the following information for Zurich: [135]
1. Income by month, beginning 1999
2. Tax returns for 2000, 2001, and 2002
3. A schedule of Marcia's out-of-pocket medical expenses and costs since 2001
4. A schedule of Marcia's medical visits since 2001
5. A current schedule of our net worth

❖ ❖ ❖

Zurich, although we have nothing to hide, are you asking for our tax records as another tactic to pressure us into accepting a lowball settlement?

❖ ❖ ❖

Saturday, May 31, 2003

Marcia's Foley catheter leaked last night. I thought I might replace it myself. I hated dealing with the catheter due to the risk of infection, but I couldn't bear having to call the Milford VNA again. So, I replaced the catheter. I was careful to avoid doing anything that might cause a urinary tract infection.

I checked the pressure ulcers and saw more bleeding, which may have been due to her increased Coumadin this week. More important, I saw white-and-blue crusting at the edges of the lower ischium pressure ulcer. I decided not to use the silver compound and just rebandaged the ulcer. If the crusting still appeared tomorrow, I would call the Milford VNA.

Cindy G. and her husband Fred came by for an hour. That cheered up Marcia, but, as expected, she was sad after they left. She stayed in bed all day.

---

[135] We have nothing to hide. However, I never could understand the legal justification that allowed the insurance companies to receive copies of our tax returns and financial net worth. Whatever law allows this financial information to be given to the insurance companies must be changed. It's not fair.

I spent the afternoon organizing the forty-six medicines that she took each day. I made four bags for each of the next seven days. It was tedious, and I had to be careful. She hated taking these medicines and vitamins each day. The meds caused her to have an irritating, unrelenting dry mouth, and many of the meds had the side effect of weight gain, which she also hated. Even worse, the growing number of medicines caused her to feel that she was not getting better.

Tuesday, June 3, 2003

With Dr. Roaf's early appointment this afternoon, Maggie and I transferred Marcia onto the commode at six thirty.

Carlotta Patten talked with Marcia while she was on the commode about the first set of interrogatories. The questions were incredibly invasive. Not that we had anything to hide, but the lawyers asked specific questions about our marriage, personal relationship, sexual activity, individual and marriage therapies, separations, and arguments. I hate this.

❖ ❖ ❖

Zurich, why are you doing this to us?

❖ ❖ ❖

At one o'clock, Marcia saw Dr. Roaf, who talked with her about several topics. She wanted Marcia to eat more bran and prunes to help her bowel program and more protein to help heal the pressure ulcers.

Dr. Roaf also wanted her to stay off the pressure ulcers; they looked much worse since the last time she examined them. She wanted Marcia to discontinue self-catheterizing until the leg cast was removed.

Marcia told Dr. Roaf I was not doing well. Dr. Roaf was sympathetic but didn't have any new advice. Marcia's and Dr. Roaf's attention to me was wonderful.

We returned home at three thirty. Marcia transferred right away into bed and then onto her side. Situated in bed in such an odd way, she was uncomfortable where the leg cast had been placed. By six, she was in tears. I gave her a Valium, sat with her, rubbed her back, and told her I would always take care of her. She was asleep by six o'clock. I was glad she went to sleep early. I needed the break.

Thursday, June 5, 2003

Marcia was melancholy last night. She cried. Life since January 9, 2002, has been emotionally and physically painful. She was worn out. At six thirty, she was still sleeping on her side, but she looked uncomfortable.

At eleven o'clock, Michelle visited. She cleaned the pressure ulcers as well as possible. She said two of them appeared larger, and they all still required much time to heal.

Friday, June 6, 2003

I woke at six o'clock, a little later than normal, but I couldn't get out of bed.

In the afternoon, we visited MetroWest Wellness Center in Natick. The visit went well, and the facility had the equipment Marcia needed for her physical therapy. She would go back next Wednesday for an intake evaluation—a definite positive.

When we returned, I transferred her back to bed to relieve pressure on the ischium pressure ulcers. She had to rest and sleep on her side, and I had to change her position every two hours.

Sunday, June 8, 2003

By eleven in the morning, Marcia had been on the commode for more than three hours. Sitting for such a long time worsened the pressure ulcers. Finally, I transferred her back into her bed and onto her side, cleaned the pressure ulcers, and rebandaged them.

While the two larger pressure ulcers were starting to heal, the redness and soreness of the other ones meant they had to be watched carefully. She began her period, so I cleaned that up as well.

Monday, June 9, 2003

Today I took stock of our situation.

What Is Working Well
1. I am more proficient at taking care of Marcia.
2. Our weekday HHA, Maggie, is competent, caring, and reliable.
3. Cindy's and Pam's friendship help Marcia immeasurably.
4. Brown Rudnick is an excellent law firm that is deeply committed to Marcia.
5. Dr. Elizabeth Roaf is an excellent physician and physiatrist who is deeply committed to Marcia.
6. The home addition, while a lot of work, is going to be wonderful for Marcia.
7. Rebecca is mostly doing okay academically at school. The support for Rebecca from the school has been great.
8. The MetroWest Medical Center provides the exact therapy Marcia will need when her leg and pressure ulcers heal.

What Is Not Working Well
1. We have not received one penny from Zurich to help Marcia get better.

2. Our dwindling cash situation is making me nervous. We had to sell some stock, use our savings, and delve into the credit line.
3. The large out-of-pocket medical expenses and costs continue to grow.
4. The DME expenses that are not covered by insurance (alternating air mattress, powered wheelchair, and EasyStand) are a challenge to pay for.
5. Not having HHA assistance on Saturdays and Sundays makes weekends difficult to manage.
6. Marcia has many conditions that are difficult to manage.
7. Marcia's chronic pain is unrelenting and worsening.
8. The pressure ulcers are unremitting.
9. Marcia's broken leg is taking forever to heal.
10. Marcia's psychological condition is worsening; her mood swings to deep sadness and depression in the evenings make me question her future.
11. My inability to get any substantial rest is taking a physical and psychological toll.
12. My own medical issues (colon, cholesterol, sleeping, weight gain, anxiety, and my painful left shoulder) are increasingly worrying me.

Marcia and Rebecca were having a strenuous time. I encouraged Rebecca to reach out to Marcia and spend time with her, but Rebecca is overwhelmed. Marcia felt abandoned and sad.

Wednesday, June 11, 2003

While Marcia was on the commode this morning, we reviewed her answers to the first set of interrogatories from Zurich. At ten o'clock, we had a conference call with Carlotta. She did a superb job of reviewing the documents and was very thorough. She seemed to appreciate our comments.[136]

Marcia and Maggie went to the MetroWest Wellness Center for her intake evaluation.

Rebecca and I are barely getting along, and I am at a loss as to what to do. We are in a horrible family situation, but what could I expect from a fifteen-year-old girl who had lost her mother?

Thursday, June 12, 2003

Michelle visited to examine Marcia's two remaining pressure ulcers. While they looked somewhat better to me, she didn't think so. They were the same size as last week, and

---

[136] I did not understand that Marcia, Rebecca, and I would be required to answer three sets of interrogatories, sometimes twice. This was the first time I had been involved in a lawsuit, and I was struck by one thought. Since Carlo Zalewski was guilty, why did we have to relive a horrible memory that our therapists are trying diligently to get us past?

yellow slough covered one of them. Marcia did her best to be on the commode for the least amount of time and then rested in bed on her side.

I worked on the materials for the interrogatories this afternoon including the excruciating details on expenses and responses.[137]

At five o'clock, Marcia was back in bed for the evening and night.

Saturday, June 14, 2003

I woke at six thirty with a splitting headache. I that know I should be wearing my mouth guard. When I didn't, I clenched my jaw all night, resulting in the worst headache. Two Percocets and two cups of coffee later, I began to feel better.

I cleaned the house before I woke Marcia at seven thirty. I transferred her onto her wheelchair and then onto the commode. My left shoulder hurt from picking up her right leg in the cast. While she was on the commode, I cleaned her bedroom, vacuumed the first floor, did three loads of wash, made dinner, took care of the dogs, and checked her wheelchair (brakes, seat cushion, and tire pressure).

At eleven fifteen, I transferred her back to bed. I washed the bathroom floor and disinfected everything. While doing my work, I thought about how I had done this nearly every Saturday since April 2002. Without any money from Zurich, I had to be Marcia's HHA on weekends.

She spent the whole day in bed, which was difficult for her. As a treat, we had Chinese food for dinner. The fortune cookie message read, *"Nature, time, and patience are the three great healers."* It was appropriate.

At around seven o'clock, Marcia started crying, as she often did at that time. As always, I gave her a Valium and sat with her for forty-five minutes. She poured out her soul. I told her everything would get better, I would take care of her forever, and I would make her strong, mobile, and independent. By then, the Valium had kicked in, and she began to feel less sad.

Monday, June 16, 2003

I woke at two thirty in the morning and checked on Marcia. She was sound asleep and snoring. She looked so content, like the Marcia I had married. When she was in bed, you would never know she was paralyzed.

Tuesday, June 17, 2003

At one thirty, I took Marcia to see Dr. Mastroianni. Marcia had had the cast on for twelve long weeks. It was nearly impossible to remember when she didn't have it. The

---

[137] Colossal Mistake #38: While I kept reasonably good financial records (on top of everything else), had I known that these records would be required for our legal case, I would have been much more careful.

technician took X-rays of both legs from foot to hip, and then Dr. Mastroianni met with us. *"I can see that the fractures in each leg have healed somewhat,"* he said. He showed us the X-ray from a month ago and today's X-ray. *"I know that you are frustrated with how long this is taking—it's one of the awful realities of spinal cord injuries. Before leaving, your leg cast will be adjusted. Please schedule a follow-up appointment for four to six weeks."*

Marcia cried, and I asked Dr. Mastroianni to excuse us so I could talk to her. She was inconsolable.

Wednesday, June 18, 2003

Because Marcia had a wound care appointment at ten o'clock, I woke at four thirty to get her onto the commode at five o'clock. I hadn't slept particularly well. (At two o'clock in the morning, I had checked on her. The TV was still on, and she hadn't taken off her glasses. Getting back to sleep took me a while.)

The doctors at the wound care center examined the pressure ulcers. The two most serious pressure ulcers hadn't healed in any noticeable manner. We were sadly disappointed. The doctor debrided them, spread ointment, and rebandaged them. His message was the same: keep weight off the pressure ulcers, continue to care for them, watch for odd coloration that might indicate an infection (besides MRSA), and make an appointment in two weeks.

On the way home, I picked up lunch for us. We talked while we ate.

Twenty years ago, I married this girl. I promised I would always care for her. Lately, I hadn't been doing such a great job.

Thursday, June 19, 2003

I realized that for the next several months while Marcia recuperated from broken legs, pressure ulcers, and other issues, she would be just existing, not living.

Every day, she sat on the commode in the morning for four hours and then went to one or two doctors in the afternoon. Today, for example, she was on the commode at seven thirty. She transferred back to bed at eleven fifteen. Michelle visited, fixed up her pressure ulcers, fixed the Foley catheter, and examined her. Michelle noticed that the new leg cast was damaging the back of Marcia's calf. Dr. Mastroianni said to bring her to his office to have a new cast put on tomorrow.

At one thirty, Marcia went to see Jill McAnulty, her therapist. When she returned home, she went back to bed for the afternoon, evening, and night until tomorrow—as she did every day. The next day started up again.

Against this backdrop, Dr. Roaf wanted her to be in bed even more. Her day now consisted of two or three hours on the commode (any bowel accidents got cleaned up), perhaps a medical appointment, and one forty-five-minute period in her wheelchair.

Friday, June 20, 2003

Like any other day, Marcia was on the commode until eleven fifteen.

I took her to the gastroenterologist. We had to find a way to speed the bowel program if for no other reason than to relieve the weight on the pressure ulcers. She had tried bran and Citrucel to no avail.

After the commode, she took a shower. Transferring her into and out of the shower required two of us. She was so depressed when she transferred back into bed. I gave her a Valium.

At one thirty in the afternoon, Maggie took her to Dr. Mastroianni to have the cast replaced. Marcia then went back to bed.

Saturday, June 21, 2003

At seven forty-five, Marcia was on the commode. At ten thirty, she was back in bed. She had developed some new blisters around the anus, several of which looked like they could open at any time. I had the unpleasant duty of telling her she needed to stay in bed all day. She was so unhappy. I had to give her a Valium to calm her down. She said those words again: *"I feel like dying."* It was so sad.

Sunday, June 22, 2003

Happy birthday, Marcia.

I saw an article in *New Mobility* magazine about a new type of wheelchair cushion called Airpulse PK by Aquila Corp.[138] Unlike Roho Cushions, which are the most widely used seat cushions for wheelchairs, the cushion connected to an air compressor, and the air cells filled and emptied to provide automatic pressure relief (like the bed mattress). The cost was $1,500. I purchased one that day—but I would pay anything to help the pressure ulcers heal more quickly.

At two o'clock, we went to a birthday dinner for Marcia. The facility's handicapped-accessible door was locked (a clear violation of the ADA), and there were chairs blocking the wheelchair-accessible entrance (another violation). I had to go through the kitchen to get inside the door and move the stacked chairs so Marcia could get in, all the while leaving her in the rain.

We returned home at four o'clock. She spent the rest of the day and evening in bed. Rebecca and I had a small birthday party for her with cake, gifts, and cards. I think she liked it.

Thursday, June 26, 2003

Marcia stayed in bed all day today. I wanted to try this to help the pressure ulcers heal. The downside was that when she defecated, she had to be cleaned up.

---

138 For more information, see www.aquilacorp.com.

Friday, June 27, 2003

For the second day, Marcia didn't use the commode. At two o'clock, she began to get ready to go to Springfield for her oldest niece's wedding on Saturday. With extensive assistance from Maggie, we left for Springfield at four o'clock. When we pulled out of the driveway, I thought: *What if we find a problem with the hotel room?* Worrying about potential problems had become my whole life.

Many of her family members would be at the wedding. I realized Marcia was feeling pressured to act as if everything was okay. It was hard for her to be honest with family members.

Fortunately, the hotel was acceptable. I transferred her to bed at eight thirty, and she was asleep in fifteen minutes.

Saturday, June 28, 2003

At seven thirty, I transferred Marcia to the toilet. This was difficult to do in the small bathroom. She was unable to defecate. Her internal hemorrhoids flared up, so every time she tried to do digital stimulation, the area around and inside the anus bled—another complication that had to be addressed. An open wound from hemorrhoids could become infected. I learned that a portable commode would have been easier.

It took forever to get going in the morning, but we arrived at the wedding reception at one thirty in the afternoon. We missed the ceremony because Marcia was on the commode for a long time. Seeing everyone was wonderful, and having everyone see Marcia was fantastic. Clearly, she was happier when she could be sociable and not stuck in bed.

We left for home at four o'clock in the afternoon. By six fifteen, she was back in bed, where I hoped she would stay until Monday. She needed the rest. The bandages on the pressure ulcers should have been changed, but I was too exhausted.

Sunday, June 29, 2003

With the plan to have Marcia stay in bed all day, I got up at eight o'clock, much later than my normal time. At eleven o'clock, it was time to wake her. I cleaned her, but she hadn't had a bowel movement. I replaced her brief and emptied the urine collection bag, and she went back to sleep. I took four Advil—I was trying to avoid taking Percocet.

By two o'clock, she still hadn't defecated. By six o'clock, she still hadn't defecated.

At nine o'clock, she didn't look well, and her stomach appeared bloated. She asked to be transferred onto the commode. I didn't want to do this. I was being selfish, but she was obviously in distress, so off to the commode she went.

She took a suppository at nine thirty. I knew I would be up for several more hours, waiting for her to finish.

These unexpected secondary medical complications—any of which could lead to serious illness—are what most people did not understand about spinal cord injury. The issue is not that Marcia would never walk again or that she had to use a wheelchair. If having to use a wheelchair was the only obstacle after the crash, her life could still be fulfilling. The secondary complications are the real problems:

1. The pressure ulcers that could easily become infected
2. The loss of bowel control, which could be complicated by E. coli, MRSA, or C. difficile
3. The loss of bladder control, which led to yeast, fungal, urinary tract, bladder, or kidney infections
4. Inter-anus or outer-anus hemorrhoids
5. A compromised immune system, which could lead to a serious infection such as pneumonia or even sepsis
6. Osteoporosis, which caused bones to break easily and fractures to heal slowly
7. Complex regional pain syndrome (CRPS),[139] which was debilitating and virtually impossible to manage

Monday, June 30, 2003

At nine o'clock, Dr. Krauth's office called with the results of the urinalysis taken last week. Marcia was diagnosed with E. coli as well as Klebsiella pneumonia—an awful, virulent, bacterial infection that was extremely serious.

I was beyond upset. Marcia was dealing with a T-12 spinal cord injury, two pressure ulcers, a broken leg, and two bacterial infections.

---

[139] This is the first time that CRPS is referenced. CRPS (also referred to as Reflex Sympathetic Dystrophy syndrome) is a disease unto itself, not a symptom of another medical issue. CRPS is maddening. The chronic pain is excruciating, but there are no FDA-approved treatments. By far, CRPS is Marcia's worst medical nightmare.

July 2003 to October 2003

Tuesday, July 1, 2003
So much has happened in the last eighteen months. I could remember only two times when Marcia could use her legs: when we married on April 16, 1983, and when she left our home on January 9, 2002. Everything else in our twenty years together had faded.

Wednesday, July 2, 2003
Marcia and I went to Cape Cod for the night by ourselves. The choice was whether to improve her psychological health by doing something fun or have her stay in bed and let the pressure ulcers heal. I didn't know the right thing to do, but we went. The wheelchair-accessible hotel room was mediocre at best. There would have been no way for Maggie to get Marcia onto the commode or onto the bed. We had to find better accommodations on the Cape.

Being with Marcia was wonderful. We went to the movies and had dinner in bed.

Thursday, July 3, 2003
After a pleasant breakfast, we went to one of the antiques stores where Marcia had been selling some collectibles. Even though the store had handicapped parking and a ramp, she couldn't navigate the small, cluttered aisles. She was furious.

We had a long drive back from the Cape through a huge traffic jam. I worried about how long she had been sitting yesterday and today. She needed to go easy this weekend.

We returned home at around four o'clock. I transferred her into bed on her side and began my chores. I was way behind on the laundry. Around eight o'clock, I gave her her meds for the evening.

At around nine o'clock, she called me to say that she had defecated and felt like she had to go more. I cleaned her. While she was three-quarters turned on her side, I performed digital stimulation to get her bowel muscles to push out the remaining bowel movement. Even though the stool was large, I was glad that this was taken care of before she went to sleep. Sanitizing everything took some time. While doing it, I thought about how clinical I had become when dealing with these sorts of complications. A year ago, they would have freaked me out.

Friday, July 4, 2003
Although a holiday for most, today was another day for us. While Marcia didn't need to get onto the commode because of last night, she did need to take a shower and have her bandages changed. She got to sleep a little later. After her shower, she went back to bed. Tomorrow, in all likelihood, she would do the same.

Saturday, July 5, 2003

I woke three times during the night to check on Marcia. With the new plan to stay off the commode to let the pressure ulcers heal more quickly, instead of getting up at seven thirty, we all slept late. Sleeping until nine thirty was beneficial.

She wanted to go onto the commode, but I strongly suggested otherwise. When she felt the need, I told her that I would digitally stimulate her so that she could stay in bed.

Marion took Lisa and Rebecca to the mall for the afternoon. It was wonderful to see Rebecca smile when she came home.

For dinner, I picked up Chinese food. We all ate together in Marcia's bedroom.

Sunday, July 6, 2003

While I was against this, Pam took Marcia to bingo tonight. I guessed that Marcia was so miserable about being stuck in bed that she had to get out of the house. At six o'clock, Pam and I helped her dress. Pam asked me, *"This is hard work. Do you have to do this every day?"*

They returned at ten o'clock. I was exhausted from waiting up. I wanted to go to bed as soon as possible, but I couldn't leave Pam to handle things. I could see that the urine collection bag was empty. Marcia's brief was soaked. Urine was on her, her dress, and all over the wheelchair.

After transferring her into bed, I carefully washed her body and put zinc oxide everywhere to prevent a fungal infection. I cleaned and rebandaged all the pressure ulcers. I replaced the brief and straightened her bed. By eleven thirty, she was cleaned up, tucked in, and ready to sleep, but I was wide awake and in pain. I took three Advil, two Percocets, and a Valium.

I heard Rebecca crying. She didn't want to go to Florida to see her grandparents. This was something for Marcia to work out with her parents, so Rebecca and I went back downstairs, and they talked. I went to bed.

Tuesday, July 8, 2003

Last night, when I emptied the collection bag, the urine was dark and pungent. I called the Milford VNA. Michelle came over and took a clean specimen for urinalysis. I thought, *Please, dear God, let there be no infections!*

Marcia and I went see Dr. Roaf, and we discussed the following:
1. Pressure ulcers—healing
2. Bladder infections—finished taking Levaquin and amoxicillin
3. Urine test this morning—results tomorrow
4. Broken leg—slowly healing
5. Air-seating system for the wheelchair—seems like a great idea

6. Bowel program—ask the gastroenterologist about a colostomy
7. Physical therapy—goals

Dr. Roaf examined Marcia. The only new issue she added to the discussion was Marcia's weight gain. She gave Marcia a prescription for a consultation with a nutritionist. She noted that Marcia was wearing makeup and was more animated.

We returned home by five, and Marcia went straight into bed. Getting her set up took more than an hour. Afterward, I felt like I was getting sick.

Someday, we would have full-time help so I wouldn't have to be her primary caregiver. Until then, taking care of her, even though I was feeling ill, was my first priority.

❖ ❖ ❖

Zurich, today is a winning day for you. Does an ordinary person have any protection against a large insurance company?

❖ ❖ ❖

Wednesday, July 9, 2003

Marcia had another dental appointment today. Because she was taking Coumadin (which might cause extra bleeding), the dentist didn't want to do any work. We had to reschedule to allow a four-day break from Coumadin.

When we came home, Maggie and she went shopping. I argued with Marcia about going out, but she wanted to. They didn't return until six o'clock, and I was disappointed that she spent so many hours out of bed.

Friday, July 11, 2003

Before bedtime, Marcia talked to me about how I was doing. I am in awful shape. I had been trying to do better, but there were days (and weeks) when I felt the weight of the world on me.[140] I regretted that I was taking her Percocet, but I couldn't deal with going to see Dr. Krauth about my own medical problems. I am lost.

❖ ❖ ❖

Zurich, do you know that the pressure from not having the money to properly care for Marcia has become unbearable? Zurich, do you know that the divorce rate after a spinal cord injury is much greater than normal? Zurich, are you using my emotional distress to increase the pressure on us? If so, you are doing a great job.

---

140 The worst was yet to come.

Sunday, July 13, 2003

Pam came over at four thirty. At dinnertime, Pam and I were together in the kitchen and out of earshot of Marcia. I did something for the first time. I complained to Pam about everything I had to do and the expectation that I would have these duties for the next thirty years. Even as the words came out, my guilt grew. I was surprised at myself for saying such awful things.[141] I didn't sleep well that night.

Monday, July 14, 2003

I was nervous about tomorrow's appointment with Dr. Mastroianni. Considering that Marcia's leg was broken in mid-February and the first cast went on in early March, she had been doubly disabled for five months. I hoped he would be able to set an end date. If not, Marcia would be infuriated. I would too.

Tuesday, July 15, 2003

The excellent news from Dr. Mastroianni was that Marcia no longer needed to have a cast on her leg. Instead, she began wearing XP Walker Aircast Boots. Dr. Mastroianni said the boots would protect her legs from another spiral fracture.[142]

When we returned home, I called Dr. Roaf with the good news. I asked her whether Marcia would be able to transfer herself without assistance when wearing the boots. Dr. Roaf said that given the extra weight, the bulkiness of the boots, and Marcia's lack of upper-body strength, it was highly unlikely she would ever be able to self-transfer.

Wednesday, July 16, 2003

I spoke to Cindi D., Marcia's friend in Florida. She asked me if I was taking care of myself. I love Cindi, but for heaven's sake, asking this question is silly. Of course I am not! How could I possibly take care of myself when all of my energy went into Marcia and Rebecca? I was at least twenty-five pounds overweight. My hair had turned gray. I have deep worry wrinkles all over my face. My left shoulder hurt. My cholesterol was excessively high due to my lousy diet. I worried all the time about everything. I am a mess.

---

141 Colossal Mistake #39: I should never have discussed my personal issues with Marcia's friends or family members. It would put Marcia in a strenuous position if she heard about my concerns from someone else.

142 I did not realize at the time the impact that the order by Dr. Mastroianni for Marcia to always wear the Aircast XP Boots would have on Marcia's long-term legal, physical, and financial needs. With the boots, an HHA was required for all transfers for as long as Marcia wore them, which apparently would be for the rest of her life. The boots also prevented Marcia from having aquatic therapy, which was excellent physical therapy.

Thursday, July 17, 2003

Michelle came by at eleven o'clock. She agreed that the pressure ulcers were beginning to heal. I took Marcia to see Jill McAnulty, her therapist.

Carlotta Patten called and requested an update on Marcia's medical visits for the legal submission. The numbers were astounding. Since coming home, Marcia had averaged 1.08 medical visits per weekday.

Friday, July 18, 2003

The attorneys sent me the first cut of the video, *"A Day in Marcia's Life."* I cried throughout it. Seeing pictures of her before and after the crash was heart wrenching. Seeing all that she had to go through each day, as well as what Maggie and I had to do to care for her, was excruciating. Watching her transfer from her bed to her wheelchair to the commode and back to bed with a cast on her leg was unbearable. The close-ups of the pressure ulcers were painful to look at.

Saturday, July 19, 2003

So, another weekend began. I wished I had the energy to do the things to take care of myself and to have some fun, but at eight thirty in the morning, all I wanted to do was go back to bed. Nevertheless, I had endless chores besides being Marcia's weekend HHA. Sitting quietly, trying to escape myself for a few hours, without Marcia calling me every few minutes, settled me down, but I am scared for the future.

What if the settlement is not enough?

What if we have to go through years of litigation before we get any money?

What happens if Marcia and Rebecca have to give depositions and appear as witnesses in a jury trial?

What happens to Marcia if something happens to me?

What are the long-term effects on Rebecca?

Am I taking too many meds?

Is my asthma getting worse?

Is my cholesterol okay, and are there related medical problems?

Would Marcia accept a live-in HHA so I could get back to a normal life?

Would the home addition be completed so Marcia and I would be happy, or are there problems yet to find?

When would I be able to go on a vacation?

We wanted to go out for an early dinner, but Marcia stayed too long on the commode. Both of us are so unhappy. As the expression went, life sucked.

Tuesday, July 22, 2003

What is the difference between existing and living? I know that we are existing, but are we living? After a year and a half, I still grappled at every moment with how our lives were.

Marcia's days are filled with mundane activities, occasional visits from friends, doctors' appointments, and little else. My life is filled with being her full-time HHA, even when Maggie was here. Outside of changing her bandages, helping her with her tampon, emptying the urine collection bag, listening to her cry, or transferring her from one place to another, we had little opportunity to be husband and wife, mother and father.

Wednesday, July 23, 2003

Maggie and Marcia went to the MetroWest Wellness Center for unsupervised physical therapy, which is medical-speak for exercising.

Before going to bed, Marcia complained about back spasms and pain. I was reasonably confident that they resulted from exercising. Perhaps she did too much too fast. With a Valium and a Percocet, she felt better. Another day came to an end. Do we really live, or do we just exist?

Saturday, July 26, 2003

At three thirty, I transferred Marcia to her wheelchair so we could all go out to dinner. The three of us had a fun time at dinner, even though the conversation was not to my liking—girl stuff. They had a wonderful time, and that was great.

We returned home around six thirty, and I transferred Marcia into bed. She painted her birdhouses for the evening but was frustrated that every time she needed something, she had to call me.

At ten o'clock, I prepared her for bed, and I went to sleep. I woke around two o'clock to check on her. She was wide awake even after taking four Restoril.

Monday, July 28, 2003

In the morning, I called Dr. Krauth's office to get the report on Marcia's urinalysis. Unfortuantely, she reported that Marcia continued to have a UTI even after taking four different antibiotics. She ordered a new antibiotic and asked Marcia to see a urologist.

Tuesday, July 29, 2003

This morning, I did what had to be the stupidest thing since Marcia came home. I never thought I was capable of such stupidity. I asked Marcia to say *please* and *thank you* when she wanted me to do something. I wanted to be treated like a husband, not like an HHA. I didn't want to wake up twenty years from now married to someone who had not been my wife, just someone I had taken care of all that time.

As the words came out of mouth, Marcia broke down in tears, showing her depression and anger about her life and me.[143] I am a complete idiot.

While this politeness was important to me, she told me she resented having to do this. She felt that given the way her life was, I was not being reasonable to have these expectations. She was utterly depressed, so just getting through the day was all I could expect. She was perfectly correct. I am not supposed to nag her; I am supposed to love her as she is.

I told her she didn't have to do anything for me but just get better. I knew one day she would thank me for everything, but not for a long time.

Wednesday, July 30, 2003

I added up our out-of-pocket medical expenses and costs since the crash. We had already spent or planned to spend more than $650,000.

❖ ❖ ❖

Zurich, why won't you pay at least some of these expenses before a final settlement is made? How do other blameless victims who do not have financial resources survive?

❖ ❖ ❖

In the 567 days that had passed since the crash, Marcia had spent 120 days in the hospital. She had made 133 doctor visits, fourteen trips to the ER, gone to sixty-one physical therapy sessions, forty-two occupational therapy sessions, had fifty-eight nurse visits, and forty-one blood tests.

Saturday, August 2, 2003

Every other week, I check our on-hand disposable medical supplies. Today, I ordered gloves, under pads, bandages, Duoderm, tape, creams, and other supplies for a cost of $728.81. Disposable medical supplies are not reimbursable by UnitedHealthcare. In addition, they are expensive—I expect we will spend more than $9,000 each year.

Rebecca, Marcia, and I went to dinner for the second week in a row. After returning home at six thirty, I transferred Marcia into bed. While rebandaging her, I saw that the pressure ulcers were still oozing blood.

Sunday, August 3, 2003

In a good move for her psychological health, Pam took Marcia to bingo for a few hours.

---

143 Colossal Mistake #40: I should never have asked Marcia to say *please* and *thank you* for medical care that she did not want but had to have. Doing so just made her feel worse.

However, when Marcia and Pam were leaving the bingo hall, the elevator broke down. Fortunately, they were not in the elevator. The bingo organizers called the Bellingham Fire Department. The firefighters had to pick up Marcia, while in her wheelchair, and carry her up the stairs to the exit level.

To say the least, Marcia was extremely embarrassed. Pam told me Marcia cried the whole way home.

Monday, August 4, 2003
Marcia's legs had swollen and the pressure ulcers worsened from being out last night.

Thursday, August 7, 2003
Michelle was here this morning. Her observations were the same as mine: one pressure ulcer was healing, one hadn't improved, and the one on the outside of Marcia's left foot had worsened.

In the afternoon, I had a long conversation with Carlotta Patten. I expressed my concern that the "Demand Letter,"[144] which presented facts about the accident in order to persuade the insurance companies to provide adequate compensation, excluded any mention of my emotional distress as Marcia's caregiver. Carlotta explained that, while Massachusetts law provided for the injured person to be compensated for emotional distress, the law did not allow for compensation for emotional distress of family caregivers. I am sure that any normal person could see how unfair the law is. Although I was being torn apart emotionally by taking care of Marcia every day, separate from any *loss of consortium*, Zurich could use my distress to its advantage.

❖ ❖ ❖

Zurich, do you realize that this is another legal area that greatly favors you?

❖ ❖ ❖

Saturday, August 9, 2003
When I woke, I didn't want to get out of bed. The only things I could think about were coffee, antidepressants, and painkillers. I dreaded weekends. I woke knowing I had many chores to do and Marcia would be in my care the whole day and the next. I woke knowing she would likely be down in the dumps because she didn't have anything to do, and I didn't have the energy to do anything with her. All I wanted to do was to watch TV and sleep.

---

144 A copy of the "Demand Letter" and the supporting volumes, can be found at www.theblamelessvictim.com.

The morning started with a horrible chore I had been delaying for more than a year. I had to put away the clothes in our closet that Marcia could no longer wear. While doing so, I saw one of my favorite dresses of Marcia's, and I cried. Before the crash, she had a perfect figure and dressed impeccably. Even when she wasn't trying, she looked stunning. All my guy friends thought so too.

I should have given the clothes to charity, but I didn't, at least not yet.

Upstairs was her office, where she used to work and where she had on display many of her best collectibles (including a phenomenal collection of Beatles memorabilia). She had not been in this room since January 9, 2002—577 days ago. The room was exactly the way it had been on that awful day. I couldn't bring myself to remove the Mac computer she had been using or her collectibles. I couldn't even have the room cleaned and dusted.

She woke at nine thirty. By ten o'clock, she, too, felt gloomy. After emptying the urine collection bag, I transferred her onto the commode and gave her breakfast and her morning meds. After I transferred her to the wheelchair and back into bed, she became melancholy. I gave her a Valium to calm her down.

We went out for dinner for the third week in a row. Rebecca and Marcia had fun together, which was wonderful to see. We went to the mall, and we all felt better when we were doing things together outside the house.

When we returned home at seven thirty and after I transferred Marcia back into bed, she became distressed once again about having little to do, being stuck in bed, and needing me to get everything for her. It was time for another Valium.

Sunday, August 10, 2003

At two o'clock, I had a therapy session with Linda Eisenberg, my therapist. More than anyone, Linda has seen how physically and emotionally worn down I was. She reminded me that I had to find time for myself. She said I had been doing much more than anyone else would ever do in a similar situation, but if I didn't get my life in order, more troubling issues would develop. She told me, in the strongest way possible, that I had to stop taking Marcia's Percocet. I was doubtful, but the message was received.

Monday, August 11, 2003

At ten o'clock, Marcia and I had a conference call with the Brown Rudnick attorneys. We listened while the attorneys explained what we should expect as compensation for her direct medical expenses, her lifelong pain and suffering, her lifelong *emotional distress*, and the *loss of consortium* with her husband and daughter. They provided what they thought would be a likely dollar range for everything.

Marcia was devastated. The tears flowed. *"Is that all?"* she asked. *"How am I supposed to live on that amount of money for the next thirty years? Do they think that Harold will ever be able to go back to work? I am so scared. Can't you get more than that?"*

Fred Pritzker recited the facts about jury awards in similar trials. He said that people in Norfolk County, where the crash occurred, would think this amount would be more than plenty.

After the call, Marcia was enraged. All I could do was give her a Valium. I felt sorrier for her than ever. I felt sorry for Rebecca and me. I hoped the attorneys were cautiously setting our expectations low, but who knew? After Marcia was in bed, she asked, *"Harold, what are we going to do about money?"*

Today was awful.

Wednesday, August 13, 2003

For a second day in a row, Marcia had no medical appointments.

Thursday, August 14, 2003

At midafternoon, I received a package from Brown Rudnick. It included a copy of the entire submission (two large volumes) and the "Demand Letter" that had been sent to the law firm representing Zurich. The material was depressing to read. It was a day-by-day, detailed account of Marcia's life from when she was born on June 22, 1955, until July 31, 2003. I had promised her I would show everything to her, but this wasn't the best time to show her the documents.

A few days earlier, the attorneys asked me if I wanted to watch the final cut of *"A Day in Marcia's Life."* They told me the folks in their office were in tears after watching it. Given Marcia's fragile mental health and my own, I said no. They were legitimately concerned the video might put Marcia and me over the edge. Someday, I would ask for a copy, but not now.

Friday, August 15, 2003

I went two days without Percocet.

Monday, August 18, 2003

After a long day, just before I was going to transfer Marcia from the wheelchair to bed, I noticed that her right leg had a raised nodule within a bruise. I didn't know what to do. The raised nodule looked serious and was warm to the touch. Consequently, at eight forty-five, we went to the ER. After an X-ray and a blood test, the doctor said the bruise was not serious but she should follow up with Dr. Krauth. We got home at one o'clock in the morning.

Dr. Crimaldi had made me promise that I wouldn't take any chances with Marcia's health and well-being. And I won't.

Tuesday, August 19, 2003

At two o'clock, Marcia saw Dr. Roaf. The appointment was uneventful except for an evaluation of the stage III ischium pressure ulcer. It appears to have worsened, with the potential to become stage IV. Dr. Roaf told Marcia she had to stay in bed and had to sleep on her side.

Wednesday, August 20, 2003

I talked with Carlotta Patten in the morning. She told me the attorneys were continuing to take depositions in preparation for a jury trial to determine *damages*.[145] The latest depositions were with Officer Boultenhouse, the flagman on duty that awful day, and Officer Kingsbury, the investigating officer.

Thursday, August 28, 2003

At the end of the day, Marcia told me about her day. Before she started, I saw tears in her eyes. While I was with Rebecca at Milford High School, Marcia tried to open the front door to let our dogs out without asking Maggie to help—bad thing number one. She then fell from her wheelchair—bad thing number two. Moreover, then she was afraid to tell me—bad thing number three. Somehow, Maggie got her back into her wheelchair. I was so frustrated. Another leg cast would be terrible.

Friday, August 29, 2003

In the late afternoon, Marcia and I went to see Dr. Mastroianni. Sadly and most unfortunately, yesterday's fall caused a fracture in Marcia's leg, even though she had been wearing the Aircast boots. She cried inconsolably.

Instead of the Aircast walking boot, a new knee-high leg cast was put on. My guess was she would have to wear it for nine weeks. She was enormously sad the whole evening. Today was horrible.

Monday, September 1, 2003

Today is Day 600 since the crash. Zurich has yet to provide any financial assistance to Marcia. We had already spent or planned to spend more than $700,000.

❖ ❖ ❖

---

[145] For more information about the jury trial to determine damages, see Timeline Three.

Zurich, how will a blameless victim, without financial resources from you, return to good health? Zurich, do you realize we are running out of money?

❖ ❖ ❖

Friday, September 5, 2003

For the first time in a long time, Marcia, Rebecca, and I had dinner together at home. Although we ordered out for Chinese, we still had fun together. Rebecca was funny and almost silly. She was so amusing.

Wednesday, September 17, 2003

I had a command appearance before Dr. Krauth today. Apparently, Marcia called Dr. Krauth and told her I have not been doing well (stress, anxiety, chronic diarrhea, and ongoing headaches). Really, I have given up on these problems. The source of my medical problems is chronic, so what really could be done? Dr. Krauth wanted to know whether there was anything she could do for me. It was thoughtful of her to ask, but at this point, who cares? She gave me a prescription for Lexapro and a new prescription for sleeping. I wanted to ask for pain meds, but I didn't.

Marcia played mah-jongg this afternoon with Cindy, Pam, and Marion. She was cranky this evening. I did not know if it was something specific, but she had an awful evening.

Sunday, September 21, 2003

All I could think about was my legal deposition on Friday, October 3. I knew the questions would be painfully intrusive. Moreover, I knew I wouldn't be able to answer the questions as well as I should, due to how poorly I was feeling.

Marcia stayed in bed all day, feeling sad. I did my best to comfort her, but even after a Valium, she was still depressed. I went to bed at eight thirty but woke at two o'clock in the morning to check on her.

Monday, September 22, 2003

Harriet Melrose called and asked that I come with Rebecca to her appointment today. Before the appointment, Marcia and I worked on the final answers to Marcia's Life Care Plan[146] for six hours, rereading it to make sure every answer was accurate. I knew we would be closely examined on every detail.

---

146   Marcia's Life Care Plan is described in detail in Timeline Three.

Then, I went with Rebecca to see Harriet. She told me Rebecca was concerned we were not going to get enough money to take care of Mom from the lawsuit. How awful that Rebecca, just fifteen years old, had been worrying about things like that.

Tuesday, September 23, 2003

Even after a great amount of research and many telephone calls, I still had not found a medical solution to Marcia's chronic pain. She is now taking a large number of powerful pain medications including Dilaudid, Fentanyl, Lyrica, Soma, and Tegretol.[147]

Wednesday, September 24, 2003

Zurich's Life Care Planner met with Marcia today. Although I was sure it wouldn't make any difference in what the planner reported, Marcia did a fabulous job of making the planner feel her pain, from the crash until now. Marcia was the most thoughtful and cogent I had seen her since the crash.

Thursday, September 25, 2003

In the afternoon, I had a long discussion with Fred Pritzker in preparation for my deposition. I did not want to be deposed. I am so afraid I might mess up.

Friday, September 26, 2003

At lunch, I asked Marcia about the Life Care Planner's visit. She said, *"I thought the whole thing was like a nightmare. I hope there won't be any more need for this, but I am more than willing to go through it again and again if it means a bigger settlement. I do not expect you to have to be the one to provide the finances to support my living a disabled life."*

Monday, September 29, 2003

At noon, the school called. Rebecca had seen the guidance counselors and explained to them why she was upset. After Maggie picked her up, Rebecca and I had a long talk. This was what Rebecca wrote:

---

147 By the end of 2010, Marcia would be taking twenty-six pills each day to manage her chronic pain. Even so, the pain continued. In 2011, we finally found an improved treatment (although non-FDA approved) for it.

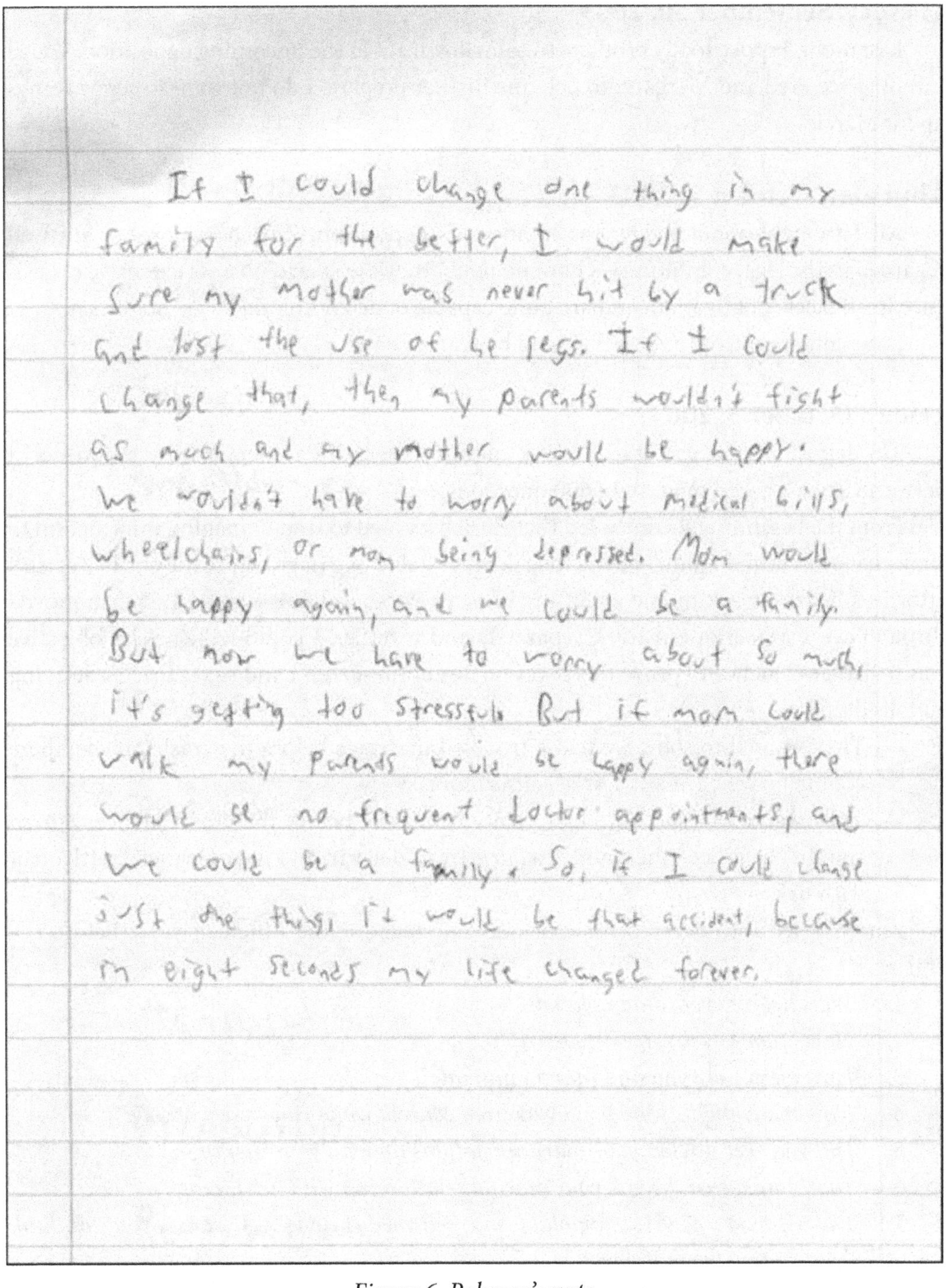

> If I could change one thing in my family for the better, I would make sure my mother was never hit by a truck and lost the use of her legs. If I could change that, then my parents wouldn't fight as much and my mother would be happy. We wouldn't have to worry about medical bills, wheelchairs, or mom being depressed. Mom would be happy again, and we could be a family. But now we have to worry about so much, it's getting too stressful. But if mom could walk my parents would be happy again, there would be no frequent doctor appointments, and we could be a family. So, if I could change just one thing, it would be that accident, because in eight seconds my life changed forever.

Figure 6. Rebecca's note.

Tuesday, September 30, 2003

Last night, I spoke to my brothers to calm down about the upcoming deposition. Today I went to see Fred and Margaret to help me further prepare. I do not want to screw things up for Marcia.

Thursday, October 2, 2003

All I thought about today was tomorrow's deposition. Zurich's attorneys are well regarded in the legal community. I have no doubt they are smart, possess extensive experience in all facets of litigation, and are quite capable of defending Zurich's interests.

I was smart enough to know I should be scared. I am.

Friday, October 3, 2003

The deposition[148] began at ten o'clock and finished at three fifteen with a few breaks in between. Zurich asked more than 600 questions.

From the beginning, I concluded that Zurich wanted to find damaging information to show that Marcia and I didn't have a long, loving, stable marriage before the crash. Zurich's attorneys began by asking me about my life, my work, and our income and then moved through every aspect of our lives, separately and together. I could tell Zurich's objective was to gather evidence to prove there was no *loss of consortium* and that Zurich's delaying actions didn't *cause* a *harm* to us.[149]

- They wanted to show we had a troubled marriage before the crash. Hence, there couldn't have been any *loss of consortium*.
- They wanted to show we had plenty of money before the crash. Hence, Zurich couldn't have been the *cause* of a *harm* by its delay in making a financial settlement with us.

Zurich pried into every crevice of our marriage for the nineteen years before the crash:

1. *"Was divorce ever contemplated?"*
2. *"How often was divorce discussed?"*
3. *"How often were you and Marcia intimate?"*
4. *"How many nights were you away from Marcia while you were working?"*
5. *"Did you ever discuss your marital relationship with your therapist?"*
6. *"Did Marcia ever discuss your marital relationship with her therapist?"*
7. *"Did Marcia's ADHD, bipolar, and self-medication ever cause you to think about ending the marriage?"*
8. *"Did you sleep in the same bedroom for the entire length of your marriage?"*

---

148 The transcript of this deposition can be found online at www.theblamelessvictim.com.
149 For brevity, a legal explanation of *harm* is not presented.

On the way home from the deposition, I had several thoughts. First, if I ever had to choose between another colonoscopy and another deposition, I would choose the colonoscopy. A colonoscopy is much less invasive and doesn't hurt nearly as much.

Second, before the deposition, I understood that our judicial system is adversarial. However, during the deposition, all I could think was there must be some ethical limits on an adversarial system based on *"zealous advocacy."*[150]

Third, I concluded that Zurich would likely ask the same questions of Marcia when she was deposed. I am deeply worried about how a deposition such as this, and trial testimony later, might set back her psychological therapy since the crash.

And that is the awful conundrum of depositions and trials. While all her health care providers have been doing their best to help her move forward, a deposition and a trial would keep her mind on the past.

❖ ❖ ❖

Zurich, are you trying to help or hinder Marcia's recovery?

❖ ❖ ❖

Tuesday, October 7, 2003

Marcia had a dental appointment at one thirty. As always, transferring her to the dental chair was formidable. We used our portable Hoyer lift.

The dentist worked to repair her teeth from the crash. When she returned to the lobby after more than two hours, she was a mess. Her teeth hurt, she was tired, and she knew there were many more dental visits yet to go. Poor thing.

Wednesday, October 15, 2003

We had an unpleasant evening. At around six thirty, Marcia became unhappy, sad, and depressed. I didn't know why, but since the crash, evenings were the worst time for her. Perhaps she was bored and tired. I gave her a Valium to calm her down.

Wednesday, October 22, 2003

At the appointment today, Dr. Krauth again increased my dosage of Lexapro. I am so depressed. I am angry at Zalewski for wrecking our lives and I am angry at Zurich for causing us financial difficulties that we shouldn't have.

---

[150] *"The zealous advocate often speaks and acts in ways that to many (people) are morally questionable, less than candid, and do not promote respect for the law in the eyes of the public."* "Ethics, Zealous Advocacy, and the Criminal Defense Attorney," lecture delivered by Robert S. Bennett (Partner, Skadden, Arps, Slate, Meagher & Flom LLP), last modified March 11, 2014, http://ww.cardozo.yu.edu/life/winter2001/bennett.

Wednesday, October 29, 2003

I took Marcia to see Dr. Mastroianni today. Unfortunately, he discovered a new displaced fracture in her left ankle (in addition to the spiral fracture in the right tibia/fibula). The fractured left ankle had to have a cast.

Marcia now has a cast on her right leg, in addition to the cast on her left foot. Again, she would require two aides for all transfers. We were both discouraged with this setback. I was so unhappy, and she had never been more depressed.

Friday, October 31, 2003

A total of 660 days have passed since the crash. This will be the final entry in my diary.

Since January 9, 2002, medical expenses exceeded $700,000, and there would be at least $150,000 of medical expenses in the next year.

I am completely overwhelmed and under psychiatric care for my depression. I have Marcia to take care of, Rebecca to take care of, UnitedHealthcare to deal with, the trial of Carlo Zalewski, the likely trial against GAF Materials Corp., Driver Logistics Services, and Carlo Zalewski, and the likely trials against Zurich and AIG.

Each day is more painful than the day before. I can just barely stand it.

TIMELINE TWO:
THE CRIMINAL TRIAL OF CARLO ZALEWSKI [151]

JANUARY 9, 2002 TO NOVEMBER 26, 2002[152]

THE EVENTS PRECEDING THE CRIMINAL TRIAL OF CARLO ZALEWSKI

Thursday, September 12, 2002

Since the crash on January 9, I had not thought much about Zalewski's criminal trial, but I did speak with the victim advocate at the Wrentham Courthouse, where the criminal trial would take place. The victim advocate told me a new, young assistant district attorney would be handling the criminal trial. I learned that after several continuances by the defense, the criminal trial had been scheduled for Tuesday, November 26, 2002, nearly eleven months after the crash.

The victim advocate asked me to speak to the Medway police officer at the courthouse. I recounted to the officer the medical issues and physical pain that Marcia had suffered as well as her difficult future. The officer was supportive and considerate. He went to all lengths to let me know they had been working on the case. He indicated that the evidence was rock solid and expected the trial to be plea-bargained.

I told the officer that our preference was to not have a trial. I didn't want to put Marcia through that.[153]

Saturday, November 20, 2002

On Wednesday, November 20, 2002, a week before the criminal trial, I met with the assistant district attorney, who said Zalewski had been charged with *"negligent*

---

151 As mentioned before, let me state that I am not an attorney, so my legal observations and conclusions may be inaccurate. For example, even this first sentence is a gross simplification.

152 A nearly complete record of the litigation documentation for Timeline Two can be found at www.theblamelessvictim.com.

153 Colossal Mistake #41: After saying this, I realized I should leave interactions with the court and police personnel to our attorneys. What I did was stupid. I should have told our attorneys that any plea bargain must include jail time.

operation of a motor vehicle." The punishment was up to two and a half years in state jail, a large fine, and a suspended or revoked driver's license. I thought that two and a half years in state jail was too large a punishment; six months would be appropriate.

The assistant district attorney indicated four potential outcomes of the criminal trial: another trial continuation, not guilty, guilty, or a plea bargain by Zalewski's *"admitting to facts sufficient for a finding of guilt,"* in which case the judge could rule *"continued without a finding."*

"Continued without a finding" means that although Zalewski was found legally guilty, if he did not violate any terms of his probation, the criminal charges against him would eventually be dismissed and expunged from his driving record.

I cringed at the idea of the judge giving a *"continued without a finding"* decision. People should know that without any time limitation, Zalewski had been found guilty of *"negligent operation of a motor vehicle,"* and his criminal actions caused catastrophic injuries to a blameless victim.

The assistant district attorney further indicated that before the criminal trial began, there would be a private meeting with the presiding judge. Zalewski's attorney and the assistant district attorney would try to informally dispose of the case.

The assistant district attorney indicated that he expected Zalewski's attorney to ask the judge to rule *"continued without a finding"* after having Zalewski *"admitting to facts sufficient for a finding of guilt."*

I thought that given the horrific facts of this case, the judge could not possibly make a decision of *"continued without a finding."* Zalewski deserved to go to jail. Other tractor-trailer drivers had to know that causing catastrophic injuries to a blameless victim in Massachusetts would be severely punished.

The Criminal Trial of Carlo Zalewski

Tuesday, November 26, 2002

So we could be at the Wrentham Court by nine o'clock, I woke Marcia at four-thirty to start her bowel program.

When we arrived, I saw Zalewski for the first time since the crash. My body shook.

The criminal trial had been assigned to Judge Thomas S. Barrett (Wrentham District Court, Massachusetts). Before the trial began, Judge Barrett met privately with John Coughlin (Zalewski's attorney) and the assistant district attorney. After the private meeting, Judge Barrett began the criminal trial.

THE COMMONWEALTH OF MASSACHUSETTS
V. CARLO ZALEWSKI
WRENTHAM, MASSACHUSETTS DISTRICT COURT
Docket No.: 0257CR0260

BEGINNING OF TRIAL TRANSCRIPT

Bailiff:

Commonwealth versus Carlo Zalewski, Docket Number 0257CR0260.

Judge Barrett:

State your name and your age, please, sir.

Defendant:

Carlo Zalewski. I am 58.

Judge Barrett:

Okay. Can I have the facts, please?

Assistant District Attorney:

Yes, your Honor. Summarizing from a Medway Police Department Report and the State Police Reconstruction Report, your honor, on the, uh, on the 9th day of January of last year at approximately 1:12 p.m., officers at the Medway Police Department were summoned to a motor vehicle accident on Route 109, a public way, in the Town of Medway, Massachusetts.

When they arrived they saw a 1997 Toyota Corolla bearing Mass. Registration 787 ELO. Uh, it was off the road into the woods down an embankment.

It took half an hour to remove the victim in that car to an ambulance to Milford Hospital. She was later transported to UMass Medical Hospital.

What had occurred, uh, there was some tree stump grinding going on the side of the road and, a, officers of the Medway Police was directing traffic. Uh, they were stopping traffic one way and allowing traffic to go. Uh, Sergeant Boultenhouse was directing traffic.

While he had stopped traffic eastbound, specifically the Toyota, uh, that I mentioned previously, he was looking westbound and he heard a crash. Looking over, he saw a tractor-trailer unit pushing the blue Toyota toward where he was standing. He ran into the woods to avoid being struck. Uh, he stated the tractor-trailer unit pushed the Toyota into the woods and that it went down the side of the embankment and came and hit a tree.

Uh, Officer Kingsbury interviewed the driver. The driver stated he thought, as he, he stated that he thought that he was driving eastbound on Milford Street; his attention was diverted to a prior vehicle that had pulled out of Trotter Drive and had proceeded westbound.

He stated he thought this vehicle was too close, was driving too close to his truck so he was watching it in the side view mirror, not watching was in front of him. He stated that when he turned his attention back before him, he saw the Toyota had stopped in front of him, but was unable to stop, striking the Toyota. He would not elaborate any further.

Uh, Trooper Jaworek conducted an investigation of the tractor-trailer unit. Uh, he found a number of administrative violations and one inoperative brake. Trooper Jaworek, according to Trooper Jaworek, this brake, one of ten brakes, would not be a factor in the accident. Trooper Jaworek concluded the condition of tractor-trailer in no way contributed to the accident, which appeared to be, which appeared to be caused by driver error.

Your Honor, uh, one final part I would like to add is that in, uh, as a result of the Trooper's reconstruction, uh, uh, it was the opinion of the reconstruction expert that driver inattention or driver distraction on the part of Mr. Zalewski was a factor in this collision, is based on the opinion that the skid mark of vehicle one, which was the tractor-trailer, uh, did not, vehicle one did not lock its brakes until impact or after impact of the vehicle two.

These are essentially the facts that the Commonwealth would prove if this went to trial, your Honor.

<u>Judge Barrett</u>:
I understand the Commonwealth is requesting a guilty, uh, with probation. Um, the defendant, uh, is requesting a continuance without a finding. Um, and, is it my understanding that, uh, this defendant has no record at all? That is what I...

<u>Assistant District Attorney</u>:
I think it is right on your right-hand side, your Honor.

<u>Judge Barrett:</u>

Uh, that is okay, I have got it here. Thank you. Alright, nothing with respect to. Okay. Alright. There is no, there is no record, um, except for this offense. I'll be happy to hear from Mrs. Rhodes.

<u>Marcia Rhodes:</u>

I cannot see how a piece of paper I wrote yesterday is going to really impact how I feel, but I'll try.

Good morning your honor. I want to begin by apologizing by having to read this statement, but there is so much I want to say, and given how I am feeling right now, I'm not sure I can get the words out.

It is always sad and disheartening when a major turning point in a person's life becomes a negative thing, and all the more upsetting if the negative change was through the negligence of another person.

I am sure that in the many years that you have been a judge, you have heard many very, very sad victim impact statements, from ordinary people, just like me. I'm sure that you've heard horrific accounts of what has happened to people just like me, as well as to our families, after negligent truck drivers, like Carlo Zalewski, fail in their driving responsibilities and cause untold tragedies to occur.

It's hard for me to imagine that anything that I am about to say will be much different from the nightmarish descriptions others have already told you, except that, what has happened because of carelessness of Carlo Zalewski, has happened to me, and to my husband, and to my daughter. So, please be patient with me while I describe for you how this truck driver's awful neglect has changed my life, not just for a few days, not for a few months, not even a few years, but for the rest of my life.

In the interest of clarity, I have broken my victim impact statement into three different areas; my life before the accident, my life as a direct result of the accident, and a typical day in my life now 11 months after the accident.

Before this accident, my life was a series of typical days filled with household chores, chauffeuring my daughter Rebecca, who was 13 at the time and working on my antiques and collectible business. I can play Mah Jongg or Bingo, attend trade shows, auctions and estate sales, as well as place my inventory out in eight different stores. I enjoyed an intimate and joyful relationship with my husband Harold, and a close loving relationship with my daughter, including all the things mothers and daughters like to do.

Before Carlo Zalewski crashed into my car on January 9, 2002, Harold, Rebecca, and I had what most people would describe as a very happy and wonderful life. We have lived in Milford for 18 years. I had my own antique and collectibles business, selling collectibles in stores all over Massachusetts.

As the district attorney said, on January 9, 2002, I was in my car, at a complete stop, on Route 109, near the Medway border, at the direction of the flagman, Officer Boultenhouse, who was directing traffic around some street work. There were no cars behind me. I was patiently waiting for the signal from Officer Boultenhouse to proceed.

Then came the horrendous crash when I was rear-ended by Mr. Zalewski's semi tractor/trailer carrying what I later learned to be 80,000 pounds of tar.

My life-altering account of the events of January 9th through the end of January is sketchy at best. I have read the front page article from the Milford News, but only one time, two days ago, and then only in preparation for this case.

I do not remember being rushed to the Milford-Whitinsville Hospital's emergency room, nor do I remember the transfer to the trauma unit at UMass Memorial Hospital. In fact, I don't remember anything of the first month it took the doctors and nurses to stabilize me, prepare me for surgery, undergo surgery, where I was treated for a T-12 spinal fracture, blood edemas, and multiple fractured ribs.

Later I learned that I was transferred to the surgical unit at UMass Memorial Hospital, where I underwent major spinal cord surgery, what the surgeon's call a T-12 spinal fusion. At the same time, I had two titanium rods inserted in my back along my spine.

When I finally awoke from all of the sedatives and painkillers after the surgery, my husband told me that I was paralyzed, that I would never walk again, and that I would be in this wheelchair for the rest of my life. Later my husband told me that, when he had to tell me that I was paralyzed for life, that this was the saddest moment of his life. The second saddest moment of his life was having to tell Rebecca that I was paralyzed.

Now I do know that I have two titanium rods in my back, which cause incessant pain and I also know about the filter near my heart, placed there in the event of re-occurring blood clots.

I don't even remember the first blood clot, but the second, which was in my left leg, was something that I will never forget. For the first five months of my recovery my left leg was so swollen, it took two people to lift it when I was transferred into my therapeutic wheelchair. This and the persistent bacterial infections were just two of the primary reasons my recovery was moving depressingly slow.

And one memory I'll always have from both UMass Memorial Hospital and Fairlawn Rehabilitation were the never ending blood samples being drawn to monitor my progress. At this point in time my arms are so scared that blood cannot be drawn from them.

When I finally got word that I was to be transferred to a rehabilitation center I wasn't scared because I knew nothing else can possibly be worse than those last three weeks in UMass Memorial Hospital. In many ways I was wrong, but I thought that I was now finally approaching a forward process toward recovery, not maintaining one.

But for six of the nine weeks I was in Fairlawn Rehabilitation Center I was in isolation due to multiple infections. This, plus my broken ribs and the enormous weight of my swollen left leg hindered any real physical or occupational therapy. People who visited me had to wear gowns, gloves, and masks. And whenever I was not in bed, I had to wear a TLSO rib chest protector which resembled a giant white tortoise shell.

Additionally, because of the negligence of Carlo Zalewski, I have had many other serious medical conditions develop, including a complete loss of bowel control, a complete loss of bladder control, a major staph infection, emergency gall-bladder surgery, pressure sores, a head edema, two blood clots, as well a yet-to-be resolved enlarged uterus. And, because of the trauma, I did not have my menstrual period for 9 months.

In total, I spent 31 days at UMass Memorial Hospital, 17 of which in the intensive care unit. You cannot even imagine the pain, the anguish, the emotional turmoil that I went through while at the hospital. Each day, as new medical conditions developed and the realization of my paraplegia grew, I hated each new day.

I then spent 66 days at Fairlawn Rehabilitation Hospital. Unfortunately, for the first 30 days, due to my MRSA infection, I was confined to my room. People who visited me had to wear gowns, gloves, and masks. I cannot do any substantive therapy at all. It was just miserable.

On last April 16th, I went home. I vividly remember this first day as if it were yesterday. When I got home into the hospital bed, it was obvious that I had done a bowel movement. My husband was completely unprepared for this; I remembered he turned white and just began to cry. I had never seen my husband so distraught, so unable to care for me. Inside, I felt like dying. How can I do this to my husband?

From April 16 until May 23, I have endured countless visits to many doctors and I have had many, many occupational, physical, and emotional therapy sessions.

Then, on May 23rd, I woke up in excruciating pain; my husband rushed me to the Emergency Room at Milford Hospital.

The next day, I had my gall-bladder removed. At the risk of sounding too melodramatic, had my back fracture been anything higher than a level T-12 break, I would not have felt the pain caused by the gangrene gall bladder and most probably would have died; those are the doctors' opinions, not mine, although I don't disagree.

I spent one week in the Milford hospital and then another two weeks at Whittier Rehabilitation Center. Finally, at the end of the third week, I was released and came home. But within a matter of weeks, I faced another major set-back.

I had developed both bursitis and tendonitis in both arms and shoulders. All physical and occupational therapy was suspended while I received several weeks of ultra-sound treatments. It wasn't until mid-July that I can finally get down to the matter of day to day living.

When I did return home, again, I had to endure even more doctor's visits, and even more occupational, physical, and emotional therapy sessions. The physical therapy took such a toll on me that I again developed very painful bursitis and tendonitis in my shoulders and arms.

I was determined to learn how to control my bowel movements. In the interest of court decorum, I won't describe how this is done, but let me say that this was, without a doubt, what I thought would be the single most personally humiliating thing that a wife must do with her husband. It is just disgusting, but I must do this every day.

I must go everywhere with a Foley catheter to hold my urine, as I do not have bladder control; this too is very humiliating. And, I have had my blood drawn so many times that I have scar tissue on the inside of my elbows.

As the weeks passed I received messages of good cheer, visitors, friends and most of all family, but I nonetheless slowly sank into a profound depression. It does not help to tell someone who is depressed that they should cheer up, that the feeling will go away, that things will get better or my personal favorite; I was lucky, things can have been worse.

People want to see you trying and want to see a stiff upper lip. Obviously these are people who have never had their lives up-ended by a debilitating physical injury.

Now, on a typical day, and solely due to the negligence on the part of the defendant Mr. Zalewski, every minute of every day has to be carefully planned for, carried out, and/or compromised.

I have a home care aid come into the house to wake me up at 8:00 a.m. She helps me out of my Air Cushioned Hospital Bed. The air cushions are there to prevent skin breakdowns, which are common to quad and paraplegics and can become a serious life threatening condition.

My care aid helps me transfer to a specially sized special order wheelchair, again with a special air cushion for dermatological reasons.

My aide then wheels me into the bathroom, where I transfer on to a padded commode and start a bowel program that I prefer not to get into specifics on, but suffice to say it takes at least 4 hours every morning. This is also when my catheter, which I must now wear every minute of every day, is emptied.

I then transfer back into the wheelchair and then transfer into a specially modeled shower that a paraplegic needs. At this point I want to tell you that somehow, in the months that followed my continuing hospital recovery, my wonderful husband managed to have the house remodeled for a paraplegic, raise our wonderful daughter Rebecca, and still tend to my physical and emotional needs.

And at the risk of digressing even further, I want to briefly touch on the subject of remodeling and how much is really involved. Tonight, as you walk through the first floor of your house, pretend you are doing it from a wheelchair / sitting position.

The sheer number of changes that have to be made to accommodate you in a wheelchair are staggering. And that presumes you aren't using the second floor or basement. Quite frankly, the up-front cost of becoming disabled is staggering.

I don't know how the less fortunate newly paralyzed victim can afford it. I've been lucky in that my wonderful husband has managed to afford to pay for the $450 wheel chair cushion, or the $350 transfer board I need to get from the bed to the wheelchair or any other seat in the house. Most people can't even dream of these 'luxuries,' which are really necessities.

But back to my typical day. After I shower, which is a very scary, I transfer back into the chair and then back into bed so my caregiver can look over my body for any skin abrasions, cuts, or bruises; this is quite an intrusive experience.

Then the caregiver puts on my 'Depends,' which are really adult diapers which I need since I still require a full-time catheter and can do a bowel movement at any time. My caregiver then helps me get the special stockings on that I must wear to tone my now unusable leg muscles and to facilitate blood circulation.

By the time I am fully clothed and back in my wheelchair it is usually around 1:00 p.m.; and the whole morning has been lost.

My caregiver has to get me lunch, since my husband and I haven't had the chance to remodel the kitchen for my use. The time between 1:00 and 3:30 is usually filled with medical appointments. Before this accident I had a wonderful General Physician and Dentist whom I saw twice yearly.

Today, I have a spinal cord specialist, physiatrist, a urologist, a dermatologist, the use of different medical labs, a radiologist, a psychologist, an endodontic specialist, and a new OB-GYN, since my previous one was unable to handle the needs of a patient in a wheelchair.

I see a Physical Therapist and an Occupational Therapist as well as also have the frequent body fluid tests, x-rays and other forms of radiation tests.

We have been fortunate in one area. Again, solely through the efforts of my loving husband, we've been able to by an electric bike for muscle stimulation, an electric wheelchair, which was prescribed because of my tendonitis and bursitis and have purchased an Easy-Stand that lets me stand in place for short periods.

Of course, we are talking thousands of dollars here. I can't begin to guess how the typical American can afford everything that's needed.

Before the accident, I'd always used the time after dinner and before bed to do things with my family or work on my business. Now I find myself with a lot of wasted time sitting in bed and, even worse it now takes a long time to fall asleep, even with medications.

From the moment I awake until I am put into bed, I am being monitored by someone. My care aid, family members, or friends. I very rarely find myself alone, which for me is one of the most devastating results of this accident.

I have always been the person who helped others out. Now, I suddenly find that I have to rely on others...and I hate it. I'm also the type of person who does not like to be the center of attention... but now I am because of this damn wheelchair and I hate it.

Before all this, others relied on me; now I must rely on others for getting me the simplest of things, or helping me do what I had always done for myself.

Before this accident, I was one of the lucky few who actually loved their work. As a dealer of antiques and collectibles much of my work was leg work, requiring me to go to estate sales, auctions, yard sales, and flea markets as well as trade shows.

I've had to give-up running my business as I did. Most stores are not wheelchair accessible, as they were built before ADA laws were passed. I dread every upcoming doctor's visit and medical test, which requires hours of preparation just to go out to and return from.

There is so much more I can say about what the negligence, the carelessness, and the imprudence of Carlo Zalewski has done to me. But, I want to also mention what Carlo Zalewski has done to my husband and daughter.

My husband is a wonderful man. From the moment of this accident, I know he has tried in every way to take care of me and to make my life worth living. He has done so many things for me while I have tried to recuperate.

He has dealt with our home remodeling, so that there would be a place for me to sleep and a disabled-accessible bathroom for me. He has dealt with insurance companies, medical personnel, legal matters, transportation, daily living issues, and so much more.

Every day, he tries to make my life easier.

But this tragedy has taken an extreme toll on him as well. First, he had to stop working; the loss of income has been substantial. Caring for me has been his full-time job.

Second, our friends and family have told me how much lack of joy there is in him now. My husband used to be the most positive, the most happy, the most loving person that I knew. Now, he, like me, struggles so hard just to find some small happiness each day.

More days than not, my husband just does his best to get through the day without getting angry and without being in pain. He is my husband and I will love him forever, but I worry about him so much. This is just so unfair to him. Carlo Zalewski has taken away my husband's joy for life.

A moment ago I mentioned what I thought was the second most personally humiliating situation. Now let me tell you what really was the most humiliating situation.

Just two weeks ago, very unexpectedly, I began menstruation again. Not at all prepared for this, my husband had to clean me up, as I cannot take care of myself. I cannot tell you how awful this was for me or for my husband; my husband had to insert the Tampax into my vagina.

Our daughter Rebecca, now 14 years and in high school, is perhaps the person who is at most risk of falling into a deep depression for a long period of her life. While she is in therapy, there is no escaping that her mom is handicapped and needs her in a way that a young child should not have to deal with.

Very unfortunately, Rebecca and I can no longer do the things together that we used to do; this disruption in our life together makes me very, very sad. I can only hope that over time, Rebecca can accept me as disabled, and to become the best person she can.

Perhaps one of the most significant changes are the ones my daughter has had to go through. She suddenly had to grow up to face and deal with something that you hope no one you love ever has to face.

Before the accident, Becca and I used to go down to the Cape, just us girls, and stay for two or three days, going to arcades, flea markets, antiquing, or just shopping at the Mall. I can't do any of these things alone with my daughter anymore. All the spontaneity we had to do fun things are now chores.

We need a ride, we need special hotel facilities, we need ramps, and we need arcade machines I can reach from a wheelchair. Shopping is a major exercise instead of a relaxing diversion. This is particularly true of our Saturday Yard sales throughout the Spring, Summer, and Fall seasons and I am particularly dreading winter.

Between the cold, ice, snow and the other typical New England conditions, I don't see much of a chance to venture outdoors in a wheelchair, with the exception of the endless doctor's appointments. There really is no place for me to go. Most of my friends' homes are not wheelchair friendly.

My life now has no spontaneity, no privacy, no intimacy with my husband, and no long-term foreseeable medical improvements in my condition. These are the things the Zalewski has cost me.

Going forward, I am completely dependent on others for nearly everything I need. I now require a home-health aide for eight hours each day to bathe me, to dress me, and to drive me.

I average 10 to 15 doctor's appointments each month for physical therapy, occupational therapy, gynecology, physiatry, orthopedics, blood tests, psycho-therapy, and others. Each night, my husband has to put me to bed, because I cannot even do this myself.

Your Honor, I know that I may sometime in the future learn how to manage my medical and hopefully my emotional problems. I may even learn how to be a paraplegic.

But, one thing that will never change, is that that man—Carlo Zalewski—because of his negligence, his carelessness, his imprudence—he has put me in this wheelchair and because of him, I will never walk again. Please find him guilty, because he is."

<u>Assistant District Attorney:</u>
Your Honor, given the profound impact this accident has had on the victim, the victim's family, her way of life, and, uh, given the facts in the case, the Commonwealth would ask that you return a verdict of guilty with conditions attached for any kind of < >, your Honor.

<u>Judge Barrett:</u>

These cases are always tough. This defendant made a mistake. We all make mistakes.

This mistake cost somebody so very much. And if there was anything I can do to go back to that day to reverse what has happened, I would certainly do that. I would not be bashful about not just imposing a guilty finding but incarcerating this individual if I thought that would somehow give you, Ms. Rhodes, back your mobility.

But, this is a criminal court.

There is nothing I can do here to give you back what you lost.

This gentleman, no matter what happens here today, is going to live with this for the rest of his life. I am sure there is not anything I can do to make it worse for him and I do not know that is really what the administration of justice is all about.

You know, he made a mistake. It was a terrible mistake. It maybe was a split-second mistake.

God knows we all make them.

I am going to continue the matter without a finding for two years.

I am going to require that he, uh, he pay $250 in court costs, that he do a, uh, some driver training, re-training. I do not know whether he will ever drive a truck again, whether or not he'll ever be capable or desire to do that, but some training certainly wouldn't hurt if he ever decides that he's inclined to want to drive a truck again.

Beyond that, there is not much I can do here. There is the civil side which will proceed, and hopefully will compensate you in some small way for what you have suffered. I cannot do that here. Okay.

<u>Bailiff:</u>
Mr. Zalewski in this matter, Docket Number 0257CR0260, on the charge of negligent operation of a motor vehicle, the matter is 'Continued Without a Finding'[154] for two years to November 25, 2004, $125 head injury assessment, $250 court costs, $50 to the Victim and Witness Fund, and you must successfully complete a driver training course for the Probation Department. Um, sir, how much time do you need to make that payment of $425?

---

154 Colossal Mistake #42: After the trial, the thought that I did not do all I could have to prevent Zalewski from harming another blameless victim caused me considerable pain. For the sake of convenience, I went along with the *"continued without a finding"* decision. I let myself, Marcia, and all future blameless victims down. Twelve years later, I still feel this distress.

<u>Judge Barrett:</u>

And, you are going to be on probation for two years. Alright. What you're saying to the Court is, listen, there are sufficient facts out there that if the Court, and if the Court believes them, I can impose a guilty finding based on what I have heard here today, and I can. Okay. I am not doing it, but I can. You are on probation for two years. If you violate probation, sir, you cannot come back and say now I want to try this case because I want to get a not guilty.

Okay, and you should also understand if you are found in violation of probation, some other judge at some other hearing can revoke this continuance and impose a guilty finding, sir, and incarcerate you for up to two years on this charge, sir. Do you understand that?

End of Trial Transcript

Tuesday, November 26, 2002

For the catastrophic injuries done to Marcia and our family, caused by Zalewski's *"negligent operation of a motor vehicle,"* Judge Barrett's punishment was as follows:

1. Pay $425 in court costs.
2. Do some driver retraining.
3. Be placed on probation with a *"continued without a finding"* for two years.

I was infuriated. According to Judge Barrett:
"This defendant made a mistake. We all make mistakes."
"I am sure there is not anything I can do to make it worse for him."
"Beyond that, there is not much I can do here."
"Mr. Zalewski in this matter, Docket Number 0257CR0260, on the charge of negligent operation of a motor vehicle, the matter is 'Continued Without a Finding' for two years to November 25, 2004."

For Marcia and our family, as well as for the citizens of Massachusetts, Judge Barrett's decision was outrageous. What worse must happen to a blameless victim in order for judge not to dispense a decision of *"continued without a finding"*?

The Death of Carlo Zalewski

Tuesday, October 26, 2009

The following obituary appeared in the *Asbury Park Press*:

"Carlo Zalewski, 65, of Hazlet, passed away, Tuesday, Oct. 27, 2009, at Robert Wood Johnson University Medical Center, New Brunswick. Born in Newark, he resided in Middletown for 40 years, before moving to Hazlet six months ago. He worked as a truck driver with several different companies for 30 years, retiring in 2008."

TIMELINE THREE:
THE PERSONAL INJURY TRIAL[155]

JANUARY 10, 2002 TO AUGUST 15, 2005

MARCIA RHODES, HAROLD RHODES, AND REBECCA RHODES (PLAINTIFFS)
V.
CARLO ZALEWSKI, DRIVER LOGISTICS SERVICES, AND GAF MATERIALS CORPORATION (DEFENDANTS)

COMMONWEALTH OF MASSACHUSETTS
CIVIL ACTION NO. 02-01159A

THE EVENTS PRECEDING THE LAWSUIT AGAINST GAF MATERIALS CORPORATION, CARLO ZALEWSKI, AND DRIVER LOGISTICS SERVICES

Thursday, January 10, 2002

The day following the crash, the insurance claims notes,[156] written by claims adjusters working at the defendants' insurance carriers, stated that Robert Manning (GAF's lead attorney within the risk management department) faxed a copy of GAF's insurance agreement with Driver Logistics Services (which leased the truck driver, Zalewski) to John Chaney, Crawford's insurance claims adjuster.[157]

---

155 As mentioned before, let me state that I am not an attorney, so my legal observations and conclusions may be inaccurate. A nearly complete record of the litigation documentation for Timeline Three can be found at www.theblamelessvictim.com.

156 In the subsequent lawsuit, Timeline Four, Judge Ralph Gants required Crawford, Zurich, and AIG to disclose most of their insurance claims notes as well as many other documents (such as Zurich's Claims Processing Manual). As will be seen, these notes and documents provide an amazing behind-the-scenes view into the claims processing operations within and among Crawford, Zurich, and AIG.

157 For clarification, Crawford and Company (Crawford), by contract, was GAF's third-party insurance administrator as well as Zurich American Insurance's (Zurich's) Agent. Zurich, by contract, was GAF's primary insurance carrier with a

Saturday, January 12, 2002

While Marcia was in the ICU at UMass Memorial Hospital, I contacted Fred Pritzker, the chair of the litigation department at Brown Rudnick. Brown Rudnick has a sterling reputation for its high ethical standards, its unfailing client representation, its comprehensive legal expertise, and its willingness to go the distance for its clients.

Brown Rudnick does not scare easily. It has had a history of winning years-long legal battles against large corporations and large insurance carriers. Fred, along with his team of trial attorneys, was appointed special assistant prosecutor in the case of *Commonwealth of Massachusetts (Plaintiff) v. Philip Morris Inc., et.al.* (Civil Action Number 95–7378). The result yielded the Commonwealth of Massachusetts more than $8 billion.

Ordinarily, Brown Rudnick represented corporate plaintiffs in complex business litigation, but on occasion, it would represent plaintiffs in a personal injury lawsuit.

Tuesday, January 15, 2002

Today, I signed the contingent fee agreement with Fred Pritzker, on behalf of Brown Rudnick, to direct any legal representation that Marcia, Rebecca, or I would need. The terms of the one-page agreement were standard: in return for providing our legal representation, Brown Rudnick would receive 33 percent of the gross proceeds (if any) plus reimbursement of direct costs.[158]

Wednesday, January 23, 2002

FORMAL NOTIFICATION OF INSURANCE CLAIM TO GAF MATERIALS CORP.

Today, Brown Rudnick formally notified GAF of the personal injury claim including copies of the Commonwealth of Massachusetts motor vehicle crash police report and the Medway Police Department incident report.[159]

---

policy limit of $2 million. As such, any insurance claim under $2 million would be paid by Zurich. To speed claims processing, Zurich, instead of doing its own initial investigation, was supposed to rely upon Crawford's investigation for insurance claims against GAF. Upon the completion of Crawford's claims investigation, Zurich could choose to further investigate any claim. AIG, by contract, was GAF's excess insurance carrier with a policy limit of $50 million. As such, the amount of any insurance claim above $2 million and below $50 million would be paid by AIG. To speed claims processing and to lower the premiums paid by GAF, AIG was supposed to rely upon Zurich's thorough claims investigation instead of doing its own investigation. AIG is a holding company that includes many subsidiaries. One subsidiary is National Union Fire Insurance Company of Pittsburgh, Pennsylvania. This property and casualty insurance company "wrote" the insurance policy for GAF. A second subsidiary is AIG Domestic Claims. This company provides the claims management services for National Union (as well as other AIG insurance companies). For simplicity, these two subsidiaries are referred to as AIG.

158 When selecting an attorney for representation in a personal injury lawsuit, ask how many times the attorney has litigated personal injuries through to a jury verdict. Some personal injury attorneys will try to settle a claim as fast possible in order to receive the attorney fees as quickly as possible, and the insurance carriers know which attorneys these are. You want the insurance company to know that your attorney does not settle easily and is fully prepared for litigation.

159 As a layperson, trying to follow the sequence and content of each litigation event was grueling, particularly while simultaneously being a full-time caregiver and patient advocate. Readers may experience the same challenge even though only the main litigation events are presented.

The Crawford Claims Progress Note stated: "We see at least three aspects of negative against the driver:

1) *Zalewski should have had sufficient view of the scene to see the roadwork ahead, but did not see it;*
2) *Zalewski was distracted by the crossing vehicle; and,*
3) *Zalewski failed to know his vehicle was unsafe for operation for week or months.*

We are contractually obligated to provide auto coverage to D.L.S. driver and the contract goes on to say we cannot subrogate,[160] *but nowhere does it say we have to defend and indemnify for their negligence."*[161]

Thursday, January 24, 2002 to Friday, January 25, 2002

The Crawford Claims Progress Note stated:

"Liability favors the claimant, no matter from where it flows."

"Zalewski's employment is terminated—'preventable' accident."

Wednesday, January 30, 2002

The insurance claims notes stated that Crawford completed its first formal report and distributed the report to GAF and to Zurich.[162]

Monday, February 4, 2002

The insurance claims notes stated that AIG was notified of the claim.

Tuesday, February 5, 2002

The insurance claims notes stated:

"Due to the nature of the claimant's injury, this claim is classified as catastrophic, and will be reportable to both GAF and Zurich." "Everything must be copied to Robert Flugger, Vice President of Risk Management at GAF."

Another insurance claim note, listed under *Damages*, stated:

"We are not fully aware of the extent of the claimant's injuries, except that we know she remains in life threatening condition at UMass Medical Hospital, is paralyzed, suffers currently from pneumonia and pancreatic infection.

---

160 "Subrogation" is the process that an insurance company uses to recover claim amounts paid to a policyholder from a negligent third party. In this instance, "cannot subrogate" meant that no how much Zurich paid on this claim, Zurich could not require the DLS driver (Carlo Zalewski) to reimburse Zurich.

161 Confusing insurance policies are advantageous to insurance carriers: resolving the confusion adds to the delay in paying the insurance claim. Opposite to the claims note, Zurich was required to pay the defense costs.

162 In Timeline Four, Crawford personnel testified that this first formal report was mailed to Zurich at its North American headquarters in Schaumburg, Illinois, in the same manner by which other insurance reports were sent to Zurich by Crawford. Zurich personnel, in their testimony, denied ever receiving this report or any other report until at least six months later. Zurich personnel testified that this "lost-in-the-mail" predicament did not unreasonably delay the start of Zurich's investigation until June 2002.

To estimate the ultimate exposure is premature, but we are aware this case will carry a high value."

Monday, February 11, 2002

An AIG Excess Claim Note by John Kurila (a manager in the segmentation department at AIG) stated:

"Facts are clear. Severity of injury/age/specials/ employer/salary/family, present med condition? Value/venue/reserve?"

Monday, April 8, 2002

The insurance claims notes stated that Crawford sent a report to Zurich and AIG recommending that Zurich's insurance reserve be set at its policy limit of $2 million.[163]

Tuesday, April 16, 2002

With Marcia's release from Fairlawn Rehabilitation Hospital, more than 2,000 pages of medical records were available to Zurich and AIG for investigation. Crawford, Zurich, and AIG did not request these medical records.

Monday, June 10, 2002

A Crawford Claim Progress Note stated:

"Defense has now been to scene, and concur that the line of sight was sufficient for D.L.S. (Driver Logistics Services) driver to have avoided the accident."

The Complaint and Demand for Jury Trial[164]

Friday, July 12, 2002

After waiting six months since the crash for a meaningful response from any of the defendants or their insurance carriers, Brown Rudnick served the "Complaint and Demand for Jury Trial" to Carlo Zalewski, GAF Materials Corp., Driver Logistics Services, and Penske Leasing.[165] I hoped that this complaint would get the attention of Zurich and AIG and that we could begin to work out a reasonable settlement.

---

163 Zurich personnel later testified that this second report was never received.

164 The timing of the submission of the "Complaint" is a conundrum for the plaintiffs. Generally, the sooner that the "Complaint" is filed, the more rapidly that money from the insurance carriers could be paid. However, the early submission of the "Complaint" would omit all unknown, perhaps large, expenses, which greatly benefits the insurance carriers.

165 During the trial, the "Complaint" against Penske Leasing was withdrawn. Because the remaining defendants had all stipulated to *fault*, the jury would only have to deliberate on the *damages* to Marcia, Rebecca, and me.

The "Complaint and Demand for Jury Trial" was also filed with the clerk of the court for the Massachusetts Superior Court of Norfolk County, Massachusetts, the geographic jurisdiction of the crash. The complaint was composed of the following sections:

1. Introduction: Marcia Rhodes, Harold Rhodes, Rebecca Rhodes
2. The Parties
   - The Plaintiffs: Marcia Rhodes, Harold Rhodes, and Rebecca Rhodes
   - The Defendants: Carlo Zalewski, Driver Logistics Services, GAF, and Penske
3. The Accident
4. Counts 1–4: Negligence by the Multiple Defendants
5. Count 5: *Loss of Spousal Consortium*—Harold S. Rhodes
6. Count 6: *Loss of Parental Consortium*—Rebecca Rhodes
7. "Demand for Relief"[166]
8. "Demand for Jury Trial"

A Crawford Claim Progress Note stated that the driver, Carlo Zalewski, was 100 percent at *fault* but indicated that Zalewski was an independent contractor.[167]

Monday, August 12, 2002

A Crawford Claim Progress Note stated that Zurich:

"Will get back to Crawford on coverage and does not want GAF to make the decision."

"Will determine if coverage and defense is owed to Driver Logistics Services."

"Is providing Penske with defense under reservation of rights."[168]

A Crawford Transmittal Letter was sent to Kathleen Fuell (major case unit consultant at Zurich), indicating a case value between $5 million and $10 million.

---

166 The "Demand for Relief" presents the amount of money that the plaintiffs would accept to settle the lawsuit. This amount is a reasonable calculation of the present value of the total of *special damages, pain and suffering, losses of consortium, loss of income*, and interest and other amounts over the life expectancy of an injured person:
Special damages include past, current, and future direct out-of-pocket medical expenses and costs. Life Care Planners, with the assistance of health care economists, are recognized as experts in determining special damages.
Pain and suffering, as well as the *losses of consortium*, is an amount of money that the plaintiff considers to be consistent with the gravity of the injuries.
The *loss of income* is a calculation by expert witnesses based upon the earnings potential of the injured person. (Because Marcia was not working, no loss of income was included the "Demand for Relief." To the great benefit of Zurich and AIG, my loss of income cannot be included, even though I had to stop working to care for Marcia.)
Interest is a calculation by expert witnesses based on the statutory interest rate (12 percent in Massachusetts) and the timing of the payments for *special damages, pain and suffering, losses of consortium*, and *loss of income*.

167 In addition to the Crawford's confusion about who is responsible for the defense costs, Crawford adds to the confusion by indicating, *"Zalewski was an independent contractor."* Whether Zalewski was an independent contractor made no difference on the defendants' *liability*.

168 *"The insurer may provide a defense to the insured, seemingly protecting the insured from the serious liabilities that may result from a civil suit. But, the liability insurer is alerting the insured defendant that insurance may ultimately not cover the resulting liability, or a portion of the liability."* "Reservation of Rights," *Wikipedia*, last modified March 11, 2014, https://en.wikipedia.org/wiki/Reservation_of_rights.

Thursday, August 15, 2002

Much to my dismay, neither Zurich nor AIG has responded to the "Complaint and Demand for Jury Trial" or the filing of our lawsuit. Even though I am consumed by Marcia's needs, I am increasingly anxious and aggravated about going to trial. I'm not sure if I can handle the stress of taking care of Marcia and the tension of a trial at the same time.

Months ago, I believed that Zurich and AIG would be good corporate citizens. For the life of me, I cannot understand why there has not been an attempt to settle this claim. There is no question about *fault*—Carlo Zalewski crashed into Marcia, and all the police reports indicated such. All we needed to talk about was a fair settlement. Why won't Zurich and AIG do this?

My stress is spilling over onto everyone. I am becoming an awful individual and a difficult person. Everybody is telling me so—even Marcia.

Friday, September 27, 2002

Now, nearly ten months after the Crash, Brown Rudnick has begun the Discovery[169] phase of our litigation by sending our First Request for Production of Documents and Things to each of the four defendants: Penske, Driver Logistics Services, Carlo Zalewski, and GAF. Per the Massachusetts General Laws, Zurich and AIG each have thirty days to respond.[170]

Friday, November 22, 2002

Although a month late, Zurich and AIG sent Brown Rudnick their responses to the discovery requests. However, Zurich and AIG provided practically none of the requested information. Nearly all of the responses included an *"objection that on the grounds that they (the requests) are vague, ambiguous, overly broad and unduly burdensome."*

Further, nearly all the responses included the statement, *"BMCA[171] states that it will produce the documents within its possession, custody, or control that are responsive to this Request."*

However, no time frame was given for the production of these documents. I guess this response is standard operating procedure for insurance carriers.

Tuesday, November 26, 2002

In his criminal trial today, Zalewski admitted to *"facts sufficient for a finding of guilt for the negligent operation of a motor vehicle."* To my dismay, the trial judge decided to continue this case without finding. This punishment is just a slap on the wrist for causing a

---

169 Discovery typically includes requests for the production of documents and things, interrogatories, and depositions.

170 Over the next several years, I learned the following: Zurich and AIG would generally not provide a timely response to any requests, responses from Zurich and AIG would generally not provide any substantial information, and a motion to compel production would generally be required to force Zurich and AIG to make an adequate response for each request.

171 BMCA is the abbreviation for Building Materials Corporation of America (GAF's corporate name).

catastrophic injury to a blameless victim. Brown Rudnick, on the other hand, was satisfied. For the civil lawsuit, the defendants are 100 percent at *fault*.

Tuesday, January 14, 2003

A Crawford Claim Progress Note sent to Kathleen Fuell stated: *"D.L.S. (Driver Logistics Services) is an additional insured under the policy because of its operation of the covered vehicles with GAF's permission."*

By procrastinating a year to clear this confusion, Zurich has been able to delay since January 9, 2002, to accept coverage responsibility for Driver Logistics Services and Zalewski.

Monday, January 21, 2003

A Zurich Claims Note included an entry by David McIntosh (a claims adjuster at Zurich):

"Please note that we will extend coverage to GAF and Driver Logistics Services. Can you please advise as to the possible exposure now that the coverage issue is resolved?"

Zurich now has accepted its insurance coverage responsibility for its insured who was 100 percent at *fault*. Through Crawford's reports, transmittals, and claims notes, Zurich must know that *damages* will exceed its $2 million policy limit. With *liability* clear, I don't understand why Zurich doesn't unconditionally tender this first $2 million to us.

More than a year has now passed since the crash. Although the crash was 100 percent the *fault* of the defendants, and the victim suffered catastrophic injuries, there has been absolutely no dialogue about settlement. We continue to be forced to use our own savings to pay for all medical expenses.

Thursday, January 23, 2003

The second step in personal injury litigation is the request by the plaintiffs to Zurich and AIG for answers to interrogatories. Today, Brown Rudnick made its first request for answers to interrogatories from Driver Logistics Services and GAF.[172]

Thursday, February 20, 2003

Crawford restated its position:

"We see this, universally for all remaining defendants, as between $5 million and $10 million."

Even with this information, Zurich and AIG made no substantive attempt at settlement.

---

172 As before, I learned, just like the requests for the production of documents and things, that Zurich and AIG would not provide timely and complete responses to any of the interrogatories. I also learned that a motion to compel production to force Zurich and AIG to make an adequate response to the interrogatories would be required for every request.

Monday, March 10, 2003

Now fourteen months after the crash, Zurich and AIG finally responded to Brown Rudnick's requests for documents made on January 23, 2003. However, the responses were devoid of any information.

Tuesday, April 8, 2003

Nearly fifteen months have passed since the crash, and there still has not yet been any serious dialogue with Zurich and AIG with regard to a reasonable settlement offer. I am so aggravated at this.

To continue discovery, Brown Rudnick sent Zurich and AIG the answers to the first set of interrogatories to Marcia and me.

Additionally, because Zurich and AIG have yet to make the request, Fred—although not legally required to do so—took the initiative to again make available to Zurich and AIG more than 2,000 pages of medical and financial information about the crash.

My anxiety continues to worsen. I am waking up in the middle of the night, worried about whether we will have enough money. I am particularly worried about how a trial, if required, would emotionally damage Marcia and Rebecca.[173] While all of Marcia's and Rebecca's therapists (and mine, too) are trying to get us to move forward, a trial would make us relive the dreadful past in excruciating detail.

Wednesday, April 16, 2003

The Brown Rudnick team continues to build the case against the four defendants for negotiating a settlement with the defendants' insurance carriers (Zurich and AIG) or for the likely jury trial.

Smartly, the Brown Rudnick team anticipated that Zurich and AIG would argue that paraplegia, while awful, would not have an overwhelmingly substantial impact on Marcia's life.

Fred and his team believed that Zurich and AIG would propound the point of view that Marcia has an excellent medical team that would enable her to achieve key rehabilitative goals such as self-transferring, self-catheterization, or being able to drive.

Fred and his team also believed that Zurich and AIG would repeatedly argue that when Marcia achieves these and other rehabilitative goals, she would have an almost normal life, therefore undeserving of substantial monies for future *pain and suffering*.

---

[173] Colossal Mistake #43: In Timeline Four, Zurich and AIG claimed that the emotional distress I felt due to Marcia's horrific medical complications could not be separated from the emotional distress that I felt as a result of the *frustration of litigation*. As such, Zurich and AIG would use this apparent lack of *causation* that would result in a *damage* as a defense against their delaying actions. I wished that I had a better understanding of this clever tactic from the beginning. I should have taken appropriate steps early on to prove that the *damages* between Marcia's medical complications and the *frustration of litigation* were separable.

To counter this argument, the team asked Dr. Roaf to write a narrative summary report as part of discovery and asked her to testify if there was a trial.[174]

Tuesday, May 6, 2003

An entry by Jodie Mills (a claims adjuster at Crawford) in the Zurich Claims Progress Note in a "Liability Transmittal Letter" stated:

"It appears we will have to indemnify the driver, D.L.S. and Penske due to the contract in place at the time of the loss."

Mills further stated that the medical records were being forwarded and that:

"Liability falls to driver, which is imputed to GAF. We see this [potential case value], universally to all remaining defendants, as between $5 Mil and $10 Mil."

Even with this information, Zurich and AIG made no attempt at settlement.

❖ ❖ ❖

This, then, is the core of what is wrong with the laws governing fraudulent business practices by an insurance carrier in Massachusetts. In our case:
1. Zurich's insurance coverage was to $2 million.
2. Zurich's own Agent, Crawford & Company, valued this case well above $2 million at between $5 million and $10 million.
3. Yet, Zurich was not legally required to tender the $2 million to Marcia. Why wouldn't Zurich send us the first $2 million and let AIG handle the rest?

❖ ❖ ❖

Wednesday, June 4, 2003

Jodie Mills, in a letter to David McIntosh, stated that the action plan was to: *"secure authority to settle both BI (Bodily Injury) claims outstanding."*

Further, the letter stated that they knew that the injury was a fracture to the twelfth vertebra, that Marcia spent three months in the hospital, and that she suffered subsequent injuries including fractured legs.

---

174 Dr. Roaf is one of the finest people I have ever known. Marcia and I will always be deeply appreciative for the wonderful care and friendship that she provided Marcia, beginning at Fairlawn in early February 2002. After discharge, Marcia saw Dr. Roaf six times per year over the next six years. Generally, doctors shy away from testifying in personal injury lawsuits. However, in most personal injury lawsuits, the dollar damage award to the plaintiffs by the jury is closely dependent on the expertise and the personal character of the doctor who testifies on behalf of the plaintiffs. Fortunately for us, Dr. Roaf agreed to provide testimony on our behalf. Trials are adversarial. During Dr. Roaf's testimony, Zurich and AIG did their very best to discredit her. Nonetheless, Dr. Roaf remained steadfast in her testimony that Marcia was an "outlier," who was not typical of persons with paraplegia. As I listened, I was dreadfully embarrassed by how Dr. Roaf was being treated by Zurich and AIG.

Monday, July 21, 2003

This afternoon, 558 days since the crash, Carlotta Patten sent me a copy of Zalewski's deposition.[175] The deposition demonstrated how smart Fred is. His questions were brilliant.

Thursday, August 12, 2003

During the preceding eighteen months, we have used a substantial amount of money from our savings. Although I could never let on to anyone, I am agonizing each day about depleting our savings well before any settlement was reached.

My frustration with Zurich and AIG is profoundly affecting my relationships with everyone close to me—the Brown Rudnick attorneys, my family, and my friends.

My therapist told me to keep everything in perspective. However, I find this just impossible to do. My anxiety level has become so devastating that I now have begun to take even stronger psych meds.

Friday, August 13, 2003

Today, Brown Rudnick sent Zurich and AIG a "Demand Letter" along with a complete package of supporting documentation and the video, *"A Day in Marcia's Life,"* so that Zurich and AIG could understand how Marcia is doing.

I hope that this package will encourage Zurich and AIG to begin a dialogue about a reasonable settlement. I just do not know if I can take this any longer.

Friday, August 20, 2003

As proof of the future medical costs, Brown Rudnick will provide to the defendants (as well as Zurich and AIG) a detailed analysis of Marcia's medical needs for the rest of her life. This comprehensive analysis (referred to as a Life Care Plan) will be developed by a recognized national expert in all aspects of spinal cord injury, Adele Pollard.[176]

Today, Pollard visited Marcia to develop the Life Care Plan. A Life Care Plan typically included a professional analysis of the patient's Functional Independence Measure (commonly referred to as "FIM"); the Functional Assessment Measure (commonly referred to as "FAM"); cost of community integration; future annual costs; future episodic costs; and, potential complications costs and associated risks costs.

---

175 A copy of the deposition, as well as many other legal documents, can be found at www.theblamelessvictim.com.

176 Adele Pollard is a registered nurse who holds a bachelor's degree in psychology and a master of science degree in health policy and planning. As well, Pollard is a licensed rehabilitation counselor (L.R.C.) and a certified case manager (C.C.M.). Pollard has experience in medical legal consulting, testimony, depositions, and in developing Life Care Plans for adults with traumatic brain, spinal cord injuries, and multiple traumas.

Based on the costs presented in the Life Care Plan, Brown Rudnick engaged an economist to determine the total expected costs throughout Marcia's lifetime. Brown Rudnick knows that Life Care Plan will be closely scrutinized by the insurance carriers.[177]

Thursday, September 11, 2003

Now 610 days since the crash, I received a call from Carlotta Patten. I learned the following:

1. Zurich wants to send its own Life Care Planner to validate Pollard's Life Care Plan. While chagrined that this would upset Marcia, I consented under the conditions that Adele prepares Marcia in advance, Adele is here, and a Brown Rudnick attorney is here.
2. Zurich and AIG want to depose me, specifically about the claim about *loss of spousal consortium*.
3. Zurich and AIG want to depose Marcia and Rebecca. I am mortified over this. I do not want anything to happen to Marcia or Rebecca psychologically or emotionally—backsliding now would take an unnecessary toll on Marcia or Rebecca.

I spoke to Fred by telephone. After the call, I realized I had to phone him again and apologize for my awful behavior. I am not handling things well. My dreadful conduct cannot be excused. Well, yes it can.

Friday, September 12, 2003

Crawford sent a letter to David McIntosh, supplementing an earlier status report:

"We wish to increase the BI (Bodily Injury) reserves to policy limits as requested. This has been our request since our 4/8/02 report. We also must increase our expense reserve, as there are four different law firms involved in this matter."

Even with this information, Zurich and AIG made no attempt at settlement.

Thursday, September 25, 2003

A Crawford Claims Progress Note in a Crawford Transmittal Letter included the following update:

"Also consortium verdicts for spouse are approximately $500K. See full case value at $5–$7 million."

---

[177] A major point of disagreement with the insurance carriers in Pollard's Life Care Plan will be Marcia's life expectancy, which will be morbidly discussed, at length, in open court in front of Marcia. I will never be able to understand how devastating this subject had to be for Marcia.

Friday, September 26, 2003

When I asked about the Life Care Plan, Marcia said the following:

"Along these lines, I would like to know what the average settlement is if the trial goes to court. Fred already told us what we can expect if we settle out of court, and I hardly think this amount even begins to cover what I feel about my personal losses and how my life has changed, not to mention the shortening of my life.

I am very tempted to go to trial. Eight million, after attorneys' fees, other expenses put forth by Harold, and taxes greatly diminishes the amount actually received, and I do not think four or five million dollars are going to cover all the future expenses, especially if the past year has been any indication on what to expect physically and emotionally.

Four million today is worth considerably less even ten years from now, and I expect at that time there will be major expenses in trying to get me to walk again, much of which I doubt the insurance company plans on paying for.

How someone can think that four million can compensate for the loss of my mobility and all the related issues, particularly those issues relating to quality time I can no longer spend with Rebecca and Harold, cover future medical costs, and help me adapt to being a paraplegic with ADHD, is an insult. I cannot begin to explain how devastating paraplegia with ADHD is. Without a cure for ADHD and for my paralysis, this will always be a major ongoing issue for me.

As far as I am considered, I want at least one million for each year I am expected to live from the time of the accident and one million for each year the accident has shortened my expectancy. I do not expect Harold to have to be the one to provide the finances to support my living a disabled life. This is why I want to know what the average settlement is if the case goes to trial."

Tuesday, September 30, 2003

Now at the end of September 2003—629 days since the crash—we have had to pay for all of Marcia's expenses since January 9, 2002, without any monies provided by Zurich or AIG.

Zurich has now been able, through one delay or another, to run the clock twenty months since the crash.

Wednesday, October 1, 2003

Six hundred thirty days after the crash, my deposition was held today in the offices of Morrison Mahoney & Miller (Boston, Massachusetts) in a nondescript conference room. The defense attorneys included:

1. Michael Smith, Morrison Mahoney & Miller—Counsel for Carlo Zalewski and Driver Logistics Services

2. John B. Johnson, Corrigan Johnson & Tutor—Counsel for Penske Truck Leasing Corp.
3. Greg Deschenes, Nixon Peabody—Counsel for GAF Materials Corp.

Before this deposition, thousands of pages of documents had been provided to Zurich and AIG as well as several sets of interrogatories from Marcia, Rebecca, and me. Presumably, the goal for this deposition is to seek additional information to enable Zurich and AIG to prepare a reasonable settlement offer.[178]

The deposition began at 10:00 a.m.

THE DEPOSITION OF HAROLD RHODES (EXCERPTS)[179]

Mr. Harold Rhodes, having been duly sworn by the Notary Public, was examined and testified as follows.

Direct Examination (excerpt) by Mr. Smith (Counsel for Carlo Zalewski and Driver Logistics Services)

❖ ❖ ❖

Mr. Smith:
And prior to the accident, in that five-year window again, did you and Marcia share the same bedroom?[180]

Witness:
No, we did not.

Mr. Smith:
Where did you sleep and where did she sleep in the house?

Witness:
There were two bedrooms side by side on the upstairs.

Mr. Smith:
And for how long had you had separate bedrooms prior to the accident?

---
178 After the deposition, I realized how wrong that I was to think this. My stupidity continues to know no bounds.
179 For simplicity, these deposition transcripts include the update changes made after the initial deposition was taken.
180 Beginning with these questions, Zurich and AIG were trying to find evidence that Marcia and I already had an unhappy marriage, proving that there couldn't be any *loss of spousal consortium*. Zurich and AIG asked similar questions at the trial in open court in front of friends and family.

Witness:

Well, again, it's hard to remember; but I would say, you know, early to mid-nineties.

Mr. Smith:

Now, is there a particular event or something that is the reason why you had separate bedrooms?

Witness:

It's a little embarrassing. I had developed a horrendous snoring problem, which even after some medical procedures can't seem to fix. My wife just can't deal with it and I completely understood.

❖ ❖ ❖

Mr. Smith:

Prior to the accident, did you ever have any family counseling or did you folks see a counselor together for any familial issues?[181]

Witness:

I—I certainly did; and on occasion, Marcia would come—would—would—would come—you know, would come along.

Mr. Smith:

Who did you see?

Witness:

Linda Eisenberg.

Mr. Smith:

For how long of a period prior to the accident were you seeing—is it Dr. Eisenberg?

Witness:

She's a licensed social worker. I don't know if she has a Ph.D. or not. Maybe we started in November, 1998.

---

[181] Zurich and AIG were entitled to know whether I have had psychological therapy as well as when the therapy began and ended. However, due to patient–therapist confidentiality, the content of the therapy sessions is privileged. Beginning with these questions, Zurich and AIG were trying to find any damaging information contained in the therapy records to prove that Marcia and I already had an unhappy marriage, proving that there couldn't be any *loss of spousal consortium*. Zurich and AIG asked similar questions at the trial in open court in front of friends and family.

Mr. Smith:
Is there a particular event or something that sticks out in your mind as to why you started seeing Dr. Eisenberg?

Mr. Pritzker:
Objection. I'm going to instruct you not to answer.

Mr. Smith:
On what grounds?

Mr. Pritzker:
On the grounds of privilege and irrelevancy.

Mr. Smith:
What privilege are you invoking?

Mr. Pritzker:
The doctor-patient privilege, privacy issues as well. Keep in mind that we are not seeking emotional distress for Harold in this.

Mr. Smith:
Well, as you recall, did you begin seeing Dr. Eisenberg as a result of difficulties in your marriage?

Mr. Pritzker:
That calls for a yes or no.

Witness:
No.

Mr. Smith:
Why did you begin seeing Dr. Eisenberg?

Mr. Pritzker:
I instruct you not to—objection. I instruct you not to answer.

Mr. Smith:
Did you go to Dr. Eisenberg on your own first?

Witness:
Yes.

Mr. Smith:
How did it come about—how did you learn of Dr. Eisenberg? How did you go see Dr. Eisenberg for the first time?

Witness:
The local counseling service in Milford is called the Milford Holliston Counseling Service. I called to make an appointment. They set me up with Linda Eisenberg.

Mr. Smith:
And you believe you first saw her in 1997; is that correct?

Witness:
I think so. Again, it's so long ago. You know, it would be approximately that time period.

Mr. Deschenes:
Nineteen—I'm sorry. I didn't hear.

Mr. Smith:
'97.

Mr. Deschenes:
'97.

Mr. Smith:
How often would you see Dr. Eisenberg?

Witness:
Once a week.

Mr. Smith:
And have you seen Dr. Eisenberg once a week from 1997 to the present?

Witness:
I'd say mostly, yes.

Mr. Smith:
And what kind of services was Dr. Eisenberg providing to you?

Witness:
In a general sense, she was helping me to look looked at things in life. So she was—

Mr. Pritzker:
I think you've—

Mr. Smith:
Fred, I haven't said anything. We talked about following the Rules of Civil Procedure today.

Mr. Pritzker:
Okay.

Mr. Smith:
As you know—

Mr. Pritzker:
Objection. I instruct you not to answer.

Mr. Smith:
Well—

Mr. Pritzker:
He's not answering the question. He's getting into privileged stuff. What you asked for is the kinds of stuff that she was doing. He's now getting into substance.

Mr. Smith:
It's his—are you saying it's his privilege that he's invoking? His doctor-client—

Mr. Pritzker:
Absolutely, yes.

Mr. Smith:
I think it's—

Mr. Pritzker:
What other privilege would there be?

Mr. Smith:
What's that? Well, I think it's relevant.

Mr. Pritzker:
I know you do and it's not. I can cite you some cases if you want but it really isn't. It would be if we were claiming severe emotional distress which we are not. We've already said that in correspondence. If you look at the claim, it's a run-of-the-mill loss of consortium claim.

Mr. Smith:
Which has to do with his relationship with his wife.

Mr. Pritzker:
Run-of-the-mill loss of consortium claims do not open up the privilege of psychiatric or psychological consultations. The law is pretty clear about that.

Mr. Deschenes:
Mike, can I make a suggestion that we go off the record just for a second and talk about this in the absence of the witness just so we can have a discussion about it?

Mr. Pritzker:
That's a good suggestion. But let's finish this line of questions first and then I'll be happy to do that.

Mr. Smith:
Do you still see Dr. Eisenberg?

Witness:
Yes.

Mr. Smith:
And how often do you see Dr. Eisenberg currently—still on a weekly basis?

Witness:
I try to see her weekly; although, recently, it's been every other week because of Marcia's—because of my responsibilities to Marcia on the weekends. So it's very difficult sometimes to see her.

Mr. Smith:
: Were your—strike that. Were your trips to Dr. Eisenberg covered by your health insurance?

Witness:
: Partially, yes.

Mr. Smith:
: Did you have a co-pay each time you went?

Witness:
: A co-pay or an out-of-network payment depending on Linda's status with UnitedHealthcare at different times.

Mr. Smith:
: Typically, what was your co-pay?

Witness:
: Ten dollars.

Mr. Smith:
: And you treatment with Dr. Eisenberg post-accident, has it changed from your treatment prior to the accident?

Mr. Pritzker:
: You can answer that.

Witness:
: Yes.

Mr. Smith:
: How has it changed?

Mr. Pritzker:
: I instruct you not to answer.

Mr. Smith:
: Do you relate your treatment post-accident with Dr. Eisenberg—strike that.

Mr. Smith:
Let's go off the record for a second.

(Off the record colloquy out of the presence of the Witness.)

Mr. Smith:
I just want to be clear on one question that maybe you responded to but I didn't hear correctly. Did you seek counseling with Dr. Eisenberg as a result of your relationship or difficulties with your relationship with Marcia?

Witness:
No.

Mr. Smith:
Did you seek counseling with Dr. Eisenberg as a result of a physical problem—your physical problem?

Mr. Pritzker:
Objection. I instruct you not to answer.

Mr. Smith:
Prior to the motor vehicle accident, did you seek counseling of any sort anywhere as a result of difficulties or problems with your marriage?

Witness:
I vaguely remember sometime in the early 1990s Marcia and I, for a very short period of time, saw somebody. I cannot remember who it was or where it was. But, you know, it was such a long time ago that I just cannot give you—I know it was for a very short period of time.

Mr. Smith:
Do you recall the reason why you sought counseling?

Witness:

To the best of my knowledge, as I remember—again, I just want to stress that this was a very longtime ago to me—this was certainly at a time when I was probably working much more than I was working at other—you know, later times.

Becca was probably, you know, four of five. Marcia—Marcia was—I was working. Marcia was trying to deal best with the child. I think we both had trouble understanding our roles and our responsibilities at this time. You know—you know, what priorities we should be setting for each other and for Rebecca and for ourselves.

Mr. Smith:
When you first saw Dr. Eisenberg, how were you feeling?

Witness:

There were a number of—there were, you know, a lot of stresses. I wouldn't call them stresses. There were a number of things I was concerned about—about realizing that perhaps the way I was looking at certain things may not be the correct way to look at certain things.

I guess I would say I was so focused and so directed and so, even I dare say narrow, that I realized that there were things that I just wasn't seeing as well as I should be seeing. That was—you know, it was suggested to me to get, you know, help in understanding more.

Mr. Smith:
How were you feeling about work at that time?

Mr. Pritzker:
Objection. I instruct you not to answer.

Mr. Smith:
It's his own feelings. It has nothing to do with his psychiatric—

Mr. Smith:
What does this have to do with a loss of consortium claim?

Mr. Smith:
It has to do with reasons—stresses in his life and the potential effect on his relationship with his wife.

Mr. Pritzker:
I instruct you not to answer.

Mr. Smith:
How were you feeling about your home life at that time?

Witness:

Oh, I dearly loved Marcia very, very much. She's, you know—you know, I haven't had a chance to say this in previous but you have to understand that Marcia, in every way, you know, completes me.

Where I am very hard-working, some have described as anal, and focused, Marcia is—before the accident, fun-loving and energetic and social. You know, she made me see things that I just had never seen before or experienced before.

She was amazing to me. I mean, you know,—I mean—I—I—she—she—you know, it was—seeing how she was with Rebecca was so wonderful. I mean, this was—in every way, this was—you know, I don't know how to describe it—a charmed life. A wonderful life that we were living.

Mr. Smith:
Other than Dr. Eisenberg, who Counsel has instructed you not to talk about, and the other doctor or the other person that you and Marcia saw, was there any other counseling or professional treatment that you sought?

Witness:
None that I recall certainly.

❖   ❖   ❖

Mr. Smith:
Do you know—strike that. When Marcia was diagnosed with ADHD, what effect, if any, did that have on your marital relationship?[182]

Witness:
I'd say the ADHD did not have any effect on our marital relationship.

---

[182] Beginning with these questions, Zurich and AIG were trying to find evidence that Marcia's preexisting medical conditions caused us to have an unhappy marriage, proving that there couldn't be any *loss of spousal consortium*. Zurich and AIG ask similar questions at the trial in open court in front of friends and family.

Mr. Smith:
At some point prior to the accident, Marcia was also diagnosed with a bipolar disorder, correct?

Witness:
That's correct.

Mr. Smith:
Do you recall when Marcia was diagnosed with a bipolar disorder?

Witness:
I can't remember.

Mr. Smith:
Was it ten years prior?

Witness:
You know, I'm sorry. I just cannot remember. You know, I just can't remember.

Mr. Smith:
That's fine. Was she on medication for her bipolar disorder?

Witness:
Yes, she was.

Mr. Smith:
What medicine—what medication; do you recall?

Witness:
I can't say.

Mr. Smith:
What effect, if any, did Marcia's bipolar disorder have on your marital relationship?

Witness:
Bipolar is—you know, it certainly affected our marriage. You know, on those times when Marcia would be depressed and my not understanding how to deal with it or what to expect from it—this was a brand new thing to me.

You know, I didn't know how to handle it or what best to do. So, you know, I mean, you know, it was—it was, you know, a challenging, you know, thing when Marcia became depressed.

Mr. Smith:
Can you describe for me your observations of Marcia's bipolar condition prior to the accident?

Witness:
Well, again, I'd say I'm no expert in bipolar.

Mr. Smith:
Absolutely not. I understand that.

Witness:
I can't really describe her bipolar. What I can talk about is the, you know, occasional times when, you know, she became, you know, you know, unhappy and—and—and, you know, not—you know, and not knowing what to do about it or how to handle it or how to be.

Mr. Smith:
I guess my question is more how did the bipolar play itself out in Marcia's activities or her personality? Just generally, you know, your understanding of Marcia and how did the bipolar play out in that?

Witness:

Again, I want to separate bipolar from depression because I was no—I can't tell you when she had—you know, she had—when she had anything having to do with bipolar. I mean, I'm no doctor. I can't—I can't see that.

But I can see times when, you know, she, you know, became depressed particularly around, you know—you know, when she had her period. You know, it—you know, she, you know, became very, you know—she became, you know, you know, unhappy and, you know, depressed. I don't know. I guess maybe—if I'm not answering your question—I'm doing the best I can.

Mr. Smith:
How long would—typically would those depressed periods last for?

Witness:
You know, you know, one or two days a month.

Mr. Smith:
How did you feel when those incidents—depressed incidents occurred?

Witness:

Well, again, over time, you know, Marcia started taking medication. When we began to realize that this was becoming a thing—you know, more than what it was before for whatever reason—she started taking medication.

So whatever she was feeling was certainly moderated a great deal. So over—you know, when it was first being experienced, I mean, it was a challenge. It was difficult. I mean, I had to figure out how to deal with this.

Over time, as she began to take medications, it abated a great deal to the point where, you know, you know, it was largely unnoticeable. So, you know, it was just a period of time that we tried to figure these things out.

Mr. Smith:
How long of a period of time was it when you first noticed these depressive episodes until she started taking the medication and there was an improvement?

Witness:
Again, you know, this was a long time ago. I can't remember.

Mr. Smith:
Was it longer than a year; if you recall?

Witness:
Oh, this was in, you know, the mid-1990s.

Mr. Smith:
Mid-nineties?

Witness:
Yes.

Mr. Deschenes:
Can we take a quick break?

Mr. Smith:
Sure.
(Off the record for a short break.)

Mr. Smith:
Other than the ADHD that we talked about and the bipolar condition, was there any other medical or other diagnoses that had an effect on the way you felt about your relationship with Marcia prior to the accident obviously?

Witness:
Again, let me say the ADHD had nothing—had no effect.

Mr. Smith:
Okay. Sure.

Witness:
And the answer is no to the question.

❖ ❖ ❖

Mr. Smith:
If the bed sores—the pressure sores get better, is it anticipated that she may be able to get some further occupational therapy and be able to self-transfer? Is that the goal?[183]

Witness:
First, her leg cast—her leg has got to heal.

Mr. Smith:
Right.

Witness:
Which is—we don't know how much longer that's going to take. Then she'll restart, as if she had come home for the first day, all of her occupational therapy, all of her physical therapy—

---

[183] Beginning with these questions, Zurich and AIG were trying to find evidence that after Marcia's expected positive rehabilitation, our spousal companionship would not be significantly diminished, proving that there couldn't be any *loss of spousal consortium*. Zurich and AIG asked similar questions at the trial in open court in front of friends and family.

Mr. Smith:
Has the—I'm sorry. Go ahead.

Witness:
—and learn to do all those things—

Mr. Smith:
Right.

Witness:
—that she needs to learn in order to have independence.

Mr. Smith:
I mean, but ultimately, self-transfer remains a rehabilitative goal from the bed to the chair and the chair to the van and be able to do all those things, correct?

Witness:
That's one of many goals. [184]

Mr. Smith:
Harold, is the goal that someday in the future—hopefully the near future—that Marcia will be able to transfer out of bed into a wheelchair, go out the front door, get in the—transfer into the vehicle that you purchased, and do what she wants to do?

Witness:

This is exactly what is described in all the spinal cord injury books that by all accounts, you know, she's handicapped, not crippled. However—and I would never say this in front of her—I just don't know.

I just don't think she'll be able to do that. I don't believe that she's strong enough or will ever be strong enough to be able to effectively do this. It's very difficult for a female to develop the upper-body strength in order to do all those things that you just described but we can hope.

---

[184] This question was difficult to answer. Zurich and AIG did a fine job in trapping me. As background, Marcia's inability to self-transfer substantially increased the required amount of HHA hours and related costs. I believe that Zurich and AIG wanted to show that Marcia would be able to self-transfer and therefore not need these additional HHA hours in order to reduce their *damages*. On the one hand, Zurich and AIG knew that Marcia has had several leg fractures, that she has osteoporosis, and that she would need to wear, likely forever, the Aircast boots. As such, she would likely never be able self-transfer. Therefore, the answer should be no. Nonetheless, from the beginning, self-transfer was a rehabilitative goal. Therefore, the answer should be yes. Last, saying *"I don't know"* would seem callous and uncaring.

Mr. Smith:
But ultimately, that is the hope and that is the goal?

Witness:
It is definitely the hope and the goal.[185]

Mr. Smith:
I think that's all I have, Harold. Thank you very much. These gentlemen may have a few questions for you.

(Off the record colloquy.)

❖ ❖ ❖

The deposition concluded at 1:30 p.m. I answered, to the best of my ability, more than 900 questions.

After a few perfunctory warm-up questions, I realized that I was not as prepared for the deposition as I would have liked. Although I did my best to just answer each question, I kept asking myself, *Why are these particular questions being asked?*

We were halfway through the deposition when I figured out that the questions were not geared toward determining a reasonable settlement offer as I had hoped. I concluded that they were asked for four reasons:

1. Is there available evidence that Marcia and I had an unhappy marriage?
2. Is there evidence in my therapy records that Marcia and I had an unhappy marriage?
3. Is there evidence that Marcia's preexisting medical conditions caused Marcia and me to have an unhappy marriage?
4. Is there evidence that Marcia's expected positive rehabilitation would show that our marriage would be unaffected by the crash?

Afterward, Fred Pritzker and Margaret Pinkham told me they thought I had done well, even though I answered several questions differently from the interrogatories. I was given a transcript of my deposition. I made these conclusions.

I didn't follow the advice of the Brown Rudnick attorneys in many of my answers. For many questions, I should have said, *"I do not know"* or *"I do not remember."* The

---

[185] This answer of yes to this question would play an important role during the upcoming trial. Later, during trial testimony, I was asked, *"But ultimately, that is your hope and that is your goal?"* Instead of saying yes, I said no, the opposite of the previous question. Everyone was aghast. This question was different from the deposition question. From day one, I was told by each health care provider that I was not to have any goals for Marcia's rehabilitation. I had to love her as she was and not nag her to achieve a rehabilitative goal. Therefore, I had no rehabilitative goals for her.

attorneys for Zurich and AIG were able to get me to open up and talk. This was the wrong thing to do as a deponent, because the follow-up questions were increasingly challenging to answer. For example, I was asked, *"And when your daughter was born, that is when Marcia stopped working full time, correct?"* I said no even though, upon reflection, I didn't know when Marcia stopped working, but I didn't want to appear like I didn't know. How stupid.

Zurich and AIG probed endlessly in this area. I should have said, *"I do not remember."* That would have stopped the follow-up questions.

I had difficulty hiding my emotions when certain questions were asked. The attorneys for Zurich and AIG must have realized that certain questions would disturb me. I would likely give an overly expressive emotional response, which, I was told, would not be taken well by the jury. For example, when I was asked, *"Were you and Marcia sleeping together?"* and *"Was it your goal for Marcia to be able to self-transfer?"* my answers were more expressively emotional than coolly rational.

Upon reflection, I could see that the order in which the questions had been asked was well determined beforehand. The most significant and perhaps the most challenging questions were asked at the end of the deposition, when I was the most worn out. Perhaps they were testing my stamina. At that point, my answers were no longer crisp and factual. They were, unfortunately, imprecise and emotional.

At the end, I was bewildered. Years later, during the testimony at the subsequent trial, I understood another objective that Zurich and AIG had for my deposition, for Marcia's deposition, and for Rebecca's deposition.

Friday, October 10, 2003

Today, Zurich and AIG brought a third-party lawsuit against the town of Medway:

"…arguing that if he (Carlo Zalewski) is found liable, the town should also be considered responsible because it provided the police detail at the work site…the officer did not properly warn drivers."

Did Zurich and AIG know, even as they brought this lawsuit, that municipalities were immune to such lawsuits? Was this a frivolous waste of time, designed to make us wait even longer?

Meanwhile, our financial situation continues to worsen.

Friday, November 7, 2003

Greg Deschenes sent an e-mail to Kathleen Fuell, attaching the "Claim Evaluation Worksheet and Pretrial Report."

Additionally, Crawford sent a letter to David McIntosh, supplementing the earlier status report:

"We wish to increase the BI (Bodily Injury) reserves to policy limits as requested. This has been our request since our 4/8/02 report. We also must increase our expense reserve, as there are four different law firms involved in this matter."

Thursday, November 13, 2003

John Chaney sent a new Crawford Claim Progress Note, which was included in the Crawford Transmittal Letter:

"We see full value of this case between 5-7 mil. It would be better if only one insurer managed a mediation of this order. By putting up the underlying policy, the single insurer will find this more manageable. Be aware that plaintiffs' counsel is a successful big case lawyer, and his demand is not unreasonable or out of hand, given the specials of just under $3 mil. He is also [redacted]."

Wednesday, November 19, 2003

A new Crawford Claim Progress Note stated:

"A conference call with AIG / Zurich / GAF / Willis."[186]

Additionally, Steve Penick (a claims adjuster at Crawford) sent an e-mail to Nicholas Satriano (a claims adjuster at AIG):

"…promising to put together a shadow copy of the file."

Monday, December 1, 2003

Twenty-three months have now passed since the crash, and there still has been no settlement dialogue. I am desperate, but I tried not to show this to anyone. I had to be strong for Marcia, but I was crumbling inside. I couldn't sleep. The medical expenses are high, but we are no closer to resolution than the day after the crash.

Why are they punishing Marcia and me?

This lack of dialogue had to be a well-planned strategy by Zurich and AIG. They want to starve us out until we are forced to settle. Horrifying.

Once again, Fred attempted to get the attention of Zurich and AIG by sending a second "Demand Letter":

"In light of what the Rhodes family has had to endure since January 9, 2002, their strong likelihood of success on the merits against each of the Defendants as described in the August 13, 2003 Demand Letter, and the fact that none of the Defendants have responded to the previous demand in the three and a half months since it was served, Plaintiffs believe that this demand is fair. This demand will automatically expire in 30 days."

---

186 Willis referred to Willis Group Holdings (New York), a large insurance broker. The job of an insurance broker is to secure for its client (GAF) the best insurance coverage at the best price. The fact that a Willis insurance broker (Fred Hohn) attended or participated in many of the discussions or actions taken by Crawford, Zurich, and AIG would play a key role later.

Tuesday, December 2, 2003

In an e-mail, Kathleen Fuell stated to Steve Penick:

"Defense counsel opines that Zalewski is 100% negligent, and was acting in the course of employment for DSL, our insured's subcontractor. They appear to have the bulk of liability, and should be paying the lion's share of the settlement. I will need all of the above clarified in order to request settlement authority within our policy limits."

Wednesday, December 3, 2003

Today, Brown Rudnick received a notice that AIG Domestic Claims, Inc.,[187] had associated in attorneys William Conroy and Russell Pollock of the law firm of Campbell Campbell Edwards & Conroy (Boston, Massachusetts).[188]

Thursday, December 4, 2003

A Zurich Claims Note included the following:

"Kathleen Fuell completes Zurich BI Claim Report notes and proposes a reserve of $2,000,000. Notes age/life expectancy of Marcia Rhodes at age 48 to be 25 years. Impression as a witness: 'sympathetic.'

In section about personal background affecting value of the claim, states 'she comes from a strong family background. She remains married. The entire family is receiving psychiatric care because of this accident.'"

"Harold Rhodes, age 49, has been treated for depression and insomnia. He helps care for his wife on a daily basis, and has suffered wage loss from impacts to his career as a marketing consultant. Rebecca Rhodes, their teenage daughter, receives weekly counseling due to anxiety over her mother's injury."

"Per defense counsel, a recent paraplegia case in Rhode Island resulted in a $19 million verdict. Jury Research cites $3.6 million verdict for intoxicated plaintiff involved in a single car accident after leaving the bar; $2 M verdict for contractor who fell through a hole where defense argued that plaintiff was negligent based on blood alcohol level and traces of marijuana; $4.5 M verdict for 59-year-old machine operator."

---

187 AIG Domestic Claims is the claims processing organization National Union (a subsidiary of AIG).

188 In Timeline Four, Nicholas Satriano will testify as to his reasons for replacing Greg Deschenes. For Marcia and me, associating in a new law firm is just another delay by Zurich. Meanwhile, our financial resources continued to dwindle.

Friday, December 5, 2003

Today, Brown Rudnick received the defendants' Life Care Plan developed by the defendants' expert witness, Dr. Jane Mattson.[189] This Life Care Plan provided for substantially less money for Marcia's care in every area of future medical expense than the Life Care Plan prepared by Adele Pollard.

I was shocked upon reading it, angered beyond all words. I couldn't believe that such a small amount of money would be contemplated as appropriate for Marcia's lifelong medical care.

For the next several months, I lived in a deep depression about her future. All I could think was that she was again being victimized. Although completely blameless, she would suffer for the rest of her life due to the negligence of their insured, but Zurich and AIG appeared unwilling to provide the money necessary to care for her.

Why hadn't a reasonable settlement offer been made?

Friday, December 19, 2003

McCarter & English[190] sent a fax to Nicholas Satriano:

"GAF asked us to examine conduct of National Union and AIG in 'responding' to GAF's nearly two-year-old demand for coverage for this catastrophic underlying claim. Although AIG received notice of the claim in February 2002, it has not yet confirmed it will provide coverage."

Unbelievable. In two years, AIG never confirmed coverage.

Monday, January 5, 2004

Kathleen Fuell sent an e-mail to Fred Hohn (the insurance broker with Willis Group Holdings) stating that she had submitted her authority recommendations to upper management.

"It is likely that we will tender our $2,000,000 limits to AIG, given the high exposure with regard to Ms. Rhodes tragic injury."[191]

Friday, January 9, 2004

Attorney Larry Boyle (Morrison Mahoney, counsel for defendants Carlo Zalewski and Driver Logistics Services) sent a letter to Jodie Mills, asking for a contact at AIG to discuss possible mediation and any settlement offer AIG would like to extend.

Two years have passed since the crash. Without a reasonable settlement offer from Zurich and AIG, our lives have been made as terrible as possible. For two years, Marcia and I have been paying for her medical expenses from our own savings. The financial pressure

---

189 Dr. Mattson's PhD is in health and social welfare policy.
190 McCarter & English is GAF's corporate law firm.
191 Tendering Zurich's $2 million to AIG, instead of to the plaintiffs without stipulation is a perfect example of where Massachusetts law must change.

on us is incredibly unfair. What would other blameless victims do if they didn't have the savings to pay for two years of medical expenses? I think that Zurich and AIG are using this lawsuit to send a loud message to other plaintiffs' attorneys that they wouldn't settle easily or quickly, even if their insured was 100 percent at *fault*.

Wednesday, January 14, 2004

McCarter & English sent a letter to AIG:
"Need coverage confirmation and to respond to settlement demand."

Friday, January 23, 2004

Kathleen Fuell made a new entry in Zurich Claims Notes authorizing Crawford to increase the reserve on the data transfer file. Kathleen Fuell also advised Crawford and Willis Group Holdings (the insurance broker) that Zurich would tender its policy limit of $2 million to AIG.[192]

Sunday, Friday 4, 2004

Attorney Anthony Bartell (McCarter & English) sent a letter to AIG:
"Still no confirmation of coverage and further delay jeopardizes settlement discussions and exposes AIG to extra-contractual liability."

Friday, February 6, 2004

Jane Gordon (in-house corporate counsel for GAF) sent an e-mail to Robert Manning and to Kathleen Fuell in which she asks for a formal notification from Zurich confirming the tender:
"We would like to be in a position to inform plaintiffs' counsel that Zurich has tendered $2 million, but that AIG will not put up a penny. The only way we are going to move this issue is for the plaintiffs' lawyer either to go ahead and schedule mediation or somehow drag AIG in front of the judge."

Monday, February 9, 2004

In response to the e-mail, Kathleen Fuell sent an e-mail to Jane Gordon referencing a conversation with Nicholas Satriano a few weeks earlier in which he stated he:
"Was not accepting any tender unless in writing."
Referring to a group teleconference on this claim in November in which Nicholas Satriano agreed to review the entire matter by December, Satriano thought that Zurich was turning over defense obligations to AIG.

---

[192] From this date until late March, Zurich tried to get AIG to accept its $2 million tender; AIG delayed accepting the tender for various reasons. Meanwhile, our financial resources continued to dwindle.

Kathleen Fuell said she was still reviewing the policy to determine if defense obligations ceased when the policy limit was offered.

Another unnecessary delay by Zurich.

Friday, February 13, 2004

Nicholas Satriano sent an e-mail to Steve Penick and Kathleen Fuell stating, *"AIG has not received a formal offer of tender in writing."*

Fuell responded to Satriano:

"A few weeks ago, I called you to advise that we were offering up our $2,000,000 policy limits. I did not state that Zurich North America was in any way relinquishing our defense obligations to the insured pursuant to the guidelines of the Business Auto Policy."

"However, as you know, we are offering up the full limits of our auto policy based on the exposure of this case, and the insured is anxious for you to take a position so a response can be made to the demand previously presented on behalf of the plaintiff."

"Regardless of whether or not you have our position in writing, you are fully aware of our assessment in this matter and should have no problem of proceeding accordingly in the best interests of our mutually insured."

Satriano then responded to Fuell, referencing Fred Hohn about contacting everyone to set up a meeting in the near future.

Friday, March 5, 2004

Nicholas Satriano handwritten notes from the meeting at GAF indicated:
"$6.6 M settlement value. $9.696 M Jury verdict."

Thursday, March 18, 2004

Anthony Bartell sent a letter to AIG, warning of a potential violation of Massachusetts General Laws Chapter 176D.[193]

Dear Nick:

We enjoyed meeting with you to discuss the Rhodes action. I write further to our brief discussion concerning AIG's statutory obligation to respond substantively to underlying plaintiffs' settlement offer.

---

[193] The fact that GAF's own outside corporate counsel had to advise AIG of the potential punishment for an unfair insurance practice is extraordinary.

I respectfully believe you misconstrue the scope of AIG's obligation and, consequently, incorrectly minimize the insurer's potential exposure to underlying plaintiffs.

Massachusetts General Law, Chapter 176D, ¶(9)(f) enumerates, as an unfair insurance practice, and insurer's "fail[ure] to effectuate prompt, fair and equitable settlements of claims in which liability has become reasonable clear." BMCA (unfortunately) faces, at the very least, reasonably clear liability for Ms. Rhodes' catastrophic injuries.

AIG, therefore, bears an affirmative obligation to commence settlement negotiations with the underlying plaintiffs. <Case Citations.> AIG bears a heightened statutory settlement obligation where, as her, underlying plaintiffs made a settlement demand, over seven (7) months ago, to which AIG never responded. <Case Citations.>

You advised that AIG refuses to extend a settlement offer because it cannot countenance underlying plaintiffs' excessive demand. The courts, however, specifically hold that 'even excessive demands on the part of the claimant...do not relieve an insurer of its statutory duty to extend a prompt and equitable offer of settlement once liability and damages are reasonably clear.' <Case Citation.>

AIG, in short, runs afoul of Chapter 176D, ¶(9)(f) by failing to respond substantively to underlying plaintiffs' settlement demand. You advised that AIG cannot violate this statute because the insurer fully protects the interests of its insured, BMCA. AIG's statutory obligations, however, run not only to its policyholder but also directly to the underlying claimants.

[A]ny person, including underlying plaintiffs, aggrieved by AIG's statutory violation may bring an action against the insurer for treble damages, attorneys' fees and costs under Massachusetts General Law, Chapter 93A, ¶(9). <Case Citations.>

We hope the above discussion clarifies AIG's statutory obligations and assists the insurer in responding to plaintiffs' settlement demand. Zurich has advised it soon will tender its $2 million liability limits toward settlement of the underlying action.

Once Zurich formalizes its tender, BMCA shall offer plaintiffs $2 million to settle their claims. Zurich will then transfer to AIG its defense costs obligations pursuant to the following provision of Zurich's automobile liability policy:

"Our duty to defend...ends when we tender, or to any claimant, or to a court of competent jurisdiction, with the court's permission, the maximum limits provided under this coverage. We may end our duty to defend at any time during the course of the lawsuit by tendering or paying *the maximum limits provided under this coverage, without the need for a judgment or settlement of the lawsuit or a release by the claimant."*

We expect AIG will cooperate fully with Zurich, BMCA, and Greg Deschenes to ensure a seamless transition of Zurich's duty to defend obligations.

If you have any questions or comments about the Massachusetts statutes outlined above, or about BMCA's plans for moving forward on the settlement front, please do not hesitate to contact me.

*Very truly yours,
Anthony Bartell*

Tuesday, March 23, 2004

Fred Hohn sent an e-mail to Kathleen Fuell confirming that Zurich's coverage counsel was in the process of drafting an official letter to tender the $2 million primary limits to AIG. The e-mail also noted that Nicholas Satriano was called up to active duty and that his manager, Richard Mastronardo (Nicholas Satriano's boss at AIG), had not returned his phone call.

Monday, March 29, 2004

Kathleen Fuell sent a letter to Richard Mastronardo that constituted Zurich's formal tender of its policy limits and that the defense obligation has been transferred to AIG.

Kathleen Fuell sent an e-mail to Robert Manning, attaching the tender letter and stating that Greg Deschenes had been authorized to extend $2 million policy limits as a settlement offer.

Tuesday, March 30, 2004

Anthony Bartell sent an e-mail to AIG and Zurich regarding the disagreement over who would pay the defense costs. According to Mr. Bartell,

"GAF will not pay own defense and that AIG and Zurich should resolve the issue."

Bartell also referenced GAF's anticipated $2 million settlement offer to the plaintiffs:

"Mr. Deschenes believes it important that BMCA, before the conference, responds to the plaintiffs' seven month old settlement proposal."

Bartell stated that if he did not hear from Zurich or AIG by 11:00 on March 31, 2004, then GAF's settlement offer would be conveyed to the plaintiffs.

Wednesday, March 31, 2004

Richard Mastronardo sent an e-mail[194] to Anthony Bartell stating:

---

194 Now Zurich and AIG are arguing about what a proper tender offer should be. Just another delay by Zurich, while our financial resources continue to dwindle.

"AIG verbally rejected Zurich's purported tender and if Zurich's policy allows them to no longer provide a defense once they tender, then it must be shifted to GAF because under the excess policy defense obligation is not triggered by a tender by the primary."

Thursday April 1, 2004

Kathleen Fuell sent an e-mail to AIG, stating that Zurich would pay for GAF's defense, with a reservation of rights against AIG.

Martin Maturine (the claims adjuster at AIG who replaced Nicholas Satriano) sent a letter to Fuell:

"Please be advised that we have reviewed the basis for Zurich tendering its primary policy limits ($2,000,000) to National Union (AIG). As stated by Mr. Mastronardo during your discussion with him earlier this week, on behalf of National Union, AIG hereby rejects Zurich's tender of its primary policy limits."

Maturine also stated that Zurich is putting its defense obligations and cost savings ahead of the interests of the insured, which is bad faith.[195]

Twenty-six months have now passed since the crash. We have spent an incredible amount of money for Marcia's out-of-pocket medical expenses and costs.

In the afternoon, I learned that Zurich offered the $2 million to Brown Rudnick, with the stipulation that this amount is to settle all claims against all of the defendants:

"Settle all claims against all defendants for $2 million."

Words could not describe my emotional breakdown. This offer was utter nonsense. Two million dollars could not possibly include enough resources for Marcia's past, current, and future medical expenses and costs, anything for her *pain and suffering*, or anything for the *loss of consortium* claims.

I couldn't, even though I had to, tell her about the offer. She is going to be devastated.

❖ ❖ ❖

Zurich, how could you do this to us? You should have offered the $2 million without any stipulations.

❖ ❖ ❖

On our behalf, Brown Rudnick rejected the offer.

---

[195] In a subsequent trial, this statement by Martin Maturine should become important evidence to then Judge Gants, but it does not.

Friday, April 2, 2004

Today, Kathleen Fuell informed GAF and all counsel that, in light of AIG's rejection of its tender, Zurich had made a business decision to continue to pay all defense costs but reserved its rights to recover its defense costs from AIG.

AIG accepted the tender of $2 million from Zurich and now is completely in charge of this lawsuit.

More than two years have passed since the crash in which a blameless victim was catastrophically injured. The person causing the crash was 100 percent at fault and was insured by Zurich.

Tuesday, April 6, 2004

Judge Cratsley, not unexpectedly, dismissed the complaint against the Town of Medway that had been filed on October 1, 2003. What a waste of time.

Friday, May 14, 2004

Martin Maturine sent a letter to Anthony Bartell:

"Everyone agreed that seeking additional discovery including the deposition of the plaintiff was important. Note that they appear to disagree about the logistics and National Union (AIG) instructed counsel to withdraw the motion to extend "pending resolution of coverage issues."

National Union (AIG) also wanted to postpone mediation until completion of discovery. Another delay.

"National Union (AIG) looks forward to participating in mediation as soon as liability and damages can reasonably be analyzed. This is not a 'new precondition' as your letter states, but rather remains the foundation on which every analysis of every claim is made.

Frankly, once discovery is complete, National Union (AIG) will participate in any reasonable attempt to dispose of the matter, with or without a third party mediator."

"Frankly, had the discovery been done in a timely manner, the proposed motion—and the correspondence surrounding it—would never have come to pass."[196]

Wednesday, May 17, 2004

AIG filed a "motion to compel" production of Marcia's mental health records.

We have nothing to hide, but obviously AIG must know that Marcia's psychological therapy records are privileged. I think AIG just wants to go on a fishing expedition to see if any damaging information could be found in her therapy records.

---

196 Now AIG is blaming Zurich for the delay. Meanwhile, our savings have become nearly depleted.

Filing this motion served a second purpose of causing additional delay.

Tuesday, June 1, 2004

Jane Gordon sent an e-mail to Kathleen Fuell, which was heavily redacted.

"It is my understanding that the motion, and the rationale behind it, have come from AIG, not from our lead counsel, Nixon Peabody."

Tuesday, June 1, 2004

The attorneys from Brown Rudnick filed the "Plaintiffs' Memorandum in Support of Its Opposition to Motion to Compel Plaintiff Marcia Rhodes to Produce Mental Health Records."

Friday, June 4, 2004

Martin Maturine sent an e-mail to Kathleen Fuell, Peter Mueller at Harwood Lloyd, Greg Deschenes, William Conroy, Jane Gordon, Ann Peri (GAF's risk manager), Steve Penick, Robert Manning, and Fred Hohn, with copied letters from May 2004, setting forth the rationale for National Union (AIG) moving to adjourn the trial.

"Our letter of April 16, 2004, attached, advised you of our association with the Campbell law firm, pro hac vice, to prepare this case for trial, as it is clear that National Union's (AIG's) policy has the greater exposure in this claim than that of Zurich's."

Yet another delay.

Tuesday, June 8, 2004

Although not required, Fred Pritzker, so astutely, offered to AIG the medical records with regard to the worsening of Marcia's ADHD and bipolar medical conditions. AIG declined this offer. Obviously, AIG had other motivations for compelling production of her mental health records.

Wednesday, June 16, 2004

A week later, and not unexpectedly, the defendants' motion to compel production of the pre-case mental health records of Marcia Rhodes was denied by Judge Chernoff.

Tuesday, July 20, 2004

THE INDEPENDENT MEDICAL EXAMINATION OF MARCIA RHODES

Even with more than 2,000 pages of medical records available, at the demand of AIG, Marcia was unexpectedly required to undergo an independent medical examination

(IME).[197] While AIG does have the right, as part of discovery, to have an IME done,[198] what part of paraplegia is Marcia faking?

Marcia had three reactions. Why couldn't this IME have been done earlier, instead of waiting until two months before trial? Why does the IME have to be conducted in a downtown Boston office in which she would have difficulty maneuvering her wheelchair? Why does the IME have to be conducted by a male (not a female) doctor?

Wednesday, August 4, 2004

THE DEPOSITION OF MARCIA RHODES[199]

As with my deposition, the defendants have a legal right to conduct a deposition of the plaintiffs. On August 4, 2004, thirty-one months after the crash, Marcia was deposed by AIG.

The purpose of this deposition, at this late date, is difficult for me to understand. I cannot believe it was required because AIG needed to learn any new information. AIG had been given thousands of pages of medical and financial records, three police reports, answers to many sets of interrogatories, investigational reports from Crawford and Zurich, and extensive information from others who had already been deposed.

I am worried that deposing Marcia might be damaging to her health. Would this deposition traumatize her again? Medical professionals from many different specialties had worked long hours to help her accept her injuries. In this one afternoon, could a major portion of her rehabilitative progress disappear?

I concluded that this deposition is being done to assess how well she would be received by the jurors and the trial judge and to evaluate her stamina when testifying at the upcoming trial. Was this deposition also to find ways to unsettle her and to make her not want to go through a jury trial? The attorneys present included:

1. Russell X. Pollock, Campbell Campbell Edwards & Conroy, counsel for the defendant, Building Materials Corporation of America, d/b/a GAF Materials Corp.

---

[197] "An independent medical examination (IME) occurs when a doctor/physical therapist/chiropractor who has not previously been involved in a person's care examines an individual. There is not doctor/therapist-patient relationship. IME's may be conducted to determine the cause, extent and medical treatment of a work-related or other injury where liability is at issue; whether an individual has reached maximum benefit from treatment; and whether any permanent impairment remains after treatment. An IME may be conducted at the behest of an employer or an insurance carrier to obtain an independent opinion of the clinical status of the individual. Workers' compensation insurance carriers, auto insurance carriers, and self-insured employers have a legal right to this request." "Independent Medical Examination," *Wikipedia*, last modified March 11, 2014, https://en.wikipedia.org/wiki/Independent_medical_examination.

[198] Dr. Joseph Hanak, who conducted the IME, confirmed the medical evidence previously provided to AIG. In fact, he made us aware of a new medical complication we had not known about. Not unexpectedly, he was never called as a defense witness at the trial. Another delay.

[199] The transcript of this deposition can be found at www.theblamelessvictim.com.

2. Grace C. Wu, Nixon Peabody, counsel for the defendant, Building Materials Corporation of America, d/b/a GAF Materials Corp.
3. Stephen J. Duggan, Lynch & Lynch, counsel for the third-party defendant, Jerry MacMillan's Professional Tree Service, Inc.
4. Lawrence F. Boyle, Morrison Mahoney, counsel for the defendant, Carlo Zalewski, Driver Logistics Services
5. John B. Johnson, Corrigan, Johnson & Tutor, counsel for the defendant, Penske Truck Leasing Corporation

The deposition began at 1:20 p.m. at the Radisson Hotel (Milford, Massachusetts). In this deposition, Marcia was asked more than 700 questions.

Thursday, August 18, 2004

Now facing trial in less than a month, AIG filed a "Joint Emergency Motion of Building Materials Corporation of America D/B/A GAF Materials Corporation, Carlo Zalewski, and Driver Logistics Services, Inc., for *In-Camera*[200] Review of Plaintiff Marcia Rhodes' Mental and Emotional Health Records and to Compel Deposition Testimony Relating to Plaintiff Marcia Rhodes' Mental and Emotional Health."

Sunday, August 22, 2004

On Sunday, August 22, 2004, AIG deposed Rebecca. It had the legal right to depose her, but like Marcia's deposition, I cannot understand the rationale for this deposition. Again, AIG had multiple sets of interrogatories from Rebecca and thousands of pages of records. Worse yet, the trial is to start in less than three weeks. What could AIG possibly learn from this deposition?

Wednesday, September 8, 2004

THE TRIAL

At 973 days after the crash, the civil trial of *Marcia Rhodes et al. v. Carlo Zalewski et al.* (Civil Action No. 02-01159A) finally began in Massachusetts Superior Court, before Judge Elizabeth Donovan.

The trial was conducted over six trial days. AIG presented only one witness.

On the first day of the trial, Warren Nitti, on behalf of AIG, offered $3.5 million ($2.5 million present value) to settle all claims.

---

200 *"In-Camera"* means having a judge review the documents and deciding if they are discoverable.

While AIG's offer might cover the past and current out-of-pocket medical expenses and costs, this amount wouldn't cover Marcia's future out-of-pocket medical expenses and costs, *pain and suffering*, Rebecca's *loss of parental consortium*, and my *loss of spousal consortium* claims. I rejected this offer.[201]

THE OPENING STATEMENTS

The trial began with the opening statement by Fred Pritzker, counsel for the plaintiffs. Pritzker described the details of the events leading up to the crash and medical issues that followed. Further, Pritzker described the four amounts to be included in the jury verdict: the amount for past, current, and future out-of-pocket medical expenses and costs; the amount for *pain and suffering*; the amount for *loss of spousal consortium*; and the amount for *loss of parental consortium*.

After Mr. Pritzker, Lawrence Boyle, counsel for the defendant Carlo Zalewski, made his opening statement. In it, he said:

"End of the day, Mr. Zalewski is totally responsible for the operation of that motor vehicle. Totally responsible for the accident and totally responsible for the injuries sustained."

After Larry Boyle, William Conroy, counsel for the defendant GAF, made his opening statement. In it, he said:

"Mr. Zalewski made a mistake. You'll hear what happened that day. This was not a question of speeding. It was not a question of drinking or drugs. He made a very unfortunate mistake and Mrs. Rhodes has paid a price for that.

And what we'll ask of you to consider through this trial and what I'll ask you to do at the conclusion of this case is to award a number that is correct and is fair.

You cannot give back to Mrs. Rhodes what she had, but with a fair and just award you can help compensate her for this loss."

THE WITNESSES

The plaintiffs presented ten witnesses:
1. Sergeant William Boultenhouse, the Medway Police officer directing traffic at the work site on January 9, 2002, testified as to the events of the crash.
2. Edward O'Hara, the Massachusetts state trooper stationed at the collision analysis and reconstruction section, testified as to the nature of the collision, its impact on Marcia's car, and the calculations made.
3. Carlo Zalewski, the defendant and driver of the forty-ton tanker-trailer, testified as to the day of crash, beginning with leaving New Jersey at 4:00 am. He

---
201 Rejecting this offer would significantly affect later legal proceedings.

further testified that he was charged with *"negligent operation of a motor vehicle"* and *"admitted to facts sufficient for a finding of guilt"* at his criminal trial.
4. Marcia Rhodes testified as to her life before and after the crash, recounting all medical issues and treatments, her ongoing *pain and suffering*, the *loss of her motherly relationship with Rebecca*, and the *loss of her spousal relationship with me*.
5. Rebecca Rhodes testified as to the *loss of her daughterly relationship* with Marcia.
6. Elizabeth Roaf, MD, Marcia's physiatrist since being admitted to Fairlawn Rehabilitation Hospital, testified as to the details of Marcia's medical conditions beginning with the crash, the lack of rehabilitative progress, and that she would always be an outlier in terms of recovery. The defense attorneys cross-examined Dr. Roaf.
7. Norman Beisaw, MD, orthopedic surgeon and professor of orthopedic surgery at University of Massachusetts Medical School, testified as to the catastrophic nature of Marcia's spinal cord injury. (Dr. Bayley, who had performed the surgery, was stationed in Iraq at this time.)
8. Adele Pollard, RN, plaintiff's Life Care Planner, testified as to the specific nature of Marcia's ongoing medical issues, the required lifelong medical support, and the costs of lifelong medical support.
9. Dana Hewins, PhD, plaintiff's economist and life expectancy analyst, testified as to the calculation of the present value of Pollard's costs of lifelong support.
10. Harold Rhodes testified as to the details of the catastrophic injury, Marcia's required home care, the financial burden, and the loss of spousal relationship.

The defendants presented just one witness. Jane Mattson, PhD, the defendants' Life Care Planner, testified as to the specific nature of Marcia's ongoing medical issues, the required lifelong medical support, and the costs of lifelong medical support. The costs that Mattson suggested were more than $1 million less than the detailed calculation by Pollard.

After examination and cross-examination of the eleven witnesses, the three attorneys made their closing statements to the jury.

Thursday, September 16, 2004

CLOSING STATEMENT BY MR. BOYLE
(COUNSEL FOR THE DEFENDANT CARLO ZALEWSKI)

Good morning, Your Honor. On behalf of my partner, John Knight, we thank you for your attention. The average Massachusetts Superior Court trial lasts about three days, and you've been here for more than twice that. A lot of people were here on that first day for jury selection, and you stayed. You did tough civic duty.

At the beginning of the case, I told you that there were very few issues in this case. We admitted liability; we admitted that she had a very serious injury and that we were responsible for it. And nothing has changed with respect to what I told you in my opening.

This case—Carlo Zalewski, who's here, and John Gonzalez, are all very sorry, and everyone in this courtroom are very sorry for this accident, and they're here to take full responsibility for the consequences and the damages this jury is going to award this morning or this afternoon.

I told you that there were—you heard about the facts of the accident, not that there is any excuse by way of explaining what happened. And I think one thing that you heard from a lot of the police was that there were no safety cones or markers of any sort, and this was at the bottom—this accident was at the bottom of this hill.

There are more cones in the front of this building on those steps than there were on Route 109 on the date of this accident. Clearly an unsafe situation. It does not make any difference. Carlo Zalewski is responsible for the accident. We are not blaming anybody else.

Now, Mrs. Rhodes suffered, and the Rhodes family suffered a tremendous loss. I am not going to in any way try to minimize that because I think that you heard fully from her physicians, there is no dispute about the injuries and the complications as to what she suffered.

Now, the question is—and a verdict you give—obviously is she's not going to walk again—your verdict would award compensatory damages to somehow make her plight, make her able to adjust to her new life. She's got a new life, and that is not going to change. Nothing we do in this courtroom is going to change that.

Now, there is a couple of things, and the Judge is going to instruct you on the law. I am not suggesting anything different. But essentially compensatory damages break down to two types. So-called special damages, which are the hard medical costs for care plan, things you can mathematically calculate.

And pain and suffering, which is an intangible, which is something we are not going to give you a cookbook and you go into that courtroom and well, paraplegia, you know, look it up at her age and somehow help you with that.

That is something that the wisdom of thirteen men and women from Norfolk County is going to have to struggle with, and that is not necessarily going to be easy because other than some—your own sense of common sense, and your own sense of your conscience is going to guide you to translate what you heard in this courtroom into a dollar award.

She should get a full award of money damages to compensate her for her loss. No question about that.

Now, the standard is what is reasonable compensation? Again, that is just a term of art, and essentially I think a fair way to look at it is not unreasonably high, not unreasonably low. And again, your conscience and your common sense, your experience in life are your only guides, and that is what you're going to have, nothing else other than exhibits in the jury room.

Now, what is not compensatory damages are something called punitive damages. It is not in this case. Where you say hey, Carlo Zalewski hit the plaintiff on the road, we are going to teach that guy a lesson, and we are going to send a message to big scary trucks, whatever.

A message of punishment that you think in some fashion might be appropriate. That is not part of this case. That is not part of this courtroom. It is not part of the law with respect to damages, not part of this case.

Secondly, what is not part of this case is awarding just on sympathy. We are all sympathetic and I am sure the plaintiff's counsel's hit—she's got all the sympathy in the world, but what she needs is money to help her adjust her life. That is not part of the damage analysis.

And lastly, what's not part of this case is wages, lost wages. It is not part of this case.

So it essentially boils down to the medicals, future and past, the shown numbers to the care plan, and pain and suffering, those two components.

Again, the application of reasonableness is standard.

Now, you've heard different testimony about care plans, what they cost, the economists reducing it to present value, and in your good wisdom, you're going to decide what's appropriate, based upon the evidence. That is your job.

They were presented to you, all of them, or both of them rather, funding for her needs for life, which is appropriate, and providing for unexpected contingencies down the road, and everything experts in this field can perceive as needs in the future.

All of that should be, I anticipate, will be part of your award, and whatever number you select will be the right one, the just one.

Now, one thing that has been a little bit of an issue in the sense of an intangible is we know where Marcia Rhodes has been, and we have heard a lot of detail about how she was the day of the accident, three months post accident in the hospital, and how she was when she was coming home and the struggles they had.

There is no question that this period of time, that was the worst. And you got that. Where is she going into the future? Unclear. Are there goals? Are there realistic goals? That is something for you to decide. And are they achievable goals?

But certainly as the experts said, it is sort of a work in progress. We are not there yet, it is certainly not the end of the day as far as improvement, and a lot of her own uniqueness will depend upon where she ends up going forward for life expectancy.

Now, I said—one of the questions I asked Mr. Rhodes, remember one of the things that Adele Pollard said, knowledge is power. And I use that at work. Knowledge is power. I want people who work with me to know how I speak and know how I think, so there are no issues at all.

This is what I am—this is what I feel about things. Knowledge is power.

And certainly there is a learning curve that both the Rhodes's are going through, the whole Rhodes family, acquiring knowledge. And this care plan is sort of a path towards acquiring knowledge to better her life, make her more independent.

And your verdict will fund a care plan. Your verdict will fund, hopefully, following the recommendation to go to either the BU program or this one in Colorado, apparently they're both top of the line programs.

But again, that is where Adele Pollard said that is where you're going to learn things that you're going to have specialists give you advice. You're going to have a dietician get involved in the diet, as opposed to something more ad hoc.

And what it boils down to essentially is a couple of things that will make her more independent. Independence meant you have more freedom in your life. People worry about having a personal care assistant always transfer you.

The goal, you want to be able to get out of bed in the morning, you want to be able to get on the toilet, you want to be able to go in the shower and transfer. That is an achievable goal. Will she make it? Who knows? That is a realistic goal.

And one of the two components, when you boil it all down, is diet and getting stronger. Her upper body's got to get stronger so she can lift herself and accomplish these transfers.

Now, with all due respect to Harold Rhodes' social worker who told—he said yesterday—my social worker told me neither to encourage or discourage my wife. I would suggest that if you go to the BU spinal cord program, they're going to say it is going to be tough love, it is going to be encouraged. Lose some weight, lift the weights.

And is it going to be easy? No, it is going to be hard. It is going to be a program of sacrifice. And I would suggest Marcia Rhodes can do it. Marcia Rhodes has been compliant. You saw on the videotape, she's exercising, she's obviously very intelligent.

So I would suggest that she's not going to give up hope. These are achievable goals.

A woman who's 45, with a dietician, can lose weight and can get stronger. Whether or not they'll be fully independent, who knows? She can take driving courses, she can become independent.

And according to Dr. Pollard, one of the life care planners, that her goal is not to have any personal care people. Be able to do things on your own. That is where you want to be. That is better for Mrs. Rhodes, that is better for Mr. Rhodes, and that is certainly better for the daughter. Again, this is the future and no one can predict it. But achievable goals.

But it is going to be not the social worker advice to neither encourage or discourage, but sort of the tough love approach. Your own experience that we have in therapy, it is not necessarily easy.

Now, the defendants never said that Mrs. Rhodes is going to be a wheelchair marathoner, or join a wheelchair basketball team or anything like that, but life care planners talked about in the universe of people with handicaps and disabilities exist, but certainly transferring upper body strength from bed to a wheelchair does not participate in the Boston Marathon necessarily. I think it is achievable to suggest the evidence—it is an achievable goal.

Now, at the end of the day, your award, and especially the Life Care Plan, is going to be a path. We do not know exactly where that path is going, but you should fund that path. And in a perfect world, she won't need seven days a week personal care help, but you should fund it, because if she does need it, the money's there.

In a perfect—and hopefully some of the things that they recommend, the independence will be achieved, and that is what you should fully fund and award her pain and suffering. And the husband and the daughter for something called loss of consortium.

And that is all damages that have been proven and what you should award for.

Now, the Judge told you at the beginning of the trial that at the end of this case, the last thing—I teach a paralegal course at night, and say the jury goes out, they're going to return something called a verdict. It is from two Latin words, 'veritas,' the truth; 'dicto,' to speak.

And that is based upon your conscience and your life experience in an effort to try to be fair to all parties in this case. And I ask that you return your verdict, and return a fair verdict for the plaintiff and a fair verdict for the defendants.

Thank you.

CLOSING STATEMENT BY MR. CONROY (COUNSEL FOR THE DEFENDANT GAF)

May it please the Court, Mr. and Mrs. Rhodes, counsel. Members of the jury, good morning.

Justice is done when compensation is fair. And that is what this case has been about from the very beginning of this trial. What is fair compensation to Mr. and Mrs. Rhodes and their daughter, Rebecca?

From the very beginning of this trial, that is what we have been here about.

It is a very unfortunate accident. We all wish we weren't here.

Mrs. Rhodes' life has been changed dramatically, in ways that are just hard to imagine.

At the beginning of this case, I told you that. I also told you that from my clients' standpoint, GAF, Building Materials Corporation, that we are responsible for what happened on that day.

Mr. Zalewski's actions that day legally flow back to us. And Mr. Zalewski's taken responsibility, his employer has, D.L.S., and my client GAF also has.

This case is about compensation, not about punishment. What happened that day was a mistake, a mistake that Mr. Zalewski regrets deeply.

Then the issue becomes well, what is fair? What is fair for this case?

It is a very difficult thing to do is to try and put numbers and assess values on things we take for granted. You've heard at length about the details Mrs. Rhodes has with her life. The issues with her bowel problems and urinary problems. Things we take for granted each day.

She cannot walk again. She cannot do things that each day she was accustomed to doing.

And these are hard, they're very hard for her. We understand that. And the challenge in this case has been to look at snapshots of how Mrs. Rhodes' life was before this accident, and what she did, and what her interests were, and to try and compare to after the accident what she does, what she is trying to do.

And at the same time, respect her limitations. And frankly, it is a challenge for us. She was badly injured. And we have placed ourselves into your hands to come up with a just and a fair verdict in this case. A reasonable verdict.

Each one of us feels very badly for what's happened to her. And we cannot put aside sympathy. It just cannot be done. And we feel the emotions in this case. But we cannot allow our emotions and ours sympathy to decide what the value is for the losses here. Because once that is done, ladies and gentlemen, the system can run amok.

I cannot suggest to you how to do it, because I do not know. That is why, as a group, we ask you to apply your collective common sense and sort through the issues and determine what you think collectively is right, what is fair, and what is just. That is all I ask on behalf of my clients. Nothing more.

If we look at Mrs. Rhodes to begin with, there has been a number of different plans presented to you. We had Dr. Mattson presenting one Life Care Plan for her future health care expenses. It was on the order of 1.2 million dollars before it is reduced to present value.

We had the higher plan that we heard from the plaintiff's expert, Dr. Pollard. That was in the range of 1 and a half to 2 million dollars. These account for that?

There is the issue of pain and suffering. And you account for that as well.

All I can tell you, ladies and gentlemen, is be fair, to be reasonable. There is expectations that Mrs. Rhodes has for the future to improve her life. She has certain goals that she's working to. There has been some complications that she's run into since this accident. Hopefully she's worked through those.

The leg fractures when she was dropped. A series of bedsores that hopefully are under control. They will be periodic. One's back again now.

You need to account for all these things, but look to the future. And no one knows what it holds for Mrs. Rhodes in terms of her level of improvement. We know what the goals are. We know what the plans are. And consider all those.

Mr. Rhodes. He has a claim here as well. And reasonably account for what he has done to help his wife through all this.

And Rebecca. Rebecca's been through a lot as well. Her relationship with her mother is changed. Though she seems to be back doing a lot of things that she did with her mom before the accident, it is different. It is a different relationship. We understand that. She's trying to move on. She's doing well in school. She plans on going to college.

But there is a value for what she's lost. And you need to sort that out. It all gets back to a question of what is fair. Not punishment in this case, but fairness and reasonableness.

You'll think back on this trial for a long time. You saw a lot of things, you learned a lot of things, and you saw a lot of sorrow. But you'll look back on this trial and you'll say to yourself, did I do the right thing with how we assessed damages? Was it fair? Was it reasonable? Was it controlled? That is what I ask of you.

Thank you.[202]

---

202 After six days of trial, after all of the witnesses, testimony, depositions, interrogatories, pretrial motions, pretrial hearings, the IME, discovery, thousands of pages of medical documentation, and mediation, all that William Conroy, on behalf of AIG, could say in his closing was: *"And the challenge in this case has been to look at snapshots of how Mrs. Rhodes' life was before this accident, and what she did, and what her interests were, and to try and compare to after the accident what she does,*

CLOSING STATEMENT BY MR. PRITZKER
(COUNSEL FOR THE PLAINTIFFS)

Ladies and gentlemen, on behalf of the Rhodes family, Margaret Pinkham, and the rest of the team, you've been a great jury. This has not been an easy thing to go through. Mr. Boyle mentioned the amount of time you've all been sitting here, and that is the sacrifice.

It is more than that. It is more than that because you've had to hear things that have been uncomfortable. You've seen things that are uncomfortable. The Rhodes family has had to bare not only their souls, but their—their intimacies, their privacy to you.

But there was no other way to do it to get you to understand what they have gone through as a family, what Marcia has and is and will be going through for the rest of her life.

This is an unusual case in a lot of ways, and probably one of the biggest ones is that there is no issue of liability in the case. All of the defendants have acknowledged their responsibility.

Mr. Zalewski has acknowledged that he was careless in the way he was driving. Driver Logistics Services and GAF have acknowledged that because of their corporate roles, they are responsible for his behavior.

So they came to you at the beginning and they come to you now and said that all they want you to do is to render a fair and reasonable verdict.

But, I'll ask you to reflect for a minute as to what they did during the trial. Because on the issue of damages, which is the only thing that you are to determine, they either low-balled the damages with their own witnesses, or did not mention them at all.

The only witness on damages that they presented to you was Jane Mattson.

And as to her, she presented her Life Care Plan. The first thing she did was choose the lowest possible life expectancy for Marcia Rhodes. And we are talking about the life expectancy after her injury.

We all know that she has a life expectancy or she had a life expectancy of approximately 82 years if it weren't for the injury. So the—Jane Mattson chose 72 years for her life expectancy.

---

what she is trying to do. And at the same time, respect her limitations. And frankly, it is a challenge for us. She was badly injured. And we have placed ourselves into your hands to come up with a just and a fair verdict in this case. A reasonable verdict."

And as reinforcement of that, they pulled out Exhibit 63, which was the report of Mr.—or Dr. DeVivo.

And the last page of that has a schedule on it. And they cross-examined Dr. Hewins as to whether or not he understood that schedule. And they also cross-examined one of the doctors on that.

And it turns out that at age 72, which happens to be 24.4 years from the time that the report was written, the survival probability is between .56 and .53. That means the survival probability is between 56 percent and 53 percent.

Or, to put it another way, Mrs. Rhodes has a better than equal chance to survive longer than age 72.

Notwithstanding that, Jane Mattson adopted that as the only life expectancy that she used in her Life Care Plan.

Now, I have to kind of jump aside for a minute because does it really matter if you use the life expectancy of age 72, the Life Care Plan is going to be less. But think about what that means. What that means is that Mrs. Rhodes is being deprived of ten years of her life.

So while the life expectancy part of the damages might be less, you now have to figure out what the worth is, what the value is for the fact that this injury rendered by the defendants who have admitted their responsibility has lowered her life expectancy by ten years.

So one way or another, it should be compensated for by the defendants.

What would happen to Marcia if you actually adopted the Life Care Plan of Jane Mattson and on her 72nd birthday she was still here? She'd be out of money. For whatever the remainder of her life was under the Life Care Plan that the defendants presented to you, she would be out of money.

Is that fair and reasonable?

Ms. Mattson provided no allowance for modifications of the home, except for the kitchen.

Now, the Rhodes family had a rather nice home before this accident. Four bedrooms and a bath upstairs. A downstairs that consisted of a living room, a den, a dining room and a kitchen.

And after the accident, when Mrs. Rhodes can no longer access the upstairs or the basement area where Mr. Rhodes had his office, it was okay with Jane Mattson that Mrs. Rhodes sleep on a hospital bed in the living room for the rest of her life. Is that reasonable?

From these defendants who have admitted liability and have said we are responsible, is it reasonable to ask a person to sleep in the living room, knowing that they're handicapped for the rest of their life?

That is what the defendants have presented to you.

There was no provision in the Mattson plan for any physical exercise club. There was no provision for added care as she got older. Her only provision health care at all or health care aide was three hours a day, even though Drs. Roaf and Biesaw both testified that it was unlikely that Mrs. Rhodes would ever be able to transfer without assistance.

Jane Mattson said gee, if she exercises, if she loses a little weight, there is no reason why she cannot transfer by herself. Let's just stop for a minute and reflect on what that means. You saw Mrs. Rhodes both at the early stage of her post-accident recovery and then six months ago trying to transfer.

And she does pretty well right now in taking two hands and being able to lift herself up. The problem is you need a third hand for the board. So the people who transfer, who are typically younger and athletic people, are those people who can maneuver so they're lifting themselves up, not with two arms, but with one arm while they're sliding the board under with the other, and then pushing themselves over on the board.

Now, Mrs. Rhodes is doing a lot better than she has. Will she ever be able to transfer independent of any help? Well, the doctors doubt it. Jane Mattson didn't, but the doctors did. And let's reflect for a minute on what Ms. Mattson said about the three hours per day, because it was relying upon the fact that well, Mr. Rhodes and the daughter are also around to help.

Is it fair, ladies and gentlemen, to impose that burden on Harold and Rebecca because of the accident that was the responsibility of the defendants? As opposed to providing more reasonable health care for seven days a week, so maybe the family would be relieved from some of that burden?

Is that fair and reasonable?

One of the most outrageous positions of the Mattson Life Care Plan, I think, was the provision for five doctors' visits per year.

Five doctors' visits per year, given what this poor lady has gone through, and given what she is expecting to go through for the rest of her life, and given the fact that today, as you heard Harold Rhodes testify yesterday, she has nine doctors that she visits on regular basis, including a psychologist, a physiatrist, which was—who was Dr. Roaf, an orthopedic surgeon, a (surgical) urologist, a gastroenterologist, a urologist for her urinary problems, a gastroenterologist for her bowel problems, a podiatrist, a wound care specialist, an her regular doctor.

Five visits a year means she cannot see her doctors even once during any given year.

Is that reasonable?

Let's look at damages if we can for a minute. You've seen most of these chalks before. There does not seem to be any dispute about the past expenses. Those are expenses that have already been expended, in order to care for Marcia, because of her injuries.

Very quickly, the $425,000 figure is for medical services and prescriptions to date, those all came into evidence by way of certified records by the medical providers, and they were unopposed. In fact, all of these figures were unopposed.

There was home care, medical equipment, medical supplies, miscellaneous stuff like a Life Care Plan that brings offers and a health club, handicap accessible van, handicap modifications to the home, which as you've already heard, probably too much now, for the three phases, that included design costs.

They do not include the kitchen because no costs were assessed, although both Jane Mattson and Adele Pollard indicated that $20,000 would be appropriate additional costs to kitchen modifications.

And the last one, the $49,000 for the basement, has not been done, although the bids are out and that hopefully will be done shortly.

That amounts to $911,458 that is been expended so far on Mrs. Rhodes' rehab.

Now let's talk about future damages. The future damages were those based upon the Pollard Life Care Plan, and Dana Hewins, the economist. The economist, by the way, who also works for both of the defendant firms in cases like this.

There was loss of household services of $292,000. And that number has been already reduced to present value. As you heard Dr. Hewins say, first he projects out what it is going to cost, and then he figures out what the award should be as of the date of the filing of the complaint, so they can take that money and use it as necessary, in order to reach the bigger cost over a period of years.

And the future medical and personal care expense also reduced to present value is Adele Pollard's Life Care Plan, and we took the 83 year age part of her plan, which was 1.997, close to 2 million dollars.

And the total of those future expenses together were $2,290,000, for future expenses that it is going to take to care for Marcia Rhodes for the rest of her life.

Now, once again, going back to Exhibit 63, the question is that an unreasonable age to pick, they have to pick some age. And I suggest to you once again, if you go back to that—to that chart, the probabilities are a lot lower that Marcia Rhodes will reach age 83, but they're not zero. They're not close to zero.

In fact, the probability is 2339, close to 25 percent, which is one in four. She has a one in four probability that she will survive beyond the age of 83.

Now, if what we are talking about is fair and reasonable compensation against those defendants who have already admitted liability, I suggest to you that using this money and rejecting the Mattson money is the appropriate thing to do.

So we take all—before I put up this next chart, let me just talk to you about what we have just seen. What we have just seen are past expenses that Mrs. Rhodes has had expended on her behalf. And a reasonable estimation of what it will take to care for Mrs. Rhodes for the rest of her life because of her injury.

And it is important to focus on the fact that what we are talking about is care for Mrs. Rhodes because of her injury. It does not deal at all with compensation for the infliction of the injury itself, something which is called pain and suffering.

Now, Judge Donovan will be instructing you on what the legal requirements are for pain and suffering, but I am going to give you a little preview if I might. Before I do that, let's look at what the total package is for the damages that you will be considering.

We have already talked about the medical bills and other injury-related expenses, those are the past expenses, of $911,000. We talked about the future care by way of both the Life Care Plan and the lost household services, which total $2,290,000.

The total of that is $3,201,000 to care for Mrs. Rhodes past and future, but all post accident. That is only to care for her because she has been rendered a paraplegic.

The last part, which we have not gotten to at all, and you've had very little talked about, is the physical pain and the emotional pain, the physical suffering and the emotional suffering, which has been given to Mrs. Rhodes because of this accident.

So we have mental and physical pain and suffering, which includes emotional distress, impairment of normal functioning, loss of life. It is her pain, her loss of function, her loss of mobility, her loss of freedom, her loss of privacy, her embarrassment at her condition, her depression and the general loss of the enjoyment of her life. That is this final portion.

That is the part that the lawyers cannot give you a number on. That is the part that you have to take the evidence that has been presented to you. You have to layer on top of that your own personal experience, and you have to come up with a fair number.

You have, however, heard some evidence that will help you. The 3.2 million dollars is a very large number, just to care for Mrs. Rhodes for the rest of her life. The pain and suffering that she has been forced to endure is huge, and it started the day of the accident. And it started before the crash.

Let's go back to that first day when Mrs. Rhodes is stopped by Sgt. Boultenhouse, then Officer Boultenhouse. He has his hand up; he's wearing his orange vest. She stops, and she looks in the rear-view mirror. And when she looks in the rear-view mirror, her pain and suffering starts. Because she sees this truck barreling down the hill.

And she has to make some quick decisions. She cannot turn to the left because the cars have started coming to her left, going in the opposite direction. If she went straight, she would have killed Sgt. Boultenhouse.

So she turned her wheel to the right. And then there was the crash. And at the moment of the crash, you heard Mrs. Rhodes talk about and describe how she heard her back break. Dr. Biesaw described it as her back bursting. She heard it. She heard the fact that she was going to become a paraplegic before she felt it.

And directly thereafter, she knew that she had no feeling, no motion from the waist down, but she sure had a lot of pain from the waist up.

You heard about the fractured ribs and you heard about the fact that she described them as knives cutting her from the inside out. She was in enough pain so she said—she testified that she was pleading for some medication, which they wouldn't give her until they were able to assess what her injuries were. That is where the pain and suffering started.

She did not deserve anything. She did not do anything to deserve that kind of pain.

As horrible and as frightening as that first day was, now let's just talk a little bit about what happened at UMass Memorial Hospital, where for the first week, all they can do is try and stabilize her and save her life.

You saw the pictures of her strapped into the rotor bed, where all they were doing was trying to prep her enough so they can then go in and operate on her and see whether or not there was anything about her spine that they can save.

And then six days after the accident, when she's finally stable enough to be operated on, you heard quite a lot of detail from Dr. Biesaw, as to what happened on the operating table. I know it was probably more graphic than you ever wanted to know, but I thought it was awfully telling as he was describing what Dr. Bayley, the orthopedic surgeon did, that he put his finger into the spine where the spinal cord was supposed to be and it was not there. And he knew immediately there'd be no repair to the spinal cord.

So what did he do? He aligned the spine, put the rods and the screws in. Dr. Biesaw talked about the functions of the spine being flexible as well as for stability to keep us upright because she's lost the flexibility. Those rods with the screws in are now just stabilizing the spine enough so she can sit up straight. She has to be that way for the rest of her life.

If that weren't enough, and it should have been enough, within a week she had other surgery because she was developing blood clots. Now, the surgery was not to correct the blood clots, the surgery was to keep the clots from traveling up to the heart, to the lungs, and to the brain, which would have killed her.

So a week after—I am sorry—two weeks after the spine surgery, she's back in the operating room again for more surgery to insert this filter through the groin. And can you imagine, ladies and gentlemen, having just come through the back surgery, what that must have entailed.

Well, she was at the UMass Memorial Hospital almost a month. And there were other complications, as you've heard, the bleeding of the brain, the air that formed between the chest wall and the lungs, just complication upon complication. You'll have all that. You'll have it in the jury room with you. I do not really expect you to go through it, but it was brutal.

Why am I reviewing all of this with you?

Because it deals with the pain and the suffering, which Mrs. Rhodes has endured since the date of this crash.

So now let's focus on Fairlawn, where she was for two and a half months. For two of those months, she was in isolation because of the development of the staph infection. So I want you to picture this. Here is the woman who is finally starting to deal with her paralysis.

She knows that she's paralyzed from the waist down, she's never going to walk again, she's never going to feel again, she probably does not yet comprehend all of the other problems that paraplegia offers. But she's trying to deal with it, and everybody who comes into her room is wearing a surgical gown and a mask. Just picture what that must be like, ladies and gentlemen. And what is it worth?

Well, the stay at the Fairlawn was not only complicated because of the isolation, but this poor woman, as you know, had her broken ribs which were being sandwiched by the body brace, which was necessary to allow the spine to heal. I cannot imagine the pain. Maybe you can. But it certainly was something that should be considered as part of the pain and suffering award.

And in addition to that, she developed a blood clot in her leg, where the leg swelled up to four times the size of her normal leg. It was so heavy, it took two people just to move the leg. And all of this while she's trying to rehab, to become as comfortable and productive as she can, in isolation except for the last two weeks of her—of her two and a half months stay at Fairlawn.

If that weren't enough, then it should be enough. Will any of us forget quickly Marcia and Harold Rhodes' 19th anniversary? That was the day that she came home from Fairlawn. That was the day that she had the bowel movement accident that neither of them expected or were prepared for.

And the worst thing about that was that here is Marcia, who is helpless in her bed, having to finally recognize that her husband is trying to move her, with difficulty, is trying to wash her, is changing her diaper, and that this will happen over and over again for the rest of her life.

What is that worth? If I were writing this as a script, I would say enough already. But two weeks later, she's back in the hospital because of a gangrenous gallbladder, a gallbladder that she cannot feel was becoming so infected that when they finally recognize what the problem is, it had to be taken out on an emergency basis. And then she had to spend two more weeks at another rehab, center, at the Whittier Rehab Hospital.

And you heard her description, amongst other things, of the fact that they put a tube in her side, in order to drain from the gallbladder cavity that they had taken out, the blood and the other fluids that they kept getting on her clothes and how embarrassing that was to her.

Well, when she came home from the second stay, they started a routine. At least they started a routine. Until she broke her legs. Not one leg as the defendants made reference to, but both legs. And if that weren't enough, she developed at about the same time the pressure sores.

And so between the casts and the pressure sores, she was forced to stay in her bed for the next eleven months, except for trips to the toilet and to the doctor.

All of this, all of this inflicted on her because of the injury. All of this in the category of pain and suffering over and above the 3.2 million dollars that was spent or will be spent for her care.

Any one of these events would justify a large pain and suffering award, any one of them. All of them together? I do not have a word, but it is enormous.

What would a fair compensation be to Marcia Rhodes for the—for one month of having to be subjected to this? What would a fair compensation be for one year of being subjected to this? What's a fair compensation for the last two and three quarters years that It is been since the accident? And what will it be for the next 33 years?

That is up to you, ladies and gentlemen.

I wish I had some guidance for you. I am glad, in a way, that I am the lawyer who's asking the questions and you're the ones that finally has to render the verdict.

But we are not through yet, because we still have to deal with the loss of consortium claims for Harold and Rebecca. And I am not going to spend a lot of time on it.

Can anyone challenge that the relationship between Harold and Marcia, previously a relationship of husband and wife, has turned into that of caregiver and manager for Harold and patient for Marcia.

Harold is there to give Marcia whatever support and help she needs, days, nights and weekends. Marcia is no longer there to give Harold the comfort, support, and care which if he does not need now, he certainly will before their relationship is over. Is she able to give that? Is she able to care for him if he gets ill? Are they able to spend time together the way they used to before the accident? That is Harold's loss of consortium claim.

And Rebecca? When Rebecca opened up and confessed to us all that she does no longer confide in her mother with her problems because her mother's problems are so overwhelming, did not that say it all? This is not about having dinner before the accident and still having dinner, mother and daughter, after the accident. This is not about taking trips down the Cape before the accident, and they've taken a trip down the Cape, a successful one, after the accident. This is about the fabric of the relationship.

And I suggest to you, ladies and gentlemen, that that fabric is torn, and it was torn because of this accident. Marcia is now consumed with her own care, and Rebecca has withdrawn.

All of this because of the actions of Zalewski, for which all of the defendants have admitted responsibility.

Finally, I want to just remind you folks, back at this opening, when I was trying to paint the picture of the accident, and you had a couple of freeze frames, and we'll go back to one of those frames, it was Marcia, stopped by Officer Boultenhouse, Zalewski is just coming over the crest of the hill. We heard from Trooper O'Hara that the rate of speed that Zalewski was traveling, that he traveled 56 feet per second. We know from Trooper O'Hara and the other officers that there were 750 feet traveled between the crest of the hill and the point of the accident.

That means that it took Mr. Zalewski 12 seconds, 12 seconds when he had a straight road, downhill, no one between himself and Marcia Rhodes, and an unobstructed view. Twelve seconds when he was not looking. Twelve seconds when he did not stop. Twelve seconds when he did not slow down. And in those twelve seconds, the Rhodes' family's life was changed forever.

I know, ladies and gentlemen, that you will render not only a verdict on the care costs, but also a fair verdict on the pain and suffering of Marcia Rhodes and the loss of consortium claims of Harold and Rebecca Rhodes. And I thank you for your attention.

Thursday, September 16, 2004 (continued)

THE VERDICT

After the closing statements on the last day of trial, at lunchtime, the jurors began their deliberations.

<u>The Court:</u>

"Madam Forelady, during the course of your deliberations if you have any questions on the law of damages, I will answer the questions on the law of damages, but It is up to you people to determine the damages. That is solely within your domain.

What we are going to do is we'll swear in our court officer. As I said, if you have any question, you write it down on a piece of paper and knock on the door and give it to our court officer. Then I am going to have counsel go over—we have to put together all those 72 exhibits, and then we'll send those in to you as quickly as we can. All right."

<u>The Clerk:</u>

"Officer Waite, do you solemnly swear that you will keep this jury in some separate but convenient place until they are agreed, that you will suffer no person to speak with them nor ask them if they are agreed, nor suffer them to disperse until they are discharged of the verdict, except by order of the Court, so help you God?"

<u>Court Officer:</u>
"I do."

<u>The Clerk:</u>
"Thank you."

<u>The Court:</u>
"All right. The jury can go out."

❖ ❖ ❖

Just after the jurors left the courtroom, Marcia and I had to go home. Because Marcia had to be seated for many hours, Marcia developed several pressure ulcers on her buttocks. I had to get Marcia home and into bed.

It took the jurors just four hours to return their verdict.

❖ ❖ ❖

The Clerk:
"May I inquire of the jury, Your Honor?"

The Court:
"Please."

The Clerk:
"Madam Foreperson, have eleven of your number agreed on a verdict?"

Foreperson:
"Yes."

The Clerk:

"May we have the papers, please. Thank you. Madam Foreperson, members of the jury, harken to your verdict as the court records it in Civil Action 02-1159, Marcia Rhodes, Harold Rhodes Individually, Harold Rhodes on behalf of his minor child and next friend Rebecca Rhodes, Plaintiffs, versus Carlo Zalewski, Driver Logistics Services, Inc., and Building Materials Corporation of America, d/b/a, GAF Materials Corp., Defendants."
Question No. 1:
"What sum of money will fairly and adequately compensate the plaintiff Marcia Rhodes for the injuries sustained as a result of the defendant's negligence?"

Foreperson:
"The amount in words: Seven million four hundred and twelve thousand dollars. In figures: 7,412,000."
Question No. 2:
"Did the plaintiff Harold Rhodes sustain the loss of consortium as a result of the injuries to his wife Marcia Rhodes?"

Foreperson:
"The answer is 'yes.'"
Question No. 3:

"What sum of money will fairly and adequately compensate the plaintiff Harold Rhodes for his loss of consortium?"

Foreperson:
"In words: One million five hundred thousand dollars. In figures: 1,500,000."
Question No. 4:
"Did the plaintiff Rebecca Rhodes sustain the loss of consortium as a result of the injuries to her mother Marcia Rhodes?"

Foreperson:
"The answer is 'yes.'"
Question No. 5:
"What sum of money will fairly and adequately compensate the plaintiff Rebecca Rhodes for the loss of consortium?"

Foreperson:
"In words: Five hundred thousand dollars. In figures: 500,000."

The Court:
"So say you, Madam Foreperson?"

Foreperson:
"Yes."

The Clerk:
"All must respond. So say at least eleven of your number?"

Jurors:
"Yes."

The Clerk:
"Thank you. The verdict has been recorded, Your Honor."

The Court:
"Thank you. Madam Forelady, members of the jury, I want to thank you very much for coming in and performing your civic duty. Under our constitution, we are all required to sit as jurors, so on behalf of all the members of the court staff and judiciary, thank you for performing your civic duty."

❖ ❖ ❖

Fred Pritzker called us at home after the verdict was announced. When the phone rang, I was taking care of the new pressure ulcers that had developed during the trial. I had to ask him to call us back to tell us the verdict.

After all these years of waiting for justice, we had to wait another ten minutes. I didn't mind this wait.

"It took but a second for a woman's life to be forever altered when her vehicle was slammed from behind by an 18-wheeler, instantly paralyzing her from the waist down. It took a jury four hours to award her more than $9 million in damages for pain and suffering, loss of consortium and the cost of future care. The $9.41 million verdict—in the case of Rhodes, et al. v. Zalewski, et al.*—tops the list of Massachusetts jury verdicts in 2004."*[203]

Was this a win for blameless victims? In some ways, it was, but in many other ways, it wasn't.

While the verdict was going to cost Zurich and AIG a lot of money, they had been able to send a loud message to all future blameless victims and their attorneys: *"If you want to win, you will have to spend years in litigation, which we still don't think you will do because of this verdict. In the end, we still come out ahead."*

Post-Trial Actions by Zurich and AIG

Tuesday, September 21, 2004

Steve Penick sent an e-mail to Kathleen Fuell stating:

"Do not know what AIG's intentions are?"

He noted that there was an offer of $6 million from AIG and plaintiffs countered with $10 million offer. With pre-judgment interest, the total award increased to $11,950,000.

Penick sent another e-mail to Fuell, responding to her e-mail saying that the third-party attorney told her that a verdict was rendered. Penick apologized for the delay.

"There were no surprises. I am waiting for the formal report as well. AIG attorneys took the lead and GAF's original attorneys simply monitored." "We are not anticipating an appeal."

Friday, October 8, 2004

Today, Zurich and AIG filed a "Post-Trial Motion" to Judge Donovan for a new trial or, in the alternative, a remittitur (a decrease in the verdict amount decided by the jurors). More than ever, I am angry. Why wouldn't AIG pay what the jury said and let us move on with our lives? Why do they keep this up? I didn't know if Marcia and I could stand anymore of this.

---

[203] "Top Verdicts of 2004 Experience 'Rebound,'" *Massachusetts Lawyers Weekly*, January 17, 2005, last modified March 11, 2014, http://masslawyersweekly.com/2005/01/17/top-verdicts-of-2004-experience-rebound.

Tuesday, October 26, 2004

Zurich and AIG filed a "Notice of Appeal" to the Massachusetts Appeals Court, requesting that a new trial be ordered due to Judge Donovan's *"abuse of her discretion."* Marcia and I were devastated to learn about this. Another year or two had to pass before the Massachusetts Appeals Court would resolve the victimization.

Before the Appeals Court could hear the appeal filed by Zurich and AIG, the six-day trial transcript had to be completed. To expedite its completion, Brown Rudnick paid additional money.

The Massachusetts judicial system is not able to produce timely trial transcriptions.[204] The completed trial transcript would take more than one year.[205] However, the post-judgment interest continued to accrue at 1 percent per month; waiting a year to settle would cost AIG an additional $1 million.

Without the trial transcript completed, AIG would continue to negotiate a lower amount with Fred.

Tuesday, November 15, 2004

Judge Donovan denied the post-trial motion by Zurich and AIG for a new trial and/or remittitur.

Wednesday, December 15, 2004

An e-mail was sent to Kathleen Fuell requesting that a funding transfer request be submitted immediately:

"As we are dealing with a Massachusetts 93A time limit demand and are accruing post-judgment interest."

Friday, December 17, 2004

Two new entries were made in the Zurich Claims Notes, noting that AIG filed a formal "Notice of Appeal." It was issuing a settlement check in response to the Chapter 93A demand to mitigate further exposure to ongoing litigation and a potential claim for treble *damages* as well as to cap post-judgment expenses.[206]

Wednesday, December 22, 2004

Nearly three years after the crash and three months after the trial, Zurich made a payment of $2 million (and $323,000 for the pre-judgment and post-judgment interest) to

---

[204] Massachusetts is recognized as among the worst in the United States. Although a well-recognized problem, this delay is a major defect in the Massachusetts justice system. For more information, see "Report of the Study Committee on Trial Transcripts" at http://www.mass.gov/courts/trialtransrep.pdf.

[205] More than five years later, in January 2010, the Massachusetts Supreme Judicial Court finally made an effort to resolve this extremely slow production of trial transcripts.

[206] I believe that these entries prove that Zurich failed to *"effectuate prompt, fair and equitable settlements of claims in which liability has become reasonably clear"* and that its failure was *willful or knowing*.

us. Zurich had successfully been able to delay making its payment for as long as possible. Zurich shouldn't be allowed to do this to a blameless victim.

Zurich must be severely penalized to prevent Zurich and other primary insurance carriers from doing the same to other blameless victims.

January 2005 to July 2005

While the jury's verdict had been made on September 16, 2004, we have heard nothing from AIG. Why won't AIG just pay the remaining amount of the jury's verdict? AIG shouldn't be allowed to do this to a blameless victim.

Like Zurich, AIG must be severely penalized to prevent AIG and other excess insurance carriers from doing the same to other blameless victims.

Thursday, July 14, 2005

Ten months after the verdict by jury and more than three and a half years after the crash, Brown Rudnick, on our behalf, accepted AIG's offer of $8.97 million. Including the $2.32 million from Zurich and the $550,000 from Jerry McMillan's Tree Company, the award totaled $11.84 million. Of that amount, Brown Rudnick received $4.1 million (including expenses and attorney fees). Yet to be paid is the negotiated reimbursement to UnitedHealthcare for the medical expenses that it has paid. Additionally, taxes will have to be paid on the interest. The remainder is the amount of money to take care of Marcia for the rest of her life.

Friday, July 15, 2005

All that I could think about is this question. If these same events happened to a different blameless victim, and if this blameless victim didn't have the funds to pay an enormous amount of money for expenses, didn't have access to a world-class law firm like Brown Rudnick, and didn't have a spouse who could afford the loss of income, could this blameless victim expect a verdict of $11.84 million?

No.

And that is my outrage. The Massachusetts judicial system has to make sure what happened to Marcia will never happen to another blameless victim.

Zurich and AIG must be substantially punished for their unfair delays so that they and other insurance carriers won't ever do this again.

TIMELINE FOUR:
DID ZURICH, AIG, OR BOTH COMMIT AN *"UNFAIR OR DECEPTIVE ACT"*?

NOVEMBER 1, 2004 TO JULY 30, 2008

MARCIA RHODES, HAROLD RHODES, AND REBECCA RHODES (PLAINTIFFS)
V.
AIG DOMESTIC CLAIMS AND ZURICH AMERICAN INSURANCE (DEFENDANTS)

CIVIL ACTION NO. 05-1360BLS IN MASSACHUSETTS SUPERIOR COURT[207]

INTRODUCTION TO INSURANCE LAW IN MASSACHUSETTS

Massachusetts General Laws state that *"unfair or deceptive acts or practices in the business of insurance"* include *"failing to effectuate prompt, fair and equitable settlements of claims in which liability has become reasonably clear."*[208]

I learned that this law has been litigated many times. Now, each word of this law has a special legal meaning.

Through these earlier judicial decisions, rather than requiring a financial settlement when *liability* was *"reasonably clear,"* insurance carriers have been able to develop

---

207 As mentioned before, let me state that I am not an attorney, so my legal observations and conclusions may be inaccurate. A nearly complete record of the litigation documentation for Timeline Four can be found at www.theblamelessvictim.com.
208 Massachusetts General Laws, Chapter 176D, last modified March 11, 2014, https://malegislature.gov/Laws/GeneralLaws/PartI/TitleXXII/Chapter176D/Section3.

clever loopholes to postpone their responsibility to effectuate *"prompt, fair and equitable settlements of claims."*[209]

For example, through one earlier decision by the Massachusetts Supreme Judicial Court (SJC), the plain meaning of the word *liability* has been redefined to separately include *fault* and *damages*.

When does *fault* become *"reasonably clear"*? Is *fault* *"reasonably clear"* when the driver of a tractor-trailer crashes into the rear-end of a stopped vehicle, witnessed by a police officer, and the driver is given a motor vehicle citation? To the great advantage of insurance carriers, *fault* is not *"reasonably clear"* until the tractor-trailer driver is convicted of, or pleads guilty to, a motor vehicle violation. A criminal trial, and the appeals, might take many months or years to finalize.

When do *damages* become *"reasonably clear"*? Are *damages* *"reasonably clear"* when the person in the stopped vehicle is immediately catastrophically injured? To the further great advantage of insurance carriers, the *damages* to a catastrophically injured person might not be *"reasonably clear"* for many months or even a few years.

Before an insurance carrier would *"effectuate a prompt, fair and equitable settlements of claims,"* Marcia would have to wait until (a) the driver of the tractor-trailer would legally be found at *fault* through a criminal trial and (b) enough time had passed such that Marcia's current and future *damages* could become reasonable clear.

Through these earlier judicial decisions, Marcia is triply harmed. First, Marcia must suffer horrible medical injuries.

Second, Marcia and I must pay all of her past, current, and future medical expenses and costs, perhaps many hundreds of thousands of dollars, without any financial support from Zalewski's insurance carrier. Likely, we will face a dire financial consequence.

Third, Marcia and I will be forced to endure extensive and unrelenting litigation instead of concentrating on her recovery and rehabilitation.

Together, insurance carriers could delay for a very long time *"to effectuate a prompt, fair and equitable settlements of claims in which liability has become reasonably clear"* with Marcia and me.

For all blameless victims, this delay will be financially overwhelming and emotionally devastating, and altogether ruinous. Insurance carriers know this. Insurance carriers use this to pressure blameless victims into an insufficient financial settlement.[210] This is a crappy system of justice for blameless victims.

---

209 For more information, see https://malegislature.gov/Laws/GeneralLaws/PartI/TitleXXII/Chapter176D/Section3.

210 On the other hand, an insurance carrier could logically and immediately conclude that the driver of a tractor-trailer who crashes into the rear-end of a stopped vehicle, witnessed by a police officer, and who is given a motor vehicle citation, is at *fault*. A criminal trial just isn't necessary to make this reasonable determination. Further, if the insurance carrier has a policy limit of $2 million and, through its claims processing experience, knows that any catastrophically injured individual will have *damages* that far exceed its $2 million policy limit must reasonably conclude that its $2 million policy limit will be paid, no matter what the final determination of *damages* is. As a good corporate citizen, this insurance carrier

❖ ❖ ❖

"Delay undermines the effectiveness of the criminal justice system by putting off the punishment of the guilty and the vindication of the innocent."[211]

❖ ❖ ❖

Monday, November 1, 2004

After the jury announced its verdict, I was often asked whether I was satisfied with the results of the trial. On the one hand, the jury completely understood Marcia's catastrophic injuries and how her life would now be. I was gratified about that. On the other hand, I was more fixated on ascertaining what could be done to prevent insurance carriers from doing to future blameless victims what Zurich and AIG did to Marcia.

LEGAL REQUIREMENTS TO PROVE AN *"UNFAIR OR DECEPTIVE ACT"*[212]

Today, I met with the attorneys from Brown Rudnick to learn what could be done to penalize Zurich and AIG for the years of delay. By publicly and substantially punishing them, perhaps the next insurance carrier would do far better for the next blameless victim. I learned that there are two relevant statutes in the Massachusetts General Laws.

MASSACHUSETTS GENERAL LAWS CHAPTER 176D[213]

Chapter 176D defines *"unfair or deceptive acts or practices in the business of insurance."* Section 3(9)(f) of this statute states: *"The following are hereby defined as…unfair or deceptive acts or practices in the business of insurance"…"failing to effectuate prompt, fair and equitable settlements of claims in which liability has become reasonably clear."*

---

could immediately provide the catastrophically injured person with its $2 million policy limit. By doing so, blameless victims would not be financially overwhelmed or emotionally devastated. Blameless victims could concentrate all of their energies on their recovery and rehabilitation.

211 Malcolm Feeley, *The Process Is the Punishment: Handling Cases in the Lower Criminal Courts* (New York: Russell Sage, 1979).

212 Understanding Chapter 93A and Chapter 176D is extremely difficult. Many attorneys (and judges) have different, sometimes opposite, understandings. Additionally, there are many legal cases that, at one time or another, have impacted the legal interpretation of Chapter 93A and Chapter 176D. Further, due to the subtle vagueness and exceptions of Chapter 93A and Chapter 176D, it is impossible to provide a brief but complete analysis. Only a brief overview relevant to this lawsuit is presented here.

213 For more information, see https://malegislature.gov/Laws/GeneralLaws/PartI/TitleXXII/Chapter176D/Section3.

While this is seemingly straightforward, the legal interpretation of Chapter 176D Section 3(9)(f) is not easily understood.

First, in the context of Chapter 176D, what does the word *liability* legally mean? For example, is the driver who is at fault for an auto accident immediately liable? Oddly, the legal answer is no.

After Chapter 176D became law, courts refined the legal meaning of the word *liability* to include both *fault* and *damages*. As such, *liability* is not established until both *fault* and *damages* have become *"reasonably clear."*

Fault is established only when a judge or jury determines a verdict of guilty or when the driver admitted to facts sufficient for a finding of guilt.

Damages is only established only when the calculation of the present value of the total of past, current, and future out-of-pocket medical expenses and costs, *pain and suffering*, *loss of parental consortium*, *loss of spousal consortium*, losses of income, and interest and other amounts, over the driver's life expectancy, has become *"reasonably clear."*

Even then, after *fault* and *damages* have been established, has the defendant's insurance carrier that failed *"to effectuate prompt, fair and equitable settlements of claims in which liability has become reasonably clear"* committed an *"unfair or deceptive act"*? Oddly, again the legal answer is no.

Second, after Chapter 176D became law, courts added a requirement before a defendant's insurance carrier could be proved to have committed an *"unfair or deceptive act."*

Not only must a defendant's insurance carrier fail *"to effectuate prompt, fair and equitable settlements of claims in which liability has become reasonably clear,"* but in failing to do so, the defendant's insurance carrier must be the *cause* of a *harm*[214] to the blameless victim.

AN EXAMPLE OF AN INSURANCE CARRIER VIOLATING CHAPTER 176D

Here is a simplistic example of an insurance carrier committing an *"unfair or deceptive act."*

1. An individual is injured in an auto accident. The driver of the other vehicle is cited for negligent operation of a motor vehicle.
2. Within six months of the auto accident, the judge at the criminal trial finds the driver guilty or the driver admits to facts sufficient for a finding of guilt. At this point, *fault*, as the first part of establishing *liability*, has been established.

---

214 As mentioned before, for brevity, legal explanations of *causation* and *harm* are not presented. These are particularly difficult legal concepts to understand for a person who is not an attorney. Although simple in appearance, the legal meanings of these words have been the subject of many earlier court decisions. As a further complication, there is increasing debate within the legal community as to whether *causing* a *harm* is even a requirement to find that the insurance carrier had committed an *"unfair or deceptive act."* For an initial understanding, see http://masscases.com/cases/sjc/445/445mass790.html.

3. Within one year of the auto accident, the plaintiff provides the defendant's insurance carrier with documentation that calculates *damages* to be $1 million. However, the defendant's insurance carrier does not respond in any meaningful way.
4. Two years after the auto accident, the plaintiff files a personal injury lawsuit, including updated documentation that calculates *damages* to be $2 million. However, the defendant's insurance carrier continues to not respond in any meaningful way.
5. Three years after the auto accident, the personal injury trial is held. The defendant's insurance carrier offers $250,000 to settle. The plaintiff does not accept the offer. The jury awards the plaintiff $2 million plus interest of $300,000.
6. The defendant's insurance carrier files a series of post-verdict motions to overturn the award. All the post-verdict motions are denied.
7. Nine months after the verdict, the defendant's insurance carrier still has not made the $2.3 million payment. The plaintiff files a Chapter 93A/Chapter 176D lawsuit contending the *"defendant's insurance carrier willfully or knowingly[215] failed to effectuate prompt, fair and equitable settlements of claims in which liability has become reasonably clear and, in doing so, was the cause of a harm to the plaintiff."*
8. Three months later (which is twelve months after the jury's verdict and thirty-six months after the filing date of the personal injury lawsuit), the defendant's insurance carrier pays $2.3 million to the plaintiff.
9. One year later, the Chapter 93A/Chapter 176D trial is held. The judge finds a violation that the defendant's insurance carrier *willfully or knowingly "failed to effectuate prompt, fair and equitable settlements of claims in which liability has become reasonably clear"* and, in doing so, was the *cause* of a *harm* to the plaintiff. As a penalty, the judge orders the defendant's insurance carrier to pay an amount of money[216] to the plaintiff.

According to Steven Bolotin,[217] Chapter 93A *"is confusing, complex, amorphous, and it is known jokingly as the lawyers full-employment act. Most 93A violations do not make it through the court system because it is hard to prove a violation is a knowing one—a major point of the law. I have in my years of practice taken only one 93A claim to a final verdict."*

---

215 For brevity, the legal concept of *willful or knowing* is not presented here. This is another particularly difficult legal concept to understand for a person who is not an attorney.

216 For brevity, the legal concept of how a judge determines the amount of money to be paid is not presented here. This is another particularly difficult legal concept to understand for a person who is not an attorney.

217 Steven Bolotin is an attorney with Morrison, Mahoney & Miller. These quotes were included in *Insurance Times*, February 6, 2001, Vol. XX, No. 3. Copyright © *Insurance Times*. All rights reserved. Reproduced without permission. In full disclosure, Bolotin's law firm represented Carlo Zalewski and Driver Logistics Services in the earlier personal injury trial.

OVERCOMING THE LEGAL AND EMOTIONAL OBSTACLES MAKES PROVING AN *"UNFAIR OR DECEPTIVE ACT"* DIFFICULT

THE LEGAL OBSTACLES

In our case, there were at least eight substantial legal obstacles to prove that Zurich, AIG, or both committed an *"unfair or deceptive act"* by *willfully or knowingly "failing to effectuate prompt, fair and equitable settlements of claims in which liability has become reasonably clear"* and, in doing so, was the *cause* of a *harm* to the plaintiff.

Powerful corporate entities. Zurich and AIG are powerful corporate entities with significant financial resources. In 2003, Zurich reported revenues of $49 billion. AIG reported revenues of $47 billion. Both companies could easily afford to drag this litigation out for many years at significant cost to Brown Rudnick.

Substantial insurance industry support. Zurich and AIG, as major leaders of the insurance industry, would have substantial support from many (if not all) of the organizations with a vested interest.

Proving a *willful or knowing* violation. In general, insurance carriers are superb at masking their actions as neither a *willful* nor a *knowing* violation. An expert witness, on behalf of the insurance carrier, often use the term *"insurance industry custom and practice"* as a defense against proving a *willful or knowing* action to fail *"to effectuate prompt, fair and equitable settlements of claims in which liability has become reasonably clear."*

The acceptance of the use of hypothetical settlements offers. During the trial, a plaintiff might be asked by the insurance carrier, *"Would you have accepted a settlement offer of $5 million?"* On the one hand, suppose the plaintiff answers *"no"* or *"I do not know"* and further suppose that the trial judge decides that this $5 million hypothetical offer would have been a reasonable settlement offer. The insurance carrier will then argue that because the plaintiff wouldn't accept this reasonable hypothetical offer, there could not have been an *"unfair or deceptive act."* On the other hand, suppose the plaintiff answers *"yes."* The insurance carrier will argue that the plaintiff didn't negotiate in good faith, because the settlement demand was larger. Again, there cannot be an *"unfair or deceptive act."*

Proving *causation* of *harm*. Even if a plaintiff can prove that an *"unfair or deceptive act"* had been committed, the plaintiff must additionally prove both that the plaintiff was *harmed* and that the actions of the insurance carrier were the *cause* of the *harm*. Proving *harm* and that the insurance carrier was the *cause* of that *harm* is difficult.

The amount of the punishment. Judges might be concerned about the negative reaction to a large financial punishment. In our case, the Defense Research Institute argued that it is *"unclear whether the Court has thought through the long-term consequences of its ruling on the insurance marketplace or the cost of such rulings to policyholders, both in terms* *of increased costs of insurance and sums that insureds may now be forced to pay through self-insured retentions, deductibles and retro-rated premiums."*[218]

Constitutionality: Cruel and unusual punishment. If the punishment to either or both Zurich and AIG is large, the punishment could be subject to the precedents concerning the Eighth Amendment of the US Constitution, regulating cruel and unusual punishment.

The excellent attorneys representing Zurich and AIG. The principal defense attorneys included Greg Varga of Robinson & Cole,[219] representing Zurich, and Anthony Zelle and Mark Cohen of Zelle McDonough & Cohen,[220] representing AIG. All three are expert litigators.

THE EMOTIONAL HURDLES

Besides the legal issues, pursuing this action against Zurich and AIG would require Marcia and me to endure terrible emotional hurdles for more than six years of litigation frustration, which will infiltrate every day of our lives.

All the anguish of interrogatories, depositions, and trial testimony would be played out once again.

To begin, there would be a trial in Massachusetts Superior Court.

Win or lose, there would be an appeal to the Massachusetts Appeals Court.

Win or lose, there would be a second appeal to the Massachusetts Supreme Judicial Court.[221]

If we won, there might be a trial before the US Supreme Court.

What choice did we have? We had to do all that we could to protect future blameless victims.

Litigation in the Massachusetts Superior Court Begins

Friday, November 19, 2004

To get Zurich and AIG to pay the jury's verdict and lay the groundwork for a second lawsuit alleging an *"unfair or deceptive act,"* Brown Rudnick sent Zurich and AIG a Chapter 93A "Demand Letter."

Tuesday, April 5, 2005

Today, Brown Rudnick filed a lawsuit with its initial complaint, on our behalf, against Zurich and AIG: *Marcia Rhodes et al. v. AIG Domestic Claims and Zurich American Insurance* (Civil Action No. 05-1360BLS).

---

218 "Massachusetts Court Raises the Stakes for Failing to Settle," Michael Aylward, last modified March 11, 2014, http://dritoday.org/post/Massachusetts-Court-Raises-The-Stakes-For-Failing-To-Settle.aspx.
219 For more information, see www.rc.com.
220 For more information, see www.zelmcd.com.
221 The Massachusetts Supreme Judicial Court is most often referred to as the "SJC."

This decision by Brown Rudnick's senior management to go up against Zurich and AIG showed magnificent resolve. For an additional six years or more, Brown Rudnick would have to accept the tremendous financial expense to litigate this lawsuit.

Massachusetts Superior Court Judge Ralph Gants, in the Business Litigation Section, will preside.

Dan Brown, a member of Fred Pritzker's litigation department, joined our team of attorneys.[222]

Plaintiffs' Discovery Begins: Zurich and AIG Refuse to Provide Requested Documents or Answers to Interrogatories

With the complaint filed, discovery began. Through discovery, Brown Rudnick sought information to understand the settlement actions by Zurich and AIG.[223] In general, the discovery requests by Brown Rudnick included the following:

- Category 1: Internal correspondence of the third-party administrators Crawford and AIG created before litigation was threatened or commenced.
- Category 2: Internal correspondence of the third-party administrators Crawford and AIG created after litigation was threatened or commenced.
- Category 3: Correspondence between and among the parties and their attorneys.
- Category 4: Communications among the defendants and GAF'S insurance broker, Willis Group Holdings.
- Category 5: Documents regarding the reserve amounts set for the underlying tort case.
- Category 6: Claims manuals.

Finally, Brown Rudnick made a "Motion to Compel" production of these documents as well as answers to interrogatories. Zurich and AIG responded with their motions to deny the motion to compel.

Tuesday, December 6, 2005

Today, Brown Rudnick served Zurich with a second request for documents, specifically detailing the types of claims manuals and guidelines requested.

---

[222] Like the other fine attorneys at Brown Rudnick, Dan Brown possesses an extraordinary legal mind. Many times, he showed an uncanny ability to recall and comprehend even the smallest of the case facts. While his legal participation would be extraordinarily helpful overall, after reviewing thousands of pages of documents, he noticed that a key document was missing from those provided by the defendants. This document turned out to be vitally important.

[223] Over the next nine months, Brown Rudnick will make multiple requests for documents as well as answers to interrogatories, nearly all of which will be unanswered.

Monday, January 23, 2006

Judge Gants decided which documents are privileged and which are not through his "Memorandum and Order on Plaintiffs' Motion to Compel Defendants to Produce Documents."[224]

He organized the documents requested by Brown Rudnick's attorneys into six categories and made a decision about privilege for each category. His decision on document production, including the insurance claims notes, enabled Brown Rudnick to have a more complete understanding of the settlement actions taken by Zurich and AIG.

Category	Privilege Determination by Judge Gants
Category 1: Internal Correspondence of the Third-Party Administrators Crawford and AIG Created Before Litigation Was Threatened or Commenced	"…until litigation has been threatened or commenced, the factual reports of investigation and the insurer's evaluation of those reports contained in the claims file are prepared in 'the ordinary line of business and duty' and not in anticipation of litigation, and thereby do not constitute protected work product."
Category 2: Internal Correspondence of the Third-Party Administrators Crawford and AIG Created After Litigation Was Threatened or Commenced	"…this Court finds that the opinion work product created by insurance company claims representatives who participated in determining the timing or the amount of the settlement offers made to the plaintiffs in the underlying case is discoverable because the conduct of these claims representatives is at issue and the need for such work product is compelling."
Category 3: Correspondence Between and Among the Parties and their Attorneys	"…this Court finds that: 1. Privileged communications shared by counsel with clients they jointly defended remain privileged; 2. Privileged communications exchanged by the defense attorneys with other defense attorneys and defendant clients remained privileged as a result of the joint defense privilege; but, 3. Communications directly between or among the defendants that were never protected by the attorney-client privilege or work product doctrine do not become privileged or protected as a result of the joint defense privilege."

---

224 For the complete decision, see http://masslawyersweekly.com/fulltext-opinions/2006/01/23/rhodes-et-al-v-aig-domestic-claims-inc-et-al/. For the complete article, see www.qoclaw.com/sw/Jul06_1.htm.

Category 4: Communications Among the Defendants and GAF's Insurance Broker, Willis Group Holdings	"…privileged communication that was copied to Willis must be disclosed to the plaintiffs because the privilege has been waived."
Category 5: Documents Regarding the Reserve Amounts Set for the Underlying Tort Case	"To the extent that the defendants are contending that reserve information may never be disclosed, even within those parameters, because the information is not relevant, this Court rejects that contention."
Category 6: Claims Manuals	"Consequently, this Court orders the disclosure by AIG and Zurich of their withheld claims manuals and claim handling guidelines."

Wednesday, February 22, 2006

Today, Zurich and AIG filed a "Petition for Interlocutory Relief," asking that a judge from the Massachusetts Appeals Court request this court to grant their petition and to reverse the trial court's order.[225]

Zurich and AIG continue to do everything possible to keep these documents from Brown Rudnick.

Monday, February 27, 2006

When Brown Rudnick received the defendants' "Petition for Interlocutory Relief," its attorneys began immediately to develop an opposition response. However, even before Brown Rudnick could file its "Opposition," Judge Dreben of the Massachusetts Appeals Court made his ruling:

"It is only in the rarest of cases that a single justice will interfere with a discovery order. This is not such a case. See the thoughtful opinion of the Massachusetts Superior Court Judge Gants. The petition is denied."

Wednesday, March 1, 2006

Although more than a month has passed since Judge Gants ordered Zurich to produce all withheld claims manuals and Zurich's "Petition for Interlocutory Relief" had been denied, Zurich still has not produced these documents.

Because Brown Rudnick would be deposing Kathleen Fuell on March 10, 2006, an emergency motion to compel Zurich to produce the Zurich claims manuals was filed.

---

225 The term *trial court* is synonymous with "Massachusetts Superior Court" as well as with "Judge Gants."

Wednesday, March 8, 2006

After nearly a year of requests, Zurich produced its claims manual, "Liability Best Practices." Importantly, this manual specified how a claim, such as ours, should be adjusted by a major case unit consultant at Zurich.

Tuesday, August 22, 2006

THE DEPOSITION OF HAROLD RHODES[226]

Marcia, Rebecca, and I again will have to endure being deposed by Zurich and AIG. My deposition was held at the offices of Robinson & Cole. The defense attorneys at the deposition included the following:
1. Anthony Zelle of Zelle McDonough (Boston, Massachusetts), representing AIG.
2. Mark Cohen of The McCormack Firm (Boston, Massachusetts), representing AIG.
3. Greg Varga and Elizabeth Sackett of Robinson & Cole (Hartford, Connecticut), representing Zurich.

Mr. Cohen began the deposition. After Mr. Cohen, Mr. Varga continued the deposition. Over the next six hours, I was asked more than 1,000 questions. When they thought I was about to wander off track, Fred Pritzker and Margaret Pinkham said, *"Just answer the question."* I got back on track. I was questioned in two particular areas:

4. What distinguishable *harm* was I alleging? Further, on what basis am I alleging that Zurich, AIG, or both were the *cause* of the *harm*?[227]
5. Hypothetically, would we have accepted an offer of six million, seven million, or $8 million to settle?[228]

Thursday, August 24, 2006

THE DEPOSITION OF MARCIA RHODES[229]

Two days later, Marcia was deposed. The defense attorneys included Anthony Zelle, Greg Varga, and Robert Maselek from The McCormack Firm.

The answers she gave had to be taken at face value. For most of the time until the first trial, Marcia was a patient in rehabilitation, suffering from one or more secondary

---

226   The transcription of this deposition can be found at www.theblamelessvictim.com.
227   Later, the Massachusetts Supreme Judicial court made a landmark ruling concerning this line of questioning.
228   Later, the Massachusetts Supreme Judicial court made another landmark ruling concerning this line of questioning.
229   The transcription of this deposition can be found at www.theblamelessvictim.com.

medical complications and taking strong medicines. Her knowledge of the details of what had transpired over the four years preceding was foggy.

The deposition began at 11:00 a.m. at the Radisson Hotel (Milford, Massachusetts) and continued until 2:15 p.m. Marcia was asked more than 350 questions.

Friday, August 25, 2006

THE DEPOSITION OF REBECCA RHODES[230]

Legally, Zurich and AIG had the right to depose Rebecca.

However, given that she had no firsthand knowledge about whether Zurich or AIG committed a *willful or knowing "unfair or deceptive act"* and had no knowledge about the *harm* that Zurich and AIG caused, like Marcia, I was not sure why Zurich and AIG wanted to depose her.

Beginning on January 9, 2002, Rebecca's therapist, psychiatrist, school counselors, and others have tried to get Rebecca past this tragedy and to focus on her future.

I am worried that a lengthy deposition could undo all the progress she had made over the last four years.

Her deposition was held at the Radisson Hotel (Milford, Massachusetts), beginning at 11:00 a.m. and concluding at 1:00 p.m. The defense attorneys included Mark Cohen and Greg Varga.

In spite of my concern, Rebecca is the smartest and most fearless one in our family. She answered one of the first questions deftly and straight to the point.

Mr. Cohen:
"What is your understanding as to what the lawsuit is all about?"
Ms. Rhodes:
"It is my understanding that this lawsuit is in regards (to) how long it took to receive money from the first trial."

Could a father be more proud? Mr. Cohen and Mr. Varga asked her more than 450 questions.

The Trial

Monday, February 5, 2007: Trial Day One

Marcia woke at 3:30 a.m. to complete her morning activities and provide us plenty of time to drive to Boston. As we entered the courtroom on the tenth floor of the Massachusetts Superior Court of Suffolk County, I was filled with trepidation. Trials are just plain scary.

---
230 The transcription of this deposition can be found at www.theblamelessvictim.com.

In addition to the Brown Rudnick attorneys (Fred Pritzker, Margaret Pinkham, Dan Brown, and Rachel Lipton), the following attorneys made appearances:
1. Gregory P. Varga, Elizabeth Sackett, and Steven Goldman of Robinson & Cole (Hartford, Connecticut), counsel for the defendant Zurich American Insurance
2. Anthony Zelle, Brian McDonough, and Robert Maselek of Zelle McDonough (Boston, Massachusetts), counsel for the defendant AIG
3. Mark E. Cohen of The McCormack Firm (Boston, Massachusetts), counsel for the defendant, AIG

Besides the attorneys, there were several individuals in the seated section. I had no idea who these people were, but I expected that they were from AIG and Zurich.

OPENING STATEMENT BY MR. PRITZKER (COUNSEL FOR THE PLAINTIFFS)

As the court now knows, almost seven years ago and one month, on January 9, 2002, Marcia Rhodes' life was irreparably changed. The liability, the injury, the potential damages were known almost immediately to the defendants.

Notwithstanding that, the first offer of settlement of any kind in this case came from Zurich Insurance Company in March 2004, two years and two months after the accident.

That was accompanied by a tender to AIG, the excess carrier, of the $2 million policy and it took AIG another, depending upon the date, six to eight months to make its first offer, which added $750,000 to the $2 million that has been tendered to it by Zurich.

What I have just stated is the overall basis for the plaintiffs' claim that both Zurich and AIG violated Chapters 176D and 93A of the Massachusetts General Laws by failing to promptly effect settlement once liability was reasonably clear.

Some key dates. Crawford & Company issued its first full formal report on January 30, 2002. As the court will see when we start to get into the evidence, that report was incredibly detailed, given the fact that it was approximately three weeks after the crash, both as to how the accident happened and Crawford's then knowledge of Mrs. Rhodes' injuries, which got only worse after that because of complications.

But the initial injuries that I disclosed earlier in my opening were known to Crawford within three weeks of the accident.

Suit was filed in July 2002. Zalewski admitted to facts sufficient to warrant a guilty claim, a finding of driving to endanger in November of '02. The defendants responded in detail to discovery in April of '03, including very, very lengthy summaries of how the accident happened, of the then injuries and complications that Mrs. Rhodes suffered, accompanied by 2,000 pages of medical reports and medical bills.

The plaintiffs issued a written demand for settlement in August of '03; a 17-page demand, again detailing in incredible detail the injuries, how the accident happened, the theories of liability, disclosing the experts that the plaintiffs intended to use and her view of what it was going to cost for life support and care for Mrs. Rhodes for the rest of her life.

Zurich offered the policy limits in March of '04, two years, two months after the—almost three months—after the accident. AIG made its first offer in August of '04. There was a trial and verdict in September of '04 and so the first offer from AIG came one month prior to the trial.

Now let me go into some more detail. As I indicated, while Crawford can set reserves, determine coverage, which I had not talked about before, and settle the claims, these all required Zurich's approval. Crawford received the notice of the accident literally the same day of the accident, started investigating, and began reporting both to GAF and to Zurich with copies to AIG almost immediately. As I indicated, Crawford's first full formal report was dated January 30, '02 and was remarkably detailed.

There were transmittal letters by Crawford that went to Zurich and to AIG, dated April 8, '02, June 10, '02, September 25, '02, December 13, '02, May 6, '03, June 4, '03, July 22, '03, September 11, '03, September 24, '03, October 9, '03, and November 13, '03. From the first transmittal letter until the time—until March of '03, Crawford was recommending to Zurich to reserve this case at the full policy value of $2 million, every single transmittal letter.

It was also, from the very first transmittal letter, attributing liability to the driver. From the first transmittal letter on, the words 'liability' clearly falls to the D.L.S. driver. By September 25, '02, Crawford had put a value on the case of $5 to $10 million.

They later, because of a glitch[231] that you'll hear about, reduced that value from $5 to $7 million, but it never went—the low end never went below $5 million.

Inexplicably, Zurich never opened a claims file on this case until August of '02. There are only three entries in Zurich's claim notes between August of '02 and January of '03, and they

---

231 This "glitch" will play a significant role in Judge Gants' ruling.

all deal with the fact that coverage counsel had been hired and that they're waiting for coverage counsel to respond.

On January 21, '03, one year after the crash, we see the first substantive note from Zurich, quote, Please note that we will extend coverage to GAF, Penske, and Driver Logistics Services. "Can you please advise of the possible exposure? Now the coverage issue has been resolved."

The first note from Zurich, a year after the accident. The person who wrote that note, David McIntosh (a claims adjuster at Zurich) who was the first claims adjuster from Zurich on this file, admitted to receiving some but not all of the proffered transmittal letters prior to writing that note.

You will hear that Crawford is sending and sometimes resending their reports all along to both Zurich and AIG.

Between January 3—January 21 of '03 and June of '03, the notes reveal that Zurich is doing virtually nothing but complaining that Crawford's reporting is inadequate. Keep in mind, Your Honor, that Crawford is the agent of Zurich for adjusting and administering this claim.

In August, the Rhodes file the transcript from David McIntosh (a claims adjuster at Zurich) to Kathleen Fuell, not because McIntosh leaves the company but only because there is a reassignment of certain claims files.

Ms. Fuell is apparently unaware that the coverage issues have been resolved. There is no handout; there <are> no memos to indicate what the open items are as to this claim when Ms. Fuell picks it up. So as she testified, and as she will testify today, she was really starting from ground zero in trying to evaluate this claim.

She begins working on the file in August or early September of '03. By that time the case—the claim had been in suit for over a year. In April of '03, as I indicated, the plaintiffs had responded to discovery with incredible detail, but apparently Zurich was not communicating with defense counsel and did not know that all of the backup for the liability and for the damages had already been produced to the defense team.

By August of '03, the plaintiffs—I am sorry. From the time that Ms. Fuell saw the plaintiffs' demand, she testified, and will again, I am sure, that she had an instinctual feeling that she should be putting up as reserves in tendering the full value of the Zurich policy.

From there it takes another four months for her to get the approval to do that. Four months. She tenders verbally at the end of January or the beginning of February of '04, now two years after the accident.

What's AIG's response and what have they been doing during all of this time? We do know that they're being copied in on all of Crawford's reports. Their first affirmative action in dealing with Zurich is to tell Zurich, "We do not take tenders verbally. You've got to put it in writing."

Ms. Fuell puts it in writing. What's their next response? We reject your tender. Why did they reject the tender? Ms. Fuell had said, "We are tendering the policy, we therefore wash our hands of any defense obligation." Zurich says, "Wait a minute, that is not what the policy says. You've got to continue paying defense counsel."

<u>The Court:</u>
I am sorry. Zurich says this or?

<u>Mr. Pritzker:</u>
Zurich.

<u>The Court:</u>
This is Zurich. Okay.

<u>Mr. Pritzker:</u>

AIG said, "You've got to continue paying defense counsel." And there is dialogue back and forth with GAF's counsel getting involved to say stop this infighting and deal with the claim itself. And the dialogue back and forth is finally resolved—well, It is not finally resolved because there is nothing in the file to indicate that AIG ever accepted the tender, although they started to negotiate using Zurich's money, so there is a de facto acceptance of the tender, but they never vary from their rejection of the tender, which was in writing.

We do know, however, also in December of '03, Zurich hired its own defense counsel to supplement the defense team.

<u>Mr. Zelle:</u>
I think you meant AIG.

Mr. Pritzker:

I am sorry. I said Zurich and I did not mean that.

AIG, having now utilized the efforts of new defense counsel, decides not to make an offer until mediation.

So from December of '03, or soon thereafter, they come to the conclusion that their best position will be furthered if they wait until mediation to make an offer, and then they say, "We are not going to mediation until we can buttress up the defense file."

Prior defense counsel has not taken Mrs. Rhodes' deposition, they have not taken Rebecca Rhodes' deposition, and we want an independent medical exam of Mrs. Rhodes.

They want, apparently, to determine once and for all, two years plus after the accident, that this poor woman truly was rendered a paraplegic, and so the mediation does not take place until August of '04, after the IME, after the depositions of Rebecca and Marcia Rhodes. And their first offer—strike that.

Prior to this, as I indicated earlier, the plaintiffs had made a demand. That was back in August of '03. And as part of that demand we disclosed that the special economic damages, the past costs incurred were—these are medical costs, not legal costs and the future life-care needs of Mrs. Rhodes were approximately $3 million.

We now know that AIG had—or at least the defense team—had retained its own life-care planner, whose Life Care Plan was approximately $500,000 less than the plaintiffs' Life Care Plan and in all other responses was almost identical—not identical, but substantially similar, and that the difference between the plaintiff's life-care planner and the defendant's life-care planner was the life span remaining for Mrs. Rhodes now that she had been rendered a paraplegic.

Further, that the numbers would have been remarkably close at $3 million. Given the knowledge of AIG of those facts, their beginning offer, their first offer in August of '04 was $2.7 million, less than the economic specialist of Mrs. Rhodes.

By the end of that negotiating session, they had come to $3.5 million, and this includes Zurich's $2 million. They come to $3.5 million, which still did not cover Mrs. Rhodes' economic damages, plus the interest which had accrued from August of—I am sorry, from July of '02 to the date, approximately 25 percent. And that was where they left it, and that is where it was left until the day trial started, where they repeated the same offer.

Now, in the interim, the plaintiffs have settled with the tree company. The plaintiffs had not sued the tree company. The tree company was brought in as a third-party defendant by the defendants. They came to the mediation. And after the mediation, the plaintiffs and the tree company settled for $550,000.

We now know that at the trial the verdict was rendered, a jury verdict, on behalf of the plaintiffs for $9.412 million, that interest on the judgment which accrued after the usual motions for new trial for remittitur, for reconsideration—I am sorry, those two motions. The interest came to approximately two and a half million dollars, for a total judgment of just under $12 million.

Did that end this case? It certainly did not. After the motions were denied, at AIG's insistence, the defense counsel appealed. Prior to the start of the trial, Zalewski, D.L.S., Driver Logistics Services, and GAF had conceded and stipulated to liability. The only issue at trial was damages and notwithstanding a defendant's appeal. The appeal took its course.

The plaintiffs filed a claim, not in court, but they served a demand under 176D and 93A to both Zurich and AIG. In December of '04, Zurich paid $2.3 million to the plaintiffs, without a release, in response to the 93A demand. And it is articulated that that payment was for the policy limits plus post-judgment interest as required under the policy.

AIG responded by offering the plaintiffs $7 million against a $12 million (verdict). And further, that $7 million was conditioned upon a release not only of the underlying accident claim but also the 93A allegations which had now been articulated against them.

That position was repeated until September—I am sorry, approximately September of '05, '05, when finally AIG paid $8.965 million, or at least they agreed to pay $8.965 million, in three payments. And I misspoke. It was in June of '05 that the settlement occurred, not September. And the payments were made in three installments: in July, August, and September.

What were the Rhodes' doing during all of this time? Well, we know that they were suffering incredibly emotionally because of the underlying accident. But there is an overlay on top of them which is easily distinguishable. Because accidents do happen, and at some point, especially for Mr. Rhodes, he was able to separate the fact that his wife was now irretrievably injured and would be for the rest of her life.

But why was not anybody talking to him? Why, after Zalewski admitted to facts sufficient to warrant a finding of guilty on driving to endanger, was not somebody coming to them and saying at least let's help you financially. And this started to dwell on him and dwell on him and dwell on him more for the next, almost two years.

That is the kind of emotional distress that you will hear Mr. Rhodes testify to. With Mrs. Rhodes it was not quite that detailed, but she also became convinced that at some point their money was going to run out, that she was not going to be able to stay in her home, and this was because even though she was sure that the liability in this case was not a question, nobody was talking to her and why on earth would they not be talking to her if, in fact, she was entitled to this money, some money to compensate her for her injuries.

You will hear from Rebecca Rhodes, and all Rebecca Rhodes can do is observe the anxiety that this was causing to her parents, and that caused her distress as well.

So is one issue that the Rhodes' were dealing with during the course of the unfair conduct of the defendants.

What else was going on? Well, we already heard that the defendants paid ultimately, when you add it all up, a total of $11,837,995. We will go through the math of this, but the judgment that was rendered by the verdict, plus pre- and post-judgment interest, only on remaining balances, because payments, as the court remembers, were now being made at various times; the first payment by the tree company, then by Zurich, and finally in three tranches by AIG.

So if you take the total amount of the verdict and then you take the interest pre-judgment and you take the post-judgment interest only on the balances that remain unpaid, it comes to $12,621,947. The shortfall that the plaintiffs accepted in order to put this case behind them was $783,952.

The plaintiffs have to testify. They had to testify at deposition. They have to testify at trial. They have to subject themselves first to strange lawyers and then to the public to stuff that they never should have had to have been subjected to, the most personal and intimate things about what had happened to Mrs. Rhodes and how Mr. Rhodes had to deal with it. And you're going to hear from them.

And it was extraordinary and it shouldn't have happened, and it is an additional burden, emotional burden that the plaintiffs had to bear.

And then finally you'll hear that the defendants also suffered the requirement that they pay the costs, the litigation costs, of this case.

And while obviously some of those litigation costs, number one, are covered by the statute, and number two, would have been incurred in any event because we filed suit, they did not have to go on and on and on not only through trial, but then the additional cost of having to order a trial transcript because of the appeal.

With all of that, Your Honor, plaintiffs are convinced that this court will find a violation of 176D and 93A against both sets of defendants, that it was willful or knowing, that as a result of that, the plaintiffs should be awarded their compensatory damages and they should be awarded punitive damages, which under the statute are either double or triple the underlying judgment, plus attorneys' fees.

The Court:
All right. Thank you. Who on the defense side is going to argue first?

Mr. Varga:
Your Honor, Greg Varga for Zurich American Insurance Company.

OPENING STATEMENT BY MR. VARGA (COUNSEL FOR THE DEFENDANT, ZURICH)[232]

Your Honor, it appears that this entire case against Zurich is about time and timing. It is not a case about Zurich appealing a verdict. It is not a case about Zurich forcing people to go through unnecessary depositions or forcing them to testify at trial. It is a question of when Zurich took steps to effectuate settlement in accordance with Chapter 176D.

Zurich first received notice of the Rhodes claim in August of 2002.[233] August of 2002. Not January, not June. August 2002.

---

232 As mentioned before, let me state that I am not an attorney, so my legal observations and conclusions may be inaccurate.

233 Zurich's first assertion is that it did not receive any information from its attorneys or from its Agent, Crawford, concerning this catastrophic claim until eight months after the crash, due to its administrative "lost-in-the-mailroom" problems—even though there was substantial evidence that Zurich did receive other mail at the same headquarters address during this period of delay. Therefore, the eight-month delay until August 2002 to begin to investigate this claim could not be found to be an *"unfair or deceptive"* act by Zurich. Importantly, Zurich admitted that it did not follow its own claims manual:
"*Pertinent policy is confirmed within one business day of receipt of claim by case manager.*"
"*Claim file is completely registered in ACCESS within one business day of receipt of the claim by Zurich.*"
"*The insured and claimant are to be contacted within 1 business day from receipt of the claim by Zurich.*"

Crawford & Company, which was the third-party administrator that was retained and selected by the insurer, GAF Building Materials, notified Zurich in August of 2002 about this claim.[234] It is undisputed, as Mr. Pritzker has already pointed out, that Zurich only had $2 million to contribution to any settlement or any judgment in this case.

Plaintiffs have stipulated, and we know now that there was never a point in time from the date of the accident until the date of the verdict in the underlying case when the plaintiffs or any of them were willing to accept $2 million or less to settle their claims against any of the personal injury defendants. That is a fact.

Zurich had no power to effectuate settlement within the meaning of Chapter 176D within its policy limits. That much is equally clear. The best that Zurich can do in these circumstances was to take steps to make its policy limits available to the excess carrier, National Union, for its use in any settlement negotiations or dialog with the plaintiffs.[235]

We know plaintiffs would never have accepted Zurich's $2 million if it was offered the day after the accident, six months after the accident, a year after the accident, or even beyond that.[236]

So what did Zurich do? Kathleen Fuell will testify, and she's in the courtroom with us today in the first bench, and she will testify, Your Honor, that after she received a Demand Package from the plaintiffs in September of 2003, a Demand Package that contained for the first time any information regarding Marcia Rhodes' future medical care or rehabilitative care needs, future expenses, forecasts of lost economic damages, information regarding Mr. Rhodes' and Rebecca Rhodes' alleged losses of consortium,[237] when she received that Demand Package and had an opportunity to evaluate it and to verify the information contained in it, she promptly took steps to effectuate settlement of this case.

---

234 As previously shown through Crawford's insurance claims notes, Zurich was sent the first of many notifications beginning January 10, 2002.

235 While not legally required but not statutorily disallowed, Zurich could have tendered its $2 million policy, without stipulation, to us as soon as Zurich determined that the damages would exceed its policy limits. Marcia and I would have greatly appreciated this. The Massachusetts legislature should require a primary insurance carrier (whose policy limit has been exposed) to tender its policy limit to the blameless victim without any condition even if the damages of the claim have not been determined.

236 This statement is incorrect. We would have gladly accepted Zurich's unconditioned $2 million policy limit at any time, especially the day after the crash.

237 Zurich's second assertion is that it had no legal obligation to begin to investigate this claim before receiving the plaintiffs' demand package (in September 2003). Therefore, the additional thirteen-month delay could not be found to be an *"unfair or deceptive act"* by Zurich.

Now in March 2004, in November of 2003, you will hear testimony from Ms. Fuell, that during a conference call, which she convened in November of 2003,[238] on the 19th to be precise, in which she involved GAF—I am sorry, GAF representatives, the insurer; defense counsel; a representative from AIG named Nicholas Satriano, and others, that she announced her intent to go to her superiors and seek authority to tender Zurich's $2 million policy limits to the excess carrier. And by 'tender' I mean to make those policy limits available to AIG, National Union for use in its settlement negotiations that they might engage in with the plaintiff.

Ms. Fuell will testify that she made that known to everyone on that conference call in November of 2003, ten months before the trial in the underlying case, because it appeared to her, based on all the information that she had received for the very first time, in September, that it looked likely that the damages in this case might exceed Zurich's policy limit. So she put everyone on notice at that time.

What she did next, as she'll testify, is she went and sought and received authority from her superiors by submitting a report. She received that authority, and eight months before the trial in the underlying action she called Nick Satriano of AIG and she said, "You have our money." Mr. Satriano, as Mr. Pritzker pointed out, rejected the tender,[239] but Zurich put the money on the table than it had previously said it was going to do so.[240]

Ultimately, Your Honor, AIG, National Union, and the plaintiffs were unable to reach a settlement of this case. And it is not for us to comment on the reasonableness or unreasonableness of anyone's position here, and we are not going to do so.

But the point is, the case did not settle because the plaintiffs and AIG cannot reach an accord, cannot reach a number. And yet we are here today, Zurich is here today, because the plaintiffs say that instead of taking steps to effectuate settlement ten months before the underlying trial, we should have done it sooner, and as a consequence, Zurich should be held responsible and pay an astonishing $24 to $36 million. That is the claim.[241]

---

238 This date was more than twenty-two months after the crash. AIG rejected Zurich's tender offer until April 2004. Zurich had to know many months earlier that its $2 million policy limit was exposed.

239 Zurich's third assertion is that, although the company internally determined in November 2003 to tender its $2 million policy limit to AIG, Zurich had no legal obligation to e-mail this tender offer to AIG for another two months until January 2004, due to the perceived difficulty in getting management approvals at that time of the year. Therefore, the additional two-month delay could not be found to be an *"unfair or deceptive act"* by Zurich.

240 Zurich's fourth assertion is that AIG was responsible for the next three-month delay until April 2004, because it was AIG that required Zurich to put into writing that Zurich would tender its $2 million policy to AIG and that Zurich would continue to pay defense costs. Therefore, the additional three-month delay could not be found to be an *"unfair or deceptive act"* by Zurich.

241 *"Zurich should be held responsible and pay an astonishing $24 to $36 million"* is the plain meaning of the laws enacted by the Massachusetts legislature. When either a primary or an excess insurance carrier is found to have committed a

What this boils down to with respect to Zurich, Your Honor, is really two questions, and I think these are the questions that ultimately will frame the court's analysis and review of the evidence with respect to Zurich.

The first question is, were the coverage issues,[242] not just whether Zurich had a defense obligation for D.L.S. or Penske or GAF or others, but also whether Zurich's policy was the only primary policy available for indemnity on this claim, or was that issue and were issues of 'fault' and issues of damages reasonably clear sooner than the point in time when Kathleen Fuell took steps to effectuate the settlement in November 2003.

The second question is, even if Zurich had taken steps before November 2003 to effectuate settlement, would it have made a difference. This is the causation analysis, Your Honor. This is the elephant in the room that plaintiffs do not want to talk about.[243] But this is the crux of the case in many respects as to Zurich.

We will prove that the answers to those two questions I just outlined for the court are both no. An earlier tender of policy limits would have made no difference in this case, and I'll go through that evidence in just a moment. In addition, there was not an earlier point in time from our perspective when liability, damages, and all of the coverage issues became reasonably clear prior to the point in time when Kathleen Fuell took steps to effectuate settlement.

I would like to address first, Your Honor, take the two questions that I raised for you in reverse order. I would like to talk about causation first.

In the summary judgment ruling that Your Honor issued not too long ago, the court acknowledged that the plaintiffs bear a burden in this case, and that burden is to establish for purposes of causation of some damage, some actual damage and actual loss, they have to prove that if Zurich had taken steps to effectuate settlement sooner than the time that it actually did, that it is more likely than not that the plaintiffs and AIG would have settled the case before trial. This is the causation test that is an essential element of their case against Zurich.

---

willful or knowing "unfair or deceptive act" that *causes* a *harm* to the plaintiff, the amount of the punishment is a mathematical calculation without regard to its size.

242 Zurich's fifth assertion is that it had no legal obligation to begin to investigate this claim until Zurich had determined that no other insurance carrier had additional insurance coverage for one or more of the defendants. Therefore, any additional delay to locate other insurance carriers that might have additional insurance coverage could not be found to be an *"unfair or deceptive act"* by Zurich.

243 Zurich's sixth assertion is that only AIG (as the excess insurance carrier) was empowered to effectuate the settlement of a claim and, as such, any delay by Zurich is irrelevant. Therefore, any delay caused by Zurich to effectuate a settlement could not be found to be an *"unfair or deceptive act"* act by Zurich.

In the absence of a causal connection between Zurich's alleged delay in making its policy limits available to AIG and National Union and the alleged damages that plaintiffs claim, including the burden of going through a trial, there can be no remedy at all against Zurich.

We made this point at summary judgment, Your Honor, and this obviously factored prominently into the court's ruling.

To answer the question of causation here, the court will consider two sources of evidence: one, Harold Rhodes and Marcia Rhodes. How much money were they willing to accept in settlement between the date of the accident and the date of trial and at what times.[244]

The second source of evidence that the court will consider is how much money was the excess insurer willing to contribute to a global settlement of the Rhodes claims against the personal injury defendants and at what times.

Now, this evidence was before the court at summary judgment and at that time Your Honor was constrained by its standard. And that standard said you have to take the evidence in the light most favorable to the non-moving party, the plaintiffs.

But that standard does not control now, and the court is not so constrained. As Your Honor is well aware, you have the privilege of making credibility judgments in this case, considering all of the evidence and weighing it. And I will submit to the court that the credible evidence in this case on a question of causation is that the plaintiffs were never willing to accept a total settlement in the range that AIG and National Union were willing to offer.

The credible evidence is that from January 9, 2002, the date of Mrs. Rhodes' terrible car accident, all the way through the mediation, which took place in August of 2004, the plaintiffs were willing to accept $8 million.

You will see sworn testimony to that effect, Your Honor. At the same time, their demand, of course, their first demand, in July of '03, which was a verbal demand over the phone, was $18.5 million.

Now, let's talk about the AIG side. What we'll see in executive claim summary a document from AIG's files that demonstrates along with testimony that you'll hear in this case, that the highest value that AIG put on this case prior to trial, and after all the discovery was completed, was $4.75 million.

---

244 This question will later be decided by the Massachusetts Supreme Judicial Court in a landmark decision.

And that value assumed and included a $2 million contribution from Zurich and a $1 million contribution from the third-party defendant, Professional Tree. That is what AIG valued the case at; right or wrong, that was their number.

The plaintiffs remember, were eight million dollars. The highest offer that AIG made to the plaintiffs prior to the trial was $3.5 million, which, again, included Zurich's $2 million primary policy.

During the trial, as the evidence was going in, AIG and the plaintiffs had additional settlement negotiations. And during that time frame, as the evidence went in and it appeared to be going in better for the plaintiffs than AIG anticipated, AIG's evaluation rose and it went from $4.75 million ultimately to six million (dollars), again, including Zurich's $2 million contribution.

The highest offer that was made to the plaintiffs in this case was made at moments before closing arguments. And I meant the underlying case, Your Honor. The highest offer was a total of $6 million.

That was made just before closing arguments after all of the evidence was known, after the witnesses' credibility had been assessed by all who observed it, and after both sides had an opportunity to fully evaluate how the case went in.

So we have a significant gap, Your Honor, at all points in the life of this case. We know plaintiffs were not going to come down into a range that AIG was willing to pay. The court will hear evidence of that. I do not think there'll be any credible evidence to the contrary.

In addition, the court will hear from one of AIG's experts, former Massachusetts Superior Court Justice, J. Owen Todd, who, with respect to the issue of timing, will tell you that in his opinion it would have been premature and imprudent for AIG to even consider settling the Rhodes' claims before August of 2003.

And his reasoning, you will hear, is that prior to that time Mrs. Rhodes' medical treatment and rehabilitation had not reached a point from which an accurate evaluation of the extent of the need for future care and future treatment costs can be adequately analyzed.

Mr. Todd will also tell you that before the Demand Package was sent in 2003, the plaintiffs had not provided medical records from Mrs. Rhodes, future care information from Mrs. Rhodes, and other related documents that would enable the insurance companies to forecast future expenses.

What all this evidence will show, Your Honor, is that even if Zurich had taken steps to make its policy limits available before August of 2003, AIG's own expert will say that it would not have been in a position to reasonably evaluate the case and engage in settlement dialogue as of August 2003.

In summary on this point, Your Honor, the evidence will show that AIG and the plaintiffs would not have bridged the gap that separated them. They would not have settled the case regardless of whether Zurich took steps in June of 2003 as opposed to November of 2003 or any point earlier than that. The timing of Zurich's efforts to effectuate settlement and tender its policy limits to AIG made no difference.

Now, if I may, Your Honor, have a few moments to discuss the first question that I outlined, and that question is the liability, coverage and damages, the three pieces of the puzzle, if you will, for assessing—or for a liability carries task in looking at a claim. Those all become reasonably clear within the meaning of Chapter 176D, at some point prior to the time when Zurich took steps to effectuate settlement.

Plaintiffs' position, as you've heard, is that this was a, quote, no-brainer. Mrs. Rhodes' car was rear-ended, it was stopped. And Crawford & Company was told by Mr. Pritzker that she was paralyzed, over the telephone they were told that.

The plaintiffs' expert will say that by April of 2002 it was clear and Zurich should have tendered its policy limits at that point in time. From his standpoint there was no need for Zurich to look at any medical records, there was not a need for it to consider any medical bills; it did not need to look at any documentation regarding what the future might hold for the Rhodes family, whether it be rehabilitation expenses, medical care needs and so forth.

A Life Care Plan, from their prospective, none of that mattered, Zurich had no need to see any of that, it should put its money on the table before it even got notice of the claim.

You will hear from Kathleen Fuell today, Your Honor, and later from our expert witness a gentleman named Karl Maser, who has been an executive at two major insurance companies and has 40-some-odd years in the insurance industry, that it is just not that simple. It is not that simple. There were several issues, critical issues that remained unresolved for a long period of time.

What where they? The first question is, was the Zurich policy in fact primary, not vis-à-vis AIG, but was it the only or the primary policy to provide defense and indemnity. In other words, settlement or a judgment payment for GAF, Driver Logistics Services, Penske and others.

That issue, you will learn, was not resolved for a prolonged period of time despite diligent efforts on the part of Zurich's coverage counsel to gather the information and put it together and provide an analysis.

On the issue of 'fault,' Your Honor, there are four different defendants in the underlying case.

Plaintiffs treat it as if it is just one, but there are four parties. There was the driver, the employer, there was GAF, and there was Penske. Now while I would not stand here and say it was terribly difficult to figure out whether the driver was going to be held somewhat responsible for causing the accident, the question of GAF's potential liability was hotly contested for a long period of time in the underlying litigation because it involved the question of vicarious liability: whether GAF exercised sufficient control over the actions of Carlo Zalewski such that it can be held responsible under tort law.

And it remained a hotly contested issue until a very important thing happened: the plaintiffs found it necessary to amend their complaint in March of 2004 to assert a different theory of liability as to GAF, Your Honor.[245] If liability was so reasonably clear at that point, why was it necessary to amend the complaint?

The last element that was not reasonably clear, Your Honor, and this is one I am going to spend some time about, is the damages picture.

The damages picture, as I have alluded to before, did not become reasonably clear to Zurich and it would not have become reasonably clear to any insurance company prior to Zurich's receipt of documentation of Mrs. Rhodes' past medical history with respect to things from this accident or without documentation of Mrs. Rhodes' future anticipated medical expenses, rehabilitative care needs and other future expenses; all of which are a significant piece of the puzzle when we are talking about a case involving paralysis.

Kathleen Fuell of Zurich and Karl Maser, our expert, will explain that it is the primary insurers— primary carrier's duty to investigate the underlying claim fully and thoroughly. And that means it is not just to investigate up to the amount of its policy limit, it has to fully investigate all aspects of the claim, including damages.[246]

---

245 Zurich's seventh assertion is that when the plaintiffs amended their complaint, Zurich was entitled to review whole claims investigation from the beginning. Therefore, any delay caused by reviewing the whole claims investigation could not be found to be an *"unfair or deceptive act"* by Zurich.

246 Zurich's eighth assertion is that it was not required to tender its $2 million policy limits to the plaintiffs without a full release of all claims by the plaintiffs, even when Zurich determined that damages exceeded its $2 million policy limit. Therefore, any delay in tendering its $2 million policy limits, without a full release of all claims by the plaintiffs, could not be found to be an *"unfair or deceptive act"* by Zurich.

You will also hear that it is inconsistent, or would have been inconsistent with good claim handling practices and industry standards for Zurich to rely on secondhand information and hearsay about the nature and extent of the injuries sustained by Mrs. Rhodes or hearsay about any other damages that the plaintiffs intended to prove.[247]

What a primary carrier has to examine—and this is imperative—is credible evidence, documentation establishing what the damages are. It cannot rely solely on secondhand information. And one of the reasons for that is illustrated by this very case, Your Honor. You will learn that in May of 2003 plaintiffs told defense counsel that Mrs. Rhodes' medical expenses had already reached a million dollars.

You will also learn when you look at the Demand Package in this case, which will be an exhibit, from August of 2003, that in fact the medical expenses were 40 percent of that number, 40 percent, which illustrates the reason why we need backup and why an insurance company has to do a thorough investigation and rely not on hearsay and secondhand information.

The evidence in this case will demonstrate Your Honor, and particularly through the testimony of John Chaney (an insurance claims adjuster at Crawford), which you'll have an opportunity to read, he was employed by Crawford & Company, GAF's third-party administrator, he will tell you that within weeks of the accident he spoke to Mr. Pritzker. And during that conversation, among other things, he asked Mr. Pritzker for something.

He said: "I will need you to provide me with information regarding Mrs. Rhodes' condition and on the information and updates on how she's doing and what the future is going to hold and what the medicals are." That was a request that was made in January of 2002, Your Honor.

For the next 12 months there was complete radio silence. Mr. Pritzker and his team provided not a single medical record, not a single medical bill, not a single update on Mrs. Rhodes's status. No information whatsoever was forthcoming during the time that Mr. Chaney (an insurance claims adjuster at Crawford) was handling the claim on behalf of Crawford.[248]

The strategy instead was to race to the courthouse, get the lawsuit filed so we can get the interest clock ticking; and that is what happened. No information was shared during that first year at all.

---

247 Mr. Varga correctly states that there was a math error in the plaintiffs' demand package. What Mr. Varga fails to state is that the amount equaled to a few hundred thousand dollars in the context of a multimillion-dollar settlement.

248 Zurich's ninth assertion is that it had no legal obligation to proactively acquire the needed information in order to thoroughly investigate this claim. Therefore, any delay in acquiring the needed information could not be found to be an *"unfair or deceptive act"* by Zurich.

Now the plaintiffs emphasize already, and I am sure they will continue to do so in this case, the reports that were sent by Crawford & Company to GAF and some of which were copied to Zurich.

Parenthetically I would note that you will hear evidence that the first two reports that Mr. Pritzker referred to, the January report and the April 2002 report, were never received by Zurich. Zurich's first notice of this claim was August of 2002.

What plaintiffs focus on the most is the notations in some of those Crawford reports as to, quote, potential case value, instances in which they make comments about the potential value of the case being between five (million dollars) to seven million (dollars) or five (million) to ten million dollars.

The evidence in this case that you will hear from the Crawford adjustors who worked on it and you'll see in the documents and the reports themselves that we'll put before you, is that when the Crawford people made those comments about potential case value and when they were making comments regarding what the reserve, the loss reserve should be in this case, they did not have a single medical record, they did not have a single medical bill, they did not have a single update on Mrs. Rhodes' condition, they did not have any documentation of her prognosis, nothing about the future potential care needs or expenses, nothing about Mr. Rhodes' loss of consortium claim or Rebecca Rhodes' loss of consortium claim.[249]

They were making these recommendations they will admit to you, based on guesswork. As I mentioned before and as our witnesses will explain, an insurance company cannot, and someone in Zurich's position as a primary, cannot rely on secondhand information.

And Zurich was aware that Crawford did not have backup and you will hear testimony, or you will read testimony, from David McIntosh, who is Ms. Fuell's predecessor in handling this file, as the oversight person for this Rhodes' claim.

You will hear that he repeatedly requested Crawford to provide backup information, information regarding exposure; he made that request in August of 2002. He made it in January of 2003; again, he made it in March, 2003, May 2003, June, July, and August, continually saying: I need something more, you have to give me documentation so I can make a reasoned rational judgment about what this case may be worth and what the disposition strategy may be.

---

[249] Zurich's tenth assertion is that it had no legal obligation to accept the claims investigation provided by Crawford (Zurich's Agent and GAF's third-party insurance administrator). Therefore, any delay caused by Zurich's determination that Crawford's claims investigation was inadequate could not be found to be an *"unfair or deceptive act"* by Zurich.

Our expert, Karl Maser, will tell you, Your Honor, that Mr. McIntosh's requests were reasonable and also consistent with good claim handling practices, both in terms of their content and in terms of their timing.

The evidence will demonstrate that Crawford continued to explain to Zurich in these reports that it was following up for medical information. Even in July of 2003, Crawford did not have the medical documentation, it did not have documentation of future care needs or anything like that, yet they continued to make these comments in their reports.

It was not until September of 2003, Your Honor, when the Demand Package arrived, which I have already mentioned to the court, 13 months after the lawsuit was filed, 19 months after the accident, when Zurich for the first time saw any medical bills or any documentation regarding damages, apart from secondhand information.

Ms. Fuell will testify that she analyzed that Demand Package very carefully, it was a voluminous package and she had to read through it very carefully and then once she completed that review she took a number of steps to move this case into a settlement mode. She took steps to effectuate settlement within the meaning of Chapter 176D.

What did she do?

The first thing she did was she sought and obtained input from defense counsel, the defense lawyer that GAF had hired to represent them, Nixon Peabody. She sought their input because they were Massachusetts lawyers and obviously would have something to say about jury verdicts in this jurisdiction as well as issues of liability, the merits of the case and damages.

In addition to seeking defense input, Kathleen Fuell obtained a copy of the defense Life Care Plan and she reviewed that very carefully, again with an effort to verify the damages that were being claimed and the information she saw in the Demand Package.

The third thing she did was convene a teleconference, and I have already explained this to Your Honor, in which she said at the end of that conference: "This is my plan, I am going to seek authority to tender my policy limits to AIG for use in settlement."

Once that authority was received she immediately called Nicholas Satriano and again said: "Now, I am formally telling you, you have my policy limits." He said, "I cannot take that, I need it in writing."

So she went back after consulting with counsel about issues relating to the tender; she then put it in writing on March 29, 2004, stating that the tender had already been made but we are in addition telling you, AIG, that we are relinquishing our defense obligation in this case.

March 29th, 2004, was the first time that that position was taken by Zurich and after AIG rejected it and there was some discussion over the course of three days, Ms. Fuell sent an e-mail, and you'll see it in this case, that as a business decision we are not willing to let GAF bear the burden of its own expenses for legal fees, so we will continue to defend. Zurich stepped up and said: "We'll keep the defense obligation, so this moves forward."

Having received a rejection of the tender by AIG, Ms. Fuell did the only thing that she can do, Judge, she made an offer through defense counsel of the policy limits to the plaintiff.[250] *After the tender, Your Honor, Zurich was never consulted on any settlement negotiations, nor did it expect to be because it had exhausted it policy limits.*

Zurich did not know about the mediation in August of 2004. Zurich was not consulted before the trial or during the trial about any settlement offers, any settlement demands that had been exchanged by the parties.

Zurich was not calling the shots on the litigation anymore because in December of 2003, just after Kathleen Fuell had explained that she intended to seek authority to tender her policy limits, AIG retained its own counsel to take over the case, Campbell Campbell & Edwards.

After the judgment was entered in this case, Your Honor, Zurich stepped up again; Mr. Pritzker already mentioned it to you. The evidence will show that Zurich paid its $2 million policy limits to the plaintiffs. In addition it paid $322,000 and change, in post-judgment interest, not on its $2 million policy but on the entire underlying judgment of $11.8 million.

Zurich did not ask for release. The evidence will show Zurich had no contractual obligation to make the payment because there was an appeal pending by AIG's designated counsel. Yet Zurich made that payment and put the money in the plaintiffs' hands.[251]

Now, Your Honor, I am not going to spend time talking about damages in this case and there is two reasons: one, I have gone on long enough, but secondly, the court correctly pointed

---

250 Mr. Varga fails to say that Zurich's offer of $2 million to the plaintiffs was conditioned on a full release of all claims against all defendants. Obviously, that condition could not be accepted.

251 This statement could easily be misinterpreted. The verdict against Zurich came on September 16, 2004. Zurich did not make payment until December 22, 2004.

out and predicated in the summary judgment papers, that plaintiffs will have an extraordinary difficult time proving damages in this case.

I am also not going to stand before you, Your Honor, and tell you that every single aspect of this case was handled to perfection. No claim is ever handled to perfection.

When we put a magnifying glass to a claim file, we always find little things that one can have done differently or save time on. But our Massachusetts Appeals Courts have made it abundantly clear that insurers in the position of Zurich are not to be held to standards of omniscience or perfection.

As the SJC said, and I would like to just for a second quote, in the Clegg case, so long as it acts in good faith—

Mr. Pritzker:
I thought this was an opening. I kept away from closing because I am prohibited from closing.

The Court:
It is an opening, I'll let him—I will also say that I read the Clegg case again on Thursday or Friday, so I do not think he's going to tell me anything that I have not already—

Mr. Varga:

Your Honor, I will spare the quote, what I will say is that the court said as long as the carrier exercises honest business judgment it is not violating 176D. We will demonstrate in this case that in overseeing Crawford & Company's administration of the Rhodes' claim the activities of Kathleen Fuell and David McIntosh were guided by honest judgment.

So ultimately even if this court were to conclude that Zurich can have taken steps before November 2003 to effectuate settlement by tendering its policy limits, and that that failure to do it sooner somehow caused this case to go to judgment, you will hear no evidence and you will see no evidence this week or next, suggesting that Kathleen Fuell or David McIntosh of Zurich willfully, intentionally, deliberately or even recklessly delayed tendering the policy limits to AIG. They exercised honest business judgment and acted in good faith. Thank you.

The Court:
I'll hear from whomever AIG or National Union wish to offer and then we'll take our break after the final opening.

OPENING STATEMENT BY MR. ZELLE
(COUNSEL FOR THE DEFENDANT, AIG)

Your Honor, there is substantial evidence of good faith and of AIG's compliance with industry practices that I would like to outline. But because I do not have the jury here as the finder of fact, Your Honor, I would like you to be patient and I am going to defer on making my opening statement until we begin to present our evidence.

That, however, will be on Thursday when we are bringing Mr. Satriano for plaintiffs' case and to avoid having to bring him back, we will present our direct evidence, our affirmative evidence, at that time. Therefore, I'll wait until then.

The only thing I would like to clarify is that I would like to open before Mr. Satriano takes the stand despite the fact that his initial testimony will be by plaintiffs' counsel, because I think it will be to the benefit of the court to hear evidence consecutively as opposed to evidence interrupted by my opening.

<u>The Court:</u>
As long as you're not commenting on testimony that is already been heard when you do open.

Tuesday, February 6, 2007: Trial Day Two
    Examination of Jodie Mills (second claims adjuster at Crawford & Co.)
    Examination of Kathleen Fuell (major case unit consultant, Zurich)

Wednesday, February 7, 2007: Trial Day Three
    Examination of Kathleen Fuell (resumed)

Thursday, February 8, 2007: Trial Day Four
    Examination of Kathleen Fuell (resumed)

Friday, February 9, 2007: Trial Day Five
    Examination of the Honorable Judge Steven Rhodes (brother of Harold Rhodes)
    Examination of Rebecca Rhodes (plaintiff and daughter of Marcia and Harold Rhodes)
    Examination of Peter Hermes (attorney for McMillan Tree Service)

Monday, February 12, 2007: Trial Day Six
    Examination of Carlotta Patten (attorney at Brown Rudnick)
    Examination of Marcia Rhodes (plaintiff)

Tuesday, February 13, 2007: Trial Day Seven
Examination of Greg Deschenes (attorney for GAF)
Examination of Nicholas Satriano (complex claims director, AIG)

Wednesday, February 14, 2007: Trial Day Eight
Examination of Nicholas Satriano (resumed)

OPENING STATEMENT BY MR. ZELLE
(COUNSEL FOR THE DEFENDANT AIG)

Your Honor, I'm going to outline our evidence. It will show that there was no unfair and deceptive claims handling practices on the part of AIG. I believe the evidence will also establish that there was not any injury, compensable injury, incurred by the plaintiffs as a result of any conduct on the part of AIG.

National Union issued an excess policy. The terms are clear; they set forth what AIG's duties are to GAF. They specifically say that AIG does not have any duty to defend, but it does have a right to associate in counsel.

The evidence is going to show that it was in November 2003 that AIG first rolled up its sleeves to get involved with this case, and AIG's involvement was precipitated by the efforts on the part of Zurich and GAF and defense to reach up to AIG and ask for AIG's involvement. Again, there will be some testimony that AIG is a claim handling administrator for National Union, which issued the policy to GAF.

The evidence will show that when AIG was informed by defense counsel and Zurich and GAF that the Zurich policy limits were available, that Mr. Satriano told Ms. Fuell that he can't accept a tender unless it was in writing. And Mr. Satriano will explain what he meant.

He'll explain that it was his supervisor's directive to obtain written, formal written tender, and he'll explain the reason for that. He'll explain that the reason that he wanted it in writing was so there was a firm understanding between AIG and the primary carrier as to their respective obligations going forward, not only in terms of control over the money but control over the defense and the payment of the defense costs.

Mr. Satriano will testify that Ms. Fuell agreed that it was important to iron out the parties' respective positions with respect to a continuing defense obligation and that Ms. Fuell told him that she would respond to him with a formal written tender which explained that. And that letter, that formal written tender, was provided on March 29, 2004.

It included a demand, the court will see, that AIG assumed the defense of the insured. However, Zurich retracted that position and three days later Zurich informed AIG that it would continue to incur the costs of defense counsel, Mr. Deschenes and defense counsel appointed to Mr. Zalewski and D.L.S. and Penske.

The evidence will also show that two days after the tender was made, the formal written tender was made to AIG, that defense counsel offered the Zurich policy limit to the plaintiffs. At that point, the tender was meaningless because AIG didn't have control over that money to use to either entice Mr. Pritzker in mediation or not.

The evidence presented by AIG will focus primarily on two time periods, the November 19 through March 2004 period where Mr. Satriano was involved, and then the April 2004 through trial and beyond when AIG, before trial, was trying to obtain information that it believed was necessary to thoroughly evaluate the claim and ultimately to settle the claim.

Mr. Satriano will testify that he wanted to get all the information that he believed was necessary to evaluate the claim before he evaluated the claim, that he was reluctant to engage in any quantitative analysis before he had that information.

He will also testify that during the time period between November and March, he worked to review the information that was provided to him. He worked to associate in counsel because he felt more comfortable having his counsel reporting to him and actually did not feel confident with Mr. Deschenes, and he'll explain the reasons why.

He'll testify that there was resistance by GAF to Mr. Conroy's association in the case, and he will explain that until the March meeting, there was not an agreement by GAF to permit Mr. Conroy to be directly involved to communicate directly with Mr. Pritzker.

His testimony will demonstrate that he diligently worked to build a team, to get up to speed personally to obtain the information that he believed was necessary to undertake a valuable assessment of the claim.

He's going to explain that there were questions concerning insurance coverage. He will testify that he requested—and as of the time that he left he did not receive an analysis that he had requested of coverage that had been performed by Zurich.

And he'll explain why that was important to his assessment, not of the value of Mrs. Rhodes' injuries, but as to the exposure to GAF under the National Union policy.

He'll testify about the efforts that he believed were necessary in March to put the case into a reasonable position to go to mediation. He'll identify the deposition of Mrs. Rhodes, an IME of Mrs. Rhodes, particularly one that is performed by a physiatrist, or a physical medicine specialist, whose job it is—whose practice area includes assessing paralysis and spinal cord injuries and recovery from those injuries.

He'll testify that there was information in the life-care plan that made projections as to Mrs. Rhodes' recovery, but that was far different from the type of information that can be provided by a medical doctor who specializes in that arena.

Mr. Satriano will testify that after he left he spoke with his supervisor, Mr. Mastronardo (Nicholas Satriano's boss at AIG), about picking up the case so there wasn't any beats missed in handling the case.

Mr. Mastronardo (Nicholas Satriano's boss at AIG) was only involved for a short time. Mr. Mastronardo (Nicholas Satriano's boss at AIG) will testify as to his involvement as to what he believed needed to be done—this was in April of 2004—to effectively resolve the case, to obtain the information, get the case into mediation and give it a shot at settlement before trial.

The period after April was initially—the claim was handled by Mr. Maturine (a claims adjuster at AIG). Mr. Maturine, the documents will show, was focused on again team building and making sure that GAF's concerns regarding the associating in of Mr. Conroy were addressed.

And as the court will see from the documents, there certainly was a rather defined dispute as between Mr. Bartell (McCarter & English) on behalf of GAF and AIG. But going back to Mr. Satriano, he's going to testify that that was a sideshow, that it didn't interfere with his efforts to evaluate the case.

Testimony will be provided by Mr. Nitti, through his deposition I believe on plaintiffs' case, also by Ms. Kelly (Vice President, AIG Domestic Claims), whose Mr. Nitti's supervisor. She'll explain that Mr. Nitti had just started with AIG that she worked with him very closely in the evaluation of the Rhodes claim.

She'll explain, Ms. Kelly will, that there are many variables that going into evaluating a claim. And she will testify that given a rather limited amount of information that AIG had that was obtained through discovery by defense counsel, it was more difficult than in most cases.

She'll testify that from the information that was available to AIG, she and Mr. Nitti did their best to evaluate the claim and develop a number to present to their supervisor—this was Mr. Pedro—to request authority to settle the case during mediation. She'll also testify that that wasn't the be-all and end-all, that in her experience, when parties, whether at mediation or at any other time when they are negotiating, are within reaching distance, that is, within a close range; a telephone call to Mr. Pedro is generally sufficient to obtain sufficient authority to close the deal.

Ms. Kelly will testify that when she was looking at the case, when she and Mr. Nitti were working with the case, one of the most difficult things for them to assess was Mrs. Rhodes' future recovery.

And there will be evidence that we will present as to Mrs. Rhodes' testimony at trial, testimony personally from Mrs. Rhodes, testimony from her healthcare professionals, that as of that time, September of 2004, she had not begun her rehabilitation process.

And there will be testimony also from the trial that we will introduce from the physicians that it was extremely unusual for paraplegics to be three years out from the accident and not to have begun their rehabilitation. And she will explain that she did her best despite having that detailed information, despite having a history of recovery, to put a value on the future loss, both the economic loss and the non-economic losses.

She will also testify, based on information that she had received through the deposition, through the independent medical examination, that she believed that there was a—that Mrs. Rhodes can make significant physical and emotional gains once she began her rehabilitation process, and that she factored that into her assessment of the value of the case.

She will testify that depositions and IME's are typically available for review by the excess carrier at the time the primary carrier tenders its limit, and that in her view they are critical to the evaluation.

She will testify in detail about her experience in evaluating cases, how she does that, and why she believed that her evaluation, which led to authority, her request for authority, of $1.75 million from AIG, which represented her view that the reasonable settlement value or a reasonable offer at the time of the mediation would be as high as $4.75 million. She'll explain why she thought that was a reasonable figure to have in her mind going into mediation.

She'll testify that she has, in her experience, a routine familiarity with jury verdicts involving paralysis cases, burn cases, quadriplegic cases, disfigurement cases, brain injury cases, very high-value claims, including information concerning Massachusetts cases.

She'll testify that she did not review any specific cases in connection with her valuing—attempting to establish a reasonable settlement value for this case, but that it was a part of her experience and her general knowledge.

She'll also testify that based on her experience, the presence of the plaintiff at the mediation increases the likelihood of settlement. And she'll testify that she was disappointed when she learned from Mr. Nitti, who attended the mediation, that Mrs. Rhodes was not present.

She'll testify that she had expected prior to the mediation to learning more about the family dynamic, about Mrs. Rhodes' recovery during the mediation. And she will explain that, in her experience, having that opportunity to speak in front of the plaintiff is often a significant issue in moving the case closer to settlement.

She's going to testify as to her basis for believing that there would be a contribution of $1 million to the settlement pool based on the insurance available to McMillan's Tree Service.

In addition, on that subject there will be expert testimony. Mr. Cormack will testify. Bill Cormack is a veteran of 40-some years in the insurance industry.

He's going to testify about standard industry practices on the primary side, on the excess side, what insurers do to evaluate cases, on the relationship between primary and excess carriers, and about the inter-workings of the insurance industry, how things generally work, the standard industry practices.

The other expert we will be presenting is Mr. Todd. He'll testify on the subject of the reasonableness of AIG's efforts to settle and specifically the reasonableness of the offers that were made.

Both Mr. Cormack and Mr. Todd will testify that it is a well-established practice that meaningful settlement discussions are not pursued until the reasonable, meaningful, thorough *analysis of the claim can be undertaken, and that attempting to do so sooner than that generally is not only futile but frustrating.*

Our other witness will be Mr. Pritzker. And he will testify, we expect, to provide a backdrop to demonstrate that the conduct on the part of AIG in presenting offers specifically, and the amount of the offers, were reasonable in light of the demands that were made.

We expect that upon consideration of Mr. Pritzker's testimony this court will conclude that the package, the negotiation package of the plaintiffs, can reasonably be understood or interpreted by an insurer, a reasonable insurer, to indicate that plaintiffs would not settle for anything less than $10 million.

As Mr. Rhodes has not yet testified, I will suggest that there will be testimony by Mr. Rhodes that following the mediation, he made the decision that he would prefer to have the jury decide the case, and he no longer wished to consider further settlement discussions or negotiations.

Following the conclusion of the evidence, your Honor, we submit that there will be no factual basis to find that this case ever reached a point where liability, as that term is used in 93A, was reasonably clear because the information provided with respect to future damages and the assessment of the value of that claim was never reasonably clear.

But more significantly, we will show that despite that, your Honor, good-faith efforts were undertaken to resolve this case and to settle this case and that fair offers were made to effectuate settlement.

The evidence will show that AIG's offers were within the range of reasonable settlement offers and that AIG satisfied its obligations as an insurer. There will be evidence that Ms. Pinkham herself expressed the view after the trial that a $2 million jury verdict award was a realistic concern.

And finally, the evidence will show, your Honor, that to the extent that there is any finding of liability for unfair and deceptive practices or any finding that plaintiffs sustained compensable damages, that this was not due to any willful or knowing conduct on the part or misconduct on the part of AIG. And consequently, there is no evidence that would support a finding of willful or knowing or an award of punitive damages.

The only evidence that plaintiffs—or that this court will have to consider at the end of the day of damages, are damages for what will be referred to as garden-variety emotional distress or lost wages, based on what we believe the evidence will show were Mr. Rhodes' commitment to be near his wife as opposed to a financial concern, and evidence of costs that are alleged to have been incurred due to the fee arrangement that the Rhodes family had with the Brown Rudnick firm.

To the extent, your Honor, that any of those are found to be causally related to the conduct of AIG, and we submit there will be no evidence to support that finding, those damages claims, even as claimed, are a infinitesimal fraction of what plaintiffs are seeking as punitive damages and therefore no punitive damage award that conforms to double or treble damages can fairly be awarded in this case.

That's all I have.[252]

Thursday, February 15, 2007: Trial Day Nine
Examination of Nicholas Satriano (resumed)
Examination of Harold Rhodes (plaintiff)

Thursday, February 16, 2007: Trial Day Ten
Examination of Harold Rhodes
Examination of Arthur Kiriakos (plaintiff's expert witness)

Friday, March 8, 2007: Trial Day Eleven
Examination of Arthur Kiriakos (resumed)

Monday, March 11, 2007: Trial Day Twelve
Examination of Arthur Kiriakos (resumed)
Examination of Janet Kelley (administrator, Brown Rudnick)
Examination of William Cormack (defendant's expert witness)

Monday, March 12, 2007: Trial Day Thirteen
Examination of William Cormack (resumed)
Examination of Tracey Kelly (vice president, AIG)

---

252 Nowhere in this opening is there any defense about AIG's post-judgment settlement actions. Later, AIG will argue that these post-judgment settlement actions did not constitute an *"unfair or deceptive act."*
A post-trial motion to Judge Donovan for a new trial, or in the alternative, for a remittitur.
A notice of appeal to the Massachusetts Appeals Court, requesting a new trial be ordered due to Judge Donovan's "abuse of her discretion."
Waiting until July 14, 2005 to offer a settlement that was acceptable.
Making its final payment not until September 6, 2005, nearly a year after the jury verdict.

Tuesday, March 13, 2007: Trial Day Fourteen
Examination of Tracey Kelly (resumed)
"She was a blameless victim, you know, whose entire life was changed."

Wednesday, March 14, 2007: Trial Day Fifteen
Examination of Tracey Kelly (resumed)
Examination of Karl Maser (defendant's expert witness)

Monday, Thursday, March 15, 2007: Trial Day Sixteen
Examination of Frederick Pritzker (attorney, Brown Rudnick)
Examination of J. Owen Todd (defendant's expert witness)

Wednesday, March 28, 2007
The final action upon conclusion of the trial testimony, but before the closing statements, was the submission of the post-trial briefs by the attorneys representing Zurich American Insurance, AIG, and the plaintiffs. While all the post-trial briefs were lengthy, these represented the final opportunity for each side to make their legal analysis of the trial clear for Judge Gants.

Friday, March 30, 2007: Trial Day Seventeen
Closing Statement by Mr. Varga
Closing Statement by Mr. Zelle
Closing Statement by Mr. Cohen
Closing Statement by Mr. Pritzker
Questions by the Court

<u>The Court:</u>

I do have some questions. Before I ask them let me say three things. First, each of your closings was excellent. So I applaud you all for three very, very fine closings. Secondly, when I do ask questions, you interpret them at your peril in terms of what you think it says as to where I am in my thinking about the case.

So I know it is natural, but I do warn you that my questions may or may not reflect any particular inclination. So I encourage you not to attempt to read too much into my questions apart from the fact that I know there are various issues, some of which I will have to reach, some of which I may never reach but potentially may and therefore may still be asking about. So I mention that as I begin to ask questions.

Third and finally, especially with regard to Ms. Pinkham's last point, I, as I am sure everybody in this courtroom does, admire the fortitude of the entire Rhodes family in terms of enduring those terrible events, both Mrs. Rhodes in getting through the day in which everything she does is made more difficult and Mr. Rhodes in keeping the family together and helping his wife and the daughter.

So while I do admire them and to some extent can appreciate and to some extent I am sure cannot appreciate what they're going through, it also is not going to decide this case. This case is about them only to the extent that what happened to them is something that the insurance company properly needed to investigate, evaluate and consider.

So it bears on my decision to that extent, but my focus is, also as I think Ms. Pinkham properly contended, to be on what is the appropriate and legal conduct of an insurance company in examining a claim; and while that bears on the Rhodes to the extent it was their claim before them. I do understand that what I am evaluating is the extent to which on insurance company or two insurance companies did or did not engage in unfair or deceptive conduct, and that is my focus.

So whatever my decision is, it is not—if the Rhodes family win, it is not because I admire them; if the Rhodes family lose, it is not because I do not.

So having said that let me now get to a number of legal questions I have.[253]

ZURICH AMERICAN INSURANCE "LIABILITY BEST PRACTICES"

The discovery order by Judge Gants required that Zurich provide its claims processing manual, "Liability Best Practices." This manual specified, in detail, how a Zurich claim was supposed to be processed and the length of allowable time. Some highlights were as follows:[254]

"*The insured and claimant are to be contacted within one business day from receipt of the claim by Zurich. The case manager must be the one to make contact with those parties.*"

---

253 For brevity, the entire trial transcript of the court's questions to the attorneys is not included. For the complete trial transcript, see www.theblamelessvictim.com.

254 For brevity, the entire manual is not included. For the entire manual, see www.theblamelessvictim.com.

"If there is representation of the claimant by counsel at the outset (including situations where the lawsuit is our first notice), initial contact with the attorney should be made over the telephone, within one business day, to obtain all available information concerning claimant's allegations relative to liability, injuries and damages."

"The case manager should develop and pursue a focused and proactive strategy to obtain all necessary evidence and information, and should not abandon the investigation to counsel or the discovery process."

"The case manager evaluates the claim exposure upon receipt of new information that potentially impacts his/her assessment of liability, injuries or damages. An evaluation is completed and documented in the file within no more than 30 days of receipt of said information."

"Estimated realistic case exposure is proactively recognized as soon as practicable, but no more than 30 days from our receipt of information evidencing that exposure."

"The case manager will develop and document a customized strategy for the resolution of the claim within 45 days of receipt of the claim."

DID ZURICH COMMIT AN *"UNFAIR OR DECEPTIVE ACT"*?

1. Zurich asserted that it did not receive any information from its attorneys or from its Agent, Crawford, concerning this catastrophic claim until eight months after the crash, due to its administrative lost-in-the-mailroom problems. Therefore, the eight-month delay until August 2002 to begin to investigate this claim could not be found to be an *"unfair or deceptive act"* by Zurich. If Judge Gants accepts Zurich's argument, then all primary insurance carriers would have their first adjudicated method to legally delay its claims processing without committing an *"unfair or deceptive act."*

    However, Zurich's delay of eight months—in violation of its own claims processing manual—to begin its investigation must be found by Judge Gants to be an *"unfair or deceptive act."* There was substantial evidence that Zurich did receive other mail at the same headquarters address during this period of delay.

2. Zurich asserted that it had no legal obligation to begin to investigate this claim before receiving the plaintiffs' demand package in September 2003. Therefore, the additional thirteen-month delay could not be found to be an *"unfair or*

deceptive act" by Zurich. If Judge Gants accepts Zurich's argument, then all primary insurance carriers would have their second adjudicated method to legally delay its claims processing without committing an *"unfair or deceptive act."*

However, waiting until the plaintiffs' demand package has been received is not legally required. Therefore, by waiting the thirteen months to begin its claims investigation, Zurich must have committed an *"unfair or deceptive act,"* since Zurich's own claims processing manual, "Liability Best Practices," requires proactive investigation, even if no demand package has been received.

3. Zurich asserted that, although the company internally determined in November 2003 to tender its $2 million policy limit to AIG, Zurich had no legal obligation to e-mail this tender offer to AIG for another two months until January 2004, due to the perceived difficulty in getting management approvals at this time of the year. Therefore, the additional two-month delay could not be found to be an *"unfair or deceptive act"* by Zurich. If Judge Gants accepts Zurich's argument, then all primary insurance carriers would have their third adjudicated method to legally delay its claims processing without committing an *"unfair or deceptive act."*

However, by waiting two additional months simply to e-mail its tender offer, just because of the perceived difficulty in getting management approvals, Zurich must have committed an *"unfair or deceptive act."* Insurance carriers do not stop their operations in November, December, and January; Zurich's own claims processing manual, "Liability Best Practices," requires speedy claims processing.

4. Zurich asserted that AIG was responsible for the next three-month delay until April 2004, because it was AIG that required Zurich to put into writing that Zurich would tender its $2 million policy to AIG and that Zurich would continue to pay defense costs. Therefore, the additional three-month delay could not be found to be an *"unfair or deceptive act"* by Zurich. If Judge Gants accepts Zurich's argument, then all primary insurance carriers would have their fourth adjudicated method to legally delay its claims processing without committing an *"unfair or deceptive act."*

However, by taking three months merely to write an e-mail just to confirm its verbal agreement with AIG, Zurich must have committed an *"unfair or deceptive act"* since Zurich's own claims processing manual, "Liability Best Practices," requires speedy claims processing.

5. Zurich asserted that it had no legal obligation to begin to investigate this claim until Zurich had determined that no other insurance carrier had additional insurance coverage for one or more of the defendants. Therefore, any additional delay to locate other insurance carriers that might have additional insurance coverage could not be found to be an *"unfair or deceptive act"* by Zurich. If Judge Gants accepts Zurich's argument, then all primary insurance carriers would have their fifth adjudicated method to legally delay its claims processing without committing an *"unfair or deceptive act."*

   However, by not simultaneously investigating this claim while looking for additional insurance coverage, Zurich must have committed an *"unfair or deceptive act."* There is no legitimate reason why proactively investigating this claim could not be done concurrently with looking for additional insurance coverage (which was never found).

6. Zurich asserted that only AIG (as the excess insurance carrier) was empowered to effectuate the settlement of a claim and, as such, any delay by Zurich is irrelevant. Therefore, any delay caused by Zurich to effectuate a settlement could not be found to be an *"unfair or deceptive act"* by Zurich. If Judge Gants accepts Zurich's argument, then all primary insurance carriers would have their sixth adjudicated method to legally delay its claims processing without committing an *"unfair or deceptive act."*

   However, by causing any unnecessary delay in investigating this claim (without regard to AIG's settlement actions), Zurich must have committed an *"unfair or deceptive act."* The logical conclusion of this sixth assertion is that a primary insurance carrier could take any amount of time to investigate a claim and then tender its policy limit, without any concern for possibly having committed an *"unfair or deceptive act."*

7. Zurich asserts that when the plaintiffs amended their complaint, Zurich was entitled to review the whole claims investigation from the beginning. Therefore, any delay caused by reviewing the whole claims investigation could not be found to be an *"unfair or deceptive act"* by Zurich. If Judge Gants accepts Zurich's argument, then all primary insurance carriers would have their seventh adjudicated method to legally delay its claims processing without committing an *"unfair or deceptive act."*

However, by delaying the completion of its claims investigation through unnecessarily re-reviewing the non-amended portion of the complaint (not just the amendment), Zurich must have committed an *"unfair or deceptive act."* The plaintiffs' amending the complaint is not a reason for a primary insurance carrier to restart its claims investigation from the beginning.

8. Zurich asserted that it was not required to tender its $2 million policy limits to the plaintiffs, without a full release of all claims by the plaintiffs, even when Zurich determined that *damages* exceeded its $2 million policy limit. Therefore, any delay in tendering its $2 million policy limits, without a full release of all claims by the plaintiffs, could not be found to be an *"unfair or deceptive act"* by Zurich. If Judge Gants accepts Zurich's argument, then all primary insurance carriers would have their eighth adjudicated method to legally delay its claims processing without committing an *"unfair or deceptive act."*

   However, by requiring a full release of all claims against all defendants in order to receive its $2 million policy limit, Zurich must have committed an *"unfair or deceptive act."* There is not a statutory prohibition against a primary insurance carrier tendering its policy limits to the plaintiffs, without stipulation, instead of to the excess insurance carrier.

9. Zurich asserted that it had no legal obligation to proactively acquire the needed information in order to thoroughly investigate this claim. Therefore, any delay in acquiring the needed information could not be found to be an *"unfair or deceptive act"* by Zurich. If Judge Gants accepts Zurich's argument, then all primary insurance carriers would have their ninth adjudicated method to legally delay its claims processing without committing an *"unfair or deceptive act."*

   However, by delaying through not proactively investigating this claim, Zurich must have committed an *"unfair or deceptive act."* Its own claims processing manual requires proactive investigation.

10. Zurich asserted that it had no legal obligation to accept the claims investigation provided by Crawford (Zurich's Agent and GAF's third-party insurance administrator). Therefore, any delay caused by Zurich's determination that Crawford's claims investigation was inadequate could not be found to be an *"unfair or deceptive act"* by Zurich. If Judge Gants accepts Zurich's argument, then all primary

insurance carriers would have their tenth adjudicated method to legally delay its claims processing without committing an *"unfair or deceptive act."*

However, by delaying by not accepting Crawford's thorough investigation, Zurich must have committed an *"unfair or deceptive act."* Crawford was Zurich's Agent. As such, Crawford must be considered an extension of Zurich's claims investigation process, as provided in its own claims processing manual.

DID AIG COMMIT AN *"UNFAIR OR DECEPTIVE ACT"*?

AIG argued that none of its pre-judgment settlement actions could be found to be an *"unfair or deceptive act."* Further AIG argued that none of the following post-judgment settlement actions could be found to be an *"unfair or deceptive act"*:
1. A post-trial motion to Judge Donovan for a new trial or, in the alternative, for a remittitur.
2. A "Notice of Appeal" to the Massachusetts Appeals Court, requesting a new trial be ordered due to Judge Donovan's *"abuse of her discretion."*
3. Waiting until July 14, 2005, to offer a settlement that was acceptable.
4. Making its final payment not until September 6, 2005, nearly a year after the jury verdict.

WAITING FOR THE DECISION BY JUDGE RALPH GANTS

With the trial concluded, Marcia and I began to patiently wait for the ruling by Judge Gants.

Monday, April 30, 2007: Thirty Days Since End of Trial
No decision by Judge Gants.

Thursday, May 31, 2007: Sixty-One Days Since End of Trial
No decision by Judge Gants. Marcia returned to a busy schedule of medical appointments. In August 2006, she was unfortunately diagnosed with severe interperineum pain. Interperineum refers to the area below the coccyx. This extraordinary pain was unexpected. With no ability to feel anything below her waist (due to the T-12 spinal fracture), how could she have any feeling in this area? Perhaps the titanium rods and screws, still bolted to her spinal column, were the cause of this severe pain.

On May 8, 2007, at St. Elizabeth's Hospital (Brighton, Massachusetts), Dr. Bayley, back from his military service in Iraq, operated on Marcia to remove the titanium rods and screws. Sadly, removing this hardware didn't relieve her severe interperineum pain.

On May 20, 2007, Marcia broke her right leg in two places, and a full leg cast was put on.

On May 29, 2007, she was hospitalized at Milford Regional Medical Center for severe interperineum pain as well as a UTI. This hospitalization didn't relieve her severe interperineum pain.

Saturday, June 30, 2007: Ninety-One Days Since End of Trial

No decision by Judge Gants.

Marcia continued with a busy schedule of medical appointments. She was transferred to Whittier Rehabilitation to begin physical therapy. This rehabilitation didn't relieve her severe interperineum pain.

Tuesday, July 31, 2007: 122 Days Since End of Trial

No decision by Judge Gants.

Tuesday, July 10, 2007, marked the one hundredth day that we have been waiting for the ruling from Judge Gants.

Marcia continues with a busy schedule of medical appointments. On July 16, 2007, she broke her left leg, and a medium cast was put on. On July 27, 2007, she was taken to the ER at Milford Regional Medical Center for an unexpected renal discharge.

Friday, August 31, 2007: 153 Days Since End of Trial

No decision by Judge Gants.

Sunday, September 30, 2007: 183 Days Since End of Trial

No decision by Judge Gants.

Marcia continued with a busy schedule of medical appointments. On September 6, 2007, she underwent a sigmoidoscopy[255] to determine the cause of the renal discharge; an anal fistula abscess was found and drained. This didn't relieve her severe interperineum pain.

On September 15, 2007, she was diagnosed with traumatic optic neuropathy (damage to optic nerve in right eye), likely caused by the cerebral hematoma that she suffered in the crash in January 2002.

---

255 "*Sigmoidoscopy is the minimally invasive medical examination of the large intestine from the rectum through the last part of the colon. A sigmoidoscopy is similar to, but not the same as, a colonoscopy. A sigmoidoscopy only examines up to the sigmoid, the most distal part of the colon, while colonoscopy examines the whole large bowel.*" "Sigmoidoscopy," Wikipedia, last modified March 9, 2014, http://en.wikipedia.org/wiki/Sigmoidoscopy.

Wednesday, October 31, 2007: 214 Days Since End of Trial

No decision by Judge Gants.

I was frustrated by the length of time. I continued to be optimistic, but now my confidence was qualified.

Friday, November 30, 2007: 244 Days Since End of Trial

No decision by Judge Gants.

Marcia continues with a busy schedule of medical appointments. On November 8, 2007, her broken leg healed and the cast was removed.

Wednesday, December 19, 2007: 263 Days Since End of Trial

No decision by Judge Gants.

Falling to the bathroom floor, Marcia suffered a transverse proximal fracture of tibia and fibula. She had another broken leg.

Thursday, January 31, 2008: 306 Days since End of Trial

No decision by Judge Gants.

Nine months had passed since the trial, and Judge Gants still hasn't made his ruling. For the last few weeks, I have been asking other attorneys about the delay. They indicated their cautious optimism that we would prevail, but I was chagrined by the delay. One attorney, whose opinion I valued, was having increasing doubts about a positive outcome.

February 5, 2008: 311 Days Since End of Trial

No decision by Judge Gants.

Today is the one-year anniversary of the start of the trial, and we still do not have a ruling from Judge Gants. I am so frustrated.

The Brown Rudnick attorneys called this morning. *"We should begin to prepare for a decision that will not be in our favor,"* one attorney said.

"This really stinks," I said. "What should I tell Marcia?"

Perhaps Judge Gants is adding his own judicial interpretation, and was doing extensive legal research. Perhaps he is concerned about the amount of punishment. Who knows?

March 1, 2008: 337 Days Since End of Trial

No decision by Judge Gants.

Sunday, March 30, 2008: 366 Days Since End of Trial

No decision by Judge Gants.

A year has passed[256] since the conclusion of the trial. There still isn't a decision and still no indication when the ruling would be made.

Marcia has had serious medical complications recently. On March 15, 2008, she was again diagnosed with sepsis (perhaps from an infected abscess on her kidney). She was hospitalized for ten days in the ICU at Milford Regional Medical Center, where she was on a respirator machine to maintain her breathing. Again, the medical team showed their magnificent resolve to keep her alive.

Wednesday, April 30, 2008: 396 Days Since End of Trial

No decision by Judge Gants.

Knowing that there will be at least two, maybe three, more appeals, win or lose, this case is not likely to be resolved until 2011. Three more years of this crap.

I have no idea how the judge is going to rule. Clearly, the facts are on our side-—at least everyone says so. I was sure the initial emotional outrage we hoped Judge Gants would have toward Zurich and AIG must have passed long ago.

Am I crazy? A decision against us would surely have been made a long time ago. Attorneys have told me that a denial requires less documentation and time.

All I can hope for now is that Judge Gants is writing the most legally definitive ruling on Chapter 176D and Chapter 93A, anticipating three appeals in the future (the Massachusetts Appeals Courts, the Massachusetts Supreme Judicial Court, and perhaps the US Supreme Court).

But that doesn't feel right. We're going to lose.

The citizens of Massachusetts are going to be at an even larger disadvantage against insurance carriers. When Zurich and AIG are not found to have committed an *"unfair or deceptive act,"* the insurance carriers will have full reign to do as they please to delay payments to future blameless victims.

This hurts so much.

Monday, May 5, 2008: 400 Days Since End of Trial

No decision by Judge Gants.

More than thirteen months have now passed since the Chapter 93A trial and we are still waiting for the decision from Judge Gants. The trial, which began in February 2007, now seems like a distant memory. Recalling the faces of the insurance defense attorneys and the witnesses is difficult. After all this time, I cannot believe that Judge Gants would rule against us.

---

256 The wait is excruciatingly unfair to Marcia. It is ironic that this case is about delay, and yet the judge's decision has been delayed for one year.

Wednesday, May 21, 2008: 416 Days Since End of Trial

No decision by Judge Gants.

Friday, May 23, 2008: 418 Days Since End of Trial

No decision by Judge Gants.

Wednesday and Thursday had to be our worst days in a long time.

On Wednesday, I sat in at Marcia's therapy session with Dr. McAnulty. I was selfish and overbearing in my discussion with Jill and Marcia. The details do not matter; I regretted not demonstrating a caring, loving attitude toward Marcia. I hurt her.

Yesterday, Marcia talked with an interventional pain specialist. This doctor said he could not do anything to help relieve her interperineum pain. We were sickened over this, because we had high hopes that he could make a difference. I can't believe that no one in medical science has found a treatment for a person who has had a T-12 burst fracture of the spinal cord and suffers from severe interperineum pain.

We are just lost—I have no idea what to do now about anything.

She must have surgery to repair the parastomal hernia (a large swelling around and under the stoma for the colostomy). At the same time, she will have surgery for a second stoma at a new location for the colostomy. After the surgery, she will be in recovery for at least three weeks.

I guess, after Marcia has recovered sufficiently, I will arrange for her to see the Lahey Hospital's interventional pain clinic; the Boston Spine Group; and another neurosurgeon.

But, in the meantime, she continues to live in awful pain.

Friday, May 30, 2008: 425 Days Since End of Trial

No decision by Judge Gants.

I continued to overly dwell, more than was healthy, on why Judge Gants was taking so much time to issue his ruling.

Tuesday, June 3, 2008: 430 Days Since End of Trial

THE DECISION BY JUDGE RALPH GANTS

"How dreadful it is when the right judge judges wrong."[257]

---

[257] Excerpted from *Antigone* (Sophocles) on Wikipedia. Translation by Richard C. Jebb, *The Tragedies of Sophocles*. Cambridge: Cambridge UP, 1917.

After fourteen months, Judge Gants handed down his decision today.[258] The decision is in three parts: Findings of Fact, Conclusions of Law, and Court Order.

I thought the Findings of Fact presented an accurate summary of all the legal and medical activities since the crash.

After reading the Findings of Fact, I was optimistic that Judge Gants, in the Conclusions of Law section, would find that both Zurich and AIG committed at least one *"unfair or deceptive act."*

But that didn't happen. Judge Gants found that Zurich did not commit even one *"unfair or deceptive"* at any time. Incredible. None of what Zurich had done to Marcia or me was even the tiniest violation.

For AIG, Judge Gants did find one *"unfair or deceptive act."* However, Judge Gants found that this one *"unfair or deceptive act"* was not done *willfully or knowingly*. Therefore, Judge Gants chose the smaller of the two possible dollar punishments.[259]

CONCLUSIONS OF LAW (EXCERPTS)

DID ZURICH BREACH ITS OBLIGATIONS AS A PRIMARY INSURER UNDER MASSACHUSETTS GENERAL LAWS C. 176D?

The Rhodes contend that Zurich's delay in tendering its policy limits violated its statutory obligation to "effectuate prompt...settlements of claims in which liability has become reasonably clear."

As noted earlier, Fuell verbally tendered to AIG the full policy limits in her telephone call to Satriano on January 23, 2004, but Satriano rejected the tender on two grounds:

(1) he wanted it in writing; and,

(2) he wanted the writing to address whether Zurich was also tendering its defense obligation.

Rather, AIG was obliged to accept the tender of policy limits and resolve separately the question of which insurer now had the obligation to pay defense costs.

The question then is whether Zurich's tender on January 23, 2004 was "prompt" within the meaning of M.G.L. c. 176D.

---

258 This judicial decision has been heavily excerpted. For the complete decision, see www.theblamelessvictim.com.
259 The calculation of the dollar punishment is difficult to understand, and even harder to explain, and there is disagreement even within the legal community.

To be sure, Zurich had effectively completed its due diligence by the November 19, 2003 meeting and Fuell knew then that she was going to recommend that Zurich tender its full limits.

However, in order to obtain authority for so large a tender, Fuell had to prepare a detailed BI Claim Report, which she did not complete until December 19, 2003.

While this Court has no doubt that Zurich can have and should have provided the required authorization for the tender earlier than January 22, 2004, it does not ford it to be an unfair act to have failed to do so.

Therefore, this Court finds that Zurich acted with the promptness required under M.G.L. c. 176D when it provided AIG with its verbal tender of policy limits on January 23, 2004.

Therefore, this Court finds that Zurich did not violate its obligation under M.G.L. c. 176D to make a prompt tender of its full policy limits and, if it did, its delay did not cause the Rhodes to suffer any injury or loss because the delay did not affect either the amount or timing of AIG's settlement offers.

As a result, judgment shall enter for Zurich in this action.

DID AIG BREACH ITS OBLIGATIONS AS AN EXCESS INSURER UNDER MASSACHUSETTS GENERAL LAWS C. 176D?

Once Fuell informed Satriano during that November 19, 2003 conference call that she intended to seek Zurich's authorization to tender the policy limits, AIG was placed on notice that the tender was imminent and that it would soon assume responsibility for the Rhodes' claim.

As earlier noted, until Satriano obtained Zurich's verbal tender on January 23, 2004, AIG, as the excess insurer, had no duty to make any settlement offer to the Rhodes.

However, once that tender was made, AIG assumed responsibility for and control over the Rhodes claim, including the responsibility to make a prompt and fair settlement offer.

By the tine Zurich verbally tendered its limits on January 23, 2004, AIG had more than two months to evaluate the case.

However, AIG cannot delay its arrangements for the IME or these depositions in order to delay its obligation to make a prompt settlement offer, especially since discovery in the case had closed and it was scheduled for trial in September 2004.

It appears that AIG had determined, at least by the March 4, 2004 meeting at GAF's headquarters, that it wished an IME, because Conroy before the meeting had looked for and found a physiatrist to conduct that IME.

Yet, AIG demonstrated no apparent urgency to schedule the IME; it was not conducted until July 20, 2004, nearly the latest possible time for the IME to be conducted and for defense counsel to have the benefit of the IME report before the mediation on August 11.

It is equally clear that AIG had not determined by that meeting that the depositions of Ms. Rhodes and Rebecca Rhodes were necessary to determine whether damages were relatively clear because, although the matter was discussed, no decision was made at that meeting as to whether to depose them.

The fact that AIG did not know whether it wished to depose these two parties even though more than three months had passed since it knew it would assume responsibility for this catastrophic claim demonstrates that AIG did not believe that their depositions were necessary to determine whether liability was reasonably clear.

Rather, the reason to depose them was simply to gauge how credible they would be at trial, and this reason was offset by the fear that deposing them would harden the plaintiffs' already tough position as to settlement.

Indeed, AIG proceeded to mediation without having ever deposed Rebecca Rhodes.

AIG also insisted that its attorneys seek discovery of Ms. Rhodes' psychological records, which AIG argued was imperative before it can determine whether liability was relatively clear.

The fact of the matter is that AIG did not delay its settlement offer in order to conduct the IME or to depose Ms. Rhodes or to obtain Ms. Rhodes' psychological records; it delayed its settlement offer because it did not want to make any offer until mediation and it wanted, for strategic purposes, to wait until nearly the eve of trial to mediate the case.

As a result, AIG did not make any settlement offer in this case until the mediation on August 11, 2004, almost exactly one year from the date that the Rhodes made their settlement demand.

The issue, then, is whether delaying the settlement offer this long satisfied AIG's duty under M.G.L. c. 176D to make a "prompt" settlement offer.

This Court finds that liability, including the extent of damages, in this case was reasonably clear by December 5, 2003, when the final version of the defense Life Care Plan had been prepared by Mattson.

By then, discovery had closed, all medical records had been produced, the plaintiffs had presented their detailed settlement demand, and the defense had their own Life Care Plan to compare with that presented by the Rhodes' Life Care Plan expert.

Therefore, liability was reasonably clear when Zurich tendered its policy limits to AIG on January 23, 2004.

This Court concludes that, even allowing a generous amount of time for AIG to become familiar with the claim, to obtain additional discovery it thought necessary to make liability reasonably clear, to resolve coverage issues, and to obtain internal approval within AIG, AIG violated its duty to make a prompt settlement offer once liability was reasonably clear by failing to make a settlement offer by May 1, 2004.

Having found that AIG breached its duty to make a prompt settlement offer once liability was reasonably clear, this Court now turns to the question of whether the settlement offer it ultimately made at mediation—$3.5 million—was a reasonable settlement offer to effectuate a fair settlement.

This Court finds it was at the low end of the reasonable range of settlement offers.

The issue the Court must now confront is whether AIG's breach of its duty to provide a prompt settlement offer by failing to make any settlement offer until August 11, 2004 caused the plaintiffs to suffer any damages.

It is plain to this Court that the delay did not cause the plaintiffs any actual compensable damages.

The final issue this Court must address is whether AIG breached its obligation to provide a reasonable settlement offer after trial.

This Court finds that AIG did precisely what Chapter 176D was intended to prevent—attempt to bully the plaintiffs into accepting an unreasonably low settlement rather than wait the roughly two years for their appeal to conclude and the judgment to be paid.

The Massachusetts Supreme Judicial Court requires that a plaintiff satisfy the elements of an intentional infliction of emotional distress claim in order to establish emotional distress damages in a Chapter 93A case.

This Court, while it finds AIG's conduct to be knowing and willful, does not find it be "extreme and outrageous."

Nor does this Court find the defendants' emotional distress to be sufficiently "severe" during the post-judgment period to warrant damages, if only because Zurich's payment of $2.32 million on December 22, 2004 alleviated the plaintiffs' immediate financial distress.

This Court does not agree that the emotional costs of litigation—the so-called "frustrations" of litigation—are compensable unless those frustrations rise to the level required for recovery of damages under an intentional infliction of emotional distress claim.

This Court further finds that AIG's $7.0 million settlement offer, including Zurich's $2 million and including a release of the plaintiffs' claims under Chapters 176D and 93A, made on December 17, 2004 and repeated in writing on March 18, 2005, was not only unreasonably low but also constituted a willful and knowing violation of M.G.L. c. 176D.

This Court finds that double, rather than treble, damages are appropriate here only because AIG later came to its senses and made a reasonable post-judgment offer before the appellate litigation began in earnest.

The final issue this Court needs to confront in this legal odyssey is whether the amount doubled is the actual damages or the amount of the judgment.

This Court finds that the appropriate amount doubled is the actual damages.

This Court understands why the Legislature in enacting the 1989 Amendment to M.G.L. c. 93A would wish to punish an insurer who, by its willful or knowing failure to make a prompt and fair settlement offer, forces a litigant to proceed to trial to obtain a reasonable judgment.

In such cases, the Legislature authorized the doubling or trebling of the underlying judgment to deter insurers from engaging in such unfair conduct.

However, when the insurer's failure to make a prompt and fair settlement offer occurs after the issuance of the judgment, it makes no sense to multiply the judgment because the insurer's conduct did not force the trial that yielded that judgment.

Consequently, this Court finds that AIG is liable only for double the actual "loss of use" damages of $448,250, which totals $896,500, plus the Rhodes' reasonable attorney's fees and costs incurred in prosecuting this Chapter 93A action.

Court Order

For the reasons detailed above, this Court ORDERS that:

This Court finds that Zurich did not violate its duty as the primary insurer under M.G.L. c. 176D "to effectuate prompt, fair and equitable settlements of claims in which liability has become reasonably clear." When final judgment ultimately enters in this case, judgment shall enter in favor of the defendant Zurich, with statutory costs only.

This Court finds that AIG, prior to the issuance of the final judgment, violated their duty as the excess insurer under M.G.L. c. 176D "to effectuate prompt…settlements of claims in which liability has become reasonably clear," but their violation did not cause the plaintiffs to suffer any actual damages.

This Court finds that AIG, after the issuance of the final judgment, violated their duty as the excess insurer under M.G.L. c. 176D "to effectuate prompt, fair and equitable settlements of claims in which liability has become reasonably clear." This Court finds that the actual damages caused by this violation are limited to "loss of use" damages in the amount of $448,250.

This Court finds that the violation found in paragraph 3 supra was willful and knowing, and that doubling the amount of actual damages is an appropriate punitive award for such violation. Therefore, this Court orders that National Union and AIG, jointly and severally, shall pay the plaintiffs $896,500 in actual and punitive damages.

This Court finds, under M.G.L. c. 93A that National Union and AIG shall also pay to the plaintiffs the reasonable attorney's fees and costs incurred in prosecuting this action against National Union and AIG.

Ralph D. Gants
Justice of the Superior Court

Wednesday, June 4, 2008

DID JUDGE GANTS FIND THAT ZURICH COMMITTED AT LEAST ONE "UNFAIR OR DECEPTIVE ACT"?

With regard to Zurich, we lost. Zurich won. Incredibly, Judge Gants found that none of Zurich's actions constituted even one *"unfair or deceptive act."* Through his decision, each of the conclusions of law was decided in Zurich's favor:

1. Judge Gants completely ignored Zurich's eight-month delay, until August 2002, to begin to investigate this claim, even though Zurich's own Agent, Crawford, provided its First Full Formal Report to Zurich on January 30, 2002.

2. Judge Gants agreed with Zurich's assertion that it had no legal obligation to begin to investigate this claim before receiving the plaintiffs' demand package in September 2003; therefore, the additional thirteen-month delay could not be found to be an *"unfair or deceptive act."*

3. Judge Gants agreed with Zurich's assertion that, although the company internally determined in November 2003 to tender its $2 million policy limit to AIG, Zurich had no legal obligation to e-mail this tender offer to AIG for another two months until January 2004, due to the perceived difficulty in getting management approvals at this time of year. Therefore, the additional two-month delay could not be found to be an *"unfair or deceptive act."*

4. Judge Gants agreed with Zurich's assertion that AIG was responsible for the next three-month delay until April 2004, because it was AIG that required Zurich to put into writing that Zurich would tender its $2 million policy to AIG and that Zurich would continue to pay defense costs. Therefore, the additional three-month delay could not be found to be an *"unfair or deceptive act."*

5. Judge Gants agreed with Zurich's assertion that it had no legal obligation to begin to investigate this claim until Zurich had determined that no other insurance carrier had additional insurance coverage for one or more of the defendants. Therefore, any additional delay to locate other insurance carriers that might have additional insurance coverage could not be found to be an *"unfair or deceptive act."*

6. Judge Gants agreed with Zurich's assertion that only AIG (as the excess insurance carrier) was empowered to effectuate the settlement of a claim and, as such, any delay by Zurich is irrelevant. Therefore, any delay caused by Zurich to effectuate a settlement could not be found to be an *"unfair or deceptive act."*

7. Judge Gants agreed with Zurich's assertion that when the plaintiffs amended their complaint, Zurich was entitled to review whole claims investigation from the beginning. Therefore, any delay caused by reviewing the whole claims investigation could not be found to be an *"unfair or deceptive act."*

8. Judge Gants agreed with Zurich's assertion that it was not required to tender its $2 million policy limits to the plaintiffs, without a full release of all claims by the plaintiffs, even when Zurich determined that *damages* exceeded its $2 million policy limit. Therefore, any delay in tendering its $2 million policy limits, without a full release of all claims by the plaintiffs, could not be found to be an *"unfair or deceptive act."*

9. Judge Gants agreed with Zurich's assertion that it had no legal obligation to proactively acquire the needed information in order to thoroughly investigate this claim. Therefore, any delay in acquiring the needed information could not be found to be an *"unfair or deceptive act."*

10. Judge Gants agreed with Zurich's assertion that it had no legal obligation to accept the claims investigation provided by Crawford (Zurich's Agent and GAF's third-party insurance administrator). Therefore, any delay caused by Zurich's determination that Crawford's claims investigation was inadequate could not be found to be an *"unfair or deceptive act."*

Each of these conclusions of law—all in Zurich's favor—appear to me to contradict Zurich's own claims processing manual; the substantial evidence presented at the trial, and Judge Gants's findings of fact. It is impossible for me to fathom how Judge Gants could find that Zurich did not commit at least one *"unfair or deceptive act"* from January 9, 2002, the date the crash occurred, until December 22, 2004, the date that payment from Zurich was received.

For example, Judge Gants found that Zurich did not commit an *"unfair or deceptive act"* for its eight-month delay (from January 9, 2002, until August 2002) to begin to investigate this claim (due entirely to Zurich's internal mailroom and administrative issues). How this action by Zurich was not an *"unfair or deceptive act"* is beyond all reason. Could every insurance carrier now claim that all transmittals and records to the insurance carrier were "lost in the mailroom" without being penalized?

Through Judge Gants's decision, primary insurance carriers are now legally empowered to do to other blameless victims what Zurich did to Marcia.

Imagine the implications: Every primary insurance carrier that commits the same delays as Zurich did cannot be found to have committed an *"unfair or deceptive act."*

The ramifications to future blameless victims are incomprehensible.

By not finding that Zurich had committed even one *"unfair or deceptive act,"* this decision not only failed Marcia, but it failed all future blameless victims.

I am crushed to the core of my being. I am angry. I am mortified.

DID JUDGE GANTS FIND THAT AIG COMMITTED AT LEAST ONE *"UNFAIR OR DECEPTIVE ACT"*?

With regard to AIG, Marcia mostly lost and AIG mostly won. On the one hand, Judge Gants found that AIG didn't commit even one pre-judgment *"unfair or deceptive act."*

For example, it is impossible for me to comprehend how Judge Gants could find that AIG did not commit an *"unfair or deceptive act"* by allowing AIG to require that Zurich put its tender offer into writing before AIG would take over the claims investigation (which enabled a three-month delay for AIG).

How this action by AIG is not an *"unfair or deceptive act"* is again, beyond all comprehension. Through Judge Gants's decision, excess insurance carriers are now legally empowered to do the same pre-judgment actions to other blameless victims as what AIG did to Marcia.

On the other hand, Judge Gants found that AIG did commit an *"unfair or deceptive act"* for the following post-judgment actions and that these actions were *willful or knowing*.

1. A post-trial motion to Judge Donovan for a new trial, or, in the alternative, for a remittitur.
2. A "Notice of Appeal" to the Massachusetts Appeals Court, requesting a new trial be ordered due to Judge Donovan's *"abuse of her discretion."*
3. Waiting until July 14, 2005, to offer a settlement that was acceptable.
4. Not making its final payment until September 6, 2005, nearly a year after the jury verdict.

Yes, Judge Gants did find that AIG did commit a post-judgment *"unfair or deceptive act."*

However, Judge Gants found that the actual *damages* caused by this violation were limited to the "loss of use"[260] *damages* for $448,250 and that this violation was *willful or knowing* such that:

"...doubling the amount of actual damages is an appropriate punitive award for such violation. Therefore, this Court orders that AIG shall pay the plaintiffs $896,500 in actual and punitive damages."

For all of its deplorable post-judgment actions, AIG would be punished by an amount less than $1 million.

Again, imagine the implications: another insurance carrier could make the same deplorable post-judgment actions but be punished in this same minor way. This penalty would not be much of a deterrent to prevent an *"unfair or deceptive act"* in the future.

I am dumbfounded by how Judge Gants determined the amount of the punishment.

While there is great confusion and perhaps earlier contradictory judicial decisions, I believe that a proper interpretation of Chapter 93A would be that if an insurance carrier commits an *"unfair or deceptive act"* that is judged to be *willful or knowing*, the basis for the penalty is not the "loss of use" *damages* (as Judge Gants applied) but the amount of the underlying verdict.

If so, the penalty for an *"unfair or deceptive act"* that is judged to be *willful or knowing* could be sizable. A significant punishment would be a substantial deterrent to prevent an *"unfair or deceptive act"* in the future—exactly the intent of Chapter 93A.

I am so angry.

❖ ❖ ❖

What should Marcia and I do?

We have been litigating against Zurich and AIG for more than seven years—perhaps 25 percent of Marcia's remaining life expectancy. At times, this litigation has been all-consuming and completely aggravating. Shouldn't Marcia have the opportunity to live the rest of her life without unnecessary frustration?

If so, the next blameless victim will suffer far more than her, because of this decision.

Because I had the hubris to believe that I could put right the injustices that Zurich and AIG did to Marcia, I never considered that we might lose or the consequences that would follow.

I am mortified at myself that I could be making the suffering of future blameless victims worse.

---

260 As before, the calculation of the dollar punishment is difficult to understand, and even harder to explain, and there is disagreement even within the legal community.

What should we do?

Since Judge Gants made his decision, Marcia's depression has been overwhelming. She just cries. She cannot find anything positive in her life to justify why this awful crash happened to her. Even though she continues to live with many medical complications, the emotional toll from this litigation has been far worse.

What should we do?

In most cases, the losing side of a lawsuit in Massachusetts Superior Court would make an appeal to the Massachusetts Appeals Court to try to reverse the lower court's decision.

An appeal would take perhaps another two or three years to litigate with less than a 50 percent chance of winning. A decision by Judge Gants[261]—the overwhelmingly recognized expert in business litigation—would be next to impossible to reverse.

If we do appeal and then lose again, we would be, yet again, just devastated.

We could make one final appeal to the Massachusetts Supreme Judicial Court (another two years). Even then, reversing two lower court decisions would be a near impossibility for the Massachusetts Supreme Judicial Court.

What should we do?

❖ ❖ ❖

---

[261] In December 2008, Judge Ralph Gants was appointed to the Massachusetts Supreme Judicial Court.

TIMELINE FIVE:
DID ZURICH, AIG, OR BOTH COMMIT AN *"UNFAIR OR DECEPTIVE ACT"*?

JUNE 1, 2008 TO FEBRUARY 1, 2011

MARCIA RHODES, HAROLD RHODES, AND REBECCA RHODES (APPELLANTS)
V.
ZURICH AMERICAN INSURANCE AND AMERICAN INTERNATIONAL GROUP (APPELLEES)

78 MASS. APP. CT. 299 IN MASSACHUSETTS APPEALS COURT[262]

UPDATE ON THE HEALTH AND WELLNESS OF MARCIA RHODES

Since November 1, 2003, when I concluded my daily diary, Marcia's medical complications continued to worsen—all because Carlo Zalewski did not stop.

09/1/2004	Stage III pressure ulcers—both ischium and buttocks.
01/5/2005	Lateral transverse fracture one and one-half inch below the left knee requiring full-time use of leg immobilizer.
09/19/2005	Urinary tract infection.
09/26/2005	Bladder infection.
08/1/2006	Severe intrauterine/back pain diagnosed.

---

[262] As mentioned before, let me state that I am not an attorney, so my legal observations and conclusions may be inaccurate. A nearly complete record of the litigation documentation for <u>Timeline Five</u> can be found at www.theblamelessvictim.com.

10/15/2006	Uterine fibroids diagnosed by ultrasound.
11/20/2006	Hysterectomy surgery at Milford Regional Medical Center to relieve intrauterine/back pain.
11/20/2006	Colostomy surgery at Milford Regional Medical Center.
05/8/2007	Surgery at St. Elizabeth's Hospital (Brighton, Massachusetts) to remove eight titanium screws and two titanium rods.
05/20/2007	Broken right leg (tibia/fibula) requiring full leg cast.
05/29/2007	Hospitalization at Milford Regional Medical Center for severe intractable back pain and urinary tract Infection.
06/06/2007	Hospitalization at Whittier Rehabilitation Hospital.
07/16/2007	Broken left leg requiring medium leg cast.
09/06/2007	Sigmoidoscopy—anal fistula found and drained.
09/15/2007	Traumatic optic neuropathy diagnosed (damage to optic nerve in right eye).
12/19/2007	Transverse proximal fracture of tibia and fibula two inches below right knee requiring full-time use of leg immobilizer.
02/05/2008	Urinary tract infection.
02/28/2008	Sepsis requiring hospitalization in the ICU at Milford Regional Medical Center (discharged on 3/13/2008).
03/15/2008	Sepsis with infected abscess on kidney requiring hospitalization in the ICU at Milford Regional Medical Center (discharged on 3/24/2008).
05/14/2008	Parastomal hernia diagnosed.
06/05/2008	Chronic regional pain syndrome (CRPS) reflex sympathetic dystrophy (RSD) diagnosed.

All because Carlo Zalewski did not stop.

Each day is a challenge for Marcia. Each day could bring a new medical setback. Each day is a struggle just to believe that we would happily see tomorrow together.

In the spring of 2008, Marcia was hospitalized twice for sepsis at Milford Regional Medical Center. Each time, as she was taken by ambulance when her temperature rose to more than 101, her blood pressure decreased dramatically, her breathing was shallow, and her oxygen saturation was low.

Twice, I watched the amazing ER medical personnel rapidly intubate her, place a central line in her groin (the first time) and in her left shoulder (the second time), and insert an intravenous line within minutes.

Then, Marcia was infused with a wide array of antibiotics, given medicine to keep her blood pressure up, and made to breathe using a ventilator. I was sure she was inches from septic shock.[263]

---

263 *"Septic Shock is a serious condition that occurs when an overwhelming infection leads to life-threatening low blood pressure."* "Septic Shock," A.D.A.M., last modified March 11, 2014, http://www.nlm.nih.gov/medlineplus/ency/article/000668.htm.

Friday, June 6, 2008

The time is 3:00 a.m., and I couldn't sleep. So much has happened in the last two days.

If even possible, yesterday was a worse day than getting the Trial Court's[264] decision.

Marcia and I went to see Dr. Krauth. She indicated that the pain specialist Marcia had seen has diagnosed Marcia's ongoing severe interperineum pain as Chronic Regional Pain Syndrome (CRPS)—Type II.

The specialist said, *"Marcia appears to have spinal injury with likely pain originating from the lower cord itself and thus a type of central pain syndrome. In some ways, it is similar to central pain from a stroke. Unfortunately, there are very few successful options in her case. Spinal cord stimulation is unlikely to work. An opioid pump is not effective. Narcotics are usually ineffective. Anticonvulsants might be of some value, but most patients I have seen over the years do not respond to drugs such as Tegretol. She needs to be maintained on chronic opioids long term. I see no good alternatives at this time."*

No medicines. No nerve blocks. No spinal cord stimulation. No pain pumps. At that moment, I could see that Marcia understood that she would have to live with pain for the rest of her life.

She was devastated. She cried in the car ride home and then for several hours more. Her life would forever be painful. I just hope she does not hurt herself.

Would she have to endure this awful pain for the rest of her life? I can't let that happen, no matter what the pain specialist said.

Twelve seconds. All because Carlo Zalewski did not stop.

Litigation in the Massachusetts Appeals Court Begins

Thursday, June 12, 2008

After an initial preliminary legal review, Brown Rudnick concluded that Judge Gants likely made reversible errors in the "Findings of Fact and Conclusions of Law." The team began to assess whether to go forward with an appeal to the Massachusetts Appeals Court.

Wednesday, July 30, 2008

After a six-week evaluation, the Brown Rudnick team told me they were satisfied that Judge Gants likely erred in his ruling and there were several particular findings of fact and conclusions of law that could likely lead to a reversal.

---

[264] Beginning with Timeline Five, to be consistent with court nomenclature, Judge Gants is referred to as "the trial court."

Monday, September 29, 2008

Today, Brown Rudnick filed our "Notice of Appeal." I began to learn about the timing of an appeal going forward.

First, we wait for the Clerk of the Massachusetts Superior Court to compose the "Record on Appeal," which will include *"the original papers and exhibits on file, the transcript of proceedings, if any, and a certified copy of the docket entries."*

Once the "Record on Appeal" is assembled, we will have ten days to docket the case with the Massachusetts Appeals Court and then forty days to file our brief.

Once we file our brief, Zurich and AIG will have thirty days to respond.

After Zurich and AIG file their responses, we will have fourteen days to file our "Plaintiffs Reply Brief." Then, we will wait for the Massachusetts Appeals Court to schedule the appellate hearing. Then, we will wait for the Massachusetts Appeals Court to issue its decision.

Even if we win the appeal, Zurich and AIG would surely make an appeal to the Massachusetts Supreme Judicial Court. If the SJC decides to hear the appeal, a final decision could take another two years.

If Zurich and AIG do lose in the SJC, an appeal to the US Supreme Court would likely be made. If it decides to hear this case, another two years could pass before a decision would be made.

By then, thirteen years—much of Marcia's remaining life expectancy—would have passed since the crash in 2002.

For now, we must wait for the Clerk of the Massachusetts Appeals Court to gather, organize, docket, and certify all of the documents and the trial transcript from the earlier trial.

Monday, March 16, 2009

After six months from the filing of the "Notice of Appeal," the "Record on Appeal" was assembled and the "Notice of Docket Entry" was filed in the Massachusetts Appeals Court.

Monday, May 4, 2009

Brown Rudnick filed our "Plaintiff-Appellant Brief" to the Massachusetts Court of Appeal, asserting the following:

> *"First, the Trial Court ignored the plain language and unambiguous intent of Chapter 93A by refusing to double the underlying judgment in calculating punitive damages even though it found 1) pre- and post-judgment "willful and knowing" violations of c. 93A and 2) the latter violation caused injury and damages to the Rhodes family.*

Chapter 93A explicitly requires that "the amount of actual damages to be multiplied by the court shall be the amount of the judgment on all claims arising out of the same and underlying transaction or occurrence." Therefore, it was clear legal error to not enter a punitive damage award against AIG of at least $22,730,668.

Second, the Trial Court committed clear legal error by failing to hold AIG liable for their pre-judgment "willful and knowing" refusal to make a prompt settlement offer. Contrary to the Trial Court's ruling, plaintiffs are not required to prove the case would have settled if a prior hypothetical offer had been made.

The finding that AIG tried to strong-arm the Rhodes family by intentionally refusing to make an offer when liability was reasonably clear is all that was required to establish liability and impose punitive damages.

Third, the Trial Court committed clear legal error in finding the Rhodes family suffered no injury from AIG's "willful and knowing" failure to make a prompt settlement offer. The Trial Court's factual findings support an award of damages in favor of the Rhodes family for emotional distress and for being forced to endure the "frustrations of litigation" in having to pursue claims under Chapters 176D/93A in order to collect their judgment.

If a court cannot calculate compensatory damages under c. 93A, nominal damages of $25 must be awarded. An award of nominal damages does not void the statutory requirement that punitive damages must be based on the underlying judgment for "willful and knowing" violations.

Fourth, the Trial Court improperly calculated compensatory damages for AIG's post-judgment violation of c. 176D. The Trial Court should have measured lost use of money damages from the entry of judgment on September 28, 2004 through the September 6, 2005 date of final payment on the judgment, rather than creating a hypothetical scenario based on when payments may have been made if AIG had complied with their statutory obligations.

Fifth, the Trial Court committed clear legal error in holding Zurich complied with c. 176D. The Trial Court's findings of facts establish, as a matter of law, that Zurich's inaction and deliberate delay from January 2002 through March 2004 constitute a "willful and knowing" violation of c. 176D/93A. The Trial Court erred in not entering a joint compensatory and separate punitive damages award against Zurich."

Monday, August 3, 2009

As expected, today, Zurich filed its "Defendant-Appellee Brief." In summary, Zurich's appeal brief indicated that the trial court's decision was perfect in its "Findings of Fact and Conclusions of Law":

"First, if the Massachusetts Appeals Court affirms the Trial Court's decision that the Plaintiffs did not suffer any actual damages as a result of AIG's violation of M.G.L. ch. 176D § 3(9)(f), then the judgment in Zurich's favor must also be affirmed.

Second, the Trial Court did not err in concluding that Zurich tendered its policy limits promptly once its liability under the policy became reasonably clear. The Trial Court properly concluded that Zurich's duty to effectuate settlement did not attach until late November 2003.

The evidence at trial amply supports the Trial Court's factual finding that damages in excess of $2 million (Zurich's Policy Limits) did not become reasonably clear until October 2003. The evidence at trial amply supports the Trial Court's factual finding that the existence or non-existence of other applicable "primary" insurance did not become reasonably clear until mid-November 2003.

The Trial Court properly concluded that Zurich acted promptly in effectively tendering its Policy Limits to AIG in November 2003 and formally tendering in January 2004.

Third, the Trial Court did not err in concluding that, even if Zurich's tender of its Policy Limits to AIG was not prompt, any delay did not harm plaintiffs because it altered neither the amount nor the timing of AIG's settlement offer to Plaintiffs and, therefore, caused Plaintiffs no injury."

Tuesday, August 4, 2009

AIG filed its "Defendant-Appellee Brief." In summary, the brief indicated that the trial court's decision was nearly perfect in its "Findings of Fact and Conclusions of Law."

"First, the Trial Court's punitive damages rulings are correct because (a) the Trial Court correctly refused to double the amount of the underlying judgment where that judgment did not reflect the actual damages caused by AIG's conduct and (b) the Trial Court correctly used the amount of actual damages as the punitive damages multiplicand for post-judgment conduct.

Second, AIG argues in its appeal brief that The United States Constitution Prohibits the Rhodes' Construction of M.G.L. c. 93A's Punitive Damages Provision because (a) The Rhodes' construction of the 1989 Amendment to M.G.L. c. 93A would violate the reprehensibility guidepost; (b) The Rhodes' requested application of the 1989 Amendment to M.G.L. c. 93A would violate the ratio guidepost; and, (c), The Rhodes' construction of the 1989 Amendment conflicts with the legislative purpose of M.G.L. c. 93A.

Third, AIG argues in its appeal brief that the Trial Court correctly determined that (a) the Rhodes' rejection of a reasonable settlement offer precluded their recovery based on M.G.L. c. 176D and (b) the Rhodes suffered no compensable emotional distress damages arising from AIG's conduct.

Fourth, AIG argues in its appeal brief that the Trial Court erred in finding that the (a) appeal of the judgment against GAF lacked merit because the Rhodes presented no evidence concerning the merits of the appeal; (b) Rhodes are not entitled to 'Loss of Use' damages because the Rhodes relinquished their claim for these damages by accepting a settlement and filing a satisfaction of judgment; and (c) assuming that the Rhodes are entitled to recover 'Loss of Use' damages, the Trial Court erred in calculating the 'Loss of Use' damages awarded to the Rhodes."

Monday, August 17, 2009

Brown Rudnick filed its "Plaintiffs-Appellants Reply Brief":

"First, AIG argues that it is correct to award punitive damages based only on 'actual' economic damages caused by its willful violation.

However, AIG and the Trial Court ignore the mandate of the statute: 'For the purposes of this chapter, the amount of actual damages to be multiplied by the court shall be the amount of the judgment on all claims arising out of the same and underlying transaction or occurrence.'

Second, AIG's due process challenge fails; an award that comports with a statutory cap is presumed constitutional even against a due process challenge.

Third, the Rhodes family proved that they were injured as a result of the insurer's willful pre-judgment violations of chapters 176D/93A. First, Zurich does not address the Trial Court's failure to find a 176D/93A violation as a matter of law. Second, the Trial Court improperly required the plaintiffs to prove a hypothetical pre-trial settlement—thereby ignoring the injurious chilling of the settlement process. Third, Zurich must be held responsible for its role in the overall injury to the plaintiffs.

Fourth, AIG's cross-appeal issues are unavailing. AIG argues that the Trial Court erred in ruling that its appeal was filed in bad faith because there was 'no evidence' presented at trial. In fact, there was ample evidence."

Tuesday, September 1, 2009

With the original docketing of this appeal on March 25, 2009, five months have passed.

With the documents filed, all I can do is to wait until the date is set for the appellate hearing before the Massachusetts Appeals Court, which would not likely occur for at least six months. The decision could take at least six months.

Tuesday, October 6, 2009

Last night, Marcia and I had a heart-to-heart talk. She was angry at me for my seemingly uncaring attitude. She saw me as increasingly more distant and less willing to do things for her. She even called Linda Eisenberg, my therapist.

I have no doubt that I am growing distant from her. After all these years, I know that I have become psychologically ill to the point I do not want to get help. The powerful psych medications I am taking are not helping anymore. I am sick.

I am distant from her and Rebecca as well as my brothers, my sister, friends, family, business contacts, and anyone else. Eisenberg diagnosed me as having post-traumatic stress disorder (PTSD) with chronic depression.

While I have had many life-changing events since the crash, losing the recent lawsuit to Zurich and AIG has caused me to question whether I am at all capable of accomplishing anything.

Although I would like to blame our loss on Judge Gants, I couldn't help but feel that I should have done more.

I am haunted each day by the answer that I gave to Mark Cohen about whether I would have accepted certain hypothetical amounts for settlement. My poor answer gave the opening to the defendants that they needed. I should have said, *"I do not know."* I am angry at myself for this.

And now comes the appeal. I do not want to even begin to contemplate what would happen if we lose the appeal. The demons in my head give me just awful headaches every moment of every day.[265]

Tuesday, October 13, 2009

I am now deeply involved in planning for Marcia's next surgery. A well-known secondary medical complication from a spinal fracture is loss of bowel and bladder control; the brain could not control the muscles that opened and closed the rectum and urethra.

For the loss of bowel control, she previously had colostomy surgery. Although successful, a tear in the stomach wall had developed that allowed the area under the colostomy stoma to protrude (a hernia). In late February 2009, she underwent surgery to close the

---

[265] Even as mentally and emotionally low as I had become, I later would sink even lower.

existing colostomy stoma, repair the hernia, and surgically make a new opening for the colostomy opening.

Since the crash, Marcia has had to use an in-dwelling catheter to manage the loss of bladder control. An in-dwelling catheter enables urine to pass from the bladder through a tube into a urine collection bag. While effective, it has two major drawbacks. The incidence of bladder cancer appears to increase with long-term use.

More critical is the significant increase in urinary tract infections, bladder infections, and kidney infections. Since the crash, Marcia has had many infections. To control them, a variety of antibiotics have been used (Tetracycline, Levaquin, Cipro, Keflex, Macrobid, and Flagyl).

Over time, the effectiveness of antibiotics to control the UTIs will decrease, making her increasingly susceptible to a deadly whole-body infection—*septic shock*. According to the Mayo Clinic, the mortality rate for septic shock is close to 50 percent.

To decrease the possibility of again contracting sepsis, on November 2, 2009, Marcia will undergo a six-hour ileovesicostomy[266] surgery (a surgical diversion of urine to a stoma. This surgery is complex:

1. The urethra is sown closed with a covering to prevent leakage.
2. A section of the small intestine is surgically removed.
3. The remaining small intestine is surgically sown together.
4. A small hole is made in the bladder.
5. One side of the removed section of the small intestine is sown to the bladder.
6. A stoma (opening) is made on the stomach wall (typically opposite the location of a colostomy).
7. The other side of the removed section of the small intestine is sown to the stoma.

In this way, urine is diverted from the urethra to a stoma. The stoma is covered by a urostomy bag (sometimes referred to as the *urostomy appliance*). Urine is captured in the urostomy bag and emptied at the appropriate times during the day. At night, a drainage bag is used instead of a urostomy appliance.

With a successful surgery, Marcia would no longer have to use an in-dwelling catheter, and the incidence of urinary tract and other infections should significantly decrease.

Marcia is enormously scared about this surgery.

Monday, November 2, 2009

The surgery at the Lahey Clinic (Burlington, Massachusetts) went as expected without complications. Marcia's quality of life should now be considerably improved.

---

[266] For more information, see www.surgeryencyclopedia.com/Fi-La/Ileal-Conduit-Surgery.html.

Saturday, November 7, 2009

After making an excellent recovery from her surgery, Marcia was discharged today.

Sunday, November 8, 2009

A number of Marcia's friends came over today. While it was tiring, she appeared to be glad to see everyone. Later in the afternoon, Rebecca came home from college, and Marcia was thrilled to see her. Worn out, I went to bed around 7:00 p.m. before the HHA helped Marcia get into bed.

Monday Morning, November 9, 2009

I awoke around 1:00 a.m. to check on Marcia. On the kitchen counter was a note from the previous evening's certified nursing assistant (CNA): *"Marcia is a bit disoriented and has a temperature of 99.9."*

I hurried to see her. She was awake but in significant distress. For the next three hours, she vomited everything that she had. While she appeared ill and had a mild fever, I didn't think these symptoms were serious enough to go to the ER.[267] I thought she had eaten something that couldn't be digested.

I stayed up all night with her until Cindy, the morning CNA, came at 8:00 a.m. Cindy called the Milford VNA, and one of the VNA nurses came over quickly. The VNA nurse said Marcia had to go to the hospital by ambulance. Her temperature was 101.5, and her blood pressure was low.

The ambulance took her to the ER at the Milford Regional Medical Center. She was given fluids to boost her blood pressure and an antibiotic for what appeared to be a UTI.

The attending physician called the Lahey Clinic. Lahey personnel requested that Marcia be transferred by ambulance back to the Lahey Clinic. Marcia and I begged the medical team not to send her back. She was scared to go back.

Monday Afternoon, November 9, 2009

Marcia was readmitted to the Lahey Clinic for what would be diagnosed as a *paralytic ileus*.[268] Treatment began with intravenous fluids and electrolytes. This helped to keep blood pressure at a normal level and provide nutrition. A tube placed in the nose and down into the stomach removed digestive fluids, which helped relieve and prevent pain and bloating. When a *paralytic ileus* occurs after surgery, the intestines usually become normal after about one to three days.

She began yet another miserable hospitalization.

---

267 Colossal Mistake #44: It had been a long time since I had made such a colossal mistake in caring for Marcia. However, this colossal mistake would be just the first of several over the next ten days.

268 *"Paralytic Ileus is a type of bowel obstruction that occurs when the intestines stop moving normally even though there is nothing blocking them. This prevents the digestion of food and the movement of waste out of the body. Ileus most commonly occurs after abdominal surgery, though it has many other possible causes."* "What Is a Paralytic Ileus?" Healthwise, last modified March 11, 2014, http://www.sharecare.com/health/digestive-diseases/what-is-ileus.

Saturday, November 14, 2009

Five days into the hospitalization, Marcia is now completely overwhelmed and overwrought. She was screaming at the nurses, out of character for her even when she is not well. The nurse indicated that she is going to request a psych consult.

While driving home, I was troubled by the episode. To me, her actions indicated that something else was wrong.

As I drove farther, thinking about the psych consult, I thought that in all the time I had been with her during the previous week, I had not seen the nurses give Marcia her prescription medications for her bipolar disorder, anxiety, or ADHD. The nurses had given her a small amount of pain medicine but no psych meds.

Sunday, November 15, 2009

When I arrived at Lahey at 7:00 a.m., I asked Marcia's nurse whether she had been getting her psych meds since her admittance six days ago. After checking the chart, the nurse looked troubled and said *"no."* Since last Monday, Marcia hadn't been given Adderall, Wellbutrin, or Focalin.

Anger seethed through every pore. Doing my best to remain calm—but not actually doing so—I pointed out that since Marcia had arrived a week earlier, she had gone cold turkey by not taking her three most important psych meds.

Denying Marcia her psych meds was a mistake of substantial proportion; missing the psych meds easily accounted for her extreme emotional distress the night before.

After a call to the attending hospitalist[269] by the nurse, her psych medications were restarted.[270]

Thursday, November 19, 2009

After nine nights, Marcia was discharged from Lahey Clinic. Sad, tired, and frustrated, and mad at Lahey Clinic, she was scared that something else would go wrong and that she would have to return to Lahey yet again.

Me too.

---

[269] According to Lahey Clinic, *"A Lahey Clinic hospitalist is a physician, board certified in internal medicine, who is responsible for all aspects of your care if you are admitted to the hospital. Hospitalists do not have a clinic practice and are easily available when you and your family have questions or concerns. The hospitalist takes the place of your primary care physician while you are in the hospital."* See http://www.lahey.org/Departments_and_Locations/Departments/Hospitalists/Hospitalists.aspx for more information. As a method to provide medical care inside a hospital, there has been a growing trend to use Hospitalists. Nonetheless, Hospitalists scare me. They have just a small understanding of Marcia's difficult medical conditions, and they have very busy schedules; on several occasions since the crash, the attending Hospitalist erred in his/her medical orders for Marcia. I beg all Hospitalists to not make any changes in a patient's medication program without speaking to a family member or patient-advocate first. I once very loudly screamed at a Hospitalist who had stopped all of Marcia's pain medications without talking with me first. The result was catastrophic.

[270] Colossal Mistake #45: This horrific mistake was my fault. The reality is that medical personnel, especially Hospitalists, make mistakes. While the Lahey medical personnel should have never made this error, I am so angry at myself. This failure to not recognize the problem with Marcia's medications is inexcusable no matter how sick I am. I would not be able to forgive myself for a long time.

Sunday, November 29, 2009

Marcia now wears both a urostomy bag for urine collection and a colostomy bag for fecal collection because Carlo Zalewski criminally crashed his forty-ton tractor-trailer into her stopped car.

With the surgery at Lahey completed, Marcia had to turn her attention to her other complications. For reasons not yet determined, her vision in her right eye continues to deteriorate. After a lengthy examination, her ophthalmologist concluded that she might have a neurological issue that could be affecting her eyesight.

She had to begin, yet again, extensive physical therapy to increase her upper body strength.

Because she could no longer use the stair lift, I have begun to plan to have an elevator installed so she could more easily get from the first floor to the basement where her antiques are. I hoped the elevator would have been installed by now, but my new goal was the end of April 2010.[271]

Monday, November 30, 2009

Three months have now passed since the materials for the appellate hearing had been submitted, but we must wait another three months for the Massachusetts Appeals Court to hear our appeal.

Tuesday, December 1, 2009

The days just drag on. Marcia continues to make her round of seeing her doctors since the surgery:
1. Dr. Donna Krauth (primary care physician)
2. Dr. Wei-Lee Liao (physiatrist, pain management)
3. Dr. Dawn Pearson (neurologist)
4. Dr. Elizabeth Roaf (physiatrist)
5. Dr. Paul Elliott (optometrist)
6. Dr. Roger Kaldawy (ophthalmologist)
7. Dr. Marc Nierman (urologist)
8. Dr. Albert Crimaldi (gastroenterologist)
9. Dr. Susan Barrett (orthopedics)
10. Dr. Xiangyang Li (psychiatrist)

Additionally, she began a program of outpatient physical therapy.

---

[271] Colossal Mistake #46: Instead of installing a stair lift, I should have had an elevator installed when our home addition was built. I wanted to believe Marcia would be able to manage a stair lift, but that did not turn out to be the case.

Thursday, December 3, 2009

The date, time, and judges have been set for our appellate hearing: Tuesday, January 12, 2010, at 9:30 a.m., in the John Adams Courthouse (Boston, Massachusetts). I know the appeals court is busy and the justices have extensive legal briefs and other materials they review. Nonetheless, I was so disappointed to learn we have just fifteen minutes to present the arguments that the trial court didn't correctly apply the law to Zurich and AIG.

Excluding holidays and weekends, this gave us twenty-nine business days. Just twenty-nine business days for Brown Rudnick to prepare for what might be the most significant court case involving *"unfair or deceptive acts"* by insurance carriers in Massachusetts.

After eight long years of waiting, we had twenty-nine business days. I spoke to Fred, and he reiterated that Brown Rudnick would be ready.

Friday, December 11, 2009

The days until the appellate hearing continue to dwindle—there are now just twenty-one business days until the appellate hearing.

Unfortunately, Marcia was diagnosed with yet another staph infection (likely MRSA) at the old stoma site. Although she had been taking Doxycycline (an antibiotic) for a week, the infection started to ooze pus.

Sunday, December 13, 2009

At about 5:00 p.m., Marcia called me frantically. *"Please come up to my bathroom and hurry."*

I saw urine all over her and the floor. Apparently, the urostomy bag overfilled before she was able to empty it. The mess was trivial to me; although urine was everywhere, a thorough cleaning was all that was needed. I am more concerned about whether urine had gotten into any wounds, her coccyx, the colostomy stoma, or the site of the previous colostomy stoma.

Urine carries MRSA bacteria and c. Diff bacteria, both of which are highly infectious. If bacteria colonized in an opening, she could easily have an infection, and any infection could lead to sepsis. Disinfecting her will be a major activity.

I will have to watch her closely for the next few days to see if she exhibits any secondary medical complications. If so, we will go straight to the ER.

Wednesday, December 16, 2009

Just sixteen business days remain until the hearing. With many attorneys working on this appeal on our behalf, I am feeling more optimistic about a positive outcome.

With regard to Zurich, I am optimistic that the trial court's decision will be reversed. There could be no doubt that Zurich committed at least one *"unfair or deceptive act"* that was *willful or knowing*. Primary insurance carriers must be penalized for delaying eight months to begin a claims investigation, their only excuse being that transmittals and reports got lost in the mailroom.

With regard to AIG, I continue to be reasonably positive that the Massachusetts Appeals Court will reverse the trial court's decision (with regard to the formula that Judge Gants used to determine the financial penalty). The trial court's misapplication of the *plain language* of Chapters 93A and 176D of the Massachusetts General Laws should be easily understandable and correctable.

Wednesday, December 23, 2009

Eleven business days remain until the hearing. I guess that I have nothing to do now but wait and try not to be depressed about the potential of a negative outcome.

Sunday, December 27, 2009

My well-being continues to suffer. I have gained thirty-five pounds since 2002 and now weigh 199 pounds. I can barely sleep at night even with extensive medications.

I rarely leave home anymore; I am just not interested in anything.

I am sure my fixation on this case has driven others to become more distant.

I feel entirely depressed about the prospect of losing yet again.

I am completely worn out.

Saturday, January 9, 2010

Today is the eighth anniversary of the crash. In some ways, it seems like an eternity since January 9, 2002. I can barely remember anything before. In other ways, the crash seems like just yesterday.

Sunday, January 10, 2010

At 8:00 a.m. when Marcia awoke, her temperature was normal at 98.5. At 8:30 p.m., it rose to 101.5. By 9:15 p.m., it rose to 103. By 10:00 p.m., it was 104.1, and she was becoming disoriented.

By 10:30 p.m., the paramedics arrived. By 11:30 p.m., now in the ER at Milford Regional Medical Center, she was examined by the attending physician. Her temperature was 104.4, and her blood pressure dropped to a scary 80/38. The urine was dark and cloudy, and it had an odor. Obviously, she had contracted—yet again—another serious infection.

Monday, January 11, 2010

Marcia's blood and urine were drawn for immediate testing. After struggling to insert an IV line in her right and left wrists, she began two IVs (wide open) of 500 mL of saline solution to try to get her blood pressure up. She was given Tylenol and Motrin to lower her temperature.

By 1:30 a.m., the initial urine test had confirmed that she had a serious urinary tract infection. This indicated that multiple bacterial organisms were rapidly growing in the urine.

She was given 200 mL of Vancomycin, 200 mL of Levaquin, and 200 mL of Tobramycin. These powerful antibiotics combat a wide spectrum of bacterial organisms. Later, after the urine was cultured, a more specific understanding of which bacterial organisms were present would determine which antibiotic to use.

By 5:30 a.m., she had been transferred to the ICU. Numerous medical personnel examined her, and additional blood cultures were taken. Marcia was terribly ill; the ICU team was making every effort to avoid sepsis.

At any moment, she could be put on a ventilator.

At 6:00 a.m., I received a call from Marcia's caregiver; she told me that she was ill and wouldn't be able to care for Marcia today.

Now 9:00 a.m., I have been awake for twenty-five hours and likely would be awake for another twelve hours caring for Marcia. Now is the exact time when I am most needed to make sure the medical personnel understand that Marcia has T-12 paraplegia, a colostomy, a urostomy, and multiple pressure ulcers. Fortunately, her blood pressure had stabilized and then had slightly increased.

At 9:30 a.m., I called Fred and told him about Marcia's condition. Obviously, she wouldn't be able to attend the appellate hearing on Tuesday.

Marcia slept most of the day, and I stayed at her bedside the whole time. By 5:30 p.m., her evening caregiver came to the hospital to relieve me. Because the next day was the appellate hearing, I was in bed by 8:00 p.m.

The Appellate Hearing

Tuesday, January 12, 2010

I arrived at the courthouse at 8:45 a.m. without Marcia. People were getting settled into the courtroom for the session to begin at 9:30 a.m. Fred Pritzker began his fifteen-minute presentation and, outlined these points:

1. Zurich should have tendered its $2 million primary policy by November 2002. Zurich knew Zalewski was completely liable. Zurich knew its agent (Crawford) had made an evaluation that exceeded $5 million. Zurich had at its disposal Marcia's complete set of medical records.
2. The trial court erred in the conclusions of law that AIG's post-judgment violation of Chapter 176D was not subject to the full weight of Chapter 93A.

3. If the Massachusetts Appeals Court found that either or both of the defendants are found guilty of a violation of Chapter 176D, the court—as a matter of law—had to impose that statutory punishment enacted by the Massachusetts Legislature, no matter the amount of money.

Anthony Zelle, on behalf of AIG, then began his seven and a half minutes. In general, he repeated the exact findings by the trial court and said the Massachusetts Appeals Court should affirm the trial court's decision.

Linda Morkan, on behalf of Zurich, then began her seven and a half minutes. Similarly, she repeated the exact findings by the trial court and said the Massachusetts Appeals Court should affirm the trial court's decision.

After the appellate hearing, we huddled for a postmortem. We all agreed Fred did a superb job; his answers were short and backed up by case law.

The decision by the judicial panel would rest on the issue the trial court had to face. If the panel concluded that either or both of the defendants committed an *"unfair or deceptive act,"* could justices have the courage to apply the full weight of Chapter 93A? Could they order a punishment of $24 million or $48 million?

The group concluded that the probability of our prevailing had improved through this appellate hearing.

I hope so.

Wednesday, January 13, 2010

I awoke at 2:00 a.m. I can't sleep.

I went to the hospital to be with Marcia at 1:00 p.m. At 3:00 p.m., I checked on her Dilaudid. I got angry at the nurse. Apparently, the doctor's order for Dilaudid for Marcia had been *"6 mg every four hours PRN."*

The order should have been *"6 mg every four hours QID."* PRN means *"when necessary"* or *"when requested"* from the Latin *pro re nata*. QID means *"four times per day"* from the Latin *quarter in die*.[272]

PRN implied that Marcia had to request Dilaudid. This important pain medicine wouldn't be given to her without such a request.

Given all her secondary medical complications (in particular her CRPS Type II), Marcia is unable to request pain medicine. She has to be given pain medications on a set schedule to make sure her pain level does not spike. Should it spike, getting her pain under control is very difficult. Therefore, she should automatically receive Dilaudid at 8:00 a.m., noon, 4:00 p.m., and 8:00 p.m.

I was home and asleep by 7:00 p.m. What a mistake that was.

---

272 I beg the medical community to please stop using Latin. Please!

Thursday, January 14, 2010

I was still awake at 1:00 a.m. and again, I couldn't sleep. I checked my voicemail. Apparently, Marcia had called four times around 8:00 p.m., and each time she sounded more upset. She is mad at me for not being there for her. I am just dreading seeing her later today.

At 4:00 p.m., after five days of hospitalization, Marcia was discharged. I could only hope that a long time would pass before she has to make another emergency visit.

Tuesday, January 19, 2010

Marcia continues to have many medical complications. When discharged last Thursday, she was given prescriptions for two antibiotics: Cipro for the UTI and Zyvox[273] for MRSA colonization in the open wound at the site of the earlier stoma.

Saturday, January 30, 2010

Dr. Liao, Marcia's new physiatrist at Spaulding Rehabilitation Hospital (Boston, Massachusetts), increased the prescription of Fentanyl (a transdermal opioid) to 175 mcg/h every forty-eight hours. I hoped this would relieve some of her chronic pain.

Sunday, February 21, 2010

Presenting a fever, flushed skin coloration, and an odd pain in her lower abdomen, for the second time in two months, I took Marcia to Milford Regional Medical Center. According to the medical testing, she has a UTI caused by pseudomonas aeruginosa[274] (a Gram-negative bacteria).[275]

Pseudomonas aeruginosa is classified as antibiotic-resistant bacteria; as such, there were no oral medications.

After confirming the diagnosis, the Hospitalist prescribed an intravenous infusion of Gentamicin.[276] Gentamicin is used to treat many types of resistant bacterial infections, particularly those caused by Gram-negative bacteria. Gentamicin is one of the most powerful antibiotics available.

After the infusion, Marcia was given two options. She could be admitted to the hospital, or she could return each day for a daily infusion of Gentamicin. She chose the latter.

The doctor could not provide a time frame for the number of days Marcia would require a daily infusion. Every day, a blood test and urine sample would be taken until the pseudomonas aeruginosa resolved.

---

273 The cost of a twenty-one-day supply of Zyvox was more than $1,100.
274 For more information, see www.answers.com/topic/pseudomonas-aeruginosa.
275 For more information, see wiki.answers.com/Q/What_is_the_difference_between_gram_positive_and_gram_negative_bacteria.
276 For more information, see www.knowledgerush.com/kr/encyclopedia/Gentamicin/.

Monday, July 12, 2010

Today marked six months from the date when the appeal was heard on January 12, 2010.

On multiple occasions, I have been told by different attorneys that writing a decision reversing the decision of a Massachusetts Superior Court judge is far easier than affirming a Massachusetts Superior Court decision. I could only speculate that with each passing day, the odds of reversing the trial court's decision diminished.

From a legal point of view, win or lose, there would be another appeal to the Massachusetts Supreme Judicial Court. Nonetheless, if the Massachusetts Appeals Court should affirm the decision by the trial court, I am certain we would be overwhelmed with depression—not just for ourselves but for all future blameless victims.

As an alternative, the Massachusetts Appeals Court might find sufficient errors in the decision by the trial court to cause the lawsuit to be remanded back to Massachusetts Superior Court for a retrial. In some ways, this could be even worse for us.

Tuesday, July 22, 2010

Today, in an effort to control the CRPS/RDS, Marcia has an appointment to receive an intravenous infusion of Lidocaine at the Brigham and Women's Hospital Pain Management Center.[277]

For 50 percent of persons with a spinal cord injury with neuropathic pain, the intravenous infusion of Lidocaine could bring days or weeks of pain relief. Pain doctors have not been able to determine how intravenous Lidocaine works or predetermine who will benefit.

Initially after the Lidocaine infusion, Marcia felt some pain relief. Within one hour, her chronic pain returned. Marcia could not contain her crying in front of the doctors.

I have absolutely no idea what to do next.

Monday, November 1, 2010

Like a splinter that could not be removed, waiting for the decision by the Massachusetts Appeals Court is unbearable.

THE DECISION BY THE MASSACHUSETTS APPEALS COURT

Tuesday, November 23, 2010

While in line at CVS to pick up medicines for Marcia, my cell phone rang.

---

[277] For more information about the services offered by The Brigham and Women's Hospital Pain Management Center, see http://www.brighamandwomens.org/Departments_and_Services/anesthesiology/Pain/Services/cpp_management.aspx.

"Harold, we got the decision from the court," Fred Pritzker said.

"Am I going to be happy or sad?"

Fred said he would e-mail the decision to me and we would talk again in a while.

I went home and started to read the decision. In a few minutes, my phone rang again.

"We lost, didn't we?" I said

"It sure looks that way," Fred said.

Except for a small victory, we lost again. While I feel terrible for Marcia and myself, I feel considerably worse for future blameless victims who will be subjected to the delaying actions of AIG, Zurich, and perhaps other insurance carriers.

ZURICH'S ACTIONS

According to the Public Case Information:[278]

11/23/2010 #33. Decision: Full Opinion (Cypher, J.). "Paragraph two of the judgment shall be modified to provide that AIGDC's and National Union's violation of M.G.L. c. 176D, § 3(9)(f), prior to issuance of the final judgment in the underlying case, was willful and knowing, and caused the plaintiffs to suffer actual damages from May 1, 2004, to August 11, 2004, as measured by the loss of use of $3.5 million during that period.

The plaintiffs do not challenge as clearly erroneous the judge's subsidiary findings regarding Zurich's actions between November, 2003, and January, 2004, and we conclude that his findings provided adequate support for ruling in Zurich's favor.

The matter is remanded to the Superior Court for determination of the multiplication of the damages award in paragraph two of the modified judgment; that is, the damages shall either be doubled or tripled. Paragraph six of the judgment shall thereupon be modified accordingly. In all other respects, the judgment is affirmed. *Notice."

AIG'S PRE-VERDICT ACTIONS

"In keeping with the statute's purpose of fostering out-of-court resolution of insurance claims, we conclude that the amount of the damages for AIGDC's tardy but reasonable offer, rejected by the plaintiffs, should not be measured by the judgment obtained in the underlying tort action, as urged by the plaintiffs, but, rather, should be measured by loss of use principles."

---

278 For more information, see www.ma-appellatecourts.org/display_docket.php?dno=2009-P-0619.

Further, the Massachusetts Appeals Court appeared to make new law, and avoid using the *plain language* of Chapters 93A and 176D, to concoct an argument that using the underlying judgment as the basis for the damage wouldn't be appropriate because:

"...settlement was reached post-verdict[279] and litigation at the appellate level had not commenced to a significant degree."[280]

AIG'S POST-VERDICT ACTIONS

"Here, however, where a settlement was reached post-verdict, and litigation at the appellate level had not commenced to a significant degree at that time, we conclude that the statutory purpose was served by measuring punitive damages according to loss of use rather than the underlying tort judgment."

Wednesday, November 24, 2010

In the weeks after the appeals court largely found in favor of Zurich American Insurance and AIG (with Justice Berry dissenting), four prominent attorneys challenged this decision.[281]

Thursday, December 9, 2010

Insurance Company Sanctioned for Late Settlement Offer
Plaintiff Paralyzed in Crash with 18-Wheeler [282]

Civil litigators say a recent Appeals Court decision involving an $11 million personal injury judgment means plaintiffs are no longer be required to prove causation and damages when making claims against insurance companies for failure to effectuate prompt settlement offers.

"One of the reasons so many people are reacting to this ruling is that it really was an open question until the Appeals Court weighed in," said Anthony R. Zelle, who represented

---

[279] The logical conclusion of this finding is preposterous. If an *"unfair or deceptive act"* is forgiven because *"settlement was reached post-verdict,"* we would never have agreed to a settlement at a discount from the jury's verdict. We would have forced AIG to pay the whole amount or forced the Chapter 93A trial to occur.

[280] This statement is incorrect. Extensive activity leading up to litigation at the appellate level had occurred. Any additional activity was dependent on the slowness of the Massachusetts Appeals Court. The logical conclusion is that as much as the Massachusetts Appeals Court is slow, the plaintiffs are not responsible. The implication is that payment for every jury decision in the plaintiff's favor could be delayed for a year or two, because the Massachusetts Appeals Court is slow.

[281] The other articles can be found at www.theblamelessvictim.com or online at:
www.boston-injury-lawyer-blog.com/2010/12/massachusetts-personal-injury-1.html#more
www.bwglaw.com/lawyer-attorney-1697177.html
www.burnsandfarrey.com/files/B&F_IssueFive_2-11.pdf.

[282] See http://newenglandinhouse.com/2011/02/02/insurance-co-sanctioned-for-late-settlement-offer/.

the defendant insurance company in Rhodes, et al. v. AIG Domestic Claims, Inc., et al. "The important thing for lawyers to recognize now is that a late settlement offer, even if it is deemed reasonable, is no longer going to remove the specter of punitive damages from a Chapter 93A analysis."

The court reversed Judge Ralph D. Gants, who was sitting in the Superior Court at the time, for improperly considering evidence that a personal injury plaintiff would not have accepted a late settlement offer of $3.5 million even if it had been made within the statutorily prescribed time period.

Hans R. Hailey of Boston, who argued a 2003 Supreme Judicial Court case heavily cited in Rhodes, said an insurance company's duty to make prompt and fair settlement offers does not depend on the willingness of the claimant to accept it.

"Even an outrageous demand on the part of the plaintiff does not relieve an insurer of their obligation to make a reasonable offer," he said. "It's nice to see such a clear statement from the Appeals Court on this question, but I'm really surprised to hear that so many lawyers and judges thought that type of evidence could be considered."

Head Scratching

Although the insurance company violated Chapters 93A and 176D by failing to make an offer once liability was clear, M. Frederick Pritzker, who represented the plaintiff in Rhodes, said Gants unfairly placed the burden on his clients to prove they would have accepted the terms if made earlier.

"When the insurer makes a late offer, which is deemed to be reasonable, the Appeals Court has now ruled quite clearly that such evidence is not relevant to the question of punitive damages," said Pritzker, a lawyer at Brown Rudnick in Boston.

To show that an insurance company has acted in good faith, defendants have long been permitted to introduce such evidence, said Zelle, who practices at Zelle, McDonough & Cohen in Boston.

"One of the reasons we are scratching our heads over this case is that the rule generally is that, if the insurance company makes a reasonable offer, they should be insulated from bad-faith damages," he said. "Even though AIG made a reasonable offer, the Appeals Court said they are still going to hit them up for damages."

David W. White Jr. of Breakstone, White & Gluck in Boston represented a plaintiff in a 2003 SJC case involving similar issues. He criticized the Appeals Court for rejecting the plaintiffs' argument in Rhodes that punitive damage awards are to be calculated by multiplying the underlying judgment.

Instead, Judge Elspeth B. Cypher, writing for the court, held that the amount to be doubled or trebled should be measured by applying loss-of-use principles, White said.

Using such a calculation, damages are determined by looking at the time between when the insurance company breached its duty to make an initial offer and the date a reasonable offer was finally made.

"The court chose a path that is most unusual and disappointing," White said. "There is no precedent for doing this."

When the Legislature amended Chapter 93A in 1990, White said, it clearly intended for the judgment to be the foundation for a damage award.

"Chapter 93A law has developed in a sort of a zigzag fashion, and it is hard for judges to figure out which way they should be looking at any given moment," he said. "What this case has done is take something that is reasonably confusing and make it even more confusing."

No Speculation

In reversing Gants, Cypher said, the causal link between AIG's unfair settlement practices and the injury to the plaintiffs was sufficiently established. She ruled that AIG failed to initiate settlement talks once the merits of the claim were clear, a strategy that deprived the plaintiffs of the opportunity to engage in a timely settlement process.

"[E]vidence that they would not have settled their claims for less than $8 million at mediation, less than a month before trial, was speculative as proof of whether they would have settled…had [AIG] put forth a reasonable offer months earlier," she wrote. "Given the uncertainty of the effect that unfair settlement practices and prolonged pretrial maneuvering may have on the claimant's circumstances and outlook when a late settlement offer finally is made, we think the plaintiffs' recovery here should not turn on conjecture as to what they might have done had [AIG] not abused its position."

AIG was willing to risk a deliberate violation of the law in the hope that the plaintiffs' mounting frustrations and financial strain would work to the insurer's benefit, Cypher said, noting that the treble damages provision of Chapter 93A was designed to deter such a strategy.

Cypher concluded, however, that damages should not be measured by using the $11 million judgment obtained at trial.

"[D]amages should be calculated between the time [AIG] breached its duty to make the initial offer, and the date the reasonable offer finally was made and rejected," she said. "This is the same result to the insurer had its late but reasonable offer been accepted."

Friday, December 10, 2010

All I could think about was that the appeals court confirmed the trial court's decision that Zurich did not commit even one *"unfair or deceptive act."* Apparently, it is acceptable for an insurance carrier to delay beginning its investigation for eight months when the insurance carriers says the claims reports were lost in the mailroom.

With regard to AIG, the appeals court rejected our argument of the *plain meaning* of Chapter 93A that punitive damage awards are to be calculated by multiplying the underlying judgment, not the "loss of use" of funds.

TIMELINE SIX:
DID ZURICH, AIG, OR BOTH COMMIT AN *"UNFAIR OR DECEPTIVE ACT"*?

NOVEMBER 24, 2010 TO FEBRUARY 24, 2012

MARCIA RHODES, HAROLD RHODES, AND REBECCA RHODES(APPELLANTS)
V.
ZURICH AMERICAN INSURANCE AND AMERICAN INTERNATIONAL GROUP(APPELLEES)

CIVIL ACTION SJC-10911 IN MASSACHUSETTS SUPREME JUDICIAL COURT[283]

UPDATE ON THE HEALTH AND WELLNESS OF MARCIA RHODES

Although nearly nine years have passed since the crash, Marcia has continued to have ongoing and sometimes serious medical complications—all because Carlo Zalewski did not stop.

11/17/2008	Hospitalization for bladder infection.
01/2/2009	Hospitalization for severe interperineum/back pain and UTI.
01/19/2009	Pneumonia.
02/24/2009	Surgery to repair herniated stoma.

---

[283] For more information, see http://www.ma-appellatecourts.org/search_number.php?dno=SJC-10911&get=Search.

03/6/2009	Hospitalization for multiple postsurgical infections.
03/28/2009	Hospitalization for UTI.
06/19/2009	Hospitalization for UTI.
07/28/2009	Hospitalization for UTI (MRSA).
10/21/2009	Bacterial vaginosis.
10/26/2009	Hospitalization for UTI.
11/2/2009	Hospitalization for ileovesicostomy.[284]
11/9/2009	Hospitalization for fecal bowel obstruction.
11/29/2009	Decubitus ulcer (Level 1)—coccyx.
1/9/2010	Hospitalization for UTI.
2/21/2010	Hospitalization for UTI.
3/2/2010	Hospitalization for UTI.
3/8/2010	Hospitalization for UTI.
5/22/2010	Hospitalization for UTI.
6/19/2010	Hospitalization for fecal bowel obstruction.
12/10/2010	Decubitus ulcer (Level 1)—gluteal fold left, gluteal fold right.
2/28/2011	Second surgery to repair herniated stoma.
5/14/2011	Hospitalization for UTI.
5/23/2011	Hospitalization for UTI.
6/16/2011	Hospitalization for UTI.
8/1/2011	Yeast infection.
8/8/2011	Hospitalization for UTI.
08/18/2011	Hospitalization for UTI, vancomycin-resistant enterococci (VRE)[285] infection, paralytic ileus.[286]

The last three years have been especially medically demanding. Since the ileovesicostomy surgery on November 2, 2009, to prevent UTIs, Marcia has been hospitalized eleven times. Ordinarily, healthy women are not hospitalized for a UTI. However, due to Marcia's paraplegia, she felt no abdominal pain with the onset of a UTI. Symptoms presented only when the UTI became serious: severe interperineum pain, fever, disorientation, very low (or very high) blood pressure, dark urine, or urine with odor. If a new UTI was not quickly treated with powerful antibiotics, the infection could move from the bladder to the kidneys and the bloodstream, causing sepsis.

---

284 For more information, see www.surgeryencyclopedia.com/Fi-La/Ileal-Conduit-Surgery.html.
285 For more information, see www.medicinenet.com/vancomycin-resistant_enterococci_vre/article.htm.
286 For more information, see www.ncbi.nlm.nih.gov/pubmedhealth/PMH0001306/.

Our Last Opportunity to Protect Future Blameless Victims

Wednesday, November 24, 2010

We lost again.

Again, I failed to protect future blameless victims against insurance carriers whose insureds were at fault. I am so depressed. I can barely talk to Marcia or anyone. I was so sure the Massachusetts Appeals Court would find that Zurich and AIG committed *"unfair methods of competition and unfair or deceptive acts or practices in the business of insurance"* by *"failing to effectuate prompt, fair and equitable settlements of claims in which liability has become reasonably clear"* which failure was the *cause* of a *harm* and which failure was *willful or knowing*.

If the Massachusetts Appeals Court believed that none of the many delays and inactions by Zurich and AIG did not constitute at least one *"unfair or deceptive act,"* that was *willful or knowing*, how much worse must the inactions of a primary insurance carrier or an excess insurance carrier be?

What else could Zurich or AIG have done to Marcia?

What have I done?

Primary insurance carriers have to be rejoicing at the decision, but future blameless victims are so much worse off than they would ever know.

The decision stated that Zurich fully comported its actions *"to effectuate prompt, fair and equitable settlements of claims in which liability has become reasonably clear."* As such, Zurich did not have to pay even the smallest punitive award for its delaying actions.

Zurich's long list of delaying maneuvers was further legally ratified by the Massachusetts Appeals Court. This long list will certainly be used as a roadmap by other insurance carriers without fear, to even further delay *"effectuat(ing) prompt, fair and equitable settlements of claims in which liability has become reasonably clear."* What was wrong with the judicial system in Massachusetts?

The Massachusetts Supreme Judicial Court has to correct the decisions by the trial court and the Massachusetts Appeals Court and find that Zurich committed at least one *"unfair or deceptive act."* Further, it had to find that at least one of Zurich's actions was *willful or knowing*. The consequences of not doing so are unfathomable. I can't imagine what life would be like for future blameless victims otherwise.

The decision by the Massachusetts Appeals Court stated that while AIG didn't fully comport its actions *"to effectuate prompt, fair and equitable settlements of claims in which liability has become reasonably clear,"* AIG's delaying actions were not *willful or knowing*. As such, the Massachusetts Appeals Court ordered AIG to pay a small punitive amount. It has to find that AIG committed at least one *"unfair or deceptive act."*

Even worse, by AIG having to pay a small punitive amount, excess insurance carriers won. AIG's inactions to settle after the jury verdict, while technically a violation, will certainly be used as a roadmap by other excess insurance carriers with little concern for a punitive award.

Did my arrogance in pursuing this legal action against Zurich and AIG make the world worse for future blameless victims? For one of the few times in my life, I am filled with guilt and self-doubt.

Did I do the wrong thing?

If we are not able to appeal to the Massachusetts Supreme Judicial Court, the earlier decisions would become the law in Massachusetts. At that point, even high-quality plaintiffs' attorneys would avoid Chapter 93A lawsuits against insurance carriers.

I hope that in a few years, a similar case will come along—perhaps better than ours—that would allow the Massachusetts Supreme Judicial Court to overturn the decisions by the Massachusetts Appeals Court and the trial court and set the bright line of justice straight for future blameless victims.

However, that could take years, if it ever happened. In the meantime, insurance carriers would likely continue *willful or knowing* failures to *"effectuate prompt, fair and equitable settlements of claims in which liability has become reasonably clear,"* hoping they could force a blameless victim to accept a lowball settlement offer and face only the risk of a small punitive award.

What have I done?

The only recourse would be to seek to amend the Chapter 93A and Chapter 176D laws. However, changing the laws in Massachusetts, while working against a powerful insurance lobby, would be fool's errand. The Massachusetts Legislature would need to be convinced that the well-regarded jurists were wrong. It would need to agree that punitive awards, no matter how large, are an acceptable means of punishing insurance carriers whose actions were found to be *willful or knowing* failures to *"effectuate prompt, fair and equitable settlements of claims in which liability has become reasonably clear."*

Monday, November 29, 2010

The first step to have the Massachusetts Supreme Judicial Court agree to review the decisions by the Massachusetts Appeals Court and the trial court is to file a petition requesting a "Further Appellate Review." Historically, the chances that it would grant a "Further Appellate Review" are less than 50 percent.

The rule governing an appeal to the Massachusetts Supreme Judicial Court is Rule 27.1 of the Massachusetts Rules of Civil Procedure:[287]

(e) "Vote for further appellate review; certification.

If any three justices of the Massachusetts Supreme Judicial Court shall vote for further appellate review for substantial reasons affecting the public interest or the interests of

---

[287] For more information, see www.lawlib.state.ma.us/source/mass/rules/appellate/mrap27-1.html.

justice, or if a majority of the justices of the Massachusetts Appeals Court or a majority of the justices of the Massachusetts Appeals Court deciding the case shall certify that the public interest or the interests of justice make desirable a further appellate review, an order allowing the application or the certificate, as the case may be, shall be transmitted to the clerk of the Massachusetts Appeals Court; upon receipt, further appellate review shall be deemed granted."

Wednesday, December 1, 2010

Marcia and I will make one more attempt, perhaps for the last time, to seek justice for future blameless victims. We will endure at least another two years of litigation. I know the odds of our prevailing are slim at best.

Litigation in the Massachusetts Supreme Judicial Court Begins

Monday, December 13, 2010

Brown Rudnick, on our behalf, filed a "Petition for Further Appellate Review" with the Massachusetts Supreme Judicial Court. Accordingly, Zurich and AIG have until December 24, 2010, to file their replies.

Wednesday, December 22, 2010

We received AIG's opposition to our "Petition for Further Appellate Review."

Thursday, December 23, 2010

We received Zurich's opposition to our "Petition for Further Appellate Review."

Friday, December 24, 2010

Now we wait for the Massachusetts Supreme Judicial Court to decide whether to grant our "Petition for Further Appellate Review." This decision usually takes a month.

If our "Petition for Further Appellate Review" is granted, the Massachusetts Supreme Judicial Court would set a date for the oral hearing. After the oral hearing, the decision could take five months or more.

Saturday, January 1, 2011

A new year begins, and the ninth anniversary of the crash is around the corner. These thoughts are on my mind:
1. Finding a financially practical, legal method to provide sustained relief for Marcia's chronic pain. The best solution is IV Ketamine. However, it is not FDA-approved

for the management of CRPS and would not be covered by UnitedHealthcare.[288] Each infusion is $2,000.
2. Having the Massachusetts Supreme Judicial Court find in our favor against Zurich and AIG by deciding that their actions were *willful or knowing* failures to *"effectuate prompt, fair and equitable settlements of claims in which liability has become reasonably clear."*
3. Increasing Marcia's fun each day.
4. Losing ten pounds to get to 185 and taking a well-needed vacation.
5. Developing a plan for Marcia should anything happen to me.

Thursday, February 10, 2011

Fred called me at nine o'clock, saying, *"Harold, I have some wonderful news. The Massachusetts Supreme Judicial Court has agreed to our Petition for Further Appellate Review."*

The Massachusetts Supreme Judicial Court could reverse the decisions by the trial court and the Massachusetts Appeals Court. The justices on the Massachusetts Supreme Judicial Court are smart; they would be able to see that, at the very least, Zurich committed at least one *"unfair or deceptive act"* and that AIG's actions, previously found to be *"unfair or deceptive act,"* were *willful or knowing*. The oral hearing wouldn't occur until at least September, but I am still overjoyed.

Wednesday, February 23, 2011

Although two weeks have passed since the Massachusetts Supreme Judicial Court granted our "Petition for Further Appellate Review," the docket number had yet to be assigned. In order for a docket number to be assigned, the clerk of the Massachusetts Appeals Court must *"forthwith transmit to the clerk of the full Massachusetts Supreme Judicial Court all papers theretofore filed in the case and shall notify the clerk of the lower court that leave to obtain further appellate review has been granted."*

Thursday, February 24, 2011

Today is my tenth birthday since the crash, and I received a great birthday present: the formal docket notification of our case, SJC-10911.[289]

Wednesday, March 2, 2011

AIG is dissatisfied with the brief filed in the Massachusetts Appeals Court on its behalf. Accordingly, its attorneys are requesting permission to file a new brief (to replace its brief to the Massachusetts Appeals Court).

---

288 This single topic could fill more than a hundred pages. In the end, UnitedHealthcare agreed to pay for Marcia's non-FDA-approved used of intravenous Ketamine infusions for relief of chronic pain. We want to thank UnitedHealthcare for its care for her.
289 For more information, see http://www.ma-appellatecourts.org/display_docket.php?dno=SJC-10911.

Friday, May 6, 2011

With the submission of AIG's new brief to the clerk of the Massachusetts Supreme Judicial Court, the Record on Appeal is complete for the further appellate review. The Massachusetts Supreme Judicial Court will schedule the date for the oral hearing, most likely during the fall 2011 term. After the oral hearing, the SJC would render its decision sometime in early 2012.

The SJC justices include Chief Justice Roderick L. Ireland, Justices Margot Botsford, Robert J. Cordy, Francis X. Spina, Ralph D. Gants, Fernande R. V. Duffly, and Barbara Lenk.[290] Two justices were automatically recused: Justice Gants (the trial court judge) and Justice Lenk (who had previously been employed by Brown Rudnick). We will need three of the five remaining justices to be convinced in order for our appeal to prevail.

Tuesday, August 23, 2011

After four months of waiting, the clerk of the Massachusetts Supreme Judicial Court scheduled the date for our hearing. It would be on October 6, 2011, at 9:00 a.m. in the John Adams Courthouse (Boston, Massachusetts).

Monday, September 12, 2011

The hearing is eighteen business days away. Other than an occasional e-mail, I have not spoken with Fred Pritzker for several weeks. During this intense preparation time, I did not bother him or his team.

Wednesday, September 23, 2011

As expected, the online court docket was updated with the recusals of Justices Gants and Lenk. Unexpectedly, Justice Duffly was recused. This leaves the court with four justices for our oral hearing: Chief Justice Ireland and Justices Cordy, Spina, and Botsford. To gain a reversal, we will need three of the four justices to decide in our favor. If the decision is split, the decisions by the Massachusetts Appeals Court and the trial court would be affirmed.

Wednesday, September 28, 2011

With the oral hearing one week away, I am consumed with fear about the future of blameless victims if the earlier decisions of the Massachusetts Appeals Court and the trial court are upheld. The damage done would be impossible to live with.

Sunday, October 2, 2011

As is my nature, I am consumed with thoughts of the oral hearing on Thursday. Contemplating that four Massachusetts state employees are going to decide not just the

---

290 For more information, see http://www.mass.gov/courts/sjc/justices.

judgment in our appeal but, more importantly, the fate of current and future blameless victims is overwhelming me.

Tuesday, October 4, 2011

Last night, we were notified that AIG's attorney has been replaced by a well-respected attorney, John Ryan (Sloan & Walsh).

Wednesday, October 5, 2011

Tomorrow's oral hearing will last thirty minutes, each side getting fifteen minutes.

In the first five minutes of the hearing, Margaret Pinkham had to convince the justices that Zurich didn't, in at least one instance, *"effectuate prompt, fair and equitable settlements of claims in which liability has become reasonably clear."* Additionally, she had to convince them that Zurich's failure to *"effectuate prompt, fair and equitable settlements of claims in which liability has become reasonably clear"* was *willful or knowing.*

In the following ten minutes, Fred Pritzker had to convince the justices that at least one of AIG's violations found by the Massachusetts Appeals Court was *willful or knowing.*

Margaret and Fred had to convince the justices that the *plain meaning* of Chapter 93A, which required a punishment that was equal to double or triple the amount of the jury verdict, had to be applied against Zurich, AIG, or both, no matter the size of the punishment.

If Margaret and Fred were successful, the earlier decisions would be reversed, and primary insurance carriers and excess insurance carriers would never again commit an *"unfair or deceptive act"* in Massachusetts without substantial punishment.

In the next seven and a half minutes, John Ryan, representing AIG, needed to convince the justices that the earlier decisions concerning AIG should be affirmed. (My guess is that AIG would be glad to pay the small punitive amount as previously ordered by the Massachusetts Appeals Court.)

In the last seven and a half minutes, Linda Morkan, representing Zurich, needed to convince the justices that the earlier decisions concerning Zurich should be affirmed.

Thursday, October 6, 2011

Marcia woke at four o'clock so that we could be at the courthouse by eight o'clock. The oral hearing began promptly at nine o'clock, and it concluded at 9:40 a.m.[291]

---

[291] To view the complete oral hearing, see http://www.suffolk.edu/sjc/archive/2011/SJC_10911.html www.theblamelessvictim.com. This transcription is not official. This transcription was developed from a later review of the oral hearing; I apologize for any errors or omissions.

BEGINNING OF TRANSCRIPTION OF ORAL HEARING FOR SJC-10911

Bailiff:

Court, all rise. Hear ye, hear ye, hear ye. All present having anything to do before the Honorable Justices of the Massachusetts Supreme Judicial Court now sitting in Boston, before the Commonwealth, draw near and you shall be heard. God save the Commonwealth of Massachusetts. The Court is now open, please be seated.

Court Clerk:

Docket No. SJC-10911; Rhodes versus AIG Domestic Claims.

Ms. Margaret Pinkham:

Good morning, Your Honor. My name is Margaret Pinkham. I will be addressing Zurich American Insurance's liability under Chapter 176D for five minutes.

My co-counsel, Fred Pritzker will address the measure of punitive damages in AIGDC's liability. With us at counsel's table is our colleague Daniel Brown.

We are here this morning on behalf of Marcia, Harold, and Rebecca Rhodes to ask this Court to enforce Chapter 176D and 93A. This case is not at the margins of the law. It squarely presents fundamental issues of consumer protection.

Marcia Rhodes was paralyzed when she was rear-ended by a tractor-tanker on January 9th, 2002. There was no uncertainty as to who was at 'fault' for the accident or that her injuries were catastrophic. Judge Gants determined that those facts were immediately apparent. Yet the Rhodes family existed in a state of uncertainty for 812 days.[292]

It took Zurich two years, two months, and 22 days to communicate a settlement offer of $2 million, on a claim that its adjuster had repeatedly valued at five to ten million dollars.[293]

Justice Margot Botsford:
What obligation did Zurich have to deal with AIGDC, before communicating with you or with your clients? Because of the excess, because of, as you say, catastrophic injuries, clearly the

---

[292] Although not stated, 812 days refers to the time from January 9, 2002, to March 31, 2004, approximately when Zurich offered the $2 million with a mandatory release of all claims against all defendants.

[293] The settlement offer required a mandatory release of all claims against all defendants, which was unacceptable. Zurich could have unconditionally tendered its policy limit to us.

excess policy is implicated and so the relationship between Zurich on that point and AIGDC in terms of them communicating with you?

Counselor Pinkham:
Well, Your Honor, I don't believe that Zurich's obligation to communicate with the plaintiffs was in any way implicated or constrained by its relationship with the excess carrier.

Justice Botsford:
Is it the case that when the policy was finally tendered it went through AIG?

Counselor Pinkham:
I don't understand what you mean by finally tendered?

Justice Botsford:
In other words, it wasn't given directly to you at the time, right?

Counselor Pinkham:
Um, the Trial Court found that there was a verbal tender made to AIG in January, 2004. That verbal tender was rejected. On March 31, 2004, Zurich communicated a settlement offer of $2 million directly to the Rhodes family.

Justice Robert J. Cordy:
To settle the whole case?

Justice Botsford:
No, that was without…

Counselor Pinkham:
They had to communicate a settlement offer and that was the settlement offer they communicated, correct.

Justice Cordy:
Right. Their whole policy.

Counselor Pinkham:
Correct.

Justice Cordy:
So what happened then?

Counselor Pinkham:
 I'm sorry, I didn't hear you.

Justice Cordy:
 So what happened? They tendered their whole policy, so what happened? What happened?

Counselor Pinkham:
 To the offer?

Justice Cordy:
 They tendered their whole policy and what then happened?

Justice Botsford:
 Did the money change hands?

Counselor Pinkham:
 No, Your Honor. And AIG then eventually took over defense of the case after a period of months in which there was some jockeying between Zurich and AIG as to who was going to pay for defense costs.

Justice Botsford:
 Ok, so you're saying but for that jockeying…and I know this isn't your claim, but I'm just trying to figure out this relationship, but for that jockeying about who was going to pay defense costs, ordinarily, once it was tendered in March, not in January, but in March, I take it, without any of the contingencies, it would have been paid to you, is that right?

Counselor Pinkham:
 No, Your Honor, not under the practice that they followed. It was available to AIG.

Justice Botsford:
 Is that part of your complaint? Is that part of your complaint that it was going through AIG?

Counselor Pinkham:
 Not as to Zurich, Your Honor. The crucial position that we take as to Zurich is that it failed to investigate the claim. It failed to act in accordance with its own policies, and that Zurich's delay…

Justice Botsford:
So when do you say, when do you say, is the sort of outside limit of when it should have tendered its policies?

Counselor Pinkham:
Your Honor, based on the...the short answer is November, 2002.

Justice Botsford:
And the accident was in February, 2002?

Counselor Pinkham:
January of 2002.

Justice Botsford:
January of 2002.

Counselor Pinkham:

Um, and I point the Court to Zurich's own policies. Under Zurich's own policies, it was required to investigate coverage, damages and liability immediately. Zurich waited until the Rhodes family made a settlement demand before it began to assess damages and coverage and liability was clear, no one had to analyze liability.

And I would ask the Court to review Zurich's Best Policy Practices. It's contained in the record appendix at 3655. And, in addition, Zurich's claims notes at page 3757 demonstrate that Zurich didn't even comply with its own policies.

Had Zurich complied with its policy, it would have complied with its statutory obligations. Now, Your Honor, the other issue I'd like to address is even if you take the Trial Court's findings of fact as they are written, the Trial Court found the damages were reasonably clear in the fall of 2003. The Rhodes family communicated settlement demands to Zurich in August and December of 2003.

Yet, as I just indicated, Zurich didn't communicate an offer to the Rhodes family until March of 2004. That delay at a point in time...

Justice Botsford:
Didn't you say that they did it earlier but it was rejected?

Counselor Pinkham:

No, that was, again, Your Honor, this is actually crucial; I thank you for asking that question.

The tender from AIG, excuse me, the tender from Zurich to AIGDC was invisible to the Rhodes family. All the Rhodes family knew in January of 2004 was that it had been two years since the accident, they had communicated two settlement demands and all that we heard from Zurich was radio silence.

The Rhodes family had no idea of what was going on behind the curtain between the primary and the excess carrier. And we would ask the Court to find that, based on Zurich's delay, even on the facts found by the Trial Court, that Zurich violated Chapter 176D. And, based on its complete failure to comply with either the duty to investigate, set forth in Chapter 176D, and its own policies, that that violation was willful and knowing.

Chief Justice Ireland:
You're going to have to leave there.

Counselor Pinkham:
Thank you, Your Honor. I will leave it to Mr. Pritzker to address the measure of punitive damages that we ask for against Zurich.

Mr. Fred Pritzker:
Good morning, Your Honor. Fred Pritzker, I am going to address the plain meaning of the governing statutes in this case, 176D and 93A.

Justice Botsford:
Are you...you briefed, but you're not going to address, whether, the issue of low end of reasonable, that is the August number?

Counselor Pritzker:
Not at all, not at all, Your Honor. Um, in fact, it doesn't matter in this case.

Justice Botsford:
No, I appreciate that fact.

Counselor Pritzker:
> But I am going to address the willful and knowing and knowing violations of AIGDC, both before and after the plaintiffs obtained an $11.365 million judgment at the jury verdict, um, in, um, 2004. What happened is, well, before we get there, the plaintiffs are seeking the mandatory doubling of that underlying judgment, under the 1989 amendment to 93A. And they seek these mandatory punitive damages because of the willful and knowing violations of AIGDC.

Justice Botsford:
> But, are you, I think this is your argument, but it's not your whole argument. You're arguing today you're focusing on post-judgment conduct, is that right?

Counselor Pritzker:
> I'm focusing on both, Your Honor, although it doesn't matter, um, because under Hopkins...

Justice Botsford:
> Well, if you take the Trial Judge's findings...

Counselor Pritzker:
> Yes.

Justice Botsford:
> It does matter. But you're saying?

Counselor Pritzker:
> Well, I suggest to the Court that while the trial judge found that there were no damages relating to the pre-judgment violation that was overruled by the Massachusetts Appeals Court.

Justice Botsford:
> Right, but we're not bound by that.

Counselor Pritzker:
> I certainly understand that. But we're in the position, and this Court is in the position, that there are two published decisions, one of which holds that there was no liability to AIGDC for the pre-judgment violation.

Justice Botsford:
> Correct.

Counselor Pritzker:
And another recorded decision that there is liability. But in both of them, um, the doubling of the underlying judgment was refused.

Justice Botsford:
Right.

Counselor Pritzker:
It was also refused in the post-judgment violation.

Justice Botsford:
Right, so, ok.

Counselor Pritzker:

And, um, I suggest to the Court that where all of the elements of 176D and 93A have been met, namely, there has been a violation of 176D.

Let's focus on post-judgment for the time being. That violation caused a loss. The Trial Court found that. That violation caused damages. They were assessed as "loss-of-use" damages.

The Court found that the violation was willful and knowing and actually described AIG's conduct as "insulting," "ridiculous," "intended to bully the plaintiffs into accepting an unreasonably low settlement." Um, all of those indicia were present, post-judgment. And yet the judge refused to double the underlying judgment.

And he did so on the basis that it makes no sense to double the underlying judgment when the insurer did not cause that judgment to occur.

I suggest to the Court that this creates an exception to Chapter 93A of rather broad proportions, which was not expressed, and I suggest to the Court, was not intended. All post-judgment violations, in all post-judgment violations, the violation never causes the judgment, because it occurs after the judgment has already entered.

So by definition, it can't cause the underlying judgment. It also is the case that for all of the third-party claims, at least the ones that I can think of, um, the underlying judgment, excuse me, is caused by the insured, not the insurer.

The claim for 93A against the insurer is on the basis that 93A enables the third-party claimant to go directly against the insurer under 93A, section 9, subsection 1.

Chief Justice Roderick Ireland:
If we agree with you, what would the rule in the case be, going forward?

Counselor Pritzker:
That where there is a willful violation and where there is an underlying judgment that um, um, is, um, achieved by the plaintiff, that for punitive damages purposes, for deterrent purposes, as they were amended in 1989, the, um, the punitive damages should be double the underlying judgment.

Justice Cordy:
Can I ask you about the Hopkins case? Explain to me how the Hopkins case fits into your analysis here?

Counselor Pritzker:
Um, it fits in…

Justice Cordy:
That would be inconsistent with your analysis, correct?

Counselor Pritzker:
No, not at all, Your Honor.

Justice Cordy:
Ok, explain.

Counselor Pritzker:
There was no underlying judgment.

Justice Cordy:
And that's because a reasonable offer was made late and accepted.

Counselor Pritzker:
Accepted, and so the case settled.

Justice Cordy:
 OK.

Counselor Pritzker:
 And where there is a settlement and no judgment, then the amendment to, um, the 1989, the 1989 amendment, doesn't apply.

Justice Cordy:
 Let's say that the AIG had come in late as it rarely did, and made an offer of $10 million, but it wasn't accepted, and the jury came back with $9 million.

Counselor Pritzker:
 Yes.

Justice Cordy:
 Would you say, "Well, their offer came in late, and therefore we do go to judgment. There still should be punitive damages, even though the offer that came in was very much on the high side, and was very reasonable and fair in the circumstances—still, because it went to trial, there was a judgment. That is what's in the statute."

Counselor Pritzker:
 Chapter 176D is a mandatory statute setting forth a course of conduct for insurers. And that course of conduct mandates under subsection 'f' that an insurer will effect a fair and equitable settlement once liability is reasonably clear. That is the mandate, and…

Justice Cordy:
 Well, so you have two prongs to that…

Counselor Pritzker:
 …it was violated.

Justice Cordy:
 …when is it reasonably clear such that an offer, a fair and reasonable offer, should be made? And the second is, is the offer fair and reasonable? So here in my scenario, we have a late offer. Should have been made earlier, but which would be viewed probably in retrospect and otherwise as fair and reasonable, but was not accepted, and the case went to judgment.

Counselor Pritzker:
Yes.

Justice Cordy:
And if it had been accepted, the punitive damages would not be calculated twice judgment. Where it hasn't been accepted, they would be calculated at twice judgment.

Counselor Pritzker:
That's, that's right, but keep in mind, Your Honor, that if it's accepted, there is no judgment.

Justice Cordy:
Well, I understand that.

Counselor Pritzker:

If it is not accepted and if the violation is willful and knowing, and I think that that's key, because what we're dealing with here is a punitive damage statute to deter this kind of behavior.

And when the willful and knowing violations are couched in terms of "insulting" and "ridiculous," I suggest to the Court that the hypothesis that the Court has just raised is really inapt.

Justice Cordy:
Well, I'm just posing a hypothetical. I'm trying to understand.

Counselor Pritzker:
I understand that.

Justice Cordy:
…when it is that punitive damages ought to apply and that this is the case, I take it that was described in the footnote 16 of the Hopkins situation, unresolved situation where it's a late but very reasonable offer which is not accepted and the case goes to judgment. How do you calculate punitives in that circumstance?

Counselor Pritzker:
Well, I suggest to the Court that footnote 16 deals with compensatory damages, and that's all that it deals with.

Justice Cordy:
 All right. Now you're going to have to explain that to me, because I really don't understand.

Counselor Pritzker:
 Ok, what we have is several, we have several layers to this statutory scheme. First, there has to be a violation. Then there has to be a loss, a loss being defined as the deprivation of a legal right.

Justice Botsford:
 But wasn't Hopkins a willful and knowing case?

Counselor Pritzker:
 I'm sorry.

Justice Botsford:
 Wasn't Hopkins a willful and knowing case?

Counselor Pritzker:
 Yes, it was, Your Honor.

Justice Botsford:
 So, how can you be sure that footnote 16 was about compensatory damages?

Counselor Pritzker:
 Because what—because the, um, footnote gave compensatory damages of "loss-of-use" funds and it said that those damages might be different if the…

Justice Botsford:
 …they doubled them, right?

Counselor Pritzker:
 No, yes—they did double them, but that wasn't what the footnote…

Justice Botsford:
 Right.

Counselor Pritzker:

...was attached to. It was attached to the, the, um, "loss-of-use" of funds, and the footnote said that those "loss-of-use" of funds might be different if the plaintiff didn't accept the offer. I'm sorry, it didn't accept the offer.

And the reason for that is that the period of the "loss-of-use" of funds would be, um, different if there's an acceptance, because that cuts off the liability, the compensatory liability to be doubled or, um, it would be different if it wasn't accepted, in which case, they continue on.

Justice Cordy:
Let me understand what you're suggesting ought to happen here. Are you suggesting, number one, that there should be the actual damages assessed for this delay period, which is what the Massachusetts Appeals Court did?

Counselor Pritzker:
And, and that's what they did. They did.

Justice Cordy:
And, and, and in addition to that, double punitive damages?

Counselor Pritzker:
Yes, Your Honor.

Justice Cordy:
Both of those assessments. Not that the double punitive damages essentially is the recovery under 93A?

Counselor Pritzker:
That's correct, Your Honor. That's our position.

Justice Cordy:
So you get both.

Counselor Pritzker:
We get both.

Justice Cordy:
Compensatory loss-of-use damage and the punitive?

Counselor Pritzker:
That's correct.

Justice Cordy:
And you say that's what 93A says?

Counselor Pritzker:
Well, 93A says that you get compensatory damages and you double those compensatory damages unless there has been an underlying judgment. And if there has been an underlying judgment, you substitute the underlying judgment for the actual damages and double those.

Justice Cordy:
Well, if you substitute—well, shouldn't that take care of everything?

Counselor Pritzker:
I don't believe that that's the way the statute reads, Your Honor.

Justice Botsford:
Wouldn't you be better off if it did?

Counselor Pritzker:
[laughs]

Justice Botsford:
We're getting to stratospheric numbers here. I just…

Counselor Pritzker:
Well, we're getting to stratospheric numbers anyway, Your Honor.

Justice Botsford:
I know we are, but it seems to me…

Counselor Pritzker:

And that's the last point that I wanted to make—that I know that the AIGDC will be arguing that there's no relationship between the stratospheric damages and their willful violation, and I suggest differently. I suggest that there is a nexus between the underlying judgment and the willful behavior, and it is this.

When you're dealing with catastrophic injuries, as an occurrence, or very, very large transaction as an underlying transaction, then the potential or actual judgment is going to be very large, and the willful or knowing, or and knowing, in this case, behavior, the insurer takes the risk that if they violate the statute, the doubling of that judgment is going to be huge.

That's what the legislature intended, and it's very clear.

Chief Justice Ireland:
Your time is up.

Counselor Pritzker:
Thank you, Your Honor, and I appreciate your consideration.

Mr. John P. Ryan:

Good morning, members of the Court. John P. Ryan on behalf of National Union Fire Insurance Company of Pittsburgh, PA, and AIG Domestic Claims, which for purposes of this argument, I'm just going to refer to as "the insurer." With me also is Attorney Anthony Zelle on behalf of the same parties.

I'd like to begin this and move away from my prepared remarks and return to the Chief Justice's questions as it ties into Justice Cordy's question, "What is the rule, or what should be the rule going forward tied into the education and points that are raised by the Hopkins case?"

And we'd suggest that the rule going forward and the answer to the question of footnote 16, respectfully, in the Hopkins case, would be that there is no meaningful distinction, and the rule going forward should be where the carrier, albeit willfully, as in Hopkins, knowingly, as in Hopkins, late, as in Hopkins, nevertheless comes forward with a reasonable offer, and there's a panoply—that can be low reasonable, mid reasonable, high reasonable, as in Justice Cordy's question—then at that point, the measure of damages should be the loss of the use of the money, and there's a very practical reason for that, because if the rule is employed as has just been suggested by learned counsel, our opponent, then the whole purpose of the statute will be defeated.

A quick illustration. If the carrier is late and delays that was found here, but comes forward six months, seven months, twelve months, with a reasonable offer as Judge Gants stated in his opinion, no intelligent plaintiff or reasonably well-represented plaintiff will accept that offer, because he or she would now know the mere lateness has exposed the carrier to a multiple of the underlying judgment under the plaintiff's proffered rule.

So it would drive the plaintiff away from the settlement process and, concomitantly, it would drive the carrier away from the settlement process, because the carrier would have no incentive once it passed the late marker on the highway knowing that, well, as a matter of law we're now exposed to the underlying judgment, there's nothing to be done, and they can anticipate that that type of offer will be used against them in a later 93A action.

Justice Botsford:
How do you explain the Granger case?

Counselor Ryan:

Your Honor, the Granger case, and I would suggest answers a question that was put to learned counsel on the other side, and the Granger case is the proper application of the statute, Your Honor, in this regard. Granger was an action against the subcontractor, general contractor against the one or the other.

In that case, Your Honor, the actual damages from the same and underlying transaction or occurrence was the breach of the contractual relationship between the parties. So it fit all the language of the statute, actual...

Justice Botsford:
But it was...the case talks about the judgment. It focuses on the judgment, doesn't it?

Counselor Ryan:
It does, Your Honor, but where there is a coalescence in this...

Justice Botsford:
It doesn't make the point that it's just because of that coalescence.

Counselor Ryan:

Your Honor, that is correct, but if we read the statute as even the amendment which requires, and we keep referring to quote, the "underlying judgment," which is not what the amendment, the 1989 amendment, says.

It says "actual damages for purposes of this chapter shall be the judgment on all claims, quote, arising out of or from the same and"—it's a conjunction—"underlying transaction or occurrence." That's the language of the statute.

Justice Botsford:
Yes.

Counselor Ryan:
In Granger, Your Honor, the underlying transaction or occurrence was in fact the breach of contract, and contract damages were the proper measure to be multiplied. In the tort case, Your Honor, in the tort case, the injuries by the plaintiff for the late but reasonable settlement offer emanate from 176D, the underlying transaction or occurrence is the lateness of the offer.

Justice Botsford:
But it seems to me you're just ignoring the word "judgment" in your analysis.

Counselor Ryan:

I don't believe I am, Your Honor, because…May I give you another illustration? If, for example, we had as Bertassi, Trempe, Wallace—the cases to which the 1989 amendment was responsible according to the decisions of this Court historically.

Those were all cases where there was a judgment which the insured had and its direct contractual relationship with the insurer. Those are cases where the courts had decided only loss-of-use damages were to be used, and the legislature amended the statute…no, no.

Where the actual damages are the contractual breach between the companies, Your Honor. That's the amount that should be, and it satisfies the same and underlying transaction, Your Honor. That's the type of judgment to which the statute speaks.

And we would say, Your Honor, that the language of the statute does not allow for the interpretation that's being proffered here by the plaintiffs in this case.

Justice Cordy:
It strikes me that looking a little bit at Justice Berry's dissent in the Massachusetts Appeals Court case.

Counselor Ryan:
Yes.

Justice Cordy:

That once you have been late and you haven't afforded a prompt, fair and reasonable offer, and you come in just before trial with an offer, that the burden on the insurer should be pretty high.

Not just a low offer, in a broad reasonable range, but literally a final offer, and one may even measure the verdict against the final offer to determine whether it was really fair in the circumstances. Why isn't that the way to look at this?

Counselor Ryan:
Because, Your Honor, first of all, we're constrained by the language of the statute, which I won't go back through, but I think it's important to realize...

Justice Cordy:
If we're constrained by the language of the statute that can be very problematic. I'm trying to figure out...OK. Go ahead.

Counselor Ryan:

Because, Your Honor, if we...let's take your illustration, respectfully. If we move along that time line, the grading of exposure to the insurer is actually increasing, because the interest is increasing. Let's say a typical serious case in the Massachusetts Superior Courts of the Commonwealth are 24 or 36 months to get reached. We reach that level.

If there's a delay just before trial, we're probably moving out of the doubling range into the trebling range because of the nature of waiting for the party to wait that long. If that offer is not commensurate, just prior to trial, then we have a factual finding that the offer was not reasonable and we have a double breach by the carrier, and that loss-of-use, Your Honor, has a larger component of interest. It has a larger component, potentially, of trebling, and the damages...

Justice Cordy:
The whole idea, the whole idea is, is to get away from the situation where insurers essentially do what is alleged to have happened here. Withhold what is obviously a case that needs to be settled at a fair and reasonable basis, draws it right down to the end, puts maximum pressure on the insured, really forces a trial, or acceptance of a very low offer. That's what the whole statutory scheme is intended to prevent, so...

Counselor Ryan:
But in this case, Your Honor, the trial was not forced by the insurer's conduct. The Trial Court...

Justice Cordy:
Oh, yes it was.

Counselor Ryan:
Well, respectfully, Your Honor, the Trial Court found as a fact that the offer that was made at the August mediation by the insurer, in this case, the 3.5 million dollars, if memory serves me correctly, was a reasonable offer.

Justice Cordy:
The low end of a...

Justice Botsford:
The low end.

Justice Cordy:
...reasonable offer.

Counselor Ryan:
Understood. Understood.

Justice Cordy:
Made on the eve of trial.

Counselor Ryan:
But a reasonable offer, Your Honor.

Justice Cordy:
Not a final offer. Not something that was in the middle range.

Counselor Ryan:
I understand, and the counter, His Honor will recall, was from, I believe, from 16.5 million to 15 million dollars, and the offer was rejected. That's perfectly appropriate for a plaintiff to decide whether or not to proceed to trial.

Justice Cordy:
And maybe that's perfectly appropriate...

Justice Botsford:
There's two weeks left till trial...

Counselor Ryan:
I understand that, Your Honor, but...

Justice Cordy:
It is perfectly appropriate, if it had been timely. Been made months, months before, and you can actually engage in narrowing that range. But, isn't that part of the problem?

Counselor Ryan:
In this particular case, Your Honor, the Trial Court found that liability was not reasonably clear in all of its elements, as I recall the facts, until May of 2004, approximately three months prior to the mediation which took place in August, and that's a finding of fact by the trial judge. So the interval of time we're talking about, Your Honor, is approximately three months, and I think it's noteworthy...

Justice Cordy:
The liability wasn't established?

Counselor Ryan:
Well, Your Honor...

Justice Cordy:
Liability wasn't established?

Counselor Ryan:

Both components have to be present. There has to be clarity with respect to the liability and damages, and the Trial Court so found, and indicated all the bases its finding that liability and damages were not reasonably clear until approximately May of 2004.

In this case, the finding by the trial judge in this case wound up in a punitive damages award of just slightly less than a million dollars. I believe it was $488,000, doubled. He might have trebled it. That was within his discretion of determination based on the conduct. And I believe the record will show an award of attorneys' fees of approximately a million dollars.

We're speaking about a sanction. With regard to the three-month interval, and then the five-month interval between the period between the mediation, I'm sorry, and after the judgment, rather a five-month interval. A total of approximately eight months when you add the two numbers together, even if we would accept the pre-verdict period for the sanction, ultimately, that's in the vicinity of about two million dollars.

So, Your Honor, we'd suggest that this statute does, by applying that measure of damages, accomplish a significant penalty against the insurer. We also believe, Your Honors, that it is consistent with decisions of this Court, most notably the Drywall decision.

In the Drywall decision, this Court will recall, that the comment was made by the Court that the amendment requires that the punitive damages element, for a judgment to be applicable, it must arise out of the same trial and underlying proceeding. And that's within the Drywall case, and that the 1989 amendment, retained the causal nexus between the event, the carrier's activity and the damages sought, the punitive damages.

Justice Botsford:
So you say it isn't the same proceeding because…Oh boy. Because the judgment was the tort action, and this is the 93A action?

Counselor Ryan:
We're saying, Your Honor, they had two separate proceedings which do not arise out of the same and underlying transaction or occurrence, which is the language of the amendment, Your Honor.

Justice Botsford:
And they don't, because?

Counselor Ryan:
Because, Your Honor, the conduct of the carrier is its lateness in making a reasonable offer under 176D. The underlying transaction for the plaintiff's rights against the defendant insured was the trucking accident itself. And we would say, Your Honor, that does not comport with the mandatory language of Chapter 93A, Section 9, as amended in 1989.

Chief Justice Ireland:
Thank you, Counsel.

Counselor Ryan:
Thank you, Your Honor.

Ms. Linda Morkan:

Good morning. May it please the Court. My name is Linda Morkan. I am an attorney with Robinson and Cole. With me is Attorney Greg Varga and, together, we represent Zurich American Insurance, an appellee in this case. Your Honors, I'd like to address two points that were made by Attorney Pinkham.

The first is that she stated to this Court that this case, as respects the plaintiffs in Zurich, is about the investigation, a poor investigation by Zurich. That is incorrect. That is not what this case is. That is not what the plaintiff's claims against Zurich were. In fact, the plaintiff tried to amend their complaint post-trial, to raise a claim of an inadequate investigation. And the Trial Court denied that motion.

Justice Cordy:
I'm sorry. Tried to raise...

Counselor Morkan:
A claim that Zurich had improperly investigated. Inadequately investigated the claim. What this...

Justice Cordy:
I'm sorry. What complaint are we talking about, here?

Counselor Morkan:
The plaintiff's.

Justice Cordy:
The 93A complaint?

Counselor Morkan:
The plaintiff's complaint against Zurich, as violating 176D.

Justice Cordy:
And when was that complaint filed?

Counselor Morkan:
It was after the resolution of the tort action, Your Honor.

Justice Cordy:
Right, so you're saying they were trying to amend that complaint?

Counselor Morkan:
At the end of…I'm sorry. I'll back up. When they brought suit against the insurers, the claim…

Justice Cordy:
They brought suit against the insurers.

Counselor Morkan:
Correct.

Justice Cordy:
Go ahead.

Counselor Morkan:
The claim against Zurich was that it failed to effectuate a prompt, equitable settlement offer after liability and damages had become…

Justice Cordy:
This claim…

Counselor Morkan:
...reasonably clear.

Justice Cordy:
...was brought after the jury verdict.

Counselor Morkan:
Correct. So the only claim against Zurich is not that it poorly investigated the plaintiff's claims, but that it failed to make a fair settlement offer after liability had become clear. That is the issue that the Trial Court reviewed, and that the Trial Court decided, finding in Zurich's favor, saying that, in fact, the roughly eight weeks that passed between the time that liability and damages were reasonably clear, and the time that Zurich tendered its two million dollar policies, was not a violation of 176D.

Justice Cordy:
OK, so give me the dates on that. When did the Trial Court judge find that damages and liability were reasonably clear?

Counselor Morkan:
On November 19, 2003. And in the Memorandum of Decision, he goes to great lengths to explaining why that was the date, for Zurich, that liability and damages were clear. Thereafter, approximately eight weeks passed until mid-January, which is when Zurich tendered its policy limits. And again...

Justice Cordy:
Now, when you say "tendered," did they tender them to the plaintiff?

Counselor Morkan:

To the excess. And that is the...In the case, we have primary and an excess insurer. That is the primary's obligation, which is to tender to the excess. And, in fact, the plaintiffs concede that point, in their reply brief. I'm sorry, Justice Botsford. I just wanted to make sure I got that out.

In their reply brief at 16, the plaintiffs specifically state what Zurich's statutory obligation is. Is to tender their limits to the excess. And that's what they did.

Justice Botsford:
So, but I thought that the argument this morning was that it was, the phrase was, "radio silence" in January.

Counselor Morkan:
> Well, it may be. It's true that it's invisible to the insured.

Justice Botsford:
> Would you say that complies with the consumer, emphasis consumer, protection laws?

Counselor Morkan:
> Indeed…well, because we're talking about a primary and an excess level, when a primary insurer tenders its policy limits, if it, as it did here, actually offers that amount to the insured, the insured, in taking that tender, must release the insurers. And, obviously, in a case like this…

Justice Botsford:
> Well, that's not…

Counselor Morkan:
> …where the damages were going to exceed those policy limits, the plaintiffs aren't…They're not in a position to make that two million dollars be final.

Justice Botsford:
> Wasn't the ultimate tender without releasing any liability…

Counselor Morkan:
> Yes, because, and that's why the tender goes to the excess. The excess puts that two million in their proverbial pocket, and then decides what, out of the excess policy, the excess insurer will offer to the insureds.

Justice Cordy:
> So once the tender is made to the excess carrier, Zurich's liability under 176D is done.

Counselor Morkan:
> It's…They're…

Justice Cordy:
> Even if that tender is never…

Justice Botsford:
> Communicated.

Justice Cordy:
...isn't tendered to the plaintiff...

Counselor Morkan:
Correct. Correct.

Justice Cordy:
...for a long time.

Counselor Morkan:
Although, in this case, Zurich did make that extra step, and said to the plaintiffs, "We have tendered our two million dollars, and we'll offer it to you..."

Justice Botsford:
In March.

Counselor Morkan:
I believe it was March, Your Honor. Although they had tendered to the excess before that.

Justice Botsford:
So how can it do that if it was obligated...I mean, how did it make that tender directly...

Counselor Morkan:
Well because the offer is, "We'll give you our two million dollars, but we need a release." That's what insurance companies need to do that to protect their insureds. And the plaintiffs are like, "Our damages are far in excess of two million dollars. We can't accept that money now and give you a release." Although it was understood, at that point, that that two million dollars was on the table, that Zurich had tendered.

Justice Botsford:
Well, the plaintiff's argument, I think, doesn't go beyond March, does it?

Counselor Morkan:
Well, in fact, it...

Justice Botsford:
Doesn't it say that March was not reasonably prompt?

Counselor Morkan:
But, in essence, what the Trial Court said is, that the terminal date wasn't March. The terminal date is January. So that period, the trigger date being November and the terminal date being January, that's the period that he investigated as, "Was that a reasonable time for Zurich to tender its limits, make that offer, under the policy?"

Justice Francis X. Spina:
Just one question.

Counselor Morkan:
Yes, sir?

Justice Spina:
A factual question. I thought that I heard Attorney Pinkham say that there was "radio silence," but you're saying that you made the tender to AIG.

Counselor Morkan:
Correct.

Justice Spina:
Because the plaintiff rejected your request.

Counselor Morkan:
I'm sorry, Justice Spina. I don't mean to be confusing. Chronologically, what happened is, in a phone call in November of 2003, which involved both representatives from Zurich and AIG, Zurich told AIG, "We're going to tender. You know, I have to get the approval from the upper chain, but we're going to tender our limits." That actually happened in January.

Justice Spina:
Tender to the plaintiffs?

Counselor Morkan:
Tender to the excess. That's what the primary does.

Justice Spina:
But did you ever make the offer to the plaintiff…

Counselor Morkan:
Yes, so in January...

Justice Spina:
...but the plaintiff refused to give you the release.

Counselor Morkan:
In March. January we tendered to the excess insurer, thereby putting the responsibility on them to go forward. And then, in March, communicated with the plaintiff directly, and said, "We're willing to pay our two million dollars." It was rejected because they weren't going to release all of their claims for that amount.

Chief Justice Ireland:
Thank you.

End of Transcription of Oral Hearing for SJC-10911

Friday, October 7, 2011

I am trying not to let my feelings about yesterday's hearing eat me up inside, but I know myself well. I am going to slowly fall into a deep depression, mortified that the Massachusetts Supreme Judicial Court might not find that Zurich or AIG committed a *willful or knowing* failure *"to effectuate prompt, fair and equitable settlements of claims in which liability has become reasonably clear."*

Marcia does not show her emotions, but I know she is distressed about yesterday. In a week or two, she will break down in inconsolable tears. This would tear me up inside.

Thursday, October 28, 2011

Three weeks have now passed since the oral hearing.

Monday, November 7, 2011

The first month of our six-month wait is over.

Monday, December 5, 2011

Two months have now passed since the oral hearing. According the its rules, the Massachusetts Supreme Judicial Court will render its decision within seventy days.

Tuesday, December 11, 2011

I try not to think about the implications to future blameless victims should Zurich, AIG, or both be found not to have violated M.G.L. c 176D. Whatever pretense might have existed to provide the citizens of Massachusetts with consumer protection against an *"unfair or deceptive act"* would be lost. The suffering would be worsened.

Saturday, December 31, 2011

Another year now comes to an end. In a few days, we will reach the unhappy ten-year anniversary of the crash, and we are still in litigation against Zurich and AIG.

Sometime in the next forty-five days, the Massachusetts Supreme Judicial Court will hand down its decision. While I remain steadfast in my belief that Zurich and AIG made *willful or knowing* violations, I continue to doubt that the Massachusetts Supreme Judicial Court would agree. In that case, what would I do?

Emotionally, I will be devastated; I am afraid of the deep depression that would befall me. I do not handle depression well, even with medication. As withdrawn as I am from the world already, I fear that I would become even more withdrawn, even from Marcia and Rebecca.

I would be impossible to live with, and that scares me.

I am sure that I would lack the energy, the motivation, and perhaps even the interest to change the law so that the next blameless victim wouldn't suffer Marcia's fate. I will become angry with myself for not standing up when asked.

Even today, I can barely live with my anxiety. I don't show it, but I am a big mess inside.

Sunday, January 1, 2012

These are my goals for 2012. I hope that I do better than last year.

1. Have the Massachusetts Supreme Judicial Court find in our favor against Zurich and AIG in making *willful or knowing* violations of Chapter 176D.
2. If appealed, have the US Supreme Court reject certification.
3. Should we lose against AIG and Zurich, seek legislative solutions to protect future blameless victims.
4. Increase Marcia's bodily strength through vigorous physical therapy.
5. Deal with Marcia's ongoing urinary tract infections.
6. Increase Marcia's fun each day.
7. Finish the sunroom for Marcia.
8. Develop "A Patient Advocate Guide."
9. Lose ten pounds to get to 185.
10. Take a well-needed vacation.
11. Develop a plan for Marcia should anything happen to me.

Sunday, January 8, 2012

Tomorrow is the ten-year anniversary of the crash. Over the last ten years, I learned more about spinal cord injury, infectious disease control, human anatomy, personal injury insurance, insurance carriers, Massachusetts General Laws, and attorneys than I ever wanted to know.

Worst of all, I have gained a grievous disregard for the judicial system in Massachusetts.

Judge Barrett, who presided over the criminal trial, let Carlo Zalewski off with a slap on the hand by making a decision to *"continue without a finding."* By now, given this ruling, Zalewski's driving record is clean.[294]

Judge Gants[295] took fourteen months for his decision. Ironically, the whole trial was about institutional delay.

The Massachusetts Appeals Court found that none of Zurich's delaying actions constituted an *"unfair or deceptive act."* It found that none of AIG's delaying actions were *willful or knowing.*

At this moment, I have no idea how the Massachusetts Supreme Judicial Court would rule. Either way, I have spent ten years of my life and Marcia's life desperately trying to make the laws of Massachusetts work for, not against, blameless victims.

Imagine ten years to resolve a rear-end crash.

It stinks.

Monday, January 9, 2012

A decade. Much against my better intuition, I visited the site of the crash. I didn't reminisce about the last ten years but thought about the next ten years. I wondered what life would be like for Marcia and other blameless victims on January 9, 2022. For her sake, no one told her that today was the ten-year anniversary. It would only make her feel worse.

Wednesday, January 11, 2012

After not speaking with Fred Pritzker for a while, we had lunch today to discuss media statements to be made based on the decision by the Massachusetts Supreme Judicial Court. Ninety-three days have passed since the oral hearing, and we could expect the decision within two or three weeks.

Toward the end of the lunch, Fred's phone rang. Ordinarily, he would not take a call at a restaurant—it was too public—but he answered this call.

He wrote down the name of a defense attorney. He wrote *"$5 million."* Then he wrote, *"not the final offer."* Fred told the attorney that he was heading to Florida and would call his clients and get back to him.

---

[294] I found out later that Carlo Zalewski had died on October 26, 2009.
[295] In April 2014, Justice Gants was appointed Chief Justice of the Massachusetts Supreme Judicial Court.

We were both happy. I pointed out that AIG was already on the hook for $3 million, so all the defense attorney did was raise the offer by $2 million.

When I returned home, I told Marcia about the call. Marcia wants the verdict by the SJC—no settlement. Who could blame her?

One thing for sure, the clock is ticking. The Massachusetts Supreme Judicial Court would hand down its decision any day.

Friday, January 13, 2012

There was no word from Fred yesterday. I am trying not to think about what might be happening, but how could I not?

Saturday, January 14, 2012

Without any response from the attorney, it seemed that this offer was an attempt to determine how desperate we are. AIG used the same maneuver in August 2004 just before the original trial. AIG spit out several lowball offers to sway us from going to trial in September 2004 and to see how desperate we were.

In any event, the Massachusetts Supreme Judicial Court's decision should come soon. The court rules indicate that decisions will be completed with 130 days except when the court waives this rule. As of today, 101 days have passed.

Thursday, January 26, 2012

Now 112 days had passed since the oral hearing, and the court still had not issued its decision. Over the last ten days, AIG has had on-again, off-again discussions about a financial settlement. AIG's latest offer is $5 million—just $1.5 million more than the amount currently due. As before, settlement is unlikely.

I will just have to wait.

Friday, February 10, 2012

Today, the Massachusetts Supreme Judicial Court rendered its decision in SJC-10911:[296]

"The case is before us on the plaintiffs' application for further appellate review. We conclude that the damages the plaintiffs are entitled to recover under c. 93A, § 9, on account of the defendants' post-judgment violation of c. 93A, § 2, and c. 176D, § 3 (9) (f), must be based on the underlying judgment in the plaintiffs' tort action, and not the loss of use of the sum ultimately included in AIGDC's late-tendered settlement offer months after the jury's verdicts.

---

[296] For the complete text of the decision, see http://caselaw.findlaw.com/ma-supreme-judicial-court/1594105.html or www.theblamelessvictim.com.

This conclusion makes it unnecessary to determine whether AIGDC's willful and knowing violation of the applicable statutes before the verdicts in the tort case caused injury to the plaintiffs, because even if, as they argue, the plaintiffs did establish the requisite causal link between AIGDC's pre-verdict violations and injury and thereby are entitled to a multiple of the underlying tort judgment as damages, the plaintiffs may not recover that amount twice.

"Conclusion. We recognize that $22 million in c. 93A damages is an enormous sum, but the language and history of the 1989 amendment to c. 93A leave no option but to calculate the double damages award against AIGDC based on the amount of the underlying tort judgment.

The Legislature may wish to consider expanding the range of permissible punitive damages to be awarded for knowing or willful violations of the statute to include more than single, but less than double, damages; or developing a special measure of punitive damages to be applied in unfair claim settlement practice cases brought under c. 176D, § 3 (9), and c. 93A that is different from the measure used in other types of c. 93A actions.

We remand this case to the Massachusetts Superior Court for a redetermination of damages in accordance with this opinion."

"So ordered."

DID AIG COMMIT AN *"UNFAIR OR DECEPTIVE ACT"*?

Today, the Massachusetts Supreme Judicial Court found that AIG's *"unfair or deceptive act"* was a *willful or knowing* violation."[297] In doing so, it reversed the decisions by the trial court and the Massachusetts Appeals Court.

On behalf of all blameless victims, I applauded the Massachusetts Supreme Judicial Court for this decision. Ideally, excess insurance carriers would heed this warning, change their behavior, and become better corporate citizens when settling with a blameless victim.

When the next blameless victim has to deal with AIG or any other excess insurance carrier, perhaps this decision would encourage a reasonable settlement much sooner.

Nonetheless, in a perverse way, AIG still won. By making Brown Rudnick wage this battle through the trial court, the Massachusetts Appeals Court, and the Massachusetts Supreme Judicial Court, AIG sent a message to all plaintiffs' attorneys:

---

[297] See Massachusetts General Laws Chapter 93A, Section 9, paragraph 3 at https://malegislature.gov/Laws/GeneralLaws/PartI/TitleXV/Chapter93A/Section9.

"We will delay settlement, and we don't care if we are punished. You must be willing to go up against us for ten years, and we know that you do not have the resources to do so. Take our lowball settlement offer."

On February 24, 2012, AIG agreed to make the full payment per the decision of the Massachusetts Supreme Judicial Court.

DID ZURICH COMMIT AN *"UNFAIR OR DECEPTIVE ACT"*?

The Massachusetts Supreme Judicial Court rendered its decision with regard to Zurich's conduct.

"Our review of the record indicates that the trial judge's findings on the issue of when liability and damages were reasonably clear, and whether Zurich tendered its policy limits promptly, were not clearly erroneous; there is no basis to disturb them.

The record also supports the judge's determination that Zurich, the primary insurer, satisfied its duty to effectuate settlement by tendering the policy limits to AIGDC, where it was clear that the case would not settle for an amount within the primary policy limits, necessitating the involvement of the excess insurer.

We affirm the judgment in Zurich's favor."

Quite unfortunately, the Massachusetts Supreme Judicial Court found that Zurich didn't commit, in even the smallest way, even one *"unfair or deceptive act."* Through this decision, primary insurance carriers have been given a perfectly legal roadmap for delay. The next time a blameless victim has to deal with Zurich or any other primary insurance carrier, the life of the blameless victim will be worsened.

After all of Zurich's heinous actions—perhaps even worse than AIG's—the Massachusetts Supreme Judicial Court made the following clear:

1. Zurich's eight-month delay from January 9, 2002, to August 2002 to begin to investigate this claim because of its asserted lost-in-the-mailroom problems was not an *"unfair or deceptive act."*
2. Zurich's further thirteen-month delay until September 2003, when it received the plaintiffs' demand package, to begin its investigation of this claim was not an *"unfair or deceptive act."*
3. Zurich's additional two-month delay from November 2003 (when it internally determined to tender its policy limit to AIG) until January 2004, to e-mail its $2 million policy limit to AIG was not an *"unfair or deceptive act."*

4. Zurich's three-month delay from January 2004 until April 2004 to fulfill AIG's request to provide both the tender offer, as well as the agreement to continue to pay defense costs in writing, was not an *"unfair or deceptive act."*
5. Zurich's delay to investigate this claim to take extended time by trying (but failing) to locate other insurance carriers that might have additional insurance coverage for one or more of the defendants was not an *"unfair or deceptive act."*
6. Zurich's assertion that any delay was irrelevant because only AIG was empowered to effectuate the settlement was not an *"unfair or deceptive act."*
7. Zurich's assertion that any delay associated with beginning the whole claims investigation again when the plaintiffs amended their complaint was not an *"unfair or deceptive act."*
8. Zurich's assertion that any delay in tendering its $2 million policy limits, without a full release of all claims by the plaintiffs, was not an *"unfair or deceptive act."*
9. Zurich's assertion that any delay caused by not proactively acquiring the needed claims information to thoroughly investigate this claim was not an *"unfair or deceptive act."*
10. Zurich's assertion that any delay caused by its determination that the claims investigation by Crawford (Zurich's Agent and GAF's third-party insurance administrator) was inadequate was not an *"unfair or deceptive act."*

THE BLAMELESS VICTIM

The Massachusetts Supreme Judicial Court ought to be ashamed of this decision favoring Zurich.

Do the justices understand what they have done to all future blameless victims?

They turned a person who was catastrophically injured, through no fault of her own, into a blameless victim.

Carlo Zalewski did not do this. The awful injuries to Marcia did not do this. The many horrific medical complications did not do this. The years of emotional suffering did not do this.

The defense attorneys did not do this. The trial court and the Massachusetts Appeals Court did not do this. Moreover, Zurich and AIG did not do this.

The Massachusetts Supreme Judicial Court is solely responsible for Marcia being a *blameless victim*. She was always blameless in terms of the crash, but because of the decision in favor of Zurich, the Massachusetts Supreme Judicial Court made her a victim.

Only the Massachusetts Supreme Judicial Court had within its power to make right this gruesome event by finding that Zurich did commit at least one *"unfair or deceptive act."*

Ten delaying actions were identified to prove that Zurich failed *"to effectuate prompt, fair and equitable settlements of claims in which liability has become reasonably clear."*

Ten times the Massachusetts Supreme Judicial Court found that Zurich was blameless. Ten times it found that Zurich was not the *cause* of a *harm* to the blameless victim.

Ten times it has made the lives of future blameless victims so much worse.

The Massachusetts Supreme Judicial Court made Marcia a blameless victim.

❖ ❖ ❖

At the beginning of this book, I wrote, *"These aren't the reasons why* The Blameless Victim *is such a sad narrative."*

The Blameless Victim is sad for one reason. On February 10, 2012, the Massachusetts Supreme Judicial Court disgraced itself for not finding that Zurich committed even one *"unfair or deceptive act."* The Massachusetts Supreme Judicial Court has made the dreadful lives of future blameless victims much, much worse.

Shame on the Massachusetts Supreme Judicial Court.

AFTERWORD

The Blameless Victim has taken fourteen years to complete. Since the decision by the Massachusetts Supreme Judicial Court on February 10, 2012, Marcia has continued to have multiple secondary medical complications. The unrelenting pain she feels each day is the worst of all. Mostly, she is unhappy each day. Occasionally, she finds something that makes her happy, even if for a short while. I am so sad for her. I can only hope that one day medical science will be able to provide a remedy to relieve her unbearable chronic pain.

Rebecca graduated from Hampshire College in Amherst, Massachusetts, and then worked for Hampshire College's Institutional Research department. She appears to have gotten over the trauma that started when she was thirteen years old, but I can tell she has been terribly wounded by seeing her parents so unhappy. She does her best to comfort Marcia but is aware of her mother's unremitting unhappiness. In October 2012, she married Integra Sinclair, and in 2014, she entered the graduate program in sociology at Columbia University.

For me, not a day goes by that I don't think about the Massachusetts Supreme Judicial Court's awful decision. Each day, I hurt for what it did to Marcia and to future blameless victims.

ABOUT THE AUTHOR

Harold S. Rhodes actively participates in organizations to help those less fortunate. He continues to be the primary caregiver for his spouse, Marcia, after she was catastrophically injured in January 2002.

In June 2012, Rhodes joined the board of directors of the Greater Boston Chapter of National Spinal Cord Injury Association, the same group that provided assistance to him and his wife in 2002. In October 2012, he was appointed a member of the Milford Commission on Disability. In March 2013, he became a member of the board of trustees of the Milford Regional Medical Center Healthcare Foundation. In January 2014, he was elected a corporator of the Milford Regional Medical Center. In June 2014, he was elected chairman of the Milford Commission on Disability. In September 2014, he joined the school council of Milford's Shining Star Early Education Center for children with special needs.

Previously, Rhodes provided business consulting for emerging and large high-tech companies. His education includes a bachelor of arts degree from Indiana University (1975) and a master of business administration degree from the Harvard Business School (1980). He and Marcia have lived together in Milford, Massachusetts, for more than thirty years.

THE BLAMELESS VICTIM WEBSITE

The Blameless Victim website at www.theblamelessvictim.com provides extensive additional information. The website includes:
1. Searchable directory of nearly all legal documents.
2. The video depositions of Nicholas Satriano and Warren Nitti.
3. The video, *"A Day in Marcia's Life."*
4. Claims Notes from Crawford, Zurich, and AIG.
5. Letters between opposing attorneys.
6. Transcriptions of all depositions.
7. Transcriptions of the five courtroom trials.

Additionally, the website includes a set of legal resources: web links to articles, written by both defense and plaintiff attorneys, that present the author's legal analysis of various judicial decisions.

The website includes the appendicies to *The Blameless Victim* that were not included in the book version.

Appendix A:	The Many Persons Involved
Appendix B:	Spinal Cord Injury: An Overview
Appendix C:	Spinal Cord Fusion Surgery
Appendix D:	Recovery from Spinal Cord Injury
Appendix E:	Living with Spinal Cord Injury
Appendix F:	Spinal Cord Injury Research
Appendix G:	Recommendations to Future Blameless Victims of Spinal Cord Injury and their Families
Appendix H:	On Being a Patient Advocate
Appendix I:	Access to Medical Care for Individuals with Mobility Disabilities
Appendix K:	The Stress of Family Caregiving: Your Health May Be at Risk
Appendix L:	The Process of Personal Injury Litigation: How Insurance Defense Attorneys Frustrate the Legal System to their Advantage

Appendix M: Massachusetts' Lacks Legal Recourse for Blameless Victims when Bad Faith Actions are Committed by the "Primary" Insurance Carrier and the "Excess" Insurance Carrier
Appendix O: The Many Preventable Victimizations of Marcia Rhodes
Appendix P: Required Changes to the Massachusetts General Laws
Appendix T: My Personal Commentaries

The website also includes a blog, where viewers can anonymously make comments or ask questions about any topic concerning *The Blameless Victim*.

Made in the USA
Columbia, SC
22 December 2023